Education, Religion, and the Discourse of Cultural Reform in Qajar Iran

Bibliotheca Iranica
Intellectual Traditions Series, No. 5

*The publication of this volume has been made possible by
generous donations from
Mr. and Mrs. Rasoul M. Oskouy
Mr. Payman Pouladdej*

Education, Religion, and the Discourse of Cultural Reform in

Qajar Iran

Monica M. Ringer

MAZDA PUBLISHERS, Inc. ◆ Costa Mesa, California ◆ 2001

Mazda Publishers, Inc.
Academic Publishers since 1980
P.O. Box 2603
Costa Mesa, California 92626 U.S.A.
www.mazdapublishers.com

Library of Congress Cataloging-in-Publication Data

Ringer, Monica M., 1965-
Education, Religion, and the Discourse of Cultural Reform in Qajar Iran/ Monica M.
Ringer.
p. cm—(Bibliotheca Iranica. Intellectual Traditions Series; No. 5.)
Includes bibliographical references and index.

ISBN: 1-56859-131-4
(Softcover, alk. paper)

1. Education—Iran—History—19th century. 2. Iran—Intellectual life—19th century. 3.
Iran—Civilization—Western influence. I. Title. II. Series.
LA1351. R56 2000
370'.955—dc21
00-045201

For my parents,
with deepest affection and respect

TABLE OF CONTENTS

Acknowledgements

While in graduate school at UCLA I enjoyed the dual tutelage of Hossein Ziai and Nikki Keddie. These teachers have helped me to become myself. Nikki Keddie kept me on the "sirat al-mostaqim" and generously shared with me her impressive knowledge of the Middle East. I have repeatedly benefited from her unerring advice, and thank her for her continued involvement in my academic pursuits.

I shall never sufficiently thank Hossein Ziai—only perhaps acknowledge my debt to him. It was a result of his class in college that I first became interested in Middle Eastern history, so in large part he started me on my intellectual journey. I thank him for this, for his encouragement and friendship, and above all, for his own standard of scholarship.

I have benefited tremendously from careful readings of my manuscript by Houchang Chehabi, Michael Fisher, Willem Floor, Nikki Keddie, Rudi Matthee, Adnan Mazarei, Michael Morony, Julia Clancy-Smith, and Hossein Ziai—all of whose own scholarship has taught me much. I have relied on more than one occasion on the kindness of my friends and colleagues for assistance, advice, and rejuvenating shop-talk. I have learned much from conversations with Iraj Afshar, Ahmad Ashraf, Shaul Bakhash, Houri Berberian, Hamid Dabashi, Jasamin Rostam-Kolayi, Holly Shissler, Amin Tarzi, Mohammad Tavakoli-Targhi and Heidi Wachler—who shared their knowledge and carefully considered the many questions I posed.

For the past three years I have been affiliated with Georgetown University's Center for Muslim-Christian Understanding. Thank you Dr. Esposito and Dr. Voll for your hospitality, and for your many kindnesses. I shall never forget the past year of teaching at my Alma Mater—Oberlin College—and the collegiality of the History and Religion departments. At the Library of Congress, I wish to thank Dr. Ibrahim Pourhadi and Manaf Sami of the Middle East and Africa

Division, and Les Vogel and Prosser Gifford of the Office of Scholarly Programs who provided me the time and leisure to work on the Library of Congress' Persian-language material. Firoozeh Kashani-Sabet graciously shared with me a number of important Qajar manuscripts that she is working on, and Saeed Damadi procured some hard-to-find books from Iran.

Every author or artist knows that creative endeavor is not simply a matter of time spent in the office—rather, it spills out into (more often than not completely inundating) the rest of one's life. My husband Adnan Mazarei encouraged and supported me throughout my years-long preoccupation with Qajar Iran. Thank you Adnan for caring that I am happy and for humoring the many thoughts that I insisted on sharing with you. Thanks also go to my daughter Soraya who, although she doesn't know it yet, put up with frequent absences in body but never in spirit.

Lastly, my parents should know how very much they have sustained me. They have read everything I have ever written, and have always stressed the value and benefit of cultural studies. I have not infrequently benefited from conversations with my father, Fritz Ringer, who has added many years of seasoned advice to this project. In particular, he helped me work out the conceptual and methodological framework of the study itself. My introduction and chapter on educational theory owe much to his expertise and clarity of thought. I like to think of this project in Iranian intellectual history as constituting an application of some of his own theories in the sociology of knowledge. Regardless of the success of my endeavor, it is a recognition of part of my intellectual debt to him. My mother, Mary Ringer, has been the willing victim of my not infrequent need to sound out ideas, and has generously agreed to read a small barrage of books on Iran that I have foisted on her. Throughout, both of my parents have shared my enthusiasm and have supported my commitment to this life. I dedicate this then, my first book, to my parents, in love and respect.

EDITOR'S PREFACE

Education, Religion, and the Discourse of Cultural Reform in Qajar Iran, is the fifth volume in Intellectual Traditions, a series aimed to provide scholars and students of Iranian Islamic heritage with new source materials. Future publications in the series will include studies in philosophy, mysticism and 'Irfân, religion, intellectual history, and literature.

This work is a comprehensive and analytical account of educational reform in 19th century Iran, and locates educational reform within the broader context of the process of modernization in a non-Western society. This study is based on a wide variety of sources and is the only history of the New Schools and Anjoman-e Ma'aref. Topics include: the Nezam-e Jadid, the Dar al-Fonun, the New Schools, foreign, missionary and minority schools, students abroad, and the Anjoman-e Ma'aref. It emphasizes the evolving attitudes of proponents and opponents of educational reform towards its benefits and dangers. The book describes modernization in Iran as an active and creative process of synthesis and adaptation. Reformers were aware of the problems of social change, political and institutional challenges to the status quo, and issues of the preservation of religious and cultural traditions. Reform was essentially a struggle to reinterpret and redefine tradition, to reexamine religious texts and to adapt foreign institutions to Iranian needs. The emphasis of this study is on the social, political, cultural, intellectual and institutional threat posed by educational reform to the ulama. It charts the dialectic between competing visions of Iranian polity, society and culture. This work accurately contextualizes the 19th century reform movement—clarifying the Constitutional Revolution and post-revolutionary reform goals as it recomplicates both reformers and their opponents' attitudes and approaches towards modernization.

I wish to extend my heartfelt thanks to Houchang Chehabi, John Esposito, Julia Clancy-Smith, and Rudolph Matthee for having read the manuscript and for their comments.

I am pleased to acknowledge Mr. and Mrs. Rasoul Oskouy, Mr. Payman Pouladdej, and the Department of Near Eastern Languages and Cultures at UCLA for supporting Bibiotheca Iranica: Intellectual Traditions Series.

H.Z.

INTRODUCTION

In 1805, Crown Prince 'Abbas Mirza conferred with Napoleon's secret agent, Knight of the Legion of Honor and noted Orientalist, Pierre Amédée Jaubert, at his court in Tabriz. The crown prince was in a state of anguish over his continuing military losses to Russian forces in the First Russo-Persian War of 1803-15. But he was clearly aware that these defeats were symptomatic of a larger problem. The young prince turned to Jaubert and surprised him with a barrage of questions, addressed as much to himself as to his French visitor: "What is the power that gives [Europe] so great a superiority over us? What is the cause of your progress and of our constant weakness? You know the art of governing, the art of conquering, the art of putting into action all human faculties, whereas we seem condemned to vegetate in a shameful ignorance . . . "[1] If the defeat of Persian forces in the Russo-Persian Wars of 1803-15 and 1826-28 jarred Iranians out of their complacency, it did not answer the prince's questions; nor did it rectify the glaring discrepancy of power. But the question had been asked, and the quest for a solution fervently begun. 'Abbas Mirza initiated a series of reforms to rectify the imbalance. Almost exactly 100 years later, Iran was wracked by a revolution. A revolution which demanded the establishment of a constitution. According to its defenders, constitutional government was the answer, the longed-for solution to Iran's "deficiency" vis-à-vis the West.

These two landmarks— 'Abbas Mirza's reform program and the Constitutional Revolution— standing just 100 years apart, signified the beginning of the process of modernization in Iran, and the culmination of this first response to its associated dilemmas. This book examines modernization in Iran— and this first response— from the asking of a loaded question by the crown prince, to the staging of a revolution. This period, roughly 1800-1906, is the crucible of modern Iran. It is thus imperative, not only to understand this period in its own terms, but also to recognize its enduring legacy as a reference point for all subsequent responses to the challenges of modernization. Before rejoining 'Abbas Mirza at his court in Tabriz and resuming our story, we must reflect upon the concept of modernization itself.

---

[1]Pierre Amédée Jaubert, *Voyage en Arménie et en Perse fait dans les années 1805 et 1806* (Paris: 1821), pp. 175-77.

Theory of Modernization— models and pitfalls

What is modernization? Following Max Weber, we may conceive of modernization as a process of rationalization that can be observed in at least four distinctive, but interrelated realms. In the economic, the rational pursuit of profit and the exploitation of formally free labor led to the rise of modern capitalism. In law, codification or rational system-atization created a calculable environment for entrepreneurial activity. In intellectual and personal life, new forms of scientific thought and of rational self-control arose. In statecraft, finally, public administration was taken over by a bureaucracy with specified ranks, spheres of competence, and educational qualifications.[2]

The usefulness of Weber's broad conceptualization of modern-ization lies both in its emphasis on rationalization as the crux and identifiable goal of modernization, and the applicability of this concept as a model. Since rationalization entails legal, administrative and economic, as well as social and intellectual change, we are able to account for the importance of institutional reforms, while at the same time emphasizing the importance of the "ethos" of modernization. That ethos is important; it interacts causally, and may in fact precede, administrative, legal and economic rationalization.

It is also clear that education enjoys a central role in the process of modernization and rationalization. Education fulfills several key functions in any society. On the one hand, it transmits and perpetuates the cultural heritage, the established social values and beliefs. Higher education embodies and passes on lifestyles and norms of conduct adopted by the social and cultural elites.[3] Primary education imbues the majority of school-going children with basic values and social mores. At all levels, therefore, the educational system is often and justly considered a vehicle of tradition and morality.

On the other hand, education can serve as an agent of change. In the modernization process, education provides new technical training and expertise for the civil service and for the advancing technology. In

---

[2]My understanding of Weber's conception of modernization as rational-ization is informed primarily by discussions with Fritz K. Ringer, and by H. H. Gerth and C. Wright Mills (eds), *From Max Weber: Essays in Sociology* (New York: Oxford University Press, 1958, 1970 printing).

[3]Fritz K. Ringer, *Education and Society in Modern Europe* (Bloomington: Indiana University Press, 1979), pp. 6-7.

selecting and channeling talent toward new employment opportunities, education can disrupt the status quo, encouraging upward social mobility. Most significantly, education can instill new cultural ideals, and serve as the institutional basis for newly emerging occupational and social elites.

Education enjoys a unique role in society; it reflects the past, informs the present, and prepares the future.[4] For these reasons, the educational system is often at the center of conflict between different social and political factions. To control the educational system is to impose educational and cultural ideals, values and identity.[5] The dominant groups try to "universalize their particular cultural ideal." A historical investigation of educational reform— and of the debates surrounding it— therefore reveals a great deal, not only about the belief system operative in a given society, but also about the social and political constellation of interests at a given time. Education, as an agent of change, and as a repository of values, was intimately connected to the larger social and political agenda of reform in Iran. Educational reform reflected the development of political and, eventually, of social objectives, and it thus cannot be understood apart from the larger parameters of the modernization process, and of the debates that surrounded it. Specifically, the type of educational reform desired was a function of the depth, breadth, and nature of the perceived "deficiency" of Iran. From the beginning of the nineteenth century, reform and modernization were indissolubly related to the processes of rationalization.

Since Weber's time, but drawing upon his work, theories of 'modernization' have emerged that are typically more categorical than Weber's own, particularly in their attempt fully to specify the causally relevant variables, and to cover all possible cases in a universal scheme. However, it is a mistake to focus the debate concerning modernization on a fixed roster of 'factors.' It is virtually impossible to distinguish those changes that are truly necessary conditions of modernization from those that often accompany modernization but are not absolute preconditions— or consequences. Even in evaluating a completed process of modernization, it is impossible to calculate which variables

---

[4]Ringer, *Education in Society*, pp. 14-18.
[5]Fritz K. Ringer, *Fields of Knowledge: French Academic Culture in Historical Perspective, 1890-1920* (Cambridge: Cambridge University Press, 1992), pp. 1-25.

were essential, which supplementary, and which merely incidental. Moreover, variables cannot be isolated— either in the present or in the past— but instead should be understood as creating unique clusters of conditions, events and effects. The passage of time further complicates the picture, since conditions change and effects interact. The *historicity* of modernization in a particular time, culture and society must be stressed. In different historical environments, a different conjunction, or cluster, of factors may lead to modernization.

The study of modernization in non-Western countries is all the more complicated by the fact that modernization has long been equated with Westernization, not only in much of Western political and developmental theory, but in non-Western countries as well. Due to the fact that a modern socioeconomic system first developed in the West, "modernization" is in some sense "Western." However, modernization *need* not be equated with Westernization. It is increasingly apparent that there are different paths towards, and varieties of modernization. The use of "the West" as a yardstick ignores the complexity of causal variables. Non-Western countries experience the process of modernization later than Western countries. They are therefore affected by retrospective analyses of Western modernization, even while they confront their distinctive chronological, cultural, and institutional environments. The non-Western experience need not fully replicate the Western experience. The attempt to isolate "causal prerequisites" in the Western experience and set them up as universally necessary in all other instances merely obscures the analysis of the unique conjunction of variables in historically and culturally specific environments.

The problem of identifying modernization with Westernization is not only a problem of scientific analysis, however. Quite apart from the debate concerning intentions, it is increasingly apparent that the West conceived of its own modernization experience as a universal model, to be replicated as far as possible elsewhere. It is also the case that modernization in non-Western countries— and here we are concerned particularly, but not exclusively with the Middle East— is often viewed as Westernization. This has two corollaries. First, agency is erroneously assigned to the West, with the Middle East as the passive 'receptor' of modernization. Second, modernization is perceived of as a series of necessary steps imposed or forced upon Middle Eastern countries by 'the West.' This approach mistakenly presents modernization as the implementation of fixed prerequisites. The idea of modernization as the approximation of the Western experience is a dangerous one. It obscures the crucial role of indigenous forces— be they individuals, associations, social, economic or cultural institutions. Modernization is in fact best conceived of as an adaptation— and a conscious and often creative one— of foreign models to indigenous contexts. This active conception of modernization allows us to emphasize the dialectical and contested nature of the *process*, to accurately attribute *agency*, and to free ourselves for the exploration of specific paths towards, and experiences of, modernization.

Crisis and Translation

Modernization entails the evaluation and choice of possible pathways of change. In the broadest sense, a society must determine what should be changed, what are the impediments to change, and the form that change should take. This involves the assessment of the continued viability of existing administrative, legal and educational institutions. What will they be modeled on? How will they be modified? If foreign models are used, how must they be adapted to suit indigenous contexts, needs and goals? Modernization challenges the very core of society; it demands cultural and intellectual reorientations, as well as institutional change. To define 'modernity' is also to define 'tradition.' Modernity is necessarily experienced as antagonistic to tradition. The process of modernization thus creates a situation of 'crisis.'

In such a period of 'crisis' where traditions and institutions are evaluated, a *debate over modernization* emerges. It is helpful to situate this debate in an intellectual field, a "configuration or network of relationships among various intellectual positions."[6] The concept of 'intellectual field' underscores the relational and contentious nature of beliefs, as well as their connection to the socio-political context. Different ideas compete with one another for dominance, or general acceptance. Individuals, schools of thought, and political groups compete within the 'field' for the "right to define what constitutes intellectually established and culturally legitimate."[7] In periods of rapid change— such as that engendered by the process of modernization—

---

[6]Ringer, *Fields*, p. 3.
[7]Ibid.

opponents force each other to defend and clarify their respective positions. The competition for intellectual dominance thus ultimately results in a process of "critical clarification."

Modernization in nineteenth-century Iran was a process of translation. In resolving questions about the adaptation of institutions and traditions, reformers attempted to "translate" foreign institutions and ideas into the Iranian context. I employ the term "translation" for two reasons. First, it accurately describes a creative process similar to that of translating texts from one language to another. A text or, in this case, an institution is selected for translation on the basis of its relevance to the context. Second, like a text, ideas and institutions change in the process of being translated from one context to another. It is no coincidence that language and texts in nineteenth-century Iran underwent a process of change. In addition to the rapid expansion of the public realm of textual discourse, the language employed was simplified, Persianized and popularized.

This book explores the debate over educational reform in nineteenth century Iran. It treats educational reform as a crucial element in the wider process of modernization. Because education was central to the process of institutional adaptation and cultural 'translation,' this book is also a social and intellectual history of Qajar Iran.

Modernization in Iran

Iran in the nineteenth century, in spite of the two Russo-Persian Wars early in the century, was marked by improved internal stability. The reestablishment of political hegemony over Safavid territory by the Qajars following several decades of internal disruption and foreign invasion led to renewed economic prosperity and increased international trade. Yet Iran's development— both political and economic— was significantly slower than that experienced by other Middle Eastern countries. Iran's government enjoyed neither the authority nor the efficient administration of Egypt or the Ottoman Empire. European influence and its impact were also far more diluted in Iran than elsewhere— due in part to questions of strategic and geographical location, and in part to the smaller number and less influential position of non-Muslim minorities in Iran. This worked both ways. On the one hand, Iran was never colonized as was Egypt. On the other hand, foreign capital investment was correspondingly lower in Iran. This also meant that Iran was not subject to the same pressures that European governments brought to bear on Egypt and the Ottoman Empire to develop the political, legal and fiscal frameworks suitable for capital investment. Communications and transportation networks likewise remained underdeveloped. The reform movements that dominated the nineteenth-century Middle Eastern landscape were concerned with both political and economic objectives. Iran's own experience of reform was thus determined by her own domestic conditions and was ultimately less successful than similar reform movements elsewhere in the Middle East.

The modernization process in Iran dates from the program of defensive military reform—the *Nezam-e Jadid*—initiated by Crown Prince 'Abbas Mirza in the first decade of the nineteenth century. In response to a series of military defeats by Russian armies and the consequent loss of Iranian territory, the prince recognized the inherent superiority of modern European standing armies, and attempted to establish such a force. From the outset, thus, Europe emerged as both an ominous threat to Iran's territorial sovereignty, as well as a model of change. The prince recruited a series of European military, medical and technical experts to train part of his military along European lines. As the value of European knowledge and technology became increasingly evident, the prince also dispatched two student missions to England— the first in 1811, and the second in 1815. At that time, the vision of educational reform was limited to the importation of technology and militarily relevant expertise.

'Abbas Mirza's attempt to establish a modern standing army as part of his larger fighting force differentiated the *Nezam-e Jadid* reforms from past attempts at adopting new military hardware and expertise— something not unknown in earlier periods. A modern army, in contradistinction to the system of local, primarily tribal levies practiced in Iran at the time, required a level of bureaucratic administration and a degree of control over financial resources which the Iranian system was unable to provide. The establishment of such a force thus necessitated a greater degree of centralization, of administrative control, and of effective central taxation than had previously been available. These considerations led 'Abbas Mirza to attempt a wide range of innovations. To the extent that the *Nezam-e Jadid* reforms attempted to

7

establish the institutional prerequisites for a modern army, they constituted the beginnings of a program of modernization.

The *Nezam-e Jadid* reforms were also as much a product of the ongoing attempt of the newly established Qajar dynasty to reassert control and consolidate power over its domains, as they were a result of military weakness in the face of Russia. The reforms began as a program of centralization and modernization that was to be continued by subsequent reformers— intensifying throughout the course of the century. The common denominator that ran across the political spectrum throughout the century was the recognition that only a strong centralized state would be capable of repelling the continued threat— political, commercial and territorial— posed by the European powers.[8] Individuals who advocated reform believed that it was essential to limit regional authorities and other power bases (the religious establishment figured prominently) that de facto limited the sovereignty of the central government.

Tension between central and provincial powers is nothing new, of course; it is found in all political systems, whether modern or traditional. However, what allows us to recognize nineteenth-century political reforms as aspects of modernization is the nature and scope of the desired reforms. The modernization process in Iran was characterized by the expansion of central government authority, which included the assertion of control over the judicial system at the expense of the religious establishment. It involved recognition by its advocates that secularization of the judiciary, the educational system, the training of a civil service, universal literacy and eventually, constitutional government were necessary.

In fact, the notion that the reforms of the nineteenth century were somehow qualitatively different from those of preceding periods was evident from the beginning of the century. Reform in nineteenth-century Iran was never about reestablishing imperfectly run existing institutions or reviving those left to disintegrate. It involved something quintessentially "new." In his travelogue written from Russia and England as part of the second student mission dispatched by 'Abbas

---

[8]On the trauma of loss of territory and the importance of "land" in the concept of Iranian nationalism, see Firoozeh Kashani-Sabet, *Frontier Fictions: Shaping the Iranian Nation, 1804-1946* (Princeton: Princeton University Press, 1999).

Mirza in 1815, Mirza Saleh Shirazi frequently insisted that "the new world situation" required reform in Iran. Although the emerging concept of a new era, *"asr-e jadid,"* remained largely undefined throughout the century, it continued to gain centrality as a reason for Iran to modernize. The "new era" seemed to require radically new solutions. Simply to reestablish previous systems of administration would not suffice to bring Iran into parity with the surging power of Europe.

Reform-minded prime ministers Amir Kabir (1848-51) and Mirza Hosayn Khan (1871-73) continued the emphasis on centralization and regularization of the administration as the first step in effecting administrative efficiency, increasing the flow of income from taxation to the central treasury, and revitalizing the armed forces. Both reformers also believed that the key to restrengthening Iran was the training of qualified administrative and military cadres, who could support the reform process. Amir Kabir founded the first state-sponsored European-style secondary school in Iran—the *Dar al Fonun*—in 1851 as part of his larger reform program. Mirza Hosayn Khan believed that European-style education was necessary adequately to prepare Iranian diplomats and other officials to meet the challenges posed by international diplomacy and by the aggressive European powers. In order to lead the country to "progress" and strength, he argued, officials had to be familiar with European sciences and languages, and knowledgeable about current international affairs.

As the century progressed, reformers' conceptions of the depth and breadth of Iranian "deficiency" developed, and led them to promote the adoption of more far-reaching educational goals. In the 1860s and 1870s, individuals advocating reform believed that Iran's backwardness stemmed from inadequate political institutions. One of the most ardent advocates of comprehensive modernization, Mirza Malkom Khan, declared that "the surging power of Europe has rendered impossible the survival of barbarian states. Henceforth all governments in the world will have to be ordered like those of Europe, or be subjugated and conquered."[9] Malkom Khan's conception of modernization as in fact constituting Westernization illustrates the difficulties inherent in

---

[9]Mirza Malkom Khan, *"Dastgah-e Divan,"* quoted in Hamid Algar, *Mirza Malkom Khan: A Study in the History of Iranian Modernism* (Berkeley: University of California Press, 1973), p. 71.

9

the use of the West as a model of change. Issues of the transferability of foreign institutions into the Iranian context would plague the reform movement throughout the century, and serve as a focus of the intensifying discourse. Mirza Malkom Khan led the way in urging the government dramatically to increase centralization, reorganize the administration according to European practice, and severely curtail the prerogatives of the religious establishment in both the judicial and educational arenas. Not surprisingly, he was the first to insist on the importance of establishing a universal, European-style system of education.

By the late nineteenth century, many reformers believed that new, European-style education was a social and political panacea. Educational reform became much more than a component in modernization and "progress." It emerged as the critical agent of change. In addition to advocating European sciences and languages, so as better to prepare Iran's administration and government officials, educational activists believed that the establishment of constitutional government depended on an increase in the level of popular literacy. These ideas culminated in the call for the establishment of constitutional law, not only because this meant fundamental change in the government system, but also because constitutional reform in turn was predicated upon a strong central government and upon a degree of rationalization of the judicial and educational systems— in other words, upon modernization.

Its association with and connection to Westernization further complicated the process of modernization in Iran. European military superiority demonstrated the need for European military technology and expertise as early as the *Nezam-e Jadid* reforms. Reformers sought to identify the "secret of European strength" and to undertake a process of modernization that would replicate European "progress." European political and commercial aggression also led reformers to recognize the need to make Iranian leadership more aware of world affairs— and norms of statecraft— so that Iran could regain a position of international respect and standing. Europe thus served as both a model of "progress" and modernization, *and* as a threat to Iranian sovereignty and territorial integrity.

Although the impetus to modernization was domestically propelled, the fact that Europe served as a model meant that the process involved adopting non-indigenous institutions and ideas. This led to the emergence of bipolar categories: modernization, Westernization and secularization were intimately connected, and were viewed as being jointly and directly opposed to tradition and Islam. The bipolar tension was further aggravated by feelings of inferiority and defensiveness that stemmed from the identification of Europe with "progress" and "civilization" and of Iran with "backwardness" and "stagnation." Insofar as Islam was linked with the indigenous culture, while modernization entailed both secularization and Westernization (the adoption of Christian customs and institutions), "progress" and "civilization" appeared as destructive of Islam and of Iranian cultural identity. The physical danger that European powers posed to Iran also reinforced the religious basis of Iranian identity, and complicated the task of legitimizing modernization.

This was an especially thorny issue in the realm of educational reform, due to the association of education with the inculcation of morality and the religious tradition. The introduction of European-style education directly threatened the cultural and intellectual hegemony of the religious establishment, as well as its institutional entrenchment in the traditional educational system. The religious establishment was thus threatened on multiple fronts by modernization and educational reform.

This conundrum led to the development of what I term the "modernization dilemma"— the desire to adopt elements of "modern" [read European] technology and institutions, while at the same time safeguarding Iranian cultural and religious traditions. Or in other words, to distinguish between modernization and Westernization. At the core of this dilemma lie the issues of culture, tradition and identity. Reformers advocating modernization, and often themselves opposed to cultural Westernization, assumed the difficult task of distinguishing between the two, and thus of legitimating modernization. Given the blurred lines between religious and cultural traditions, and between institutional and cultural opposition to modernization, reformers found themselves in a difficult and essentially defensive position.

The emergence of oppositional categories, in which modernization and Westernization stood opposed to indigenous cultural traditions, has been mimicked to some extent by the historiography of the nineteenth century. There is a pronounced tendency among contemporary scholars to simplify debates concerning reform as obviously salutary or plainly

11

destructive. Reform-minded ministers are described as enlightened, secular, and progressive, and their opponents— identified as principally the ulama— disparaged as backward and reactionary. Much Qajar history also concentrates on the *implementation* of reforms as the crucial factor in evaluating the modernization process in the nineteenth century. I hope that the use of educational reform as a tool of inquiry and a window upon the intellectual debates of the time will problematize our understanding of this critical period, and at the same time, recontextualize the first formulation of the response to the challenges of modernization.

Rather than positing a simple antithesis between modernization and reaction, I attempt to empirically uncover a spectrum of responses. And a constantly undulating spectrum at that. While the majority of reform-minded individuals were government ministers or high-level officials, it is no less true that reformers increasingly were drawn from a broader socioeconomic spectrum and included many lower-ranking ulama, as well as merchants. Furthermore, one should not equate advocacy of modernization with the absence of religious belief. Nor with a solitary and uniform approach to the role of religion in modern society. Many of the most ardent reformers were devout Muslims, and it would be misleading to present them otherwise.

Conversely, opponents of reform did not consist solely of ulama. There were various reasons, some institutional or political, and some cultural and intellectual, behind the opposition to modernization. Often the preservation of privileges was at stake, and members of the political elite were amongst the most ardent opponents of reform. Furthermore, while the language of debate centered upon Islam, religious language was not the exclusive preserve of the ulama. Islamic symbols, texts, and claims to identity were drawn upon *across the entire spectrum of debate, regardless of the real bases of the positions defended.* It is nonetheless the case that no group was more threatened by modernization than the ulama on particularly numerous fronts— institutional, social, cultural and intellectual— and that the ulama comprised the largest and most vocal resistance to modernization.

There were also many points of agreement between reformers and their antagonists. There was a general consensus, for example, on the need to restrengthen Iran against foreign encroachment, particularly upon Iran's financial and political sovereignty. In addition, even the

12

most ardent advocates of comprehensive modernization displayed a marked ambivalence concerning the effects of Westernization, and this was not only due to tactical maneuvering on their part. Although the much-discussed cultural divide between proponents and opponents of modernization— or what has elegantly been called "cultural schizophrenia"— was a reality to some extent, we should not de-historicize this phenomenon.[10] In the nineteenth century, this cultural divide existed only in embryonic form, and the distance between reformers and opponents was certainly much shorter than it would become in the twentieth century.

In seeking to recontextualize the history of modernization in Qajar Iran, we should also guard against seeing the significance of the period entirely in practical successes of the reform movement. Without questioning the enormous importance of the *failure* of reform, or overstating the successes achieved (especially in contrast to comparable processes of reform in the Ottoman Empire and Egypt), I believe that the ultimate import of the period lies in the intellectual *debate* about modernization and in its impact upon subsequent formulations of the same issues and dilemmas. Even today, no absolute solutions to these questions exist, nor should we expect them to. Rather, the question of culture and tradition is by nature contested, and perpetually renewed.

---

[10]The phenomenon of "cultural schizophrenia" was developed by Daryush Shayegan in *Qu'est-ce qu'un révolution religieuse?* (Paris: Les presses d'aujourd'hui, 1982).

CHAPTER I

GENESIS: THE *NEZAM-E JADID* UNDER
'ABBAS MIRZA AND MOHAMMAD SHAH

The introduction of European-style education in Iran began as part of the reforms initiated by Crown Prince 'Abbas Mirza after his troops suffered a series of military defeats by Russian forces. In conscious imitation of a similar process of reform underway in the Ottoman Empire under Sultan Selim III (r. 1789-1807), 'Abbas Mirza instituted a defensive military reform program entitled "*Nezam-e Jadid*" (The New Order). Just as in the Ottoman Empire, the *Nezam-e Jadid* consisted of the introduction of European military technology and modern methods of training troops. It also served as a catalyst for the introduction of a number of other measures, such as the translation of European books, the establishment of a printing press, the publication of a newspaper, as well as attempts to regularize the tax system, which were believed to be necessary prerequisites to substantive military reform. 'Abbas Mirza also took the unprecedented step of sending a number of Iranians to study in Europe. The *Nezam-e Jadid* therefore marked the importance of European-style education in the process of modernization and reform. Furthermore, the fact that these reforms were *predicated* on the perception of military and technological deficiency vis-à-vis Europe meant that Europe emerged as both a model of change, as well as a threat to the consequences of inaction. This paradoxical relationship to Europe and European technology and culture emerged as the dilemma concerning modernization and Westernization. An investigation of the *Nezam-e Jadid* is therefore crucial to understanding the parameters of the inherently conflictual responses to the challenges of modernization and change as they first developed in Iran.

In 1797 when Fath 'Ali Shah succeeded his uncle Aqa Mohammad Khan Qajar to the throne of Iran, he inherited not only a minimal state structure, but also serious challenges to his authority. Following the overthrow of the Safavid dynasty in 1722 by Afghan invaders, Iran entered a period of domestic turmoil and the disintegration of central authority which continued for the duration of the century. Nader Shah (r. 1736-47) reconquered many Iranian territories that had renounced central control in this period. It was not until the end of the century, however, that Aqa Mohammad Khan Qajar (r. 1779-89) succeeded in forcing the majority of outlying provinces of the Safavid Empire to submit to restored central government control. Nonetheless, the provinces of Mazandaran, Azarbayjan and Khorasan, as well as the vassal state of Georgia, still resisted Qajar domination.

The prolonged period of wars of succession had also adversely affected commerce and agriculture in many regions. Some provinces such as Azarbayjan had experienced serious depopulation as a result. This decline in prosperity led to popular discontent and greatly restricted the ability of the central and provincial governments to collect taxes.

Upon assuming the throne, Fath 'Ali Shah was confronted with a multitude of challenges. His primary objectives were first, to assert Qajar sovereignty over all his domains, and second, to reestablish central administrative structures in order to expand central governmental hegemony. It was in this political and economic context that Fath 'Ali Shah repeatedly dispatched Crown Prince 'Abbas Mirza to Azarbayjan and Mazandaran to quell local rebellions. Beginning in 1804, when Fath 'Ali Shah named 'Abbas Mirza governor of Azarbayjan, the crown prince took up permanent residence in the capital city of Tabriz. There, 'Abbas Mirza attempted to expand the central administration and increase agricultural productivity. At the same time, the crown prince was confronted with a new and entirely different challenge in the form of Russian territorial advances.

Since the time of Peter the Great, Russian rulers had entertained hopes of extending their territory south into Iranian-controlled lands. The collapse of the Safavid state provided an opportunity for Russian expansion southwards into the Iranian vassal state of Georgia, which was formally annexed by Russia in 1803.[1] The Qajars were thus faced with loss of land and sovereignty over their northern territories.

In 1803, when hostilities between Russian and Iranian troops escalated into the First Russo-Persian War of 1803-15, Russian tactical

---

[1]Russian annexation was facilitated by the Georgian rulers themselves. In 1783 the Georgian ruler, taking advantage of weak Iranian central goverment, renounced all duties towards Iran and declared Christian Georgia a vassal state of Russia. Again during Fath 'Ali Shah's rule, the king of Georgia abdicated and declared Georgia to be part of Russia. See R.C. Watson, *A History of Persia from the Beginning of the Nineteenth Century to the Year 1858* (London, 1866), pp. 89, 142.

and technological superiority became obvious. According to a diplomatic envoy in Iran, "['Abbas Mirza] said, that he soon found out that it was in vain to fight the Russians without soldiers like theirs; and that their artillery could only be opposed by artillery; and that all his efforts to make an impression on them with his undisciplined rabble had uniformly been unsuccessful."[2] The crown prince correctly recognized that the basis of Russian military superiority was not merely a question of the quality of leaders, luck, and the number of troops engaged. Rather, the prince's Azarbayjani forces had come face to face with the superior power of a modern standing army. The Russian forces consisted of professional soldiers, drilled tactical maneuvers and trained to use the latest weaponry. Russian troops enjoyed the advantage of an established chain of command which allowed for a systematic and effective campaign. In contrast, 'Abbas Mirza's troops were in effect a conglomeration of individuals— each equipped as best he could and serving only for the duration of the conflict. Moreover, they were entirely untrained as a unified fighting force— the essence of a modern soldier. The fact that the troops were organized by tribe also meant that loyalty was owed to tribal leaders, not the court-appointed (and often notoriously incompetent) military commanders.

The conflict in command and lack of professional training led to disastrous incidents of disorder, confusion and ultimately, death and defeat. Lack of corrdination, combined with traditional methods of military engagement also meant that Iranian troops, unlike their Russian counterparts, did not establish security precautions, patrols, or night guards. In addition, while Russian armies were often under provisioned, 'Abbas Mirza's troops lived off the land and considered the primary goal of military encounters to be the capture of enemy booty— traditions which led to more than one military reversal, not to mention to hardships inflicted on the peasantry.[3] 'Abbas Mirza correctly understood that the Russian army was an example of the standing professional conscript army as first developed by Napoleon. Indeed, he was well aware of Napoleon's military exploits both in Europe, and in Egypt. He was also informed of the measures taken by Ottoman Sultan

---

[2]James Morier, *A Second Journey Through Persia, Armenia, and Asia Minor, to Constantinople, Between the Years 1810 and 1816* (London: 1818), p. 211.

[3]Muriel Atkin, *Russia and Iran, 1780-1828* (Minneapolis: University of Minnesota Press, 1980), pp. 110-111.

Selim III to modernize his armed forces using European military instructors in what was known as the "New Order," or *Nizam-i Jedid*.

The crown prince and his vizier, Mirza Bozorg Farahani Qa'em Maqam, concluded that continued Iranian military inferiority would jeopardize Iran's territorial integrity, if not her absolute sovereignty. Their resolution was reinforced by their knowledge of European military exploits elsewhere, particularly by British victories in India, and Napoleon's ease in conquering Egypt in 1798. The defeat of the Egyptian Mamluks at the hands of the French, in particular, convinced 'Abbas Mirza of the need to adopt European military techniques. If, he reasoned, the Mamluks with their renowned military prowess were so easily defeated by Napoleon's forces, then Iranian troops would surely suffer a similar fate should Iran be invaded by a European power.[4]

The solution, they determined, was to undertake a reorganization and reform of the Azarbayjani military along European lines similar to that underway in the Ottoman Empire. Some initial attempts at improving Iranian troop performance were made by having Russian prisoners of war and/or deserters lead drills.[5] 'Abbas Mirza was also interested in acquiring a European ally who could serve as a source for military and technical assistance in his conflict with Russia.

The opportunity to enlist European assistance in revamping Iranian troops presented itself as a result of renewed European interest in Iran in the early nineteenth century. European countries had refrained from diplomatic contact with Iran during the period of political instability that followed the collapse of the Safavid government. The restoration of order under Fath 'Ali Shah prompted European powers to revive diplomatic relations. At the same time, Great Britain, France and Russia were becoming increasingly involved in the expansion of their political, military, and commercial interests throughout the region. Consequently, each of these three European powers recognized the geopolitical importance of Iran to its own strategic and commercial interests.

The Napoleonic Wars in Europe (1803-15) exacerbated intra-European rivalry and led to a series of rapid shifts in the making and breaking of standing European political alliances. European powers

---

[4]Pierre Amédée Jaubert, *Voyage en Arménie et en Perse fait dans les années 1805 et 1806* (Paris: 1821), p. 179.

[5]On the incidence of desertion of Russians and their employment by 'Abbas Mirza, see Atkin, *Russia and Iran*, p. 106.

evidenced increased willingness to intensify their relations with Iran. As a result, Iran was catapulted into a new and formidable international political arena. According to Atkin, Russia was aware of the advantages of colonies and thus was "consciously imitative of Western overseas expansion."[6] France, under Napleonic rule, was interested in countering British colonial power. Iran was thus a potential ally (as was the Ottoman government) against France's own enemies in the Napoleonic Wars— alternately Russia and Great Britain. Napoleon thus sought to "establish a presence in Persia which might check the advance of [Russia] and prevent the influence of [Britain]."[7] Napoleon also entertained the idea of invading British India overland through Iran. Firmly ensconsed in Egypt in September of 1798, Napoleon confidently predicted that "France will sooner or later become the ruler of India. The London cabinet is fully aware of that."[8] Whether or not British official policy was in fact convinced of an overland invasion of India by Napoleon has been a matter of some debate. Ingram maintains that in fact British official policy did not take the possibility of such an invasion seriously. Rather, British recognized their own strategic interest in maintaining a power equilibrium in the Middle East. For this reason, British policy was primarily oriented towards preventing any European powers from establishing too close an alignment with Iran.[9] The British government also believed that an alliance with Iran against her European rivals (Russia and especially France) would help her win the Napoleonic Wars.

'Abbas Mirza and Fath 'Ali Shah successfully parlayed European interest in Iran into diplomatic agreements for mutual aid and assistance in furthering the *Nezam-e Jadid* reforms. After a tentative agreement with Great Britain failed to materialize, Fath 'Ali Shah and 'Abbas Mirza negotiated an alliance with France that was ratified in 1807 as the Franco-Iranian Treaty of Finkenstein. This treaty established cooperation between Iran and a European power at an unprecedented level. In articles six and seven, France agreed to provide

---

[6]Atkin, *Russia and Iran*, p. 163.

[7]Iradj Amini, *Napoleon and Persia: Franco-Persian Relations Under the First Empire* (Richmond: Curzon Press, 1999), p. 15.

[8]Amini, *Napoleon*, pp. 31-32.

[9]Edward Ingram, *Britain's Persian Connection 1798-1828: Prelude to the Great Game in Asia* (Oxford: Clarendon Press, 1992), p. 5.

military training and weapons to 'Abbas Mirza's Azarbayjani military which Fath 'Ali Shah had for some time been requesting in his diplomatic letters to Napoleon.[10] In accordance with terms of the treaty, Napoleon dispatched Lieutenant-Colonel Auguste de Bontemps to Iran to begin reorganizing 'Abbas Mirza's troops. This mission was followed up with a more formal one under the command of General Gardane later in the year.[11] The French Foreign Minister, in his directive to Gardane, instructed him "not to lose sight of the fact that our important object is to establish a triple alliance between France, the Porte and Persia, to clear the way to India and to obtain auxiliaries against Russia."[12]

The Gardane mission provided the first systematic training of Iranian troops by European officers. It also inaugurated 'Abbas Mirza's *Nezam-e Jadid* reform program. The mission consisted of fifteen political envoys and fourteen military officers, including engineers, mappers, artillery, cavalry and infantry experts. French officers drilled 'Abbas Mirza's troops in the new European military arts. Members of the mission also translated treatises on military tactics and theories of fortification. Technicians accompanying the Gardane mission drew up a geographical map of Azarbayjan, made plans to construct two military forts, and began a cannon foundry.

The British government, alarmed by the signing of the Franco-Iranian Treaty of Finkenstein, dispatched Harford Jones Brydges to Iran in 1807. His goal was to effectively eliminate any possibility of French attack on India via Iran. He was commissioned to secure British influence in Iran by replacing the Treaty of Finkenstein with an Anglo-Iranian alliance.[13] Brydges succeeded in negotiating the Preliminary Treaty of Friendship and Alliance between Britain and Iran in 1808. According to the terms of this agreement, Britain replaced France as the provider of military weaponry and expertise. According to Brydges, 'Abbas Mirza and his prime minister, Mirza Bozorg, requested that he impress upon Fath 'Ali Shah the necessity of revamping and

---

[10]For the complete text of the treaty, see Amini, *Napoleon*, Appendix 2, pp. 205-8.

[11]On Bontemps' mission, see Jaubert, *Voyage*, pp. v-vi. For a complete list of members of the Gardane mission, see Amini, *Napoleon*, pp. 104-5

[12]Talleyrand to General Gardane as quoted in Amini, *Napoleon*, p. 106.

[13]See Sir Harford Jones Brydges, *An Account of the Transactions of His Majesty's Mission to the Court of Persia in the Years 1807-11* (London: 1834).

modernizing the Azarbayjani troops. In an audience with the shah, Brydges argued that the Iranian military was in too poor a state to attack Russian forces, and should therefore assume a purely defensive stance. He also convinced the shah to allow British military aid and financial assistance to be earmarked solely for the training of 'Abbas Mirza's troops in Azarbayjan since they were actively involved in the Russo-Persian War.[14] Britain agreed to pay a financial subsidy and provide British military training to Iranian troops. Crown Prince 'Abbas Mirza's secretary recorded that,

> As part of the treaty, it was established that . . . England, for the preparation of an orderly and powerful army, will provide each year the amount of 200,000 tomans in gold . . . and with respect to the training in military technology, qualified leaders and accomplished teachers of infantry, cavalry, artillery and engineers, weaponry experts, and carpenters will be appointed and essential weapons will not be spared.[15]

The Brydges mission consisted of three political envoys, six cavalry officers and two surgeons. Like their predecessors in the Gardane mission, members of the Brydges mission trained and instructed the crown prince's Azarbayjani troops. Sir James Sotherland held classes on surveying, mapping and geography; Dr. Campbell provided medical care and taught English; and Sir Henry Willock supervised the drilling of the troops.

Two years later, British ambassador Sir Gore Ouseley arrived in Iran to finalize negotiations of the Anglo-Iranian Treaty of Friendship. Both Ouseley and mission member James Morier noted the progress that had been made in training 'Abbas Mirza's troops. Morier, who had left Iran only a year previously, was impressed with the number and quality of the newly disciplined and systematically organized troops. Approaching Tabriz, Morier wrote that "another surprise that awaited us was the sight of a troop of Persian horse-artillery, dressed like Europeans, with shaven chins . . . headed by an English officer [who] had come to salute the Ambassador."[16] Ouseley was similarly impressed by the official military reception. He described the encounter with

---

[14]Brydges, *An Account* pp. 268-87.
[15]Provisions of the treaty are recorded by Mirza Mas'ud, in Mirza Mostafa Afshar, *Safarnameh-ye Khosrow Mirza beh Petersburg* (ed) Mohammad Golbun (Tehran: Ketabkhaneh-ye Mostowfi, 1349), p. 99.
[16]Morier, *A Second Journey*, pp. 210, 226.

British Captain Lindsay and the Azarbayjani troops under his command as follows: "With about two hundred of his horse-artillery; all Persians, whom that brave and excellent officer had admirably disciplined; they were uniformly clothed in blue jackets, with red caps and yellow lace, and managed their horses in the style of our English dragoons."[17] Not all European observers were so enthusiastic about the *Nezam-e Jadid* troops, however. Jones and Malcolm and Ousely elsewhere in official correspondence indicated that the Iranian troops were more effective using their traditional methods, since the new, European-style training was as yet incomplete. It would take much longer, they argued to Fath 'Ali Shah and 'Abbas Mirza, to unlearn the traditional methods of discipline which continued to plague the *Nezam-e Jadid* troops.[18]

'Abbas Mirza's *Nezam-e Jadid* reforms were not limited to the training of troops by European military officers. Alongside military drills, the *Nezam-e Jadid* troops were instructed in military technology and related skills such as cannon foundry, mapping and surveying. Drouville, a French officer in the crown prince's service in 1812-13, noted that the crown prince "has divided his time for the last two years between studies, and infantry and artillery maneuvers organized by the European officers." Maurice de Kotzbue, the Russian envoy to Iran in 1818, wrote that "'Abbas Mirza studied military tactics, mathematics and could speak some English."[19] In order to overcome the problem of language barriers and to facilitate instruction, 'Abbas Mirza ordered European military and technical treatises to be translated into Persian.[20] Significantly, the crown prince instructed an elite group to study

---

[17]Sir Gore Ouseley, *Travels in Various Countries of the East; More Particularly Persia*, 3 vols. (London: 1819), vol. III, p. 394.

[18]See Atkin, *Russia and Iran*, p. 135. Nor were they the only negative reports. See Rudi Matthee, "Firearms" *Encyclopaedia Iranica*, pp. 623-24.

[19]Gaspard Drouville, *Voyage en Perse fait en 1812 et 1813*, 2 vols. (Paris: 1828), vol. I, pp. 242-3; and Maurice de Kotzbue, *Mosaferat beh Iran* (trans) Mahmud Hedayat, p. 106 as cited in Mohammad Esma 'il Razvani, "Enqelab-e Fekri-ye Iran dar Dowran-e Fath 'Ali Shah," *Rahnema-ye Ketab*, vol. 7, no. 1 (1343), pp. 13-18.

[20]For partial listings of military treatises translated on orders of the crown prince, see Drouville, *Voyage*, vol. I, p. 242; and James Morier, *A Journey Through Persia, Armenia, and Asia Minor to Constantinople* (London, 1812), p. 283. For a complete list of all books and manuals translated in this period, see Hosayn Mahbubi-Ardakani, *Tarikh-e Mo'assesat-e Tammaduni-ye Jadid dar Iran*, 2 vols. (Tehran, 1975), vol. I, pp. 224-29.

military-related subjects with a French officer in the prince's service. According to 'Abbas Mirza's court chronicler,

> Several youths remarkable for sagacity and talent, chosen from the respectable families of the country, were selected to learn mathematics, military architecture, and to make themselves acquainted with the theory of war, fortification, and tactics.[21]

The shifting alliances between European powers confirmed the age-old Iranian conviction of the necessity of self-reliance. 'Abbas Mirza was concerned about the danger of military inferiority should Iran be forced to defend herself against a European army without outside assistance. As quoted in the court chronicle, the crown prince imagined a time when Iranians "would not be in need of other countries in their affairs, its intelligent masters and craftsmen would not look up to foreign countries, and would produce what they needed in this country."[22] While 'Abbas Mirza was obliged to import European-made weapons for the duration of the two Russo-Persian Wars, he aimed at becoming self-sufficient in arms manufacture. Under the guidance of European officers, various workshops were established for the production of gunpowder and weapons, using modified European models. The crown prince also accumulated a collection of different European weapons, maps, and models of machines.[23] He also encouraged European tradesmen and artisans to settle in Iran.[24]

'Abbas Mirza's goal of establishing a disciplined, standing force necessitated more than military drills and technical instruction. To an unprecedented degree, the *Nezam-e Jadid* required the mobilization of financial and administrative resources. Under the existing military levy

---

[21]'Abd al-Razzaq Donbali, *Ma'athir al-Soltaniyyeh*, translated by Sir Harford Jones Brydges and cited hereafter as *Dynasty of the Kajars* (London, 1833), p. 312.

[22]Donbali, *Dynasty*, p. 143 as quoted in Mohammad Farhad Atai, "The Sending of Iranian Students to Europe, 1811-1906," (Ph.D. diss. University of California, Berkeley, 1992), p. 21.

[23]Drouville, *Voyage*, vol. I, p. 247, and Morier, *A Journey*, p 283. 'Abbas Mirza wrote to Napoleon requesting 12,000 rifles and 10 cannons. He later made a similar request to Austrian Foreign Minister Metternich, who apparently sent him samples of various weapons. For texts of these letters, see Nafisi, *Tarikh-e Ejtema'i*, vol. I, pp. 151 and 263, respectively.

[24]'Abbas Mirza instructed Mirza Saleh Shirazi to place a notice in the London *Times* to this effect in 1823. See the *Times*, no. 11921, July 11, 1823.

system, troops were assigned to governors' and the shah's armies by local tribal and governmental authorities. The men who reported for duty were responsible for supplying their own equipment, and often were left to acquire their own food and provisions. Although payment was in theory intended for the troops during their military service, in practice it was often in arrears. The troops thus relied on their prerogative of plunder, and often caused much destruction of property and resources in the areas that they passed through— including in friendly territory. 'Abbas Mirza proposed to train, equip and provision a standing force that would be paid regularly, whether in training or engaged in a military campaign. In addition, he envisioned a force equipped with the latest European armaments. The cost of supporting his *Nezam-e Jadid* troops was therefore substantially higher than that of employing traditional levies. Moreover, the success of such an enterprise required an administrative structure capable of managing not only the provision and coordination of a standing army, but of collecting and distributing the necessary tax revenues.

As governor of Azarbayjan, the crown prince was faced with similar challenges as those confronting Fath 'Ali Shah on a national scale. 'Abbas Mirza's authority was contested by frequent border disputes, Russian territorial incursions, and the alliance of some provincial authorities with the Russians. Even some of the ulama of Tabriz collaborated with Russian forces.[25] The resources of the province, already weakened from the upheavals surrounding the wars of succession and more recently, Aqa Mohammad Khan Qajar's reconquest of the province, were further depleted by the prolonged Russo-Persian Wars of 1803-15 and 1826-28. The assistance of British officers in training the new troops and the funding promised by Great Britain as part of the Treaty of Friendship and Alliance was not enough to compensate for the huge expense of the wars. Fath 'Ali Shah, while supportive of 'Abbas Mirza's military campaigns, was also mindful of the potential security threat that 'Abbas Mirza posed— both as a destabilizing force in the ranks of the princes should he become too powerful, and also as a potential insurgent against the royal throne itself. For this reason, Fath 'Ali Shah never accepted primary responsibility for funding the Russo-Persian Wars, nor the *Nezam-e*

---

[25]Abbas Amanat, "Russian Intrusion into the Guarded Domains," *Journal of Asian and Oriental Studies* 113 (1993): 39-56.

Jadid, and permitted princely rivalry as a means of reigning in 'Abbas Mirza's potential ambitions.[26] The crown prince's precarious financial situation was further compounded by Iran's defeat by Russia, and by the resulting war indemnities that Iran was forced to pay. Moreover, by 1815, Britain had completely neglected her promised payments to 'Abbas Mirza.[27]

The goals and scope of the *Nezam-e Jadid* reforms cannot be divorced from the crown prince's attempts at expanding his authority and centralizing the administrative apparatus. The *Nezam-e Jadid* required centralization measures, and at the same time, was intended to enhance the prince's control of the province. Funding was crucial for the success of this interactive process. 'Abbas Mirza and Mirza Bozorg recognized the importance of overhauling the system of taxation in order to augment and regularize revenues, which could then be used to finance the *Nezam-e Jadid*. In a conversation with Brydges, Mirza Bozorg discussed the problem of collecting enough revenue to support the military campaign against Russia, as well as the *Nezam-e Jadid* reforms. According to the prime minister, treasury accounts were in a state of confusion and disorganization. Moreover, the system for collecting taxes was inefficient. As a result, the amount of revenue varied significantly from year to year, thereby preventing investments and making uncertain how to actually implement the plan of building up a strong military. Mirza Bozorg also evinced concern for the lack of security of the peasantry, which directly affected their ability to pay taxes.[28] Despite attempts to establish a detailed fiscal register to accurately assess local revenues, 'Abbas Mirza was unsuccessful in substantially improving the taxation system.[29] Morier records the prince complaining of his failure to regulate the amount of taxes to be paid, both by peasants and by the provincial governors.[30] The crown prince in fact never succeeded in establishing a strong financial base for his *Nezam-e Jadid* reforms. Throughout 'Abbas Mirza's governorship, the

---

[26]Atkin, *Russia and Iran*, pp. 117, 119.

[27]Vanessa Martin, "An Evaluation of Reform and Development of the State in the Early Qajar Period," *Die Welt des Islams*, vol. 36, no. 1 (1996), p. 15. In 1822 Mirza Saleh Shirazi was dispatched by 'Abbas Mirza to resecure British payments.

[28]Brydges, *An Account*, pp. 282, 317, 403.

[29]On 'Abbas Mirza's tax reforms see Martin, "An Evaluation," pp. 1-24.

[30]Morier, *A Second Journey*, p. 240.

persistent scarcity of funds constantly threatened the successful implementation of his reform program.

Students Abroad

'Abbas Mirza's decision to dispatch Iranian students to Europe was grounded in his *Nezam-e Jadid* reform program. The dispatch should be seen as constituting evidence of the prince's commitment to change. It also indicated the widening of the parameters of the perception of Iranian "deficiency" vis-à-vis Europe.

The impetus behind the first dispatch of Iranians to study in Europe arose initially out of a mutual desire on the part of Napoleon and Fath 'Ali Shah to cement their diplomatic ties. In 1808 Fath 'Ali Shah suggested to General Gardane that one of the royal princes be sent to reside at Napoleon's court. This practice of exchanging and/or assigning a member of the royal family to live in an allied court was intended as a guarantee of good intentions and to solidify the relationship between the rulers. Gardane, however, seized the opportunity to promote French influence in Iran. He made a counter-proposal to the shah that seven or eight sons of Iranian notables be sent to France for their education under the chaperonage of a member of the religious establishment.[31] Gardane, in making this proposal, was pursing established policy set by Napoleon in his relationships with non-European countries. For example, upon capturing Malta in 1798, Napoleon ordered 60 youths to be sent to France to be educated. A similar arrangement was made with Egypt. In his own words, Napoleon described the advantages of encouraging Egyptian elites to be trained in France. He wrote that, "after a couple years residence among us, these individuals would be dazzled by our greatness. Having mastered our language and adopted our culture, they would become the sturdiest champions of our cause on their return to Egypt."[32] It is also clear that

---

[31]Gardane to Champagny, April 5, 1808, Ministère des Affaires Etrangères, *Correspondance Politique, La Perse*, vol. 10, as noted in Colin Meredith, "The Qajar Response to Russia's Military Challenge, 1804-28," (Ph.D. diss. Princeton Uni-versity, 1973), pp. 185-86.

[32]Napoleon Bonaparte, *Correspondance*, V, no. 4374, as quoted in Alain Silvera, "The First Egyptian Student Mission to France Under Muhammad 'Ali," *Middle Eastern Studies*, vol. 16, no. 2 (1980), p. 4.

Napoleon deliberately allowed Gardane a great deal of latitude in cultivating relations with Iran.[33] 'Abbas Mirza welcomed the opportunity, and agreed with General Gardane that as part of French aid to Iran, a number of Iranians would be sent every year to Paris for instruction.[34] These plans never materialized, however, as the French relationship with Iran deteriorated and the Gardane mission returned to France.

Two years after the signing of the Preliminary Treaty of Friendship between Iran and Great Britain in 1809, a similar provision for the training of Iranians in Europe was negotiated between 'Abbas Mirza and Sir Harford Jones Brydges. Unlike the first arrangement with the French, the initiative to send students abroad was 'Abbas Mirza's.[35] The British were willing to accommodate this request, and offered to pay the costs of the students' journey, as well as a monthly stipend.[36] Like Napoleon, the British clearly perceived the education of Iranians in England as a means of furthering their diplomatic leverage in Iran. In a letter to Brydges, Marquis Wellesley, Governor General of India, counciled him to win over the students' affinities by making sure they became acquainted with the English Prince Regent, and that they learn English and study English literature.[37] Major Sotherland, who was placed in charge of the students in England, decided that in addition to sciences and mathematics, the students should be instructed in English literature, hoping that this would make them "confidential agents" of the British.[38]

'Abbas Mirza, on the other hand, was not interested in sending students abroad in order for them to develop sympathies towards French or English cultures or governments, but rather to acquire specific skills. Accordingly, in 1811, Mohammad Kazem and Hajji Baba

---

[33]See a Persian translation of Napoleon's instructions to General Gardane concerning his impending mission to Iran, in Nafisi, *Tarikh-e Ejtema'i*, vol. I, pp. 102-6.

[34]Mahbubi-Ardakani, *Tarikh-e Mo'assesat*, vol. I, p. 122.

[35]Meredith, "Qajar Response," p. 185.

[36]Mahbubi-Ardakani, *Tarikh-e Mo'assesat*, vol. I, pp. 124-25.

[37]See Mojtaba Minovi, "Avvalin Karevan-e Ma'aref," in Mojtaba Minovi, *Tarikh va Farhang*, vol. 3 (Tehran: Sherekat-e Shami-ye Entesharat-e Khawrazmi, 1973), pp. 380-438.

[38]Dennis Wright, *The Persians Amongst the English* (London: IB Tauris, 1985), pp. 72-74.

Afshar were selected to travel to England to study painting and medicine, respectively. Mohammad Kazem was the son of 'Abbas Mirza's court painter and had already received some training in Persian technique. The crown prince intended for Mohammad Kazem to be able to paint royal portraits and battle scenes in the style of European painters on his return. Hajji Baba Afshar was the son of one of 'Abbas Mirza's officials. The presence of European doctors as part of the diplomatic missions to Iran had heightened the crown prince's awareness of their value, and no doubt influenced him to instruct Hajji Baba Afshar to study European medicine and pharmacology. In selecting the subjects of study for the two individuals, 'Abbas Mirza clearly wanted the subjects to be of immediate use in Iran. As quoted by a member of the Brydges mission, 'Abbas Mirza wanted the students to learn "something that would be useful to me ['Abbas Mirza], the students [themselves], and their country," although he added that their studies need not be limited to their specific fields.[39]

'Abbas Mirza's decision to dispatch a second, larger group of Iranians to study in Europe in 1815 is evidence of his increasing commitment to reform in Iran. In 1815, he requested that Colonel D'Arcy, a member of the Brydges mission, escort ten Iranian students to England and arrange for their studies. D'Arcy agreed to accompany only five students to England, but he assured the crown prince that the British government would pay the students' expenses. When, however, Mirza Bozorg wrote to Morier, the British representative in Iran, for confirmation, Morier declared that he could not agree to the dispatch without the prior assent of the British government. Despite lack of official British support, D'Arcy convinced 'Abbas Mirza and Mirza Bozorg that his own political connections would enable him to procure the necessary financial resources once in England. 'Abbas Mirza agreed to pay travel costs and the first year's expenses for each of the students.

Five Iranians were chosen to travel with D'Arcy back to England: Mirza Saleh Shirazi, Mirza Sayyed Ja'far, Mirza Mohammad Ja'far, Mirza Reza Soltan Tupkhaneh and Ostad Mohammad 'Ali. Not much

---

[39]Letter from Sir Harford Jones Brydges to Cooke April 25, 1812 in British Foreign Ministry Archives group 5, letter 65, as noted in Feridun Adamiyat's introduction to Mirza Saleh Shirazi, *Majmu'eh-ye Safarnameh-ye Mirza Saleh Shirazi* (Tehran: Nashr-e Tarikh-e Iran, 1985), p. 3.

information is available concerning how the students were selected.[40] However, at least three of the five had been in contact with the British mission in Tabriz, and were known personally by D'Arcy. Mirza Saleh Shirazi had been a personal secretary for both Captain Lindsay and D'Arcy; and Mirza Reza and Ostad Mohammad 'Ali had been trained under D'Arcy's supervision at the weapons manufacturing workshop in Tabriz.

Regarding social origins, Mirza Saleh Shirazi's father, Hajji Baqer Khan Kazeruni, was a commander in the army and Mirza Sayyed Ja'far's father, Mirza Taqi Hosayni, was governor of Tabriz. The travel and living expenses designated by the crown prince for each of the students suggest that the first four were from comparable backgrounds and social status, while the fifth, Ostad Mohammad 'Ali, was from a less prominent family.[41] The subjects studied by the students and their subsequent careers further substantiate this supposition: Mirza Sayyed Ja'far studied engineering; Mirza Mohammad Ja'far studied medicine; Mirza Reza Soltan Tupkhaneh studied artillery engineering; Mirza Saleh Shirazi studied European languages and natural sciences in order to become a government translator; and Ostad Mohammad 'Ali studied gun making.

The students remained in England until 1819 when they were recalled by the crown prince back to Iran. In his account of his stay in England, Mirza Saleh Shirazi does not give a specific reason why the students were recalled. However, he discusses at some length the level of concern evinced by the crown prince concerning the students' behavior and course of study, which he attributed to the negative reports circulated by D'Arcy. 'Abbas Mirza and Mirza Bozorg apparently believed that the students were not applying themselves to their studies, and should therefore return home.[42]

---

[40]According to Mirza Saleh Shirazi, D'Arcy made the selection. However, it is likely that 'Abbas Mirza was also involved.

[41]According to D'Arcy, 'Abbas Mirza allotted Ostad Mohammad 'Ali 50 tomans for travel and 180 tomans for first year expenses, while he gave 100 tomans for travel and 250 tomans for first year expenses to each of the other four students. See his letter to Morier as quoted in Mahbubi-Ardakani, *Tarikh-e Mo'assesat*, vol. I, p. 133.

[42]Shirazi, *Safarnameh*, pp. 172, 175.

Subsequent Occupation of the Students

The occupation of the students after their return to Iran is evidence of their level of academic achievement, and of the value placed on their European experience. Hajji Baba Afshar returned to Iran after five years of studying medicine in England. Although he initially experienced a great deal of difficulty in his studies due to lack of prior training, he successfully completed a medical degree at Oxford University. On his return, he became 'Abbas Mirza's chief physician. The crown prince also selected him to serve as a translator for visiting British diplomatic missions in Iran, and in 1829 appointed him to the Iranian delegation to St. Petersburg headed by Prince Khosrow Mirza. After the death of 'Abbas Mirza in 1833, Hajji Baba Afshar, also known as Mirza Baba, became the chief physician at the court of Mohammad Shah.

Mirza Saleh Shirazi was considered particularly learned in European languages and in the general political and historical situation of Europe. Upon returning from England in 1819, he was given the title "*Mohandes*" (engineer). In addition to offering language instruction, Mirza Saleh Shirazi worked as an official translator for 'Abbas Mirza. Because of his knowledge of Europe, Shirazi was immediately drawn into the political sphere and served as a liaison between 'Abbas Mirza's court, Fath 'Ali Shah's court, and European missions to Iran. For example, in 1832-33 Shirazi was appointed as official host to Count Simnavinch, the Russian minister plenipotentiary to Iran. Shirazi was also entrusted with important diplomatic missions on a number of occasions. In 1822 he was sent by the crown prince as a diplomatic envoy to Great Britain, and in 1829 he was also selected to accompany Prince Khosrow Mirza to St. Petersburg on a particularly sensitive diplomatic mission. Shirazi was also employed in the service of Mohammad Shah, who bestowed on him the title "*Mostoufi-ye Nezam*" (government accountant) and appointed him as the "Minister of Tehran."[43] Shirazi is also credited with having established one of the earliest printing presses in Iran, and with founding the first newspaper.

Mirza Sayyed Ja'far was given the honorary title "*Moshir al-Dowleh*" by 'Abbas Mirza, and later was given the title "*Me'marbashi*" (head

---

[43]See Mahbubi-Ardakani, *Tarikh-e Mo'assesat*, vol. I, pp. 176-79; and Wright, *The Persians*, pp. 81-83.

architect). For the first few years after returning from England he taught mathematics and engineering in Tabriz to sons of nobility. He later provided similar instruction to Mohammad Shah. Mirza Sayyed Ja'far Khan was also entrusted with diplomatic functions by Mohammad Shah and Naser al-Din Shah. Between 1836-37 and 1843 he served as ambassador to the Ottoman court in Istanbul, where he was responsible for negotiating two treaties of friendship with Belgium and Spain, in 1841 and 1842, respectively. From 1843 until the death of Mohammad Shah in 1848, Mirza Sayyed Ja'far was employed in Tabriz in the service of Crown Prince Naser al-Din Mirza. In 1851, the prime minister (Amir Kabir) selected him to go to Baghdad to serve as the Iranian representative in border negotiations. Mirza Sayyed Ja'far became one of Naser al-Din Shah's closest advisors. When the shah decided to establish several ministries and also a consultative council in 1858, he charged Mirza Sayyed Ja'far with drawing up the plans, and with heading the council. He retained this position despite his additional appointment as ambassador extraordinary to London in 1861. Upon his return a year later, Mirza Sayyed Ja'far was awarded the honorary position as head of the Imam Reza shrine in Mashhad where he remained until his death in 1863.

Mirza Reza Soltan Tupkhaneh was given the position of *Mohandes-e Tupkhaneh* (artillery engineer) upon his return to Iran in 1819. He was appointed chief engineer in 'Abbas Mirza's army, and is credited with having designed the building for the first European-style educational institution founded in Iran, the *Dar al Fonun* (a polytechnic college). Clearly, therefore, Mirza Reza had attained a high degree of knowledge of engineering during his studies in England. He also reached a level of proficiency in English and French sufficient to enable him to translate books from both languages into Persian. Unlike his fellow students, Mirza Sayyed Ja'far and Mirza Saleh Shirazi, Mirza Reza was not charged with diplomatic duties, because he had neither the same social position, nor was he particularly connected to 'Abbas Mirza's court.

Ostad Mohammad 'Ali returned to Iran in 1819 well versed in gun manufacturing. He worked in an arms manufacturing workshop in Tabriz and in 1835 was placed in charge of the royal foundry in Tehran. Despite the fact that he returned to Iran with an English wife, his social standing did not suffer. In fact, Ostad Mohammad's technical proficiency earned him a great deal of prestige, and he was given the title *qurkhanehchibashi* (head of the arsenal) in addition to having "Khan" attached to his name.

Mirza Mohammad Ja'far, who remained in England to pursue his medical studies, apparently left England a year later, but there is no information on his subsequent career.[44]

The dispatch of students abroad did not end with the return of the 1811 and 1815 student missions in 1819. 'Abbas Mirza sent an additional four students to Europe during his lifetime. In 1819-20 he sent Hajji 'Abbas Shirazi, a painter by profession, to Paris to learn papermaking. In Paris, Hajji 'Abbas Shirazi worked in a number of papermaking workshops, but failed to master the craft. In order to return to Iran with the requisite skills, however, he brought back with him a French woman paper maker.[45] In 1822-23 the crown prince sent Mirza Ja'far Tabrizi to Moscow to learn printing. On his return he brought back a printing press which he set up in Tabriz. Two other students were dispatched to Europe, although the exact dates are unknown. Ja'far Qoli Beg Afshar, reputedly the brother of Hajji Baba Afshar, was sent to learn mining in Russia. Upon his return, he worked in an ammunition workshop. 'Abbas Mirza also dispatched Bahram Khan abroad to learn medicine. No information is available concerning the dates, duration, or location of his studies; however, upon his return, he reputedly practiced medicine in Tabriz.[46]

A number of general conclusions can be drawn from the information available concerning the studies and subsequent careers of the first seven students sent abroad in 1811 and 1815. First, the subjects that 'Abbas Mirza selected for the students were practical ones, and nearly all had military applications. Of the seven students dispatched in 1811 and 1815, three pursued studies with direct military applications: two students studied engineering, one gun making; and

---

[44]According to Mahbubi-Ardakani it is not clear even if he returned to Iran. See his *Tarikh-e Mo'assesat*, vol. I, p.187. Minovi, however, believed that he did return. See Minovi, "Avvalin Karevan," p. 422. Wright records that he boarded a ship bound for Iran on April 27, 1820. See Wright, *The Persians*, p. 80.

[45]Mahbubi-Ardakani, *Tarikh-e Mo'assesat*, vol. I, pp. 178-79.

[46]Information on these additional four students can be found in Mahbubi-Ardakani, *Tarikh-e Mo'assesat*, vol. I, pp. 187-89; and in Mahbubi-Ardakani, "Daramuzan va Daneshjuyan-e Irani dar Rusiyeh dar Zaman-e Qajariyeh," *Rahenema-ye Ketab*, vol. 6, no. 10 (1346), pp. 564-76.

two pursued medicine. Only two of the seven pursued studies removed from direct military applications (painting, European languages and natural sciences), although certainly these skills were valuable to 'Abbas Mirza and his court. In particular, Mirza Saleh Shirazi's extensive language training provided important diplomatic skills. None of the seven students pursued studies which were not immediately practical in nature. The crown prince made clear that study abroad was for the sole purpose of gaining useful skills. He and Mirza Bozorg were concerned that the students not waste time abroad, but apply themselves to their studies and return to Iran.

Second, upon returning to Iran, the students were given positions in accordance with their studies. They were also given marks of distinction, and honorary titles. The students returned from Europe with skills that proved nearly as valuable as their designated fields of study. The language skills and general familiarity with Europe and European customs made the students valued diplomats and government advisors. Hajji Baba Afshar, Mirza Saleh Shirazi, and Mirza Sayyed Ja'far were all given a number of sensitive diplomatic appointments, and enjoyed continued prominence under a succession of monarchs. It must be pointed out, however, that those individuals who did attain governmental and diplomatic prominence were also from powerful families with court connections. Those students without court connections were not awarded the same positions of distinction upon their return. For example, Mirza Reza received a similar education in Europe as did Mirza Sayyed Ja'far, but never rose to governmental prominence. Ostad Mohammad 'Ali, while certainly gaining marks of status upon his return, was sent to Europe to learn a trade, not a profession, and was clearly of a different social stature than the other students.

The information concerning the additional four students sent abroad by 'Abbas Mirza is too sparse to permit any conclusions to be drawn concerning their careers after returning from abroad. It is noteworthy, however, that the four dispatched individually to Europe after the return of the 1811 and 1815 missions were by and large skilled workmen. In addition, they were sent to master specific skills, rather than to engage in lengthy studies. None of these students were sent to learn engineering, or military technologies, but rather were engaged in support technology. The fact that two of the four were sent to Russia is partly a result of the general cooling off of Anglo-Iranian relations, partly a result of the considerable expense of sending students to England, and partly due to the nature of the skills they sought which could be satisfactorily acquired in Russia.

The students' language skills also provided an impetus to further translation of European works. As mentioned previously, 'Abbas Mirza had requested a number of translations of military treatises prior to sending the students abroad. However, upon their return the students themselves undertook a number of translations. In addition, the subject of the translations was no longer purely military in nature, but broadened to include European history and geography.

Publishing

In addition to the students' language skills and familiarity with Europe, the most important side benefit of 'Abbas Mirza's dispatch of students to Europe was the impetus this provided to publishing in Iran. Mirza Saleh Shirazi was largely responsible for this since he brought a printing press back with him from England in 1819. Prior to this time, printing did exist in Iran. European travelers Chardin and Tavernier in their accounts of their voyages to Iran in the Safavid period both mention the existence of printing presses.[47] However, printing was undertaken by religious minorities and did not include anything in Persian.[48] The first definite printing press to print in Persian was established in Tabriz in 1816-17 by Aqa Zayn al-'Abedin Tabrizi under the protection of 'Abbas Mirza. The first books published were the *Fathnameh* (Book of Conquest) and *Jehadiyyeh* (Fighters Against the Infidels) by Mirza Bozorg in 1817.[49]

In 1819 Mirza Saleh Shirazi returned from England bringing back with him the second printing press to be established in Iran. In his travel diary, Mirza Saleh Shirazi explained his motivations:

---

[47]Sir John Chardin, *Travels in Persia, 1643-1713* (London, 1927); Jean-Baptiste Tavernier, *The Six Voyages of Jean-Baptiste Tavernier* (London, 1678).

[48]Carmelites in Isfahan wrote and printed books prior to 1648. In addition, Armenians in Julfa, Isfahan established a printing press in 1637. See Willem Floor, "Chap," *Encyclopaedia Iranica*, vol. 6, pp. 760-64; and *A Chronicle of the Carmelites in Persia* 2 vols. (London: Eyre & Spottiswoode, 1939).

[49]It has not been ascertained which book was published first. See Floor, "Chap," pp. 761. See also Willem Floor, "The First Printing Press in Iran," *Zeitschrift der Deutschen Morgenländischen Gesellschaft*, vol. 130 (1980), pp. 369-71.

I became convinced that our return to Iran was a foregone conclusion. I thought to myself that, apart from my studies, it would be good if I could bring something else back to Iran from this land that would be useful for the exalted government. And for some time I had been thinking of bringing a printing press and the art of setting type back with me.[50]

Mirza Saleh Shirazi clearly states that his intention was to bring back something useful. The fact that his decision occurred near the end of his trip (in November, 1818) indicates that he had not been instructed to learn printing by 'Abbas Mirza as part of his studies, but rather that his decision resulted from his understanding of his general purpose for having been sent to England, as well as his belief in the desirability of a printing press for Iran.[51]

Accordingly, Shirazi proceeded to learn the process of printing in order to be able to set up a working press in Iran. Shirazi makes it clear in his travel account that learning printing was difficult and took time away from his other studies. Indeed, in order to make the most of his remaining time in England, he was constantly engaged in his studies and in learning printing:

From five hours before midday when I woke up until ten in the morning I studied French at Mr. Balfour's house. After lunch I again studied and after that until two in the afternoon I read other French books. Afterwards I changed into English style clothes and went to the home of my printing master, where I remained in the printing workshop until four thirty in the afternoon. After this I ate dinner at a public house (*mehmankhaneh*), returned home, read some Roman, Greek, Russian, Ottoman and Iranian history and some stories in English, and then translated a page from French to English.[52]

Had he known of the existence of an operational press already established in Iran, it is doubtful that he would have gone through so much trouble to learn the trade himself. Just prior to Shirazi's departure from England, his instructor Mr. Danes and Sir Gore Ouseley gave him

---

[50]Shirazi, *Safarnameh*, pp. 344-45.
[51]See Shirazi, *Safarnameh*, p. 353. Mohammad Isma'il Razvani, "Mirza Saleh Shirazi va Ruznameh-negari," in the introduction to Shirazi, *Safarnameh*, and Mahbubi-Ardakani, *Tarikh-e Mo'assesat*, vol. I, pp. 212-14, agree with this interpretation.
[52]Shirazi, *Safarnameh*, p. 345.

with a small printing press and all the necessary materials with which to establish a working press in Iran.[53]

Upon returning to Iran, Mirza Saleh Shirazi initially occupied himself with setting up the printing press. On his trip to Russia in 1829 as a member of Khosrow Mirza's diplomatic mission, Mirza Saleh Shirazi brought additional presses back with him to Iran. Mirza Saleh Shirazi, however, was too busy with other political and administrative duties to personally oversee printing operations, and he therefore requested that Mirza Asadollah be sent to St. Petersburg to learn the printing trade. On his return, Mirza Asadollah established a press in Tabriz, and at the request of Mohammad Shah, moved it to Tehran after five years.

An additional printing press was established by Mirza Ja'far Amir, who had been dispatched by 'Abbas Mirza in 1822-23 to Moscow to learn printing. In 1824-25 he published Sadi's *Golestan*. The press first established by Aqa Zayn al-'Abedin continued operation until 1824-25 when Fath 'Ali Shah requested he move it to Tehran. There, he became acquainted with Manuchehr Khan Gorji (later Mo'tamad al-Dowleh) who aided him in his publishing activities. While a number of presses were established and operated in this period, printing was not continuous, nor was the number of books large. Presses lapsed into disuse, and were periodically revived by others individuals. In no sense, therefore, was any publishing industry established, and publication continued to depend on individual effort and commitment.[54]

Books printed in the Fath 'Ali Shah period for the most part concerned religion, current events, and fables. However, travel accounts and other information on Europe gradually made its way into circulation. For example, in addition to some popular works such as *A Thousand and One Nights* and *Layla and Majnun*, *Tohfat al-Alam* (The Covenant of the World) by 'Abd al-Latif Shushtari became available in 1800, and in 1808 Aqa Ahmad Behbehani's *Mer'at al-Ahval-e Jahannema* was written.[55] In addition, the travel accounts of both Mirza Saleh

[53]Ibid, p. 353.

[54]Mahbubi-Ardakani, *Tarikh-e Mo'assesat*, vol. I, pp. 209-22.

[55]Aqa Mir 'Abd al-Latif Khan Shushtari, *Tohfat al-'Alam va Dhayl al-Tohfehl* (Tehran: Tahuri, 1363/1984), and Aqa Ahmad b. Mohammad 'Ali Behbehani, *Mer'at al-Ahval-e Jahannema*, Tehran: Amir Kabir, 1370/1991). On Shustari, see Juan Cole, "Invisible Occidentalism: Eighteenth-Century Indo-Persian Constructions of the West," *Iranian Studies*, vol. 25 (1992), pp. 3-16; on

Shirazi and special envoy Mirza Abu al-Hasan Shirazi to Europe were widely read amongst court circles, attesting to the increase in interest concerning Europe.[56]

In 1837 Mirza Saleh Shirazi printed the first Iranian newspaper, the *Kaghaz-e Akhbar*, using the printing press he brought back from London in 1819.[57] In the announcement for the newspaper, Mirza Saleh Shirazi emphasized the importance of Iranians to become aware of world events, and to import new technology from Europe. The paper was published so that "the inhabitants of the protected domains [Iran] shall become instructed."[58] The paper declared that: "the greatest instruction is teaching about the affairs of the world, to this end, in accordance with the imperial order, a news paper (*kaghaz-e akhbari*) containing news of the East and of the West will be printed at the printing house and distributed to the outlying areas and regions."[59] Due to lack of support from Mohammad Shah, however, the *Kaghaz-e Akhbar* stopped being printed less than two years later.

Opposition and the Emergence of the Modernization Dilemma

The *Nezam-e Jadid* reforms initiated by 'Abbas Mirza and Mirza Bozorg were essentially an example of the phenomenon of defensive military reforms. Elsewhere in the Middle East, Egypt and the Ottoman Empire also recognized the need to revamp their troops along European lines after suffering military defeats by European armies.[60] As

---

Behbehani, see Juan Cole, "Mirror of the World: Iranian 'Orientalism' and Early 19th-Century India," *Critique*, vol. 8 (Spring 1996), pp. 41-60.

[56]Morier, *A Second Journey*, p. 405.

[57]The first newspaper in Persian was published in India sometime in the late 18th or early 19th century. The first Egyptian newspaper, *Vaqaye' Misriyya*, was published in Cairo in 1828. The first Ottoman newspaper, *Taqvim-i Vaqayi*, was published in Istanbul in 1823. On early newspapers in the Middle East, see Feridun Adamiyat, *Amir Kabir va Iran*, 2d ed. (Tehran: Amir Kabir, 1955), pp. 368-77; and Peter Avery, "Printing, the Press, and Literature in Modern Iran," *Cambridge History of Iran*, vol. 7, pp. 815-69.

[58]Quoted in Adamiyat, *Amir Kabir va Iran*, p. 370.

[59]Ibid.

[60]See David Ralston, *Importing the European Army: The Introduction of European Military Techniques and Institutions into the Extra-European World, 1600-1914*

in these other instances, military reform in Iran naturally led to a need for related technology and skills such as European-trained doctors and the translation of European technical manuals and other texts. 'Abbas Mirza and his prime minister also recognized that structural problems impeded substantive military reform; they attempted to improve the taxation system and strengthen the central administration. From the outset, therefore, the *Nezam-e Jadid* reforms were intimately connected to 'Abbas Mirza's attempt to consolidate his own authority in the province of Azarbayjan. The dispatch of students abroad is further evidence of the perception of a "deficiency" in Iran and testifies to 'Abbas Mirza's commitment to effect substantive change. The dispatch was also the result of the internationalization of Iran's diplomatic arena. The crown prince realized that in order to meet the challenges of this new diplomatic situation, it was necessary to acquire both political expertise and a familiarity with European languages.

The *Nezam-e Jadid* reforms were thus highly ambitious— both in terms of the depth of change desired, and of the range of spheres effected— whether military, technological, diplomatic or administrative. Precisely due to its intended scope, the *Nezam-e Jadid* reforms engendered fierce opposition. An examination of the nature of this opposition reveals both the ideological and political obstacles to reform in early Qajar Iran. There were three principle bases of opposition to the *Nezam-e Jadid* reforms. First, princely and court rivalry with 'Abbas Mirza and his prime minister. Second, groups with vested interests in the political status quo were threatened by centralization measures. And third, the reforms were perceived as offensive to Iranian cultural and religious sensibilities.

Fath 'Ali Shah's reign was characterized by strong rivalry amongst the Qajar princes over the issue of succession. Princely competition was of such manifest proportion that many European travelers to Iran predicted military conflict upon the death of the shah.[61] According to 'Abbas Mirza, the most vehement enemies of the *Nezam-e Jadid* reforms

---

(Chicago, University of Chicago Press, 1990). On this process in Egypt, see Khaled Fahmy, *All the Pasha's Men: Mehmed Ali, His Army and the Making of Modern Egypt* (Cambridge: Cambridge University Press, 1997).

[61]Drouville, *Voyage*, vol. I, p. 204; Ouseley, *Travels*, vol. III, p. 56. A Russian nobleman, encountered by members of Prince Khosrow Mirza's mission to Russia in 1829, expressed similar fears. See Afshar, *Safarnameh*, pp. 237-38.

were other royal princes who were contenders for the throne.[62] The most powerful, and also therefore 'Abbas Mirza's greatest rival, was his half-brother Mohammad 'Ali Mirza, who considered himself to have been usurped in the position of crown prince (*vali ahd*).[63] The princes believed that the military reforms would strengthen 'Abbas Mirza's claim to the throne by providing him with a strong power base in Azarbayjan as well as the troops to ensure his succession by force. They were also concerned that a successful military operation against the Russian forces by the new *Nezam-e Jadid* troops would enhance 'Abbas Mirza's standing with the shah. Personal antagonisms between Mirza Bozorg and Fath 'Ali Shah's prime minister, Mirza Shafi', also contributed to the royal court's opposition to the *Nezam-e Jadid* reforms.

In addition to personal antagonisms generated by rivalry, the reforms were opposed due to the reinforcement they provided to the crown prince's centralization measures. In particular, regional powers in Azarbayjan resented 'Abbas Mirza's attempts to regularize the system of taxation. In their pragmatic view, such reform would threaten their authority in tax collection, not to mention requiring additional payments to the crown prince's court. Although a number of Qajar princes employed Europeans to train small segments of their troops in the European fashion, they were unwilling to assume the financial burden that the establishment of a standing army entailed.[64] In the absence of sufficient financial resources, the existence of large numbers of troops was dangerous as they might resort to looting if they did not receive payment.[65] The prince-governors were also reluctant to

---

[62]Jaubert, *Voyage*, p. 174.

[63]While actually older than 'Abbas Mirza, Mohammad 'Ali Mirza's mother was not, unlike 'Abbas Mirza's mother, from the Davalu groups of Qajars. This contributed to the selection of 'Abbas Mirza as crown prince. In addition, Fath 'Ali Shah was no doubt influenced by the strong preference for 'Abbas Mirza over Mohammad 'Ali Mirza demonstrated by Aqa Mohammad Khan Qajar.

[64]Drouville, *Voyage*, vol. II, p. 25. Mohammad 'Ali Mirza employed European officers to drill a corps of regular infantry in Kermanshah, and Hosayn 'Ali Mirza Farmanfarma had European military officers in his service in 1832. See Robert Ker Porter, *Travels in Georgia, Persia, Armenia, Ancient Babylonia During the Years 1817, 1818, 1819. 1820* (London, 1821), vol. II, pp. 582, 88; and George Curzon, *Persia and the Persian Question* (London, 1892), p. 581, respectively.

[65]Martin, "An Evaluation," pp. 18-19.

antagonize the ulama, local landowners, officials and tribal leaders that a military and administrative centralization and reorganization along the lines of 'Abbas Mirza's *Nezam-e Jadid* necessarily entailed. The princes preferred, therefore, to retain the existing system of tribal levies in times of need.

Local tribal leaders also opposed any change in the system of military levies. Their position as local leaders was directly threatened by the "state" attempt to establish a regular, standing army. They would thereby lose their leverage as traditional providers of troops. In addition, a regular army where obedience is defined by a hierarchical structure challenged the traditional primary allegiance of troops to their tribal leaders. Morier identified conflict in troop loyalties between their traditional and their new military leaders as a primary impediment to military reform in Iran.[66] Moreover, a regular army would destroy the established reciprocal relationship between the tribes and the central as well as provincial governments.

In addition to the explicit threat of the *Nezam-e Jadid* reforms to existing interests and prerogatives, the reforms initiated by 'Abbas Mirza constituted an implicit threat to Iranian cultural sensibilities. This is attested to by the arguments employed and the type of language used in the debates surrounding the reforms. Opponents attempted to delegitimize the reforms by representing them as in conflict with shared social and religious attitudes. Propaganda spread by opponents of the *Nezam-e Jadid* reform attacked the apparent "Europeanization" of the new troops. At issue were the European uniforms, and the enforced shaving of beards by the troops.[67] Traditionally, beards were perceived as demonstrating religious belief, as they imitated the Prophet's own behavior.[68] Even 'Abbas Mirza had reservations about forcing his men to abandon this custom. As recounted by Morier,

> It was only upon the article of shaving off beards, that the Prince was inexorable; nor would the sacrifice of them have ever taken place if it had not happened, that on firing the guns before the Prince, a powder horn

---

[66]Morier, *A Second Journey*, p. 213.

[67]Ouseley, *Travels*, vol. III, p. 394.

[68]While not prohibited, shaving was discouraged by a series of Shi'ite religious edicts. See for example, Mohammad Baqer al-Majlesi, *Bihar al-Anwar* and *Hilyat al-Muttaqin*. Based on a Prophetic hadith, the wearing of a beard was encouraged by generations of Iranian ulama.

exploded in the hand of a gunner, who by good luck had been gifted with a long beard, which in one instant was blown away from his chin.[69]

Although the *Nezam-e Jadid* troops did eventually adopt European-style uniforms, they refused to give up their customary hats. 'Abbas Mirza's personal loyalty to Iran was questioned when "his enemies said of him that he did not deserve the throne because he had become *'farangi,'* which is to say [in a pejorative way] 'Europeanized,' and that he already wore [European] boots."[70] There was also resentment against the crown prince for giving European officers authority over Iranian troops.[71]

Opposition to the visible "Europeanization" of 'Abbas Mirza's *Nezam-e Jadid* troops was reinforced by the equation of cultural trans-gressions with the violation of Islamic tenets. For example, Mirza Bozorg complained about the resistance to the European uniforms. "They [the troops] say, 'this man is a Christian, and wishes to make us Christians. It is for this reason that he gives currency to the customs of the Christians, and causes us to wear their dress.'"[72] Mohammad 'Ali Mirza also portrayed the reforms as un-Islamic. In a conversation recorded by Ouseley, 'Abbas Mirza complained that "Muhamad 'Ali Mirza . . . had endeavored to render him and his nizam odious . . . by attempting to show that in adopting the customs of the infidels he was subverting the religion of Islam." In a letter written to a collegue in 1839 an Iranian official asked rhetorically: "Can we reform our dress without offending our divine religion?"[73]

'Abbas Mirza attempted to legitimate his reforms by portraying them as in accordance with Islamic principles and tradition. For example, the crown prince explained to Ouseley that he "caused a passage in the Koran that is favorable to the improvement of the means of attack and defense in the cause of religion, to be copied, to be

---

[69]Morier, *A Second Journey*, pp. 211-12.

[70]Drouville, *Voyage*, vol. I, p. 241.

[71]Drouville, *Voyage*, vol. II, p. 131.

[72]Abu al-Qasem Qa'em Maqam, *Munsha'at* (ed) Jahangir Qa'em Maqami (Tehran, 1337/1958-9), quoted in Hamid Algar, *Religion and State in Iran* (Berkeley: University of California Press, 1969), p. 78.

[73]Letter from a Mirza Sadeq to a Mirza Hosayn, reprinted and translated into French by Eugène Boré, in *Correspondance et mémoires d'un voyageur en Orient* 2 vols. (Paris: Olivier-Fulgenie, 1840), vol. II, p. 138.

sealed and approved by the chiefs of the law in Persia, and disseminated throughout the country."[74] In another instance, 'Abbas Mirza moved to preempt claims that his military reforms violated Islamic tenets, by having the newly-introduced European-style flags blessed by a leading religious authority in front of the entire army.[75] 'Abbas Mirza's court chronicler recorded the crown prince's attempt to present his reforms not as innovations, but rather as the re-establishment of traditional systems as exemplified (and thereby legitimized) by the Prophet's own military successes. Significantly, the crown prince was compared to the Prophet:

> It was by such rules and principles [as the *Nezam-e Jadid*] that the orthodox armies in a short time overthrew the neighboring sovereigns . . . and caused to circulate in the channel of the worked the stream of Tradition and Faith derived from the pure fountain of truth and certainty.[76]

Given the vehemence of the opposition to the "Europeanization" of the *Nezam-e Jadid* troops, it is curious to note the absence of opposition to the dispatch of students abroad to Europe.[77] The dispatch of students abroad was not considered to be as significant, or as threatening, as were the military changes taking place for two reasons. First, there had been occasional Iranian travelers to Europe, and vice versa, for hundreds of years. These travelers consisted of merchants and occasionally official emissaries.[78] 'Abbas Mirza's student dispatch was seen as a continuation of this same precedent. The prevailing lack of alarm concerning the students was also the result of the enduring conviction amongst most Iranians that Europe culturally speaking, was inferior to Iran, and thus would not constitute a real

---

[74]This conversation is recorded in Morier, *A Second Journey*, p. 213. For the Qur'anic passage most probably employed, see Donbali, *Dynasty*, p. 307. Selim III employed the same Qur'anic passage in a similar attempt to refute criticism of his *Nizam-i Jedid*.

[75]Drouville, *Voyage*, vol. II, p. 133.

[76]Donbali, *Dynasty*, pp. 306-7.

[77]Mahbubi-Ardakani, *Tarikh-e Mo'assesat*, vol. I, p. 176. Even from European travel accounts, the dispatch of students abroad receives little attention. Iranian chronicles, including those of 'Abbas Mirza's secretary, Mirza Mas'ud, and Donbali, contain few references to the student missions.

[78]For records of Iranian travelers to Europe prior to 'Abbas Mirza's student dispatch, see Mahbubi-Ardakani, *Tarikh-e Mo'assesat*, vol. I, pp. 229-35; and M. K. Sadre, *Relations de l'Iran avec l'Europe* (Paris, 1937).

attraction for the students. That this in fact turned out not to be an accurate assessment of the appeal of Europe, illustrates the changing relationship of Iran to Europe— a relationship which will be explored in the following chapter.

Secondly and more importantly, the dispatch was not considered a threat due to the small numbers involved. By contrast, the military reforms involved not only a substantial number of individuals, but also represented a visual testimony to change. A continuation of the military reforms threatened to involve increasing numbers of individuals, and also threatened the status quo of various interest groups and institutions. The dispatch of students did not challenge any political, social or economic groups, and its results were confined to a very limited number of individuals. While the *language of debate* concerning opposition to military reforms centered on fears of European cultural encroachment, the students sent abroad at this time, unlike the arrival of European military advisors in Iran or the sartorial "Europeanization" of the *Nezam-e Jadid* troops, were *not* viewed as carriers of European culture back to Iran.

It is evident from the language and type of arguments employed in the conflict over the *Nezam-e Jadid* reforms that both proponents and opponents recognized the enormous emotive and symbolic value of both Islamic and Iranian cultural traditions. Moreover, these traditions formed a core basis of identity as both sides jostled to harness their legitimacy and appropriate for themselves the role of guarantors of national interests. Conflict between proponents of change and defenders of the status quo is nothing new. However, what distinguishes the *Nezam-e Jadid* reform controversy is that for the first time, reform (albeit to a limited degree) was associated with Westernization. This led to the emergence of a paradoxical relationship to reform. On the one hand, Europe was both the model of strength, and a new source of technology and skills. On the other hand, Europe represented a cultural threat, not to mention a political and territorial danger. Both the proponents and the opponents of the *Nezam-e Jadid* reforms concurred that "Westernization," in terms of the adoption of European cultural and/or social traditions, was undesirable. The dilemma thus became how to adopt European technological advances without at the same time importing European culture. It was at this time that the fault lines concerning modernization and Westernization began to emerge.

'Abbas Mirza's opponents— whether on grounds of personal rivalry or the maintenance of the political and administrative status quo— were able to capitalize on the negative cultural implications of the reforms. This forced the proponents to adopt a defensive position in an attempt to refute the connection between modernization and Westernization. 'Abbas Mirza tried to tactically circumnavigate this connection by having the reforms sanctioned by religious leaders and by portraying them as a revival of Islamic tradition. However, at this time, the modernization dilemma was neither fully perceived, nor were its ramifications explored. There was little awareness of the socio-historical context of European institutions and technology, and less still of their cultural implications. It was not until a later period when continued contestation of reforms resulted in a clarification of this process.

The Failure of the *Nezam-e Jadid*

Following 'Abbas Mirza's premature death in 1833, his reform program for the most part came to a halt. The crown prince never succeeded in establishing the foundations for substantive reform. Unlike his counterparts in Egypt and the Ottoman Empire, he did not enjoy a strong central governmental apparatus, or the necessary funds to spear-head reform. Powerful opponents and perennial financial shortages combined to cripple the *Nezam-e Jadid*. The failure of the *Nezam-e Jadid* troops under 'Abbas Mirza's leadership in the two Russo-Persian Wars further discredited the reform program. The *Nezam-e Jadid*, as it constituted a threat to established prerogatives and cultural sensibilities, lapsed into dissolution.

Mohammad Shah and the *Nezam-e Jadid*

Mohammad Shah (1834-1848) continued his father 'Abbas Mirza's efforts at adopting European military and technological advancements. He also recognized the need to regularize and strengthen the central governmental administration. Due to opposition to change, financial problems and continued internal revolts, however, Mohammad Shah was unable to effect substantive change. His focus, moreover, continued throughout his reign to be the importation of European military technology.

Mohammad Shah's commitment to military reform was a result of his attempts to reconquer Herat and thus partially make up for the recent loss of Iranian territory in the first and second Russo-Persian Wars of 1803-15 and 1826-28. Iranians still considered Herat to constitute part of Iran. The reconquest of Herat was not a new goal. 'Abbas Mirza had been in the process of besieging Herat when he died in 1833.

Immediately upon assuming the throne, Mohammad Shah made his intentions clear. As recounted by Major Rawlinson, a British officer in the service of the shah:

> So notorious was the young Shah's passion on this subject [retaking Herat], that the coronation anthems rang with prophetic paeans of victory over the Uzbegs and Afghans; and His Majesty's speech, delivered from the throne before the foreign Missions on the first occasion of a public durbar, dwelt rapturously on the same theme.[79]

Following his accession to the throne, the British granted the Iranian government funds in order to reestablish cannon and munitions foundries, and additional weaponry was sent from England. Two years later, in 1836, nine British officers arrived in Iran to engage in military instruction of Iranian troops.[80] Just as in the military reforms instituted by Crown Prince 'Abbas Mirza previously, Mohammad Shah sought religious sanction for the introduction of European-style military uniforms.[81] Without sensing any inherent contradiction, he also attempted to present the new uniforms as having pre-Islamic Persian origins, by pointing out their similarity with uniforms of soldiers engraved at Persepolis.[82]

The siege of Herat in 1836-38 furthered Mohammad Shah's awareness of the technological gap between Iranian and European militaries.[83] Military and diplomatic conflict with Great Britain led him

---

[79] Henry Creswicke Rawlinson, *England and Russia in the East* (London: John Murray, 1875), p. 51.
[80] Curzon, *Persia*, p. 583.
[81] Algar, *Religion and State in Iran*, p. 120.
[82] Boré, *Correspondance*, vol. II, p. 129.
[83] Adamiyat, *Amir Kabir va Iran*, p. 186.

to seek technical assistance from the French government. In 1839 Mohammad Shah dispatched Mirza Hosayn Khan Ajudanbashi to France to request French military instruction, and to seek French diplomatic intervention with Great Britain concerning Iranian claims to Herat. The French government, not wishing to jeopardize its relations with either Great Britain or Russia, refused to dispatch an official military mission to Iran. However, the French government did agree to facilitate an arrangement for military instruction between a group of former French army officers and the Iranian ambassador. An agreement was signed on August 9, 1839 whereby eleven former officers would be engaged for the period of eight years in instructing Iranian troops in infantry, cavalry and artillery techniques.[84] This group of French officers did not effect any substantial improvement in the Iranian military, however.[85] Years later, Iranian Prime Minister Mirza Aqasi reiterated his desire for stronger Franco-Iranian relations, and urged the French ambassador to send additional French military instructors to Iran. In a letter to the French ambassador, Comte de Sartiges, in 1844 Mirza Aqasi wrote: "That which I give importance to above everything else is that French instructors come and train [our] troops."[86]

In addition to military instruction, Mohammad Shah continued 'Abbas Mirza's policy of acquiring European artisanal skills by inviting French technicians to come settle in Iran. When Félix Eduard Comte de Sercy, the French ambassador to Iran, arrived in 1840, he brought along experts in candle making, papermaking, glass making and cotton spinning as had been requested.[87] In addition, one of the concessions granted to the French by Mohammad Shah during Sercy's mission to Iran was that French craftsmen in Azarbayjan would receive official protection for fifteen years.[88] Mohammad Shah's continued attempt to attract skilled French craftsmen from France is illustrated by the fact that the Iranian ambassador to France in 1847, Mohammad 'Ali Khan

---

[84]Homa Nateq, *Iran dar Rahyabi-ye Farhangi, 1834-48* (Tehran: Khavaran, 1368), pp. 112-14.

[85]According to Curzon "the experiment was a complete failure." See *Persia*, pp. 585-86. Nateq asserts that the French officers were essentially adventurers hoping to make money in Iran. See *Rahyabi*, p. 113.

[86]Quoted in Nateq, *Rahyabi*, p. 128.

[87]Ibid, p. 112.

[88]Ibid, p. 118.

Shirazi, requested that a variety of French craftsmen be dispatched by the French government to Iran. Guizot, the French minister of foreign affairs, agreed to send a number of craftsmen and engineers to Iran.[89] However, the death of Mohammad Shah on September 4, 1848, and the subsequent cooling-off of Franco-Iranian relations prevented the fulfilment of this agreement.

Students Abroad

Mohammad Shah, like 'Abbas Mirza, recognized the importance of sending students abroad to study. In 1839 he considered sending a contingent of 40-50 students to Egypt for training. The Iranian ambassador to the Ottoman Empire, Mirza Ja'far Khan Moshir al-Dowleh (himself a former student in England), engaged in negotiations with the Egyptian government of Mohammad 'Ali Pasha. In an official letter to Prime Minister Mirza Aqasi, Mirza Ja'far Khan wrote:

> You should make certain that a number of people will be specified and determined and have been careful that to the extent possible, [that they be] sons of nobility, literate, and educated, and [also] that in addition, two capable, qualified, trustworthy and experienced men will accompany [this group of students].[90]

Mohammad 'Ali Pasha had established a number of military training academies in Cairo by this time, and the Iranian students would no doubt have been sent to one of these. Discussions with Mohammad 'Ali Pasha broke down, however, due to protests by the British and Ottoman authorities who were concerned about the possible impetus the student mission would give to improved Iranian-Egyptian relations.[91] As a result, this group of students was never sent to Egypt. Nonetheless, Mirza Ja'far Khan's letters concerning these negotiations testify to Mohammad Shah's awareness of similar processes of adoption of European technology and military training in other Muslim countries and his desire to affect similar improvements.

The first official dispatch of students by Mohammad Shah occurred in 1845. In line with his foreign policy objectives, France was chosen as

---

[89]See Feridun Adamiyat, *Fekr-e Azadi va Moqademeh-ye Nehzat-e Mashrutiyat dar Iran* (Tehran: Sokhan, 1340), pp. 41-43. See also Nateq, *Rahyabi*, pp. 125-27.
[90]Quoted in Adamiyat, *Fekr-e Azadi*, pp. 40-41.
[91]Adamiyat, *Amir Kabir va Iran*, p. 164.

the students' destination. This was primarily a consequence of the shah's attempt to establish a close relationship with France in order to offset both British and Russian influence in Iran. Mohammad Shah was also reputed to have favored France over Britain since childhood. He learned French, French history and some geography as a child at Crown Prince 'Abbas Mirza's court in Tabriz.[92]

Negotiations with the French government undertaken in France by Iranian Ambassador Hosayn Khan Ajudanbashi in 1839 led to an agreement to send students to France for training. Five Iranians from amongst the nobility were selected: Hosayn Qoli Aqa, Mirza Zaki, Mirza Reza, Mirza Yahya, and Mohammad 'Ali Aqa.[93] Mohammad Shah selected the subjects of study for all five students. Hosayn Qoli Aqa was sent to learn infantry and artillery, Mirza Zaki Mohandes artillery, Mirza Reza medicine and mining, Mirza Yahya medicine and surgery, and Mohammad 'Ali Aqa mining, gunpowder making, and watchmaking. Since Mirza Reza was a painter, Mohammad Shah permitted him to pursue some training in painting as well.

Mohammad Shah ordered the students not to spend time learning about Europe, but instead to limit their time to their chosen studies. The government directive ordering the dispatch of this group of students states: "pursue [your] studies in Paris and do not engage in useless and frivolous activities so that you do not lose your religion."[94] Clearly, Mohammad Shah was concerned about the possible negative influence of study abroad in Europe. The fact that he viewed study in Europe as possibly resulting in a loss of "religious belief" is further testimony to the fact that in this period the desire to adopt elements of European education was limited to technological advances. In this directive, Mohammad Shah exemplifies the position that not only was Westernization not the objective of student missions, but that in

---

[92]Mohammad Shah learned French from a Mme. Lamarinière, who spent twenty years at 'Abbas Mirza's court. See Nateq, *Rahyabi*, p. 105.

[93]Information on the student dispatch of 1845-8 and the students' subsequent careers can be found in Mahbubi-Ardakani, *Tarikh-e Mo'assesat*, vol. I, pp. 189-195; Mahbubi-Ardakani, "Dovvomin Karevan-e Ma'refat," pp. 592-98; Atai, "Iranian Students," pp. 55-60; and Adamiyat, *Fekr-e Azadi*, pp. 40-44.

[94]This directive was written by Aqa Hosayn 'Ali Ghaffari Mo'aven al-Dowleh and approved by Mohammad Shah. For a copy of this directive, see Mahbubi-Ardakani, "Dovvomin Karevan," pp. 592-93.

addition, it was perceived as a cultural threat and thus potentially dangerous.

The death of Mohammad Shah in 1848 and the outbreak of unrest in Paris in the same year prompted the return of the students to Iran after less than three years in France, despite the fact that they had not completed their studies. The students all began successful careers in government service on their return to Iran. Mirza Zaki became a translator at the *Dar al Fonun* after it opened in 1851. He also was an artillery officer and taught artillery at the *Dar al Fonun* as well. Mirza Reza was employed as a translator on a diplomatic mission to France. Hosayn Qoli Aqa entered service in the army. Mohammad 'Ali Aqa, who had attended the prestigious French military academy of *Saint Cyr*, also entered military service. He was also employed in the Ministry of Foreign Affairs by Mirza Hosayn Khan as a translator. Mohammad 'Ali Aqa accompanied Farrokh Khan Amin al-Molk to Europe in 1856, and in 1861 went with Sayyed Ja'far Khan Moshir al-Dowleh to London in the capacity of second deputy. Mirza Yahya enjoyed a distinguished career in the government of Naser al-Din Shah. He attained positions as minister of foreign affairs and minister of justice, and was governor of both Fars and Yazd provinces.

The dispatch of 1845-48 was not the only official dispatch of students abroad by Mohammad Shah. Independently of the official mission of 1845, a number of individuals were sent abroad for study. In 1843 Abu al-Hasan Naqqashbashi was sent to Italy to learn European-style painting where he remained for five years until Mohammad Shah's death in 1848. Prior to the return of the 1845-48 group of students from France, Mohammad Shah dispatched two additional students abroad. In 1847 Mohammad Hosayn Beg Afshar was sent to Russia to learn glass making and sugar making. In the same year, Mirza Sadeq was sent to England to study medicine. On his return after the death of Mohammad Shah, Mirza Sadeq was sent by the prime minister, Amir Kabir, to Azarbayjan to practice and instruct medicine. In addition, Mirza Zayn al-'Abedin Tabrizi was sent to Europe to learn paper-making and cloth making.[95]

---

[95]For dates, studies and biographies of the students, see Atai, "Iranian Students," pp. 55-65; and Mahbubi-Ardakani, "Dovvomin Karevan," pp. 592-98.

Significantly, it is in the Mohammad Shah period that families for the first time sent their sons abroad to Europe for study at their own expense. Mirza Nabi Khan Qazvini Amir Tuman, sent his two sons to Europe: Mirza Hosayn Khan (later Sepahsalar) and Mirza Yahya Khan (later Moshir al-Dowleh). Mirza Yaqub Isfahani, an Armenian translator, sent his son Mirza Malkom Khan to Paris for ten years where he studied engineering. In addition, Iranian Ambassador Mirza Hosayn Khan Ajudanbashi, on his diplomatic mission to Europe in 1839 brought along his nephew, Aqa Mohammad Hasan Khan. Both he and the son of another diplomat on the mission, Mirza Ibrahim, hoped to enroll in a military school in France.[96] The fact that families sent their sons abroad for study suggests that study in Europe began to be viewed as a route to prestigious government positions. It is also evidence of the growing value attributed to knowledge of European languages and international diplomacy in this period.

Although no other students were dispatched to Europe by Mohammad Shah, he had intended to send an additional ten students to France for study. In 1847 Mohammad 'Ali Khan Shirazi, minister plenipotentiary to France, engaged in negotiations with the French minister of foreign affairs, Guizot, concerning the details of a future dispatch of students to France. It was agreed that Iran would send a number of students to learn technical skills and engineering for a period of five years. Iran agreed to pay a yearly stipend of between 150 and 180 tomans. Guizot requested that additionally, Iran send along a supervisor for the students, just as Mohammad 'Ali had for the Egyptian students studying in France at the time. Guizot made a point of urging Mohammad Shah to select students who were sons of tradesmen, rather than nobles, as he believed that they would be more attentive to their studies.[97] However, Mohammad Shah's death led to the termination of this agreement.

In conclusion, Mohammad Shah's goals with regards to the introduction of elements of European-style education did not differ significantly from those of 'Abbas Mirza. Mohammad Shah followed a

---

[96]Nateq, *Rahyabi*, pp. 110-11.

[97]Mirza Mohammad 'Ali Khan, *Ruznameh-ye Sefarat-e Ma'mur-e Iran beh Faranseh*, as quoted in Adamiyat, *Fekr-e Azadi*, pp. 41-42. Guizot's preference for sons of tradesmen rather than the nobility was in line with the importance the French government attributed to the bourgeoisie at the time.

policy of recruiting European military instructors and tradesmen in order to increase the quality of his military. Like 'Abbas Mirza, Mohammad Shah believed that Iranian "deficiency" was restricted to military techniques and technology. European education in this period remained limited to the adoption of selected military and practical skills. The students dispatched, with the exception of one painter, all studied military or military-related technology, such as medicine. Despite the fact that the two most ambitious programs to send students abroad did not materialize, the relatively large numbers intended (between 60-70 as compared to the 11 dispatched by 'Abbas Mirza), testify to the growing awareness of the importance of European technology and training. This was not translated into practical improvements, however, as Mohammad Shah was unable to substantially improve central government authority. The end of his reign saw a growth in the sale of provincial governorships and governmental offices, with only two provinces remitting taxes to the central government.

CHAPTER II

EARLY QAJAR TRAVEL LITERATURE AND THE
PERCEPTION OF "DEFICIENCY"

The defensive military reforms undertaken by Crown Prince 'Abbas Mirza and Mirza Bozorg Farahani, and continued to some extent by Mohammad Shah, resulted from a perception of military weakness vis-à-vis modern European armies. As discussed in the previous chapter, the *Nezam-e Jadid* reforms aimed to remedy this situation by adopting European military and military-related expertise. The dispatch of students to Europe further expanded the connection between reform, education and technology. The growing perception of "deficiency" in the early Qajar period was directly connected to views of Europe. The modernization dilemma— adopting European technology and expertise yet regarding European customs and institutions as undesirable— further complicated this relationship. In order to identify the emerging spectrum of beliefs concerning the type of change desired in Iran and the associated cultural threat this implied, it is important to examine ideas concerning the cause, nature and proposed solutions to perceived Iranian "deficiency."

Travel literature provides a particularly rich source for the understanding of attitudes towards Iranian "deficiency." Due to its very nature as description of travel to Europe, the accounts contain (either explicitly or implicitly) comparisons with and evaluations of Europe. Travel literature is by nature a vehicle for the construction of the "Other," and for the related process of constructing the "Self." Witht the emergence of the perception of "deficiency" travel literature took on new meanings.[1] Indeed, the early nineteenth century witnessed a substantive shift in the genre of travel literature.

Most remarkable in this shift was a change in purpose. Previously, travelers voyaged abroad (usually charged with a diplomatic mission) with a clear sense of social and cultural superiority— a veiw in which

---

[1] On the shift in genre of travel literature in the early nineteenth century and its connection to the reform agenda, see Monica Ringer, "The Quest for the Secret of Strength in Iranian Nineteenth-Century Travel Literature: Rethinking Tradition in the *Safarnameh*," in *Iran and the Surrounding World 1500-2001: Interactions in Culture and Cultural Politics* (eds) Nikkie Keddie and Rudi Matthee, forthcoming.

Europe was irrelevant in the sense that Iran had little to gain from anything European. A view which thus left little room for the evaluation of Europe as a model of change. The Russo-Persian Wars in some sense shattered this vision. 'Abbas Mirza, who clearly experienced Iranian "deficiency" first-hand, dispatched two travelers with novel mandates. They were to seek to evaluate the secret of European strength. Europe, as a model of change, became relevant to the Iranian context. These two travelers, Mirza Saleh Shirazi and Mirza Mostafa Afshar, were both associated with 'Abbas Mirza's court, and their travel accounts inaugurated an entirely new phase of the perception of Iranian "deficiency." Mirza Saleh Shirazi's *Safarnameh-ye Mirza Saleh Shirazi* (The Travelogue of Mirza Saleh Shirazi) and Mirza Mostafa Afshar's *Safarnameh-ye Khosrow Mirza beh Petersburg* (The Travelogue of Khosrow Mirza to St. Petersburg) were predicated on the perception of a "deficiency" and consciously sought to accurately evaluate its causes and potential resolution. Both accounts also presented a new understanding of the nature of Iran's problems, the key to which was the notion of "progress."

Mirza Saleh Shirazi

When Mirza Saleh Shirazi departed from Iran in 1815, his mandate was clear. As part of a student mission dispatched to England by Crown Prince 'Abbas Mirza, Shirazi had been instructed to learn European languages and sciences, as well as any other information that he found "useful" for Iran. Throughout his account, Shirazi seeks to understand the source of European strength, and to identify which aspects of Europe Iran might benefit from. In his account of nearly four years of residence in England, Shirazi recorded his observations, as well as detailed descriptions of European history, society, institutions and technology. He devoted substantial portions of his *Safarnameh* to the history of Russia, Britain, and the rise and subsequent career of Napoleon. Public works, schools, libraries, and hospitals also received particular attention.

Shirazi's travel through Russia en route to England provided his first opportunity to explore the secret of European strength. The recurring leitmotiv in Shirazi's lengthy discussion of Russian history is Russian rulers' increasing commitment to reform. Shirazi described how Peter the Great recognized Russia's military disadvantage compared with Western Europe and was convinced that the solution lay in the adoption of (Western) European science and technology. Recalling the Russian tzar's reasoning, Shirazi wrote: "[Peter the Great believed that] the reason for the glory of the Western countries is the spread of science and industries and arts."[2] To remedy Russia's technological "deficiency," Peter the Great recruited Western European military advisors and instructors and instituted a process of "Europeanization." This reform effort was continued by subsequent Russian rulers. Shirazi described how the current tzar, Alexander I, continued to promote the Europeanization and modernization of Russia by bringing "great numbers of masters of technology and new inventions to his workshops . . . He continues to import a great number of machines and mechanisms from Europe."[3] In his presentation of Russian reform, Shirazi clearly identified education as an important ingredient in Russian military strength. He devoted much attention to the schools he visited in Russia, describing in detail their curriculum, student body and the disciplines studied.[4]

Throughout Shirazi's discussion of Russia, modernization is equated with Westernization. Moreover, he identified "progress" (taraqqi) with the implementation of such a process of change. Iran's weakness was therefore attributed to its failure to undergo modernization. In Shirazi's view, the world had entered a new phase where modernization (read Westernization) was essential for progress. "Deficiency" in the Iranian context could not be resolved by the reestablishment of traditional order, but rather required something fundamentally and essentially new— modernization.

The Russian experience of modernization and the promotion of "progress" was upheld by Shirazi as a model for Iran. Geographically, Shirazi described Russia as located partly in Asia and partly in Europe. However, in keeping with the traditional Iranian worldview, he consistently differentiated between Western Europe, "farang," and Russia. The fact that Russians, described as "backward" and uncivilized— the "Uzbegs of Europe"— had successfully adopted

<hr>

[2] Mirza Saleh Shirazi, Majmu'eh-ye Safarnameh-ye Mirza Saleh Shirazi (Tehran: Nashr-e Tarikh-e Iran, 1985), p. 130.
[3] Ibid, pp. 138-39.
[4] Ibid.
[4] Ibid, pp. 138-9, pp. 142, 146.

Western European science and technology and had thus launched themselves onto the path towards progress, meant that Iran could potentially do the same.[5] By making this assertion, Shirazi assumed that science and technology are lacking cultural context and therefore could be easily transferred from their place of origin (Europe) to other countries without at the same time entailing the adoption of European culture.

Shirazi's lengthy stay in England afforded him the opportunity to refine his perceptions of the secret of European strength. Unlike Russia, which was a *recipient* of European science and technology, England is presented as a principal source of new knowledge. England's power is identified as stemming from her military (and more specifically her navy). What Shirazi found particularly remarkable about England, however, was the number of social services provided by the government. His account of England is full of descriptions of hospitals, insane asylums, schools, orphanages, fire stations, welfare societies, guilds, the postal service, and transportation systems. The British government, he concluded, promoted a smoothly running society which, together with the powerful navy, facilitated commercial prosperity.

Shirazi's stay in England, as well as his own studies at Oxford University, provided him with the opportunity for close observation of the British system of education. The *Safamarneh* is full of descriptions of educational institutions, including elementary and secondary schools, public and private schools, universities, military academies, medical schools, and libraries. In his description of English schools, Shirazi emphasized the compulsory nature of primary education, and noted that its provision was considered to be the responsibility of the state. Shirazi also pointed out the existence of established standards and well-defined qualifications for advancement— not only in colleges— but even at the secondary school level.

Particularly noteworthy is Shirazi's commentary concerning the value that the English place on education. He emphasized that although providing universal education for girls and boys is expensive,

---

[5] For a discussion of Iranian views of Europeans in the Safavid period and the denigration of the Russians, see Rudi Matthee, "Between Aloofness and Fascination: Safavid Views of the West," *Iranian Studies*, vol. 31, no. 2 (Spring 1998), pp. 219-46.

the English considered it worthwhile. According to Shirazi, "such a land goes through so much effort and trouble for the education of its children, though certainly after the boys and girls have been to school they emerge duly accomplished."[6] Shirazi even ventured to suggest that education and love of knowledge led to the betterment of the soul (*nafs-e khod ra taraqqi midadand*). The effect of education on the development of the individual was discussed by Shirazi elsewhere. He explained that,

> Each youth that goes to [primary] school for some time and talks with his companions and associates, of course this leads to the progress of his soul, and he is more elevated than his fellow men, and in their opinion is praiseworthy. . .the sign of a noble person is someone who is skilled in the visible and meaningful accomplishments . . . Every man or woman in school behaves in a certain manner that makes everyone else envious [of their comportment].[7]

Education thus was an avenue for the improvement and ennoblement of a person's character, as evidenced by their distinguishing comportment and manners. This passage by Shirazi is the first to discuss education and its role in the shaping of individual character (of both men and women), in addition to its role as training skilled technicians and soldiers.

The *Safarnameh* provides many insights into Shirazi's beliefs concerning European strength and the concomitant "deficiency" in Iran. Shirazi limited Iran's "deficiency" to the absence of new technology and the failure to promote "progress." The "deficiency" therefore did not extend to Iran's *social* (as opposed to political) institutions. Shirazi did not exhibit any notion of Iranian "backwardness" or "inferiority." On the contrary, he was conscious of his dignity as a member of 'Abbas Mirza's student mission. Shirazi upheld his role as representative of the crown prince on a number of occasions. Once, when he was offered a position as tutor, he declined in order to maintain 'Abbas Mirza's honor, arguing that it would be inappropriate and would, furthermore, jeopardize his mission in England.[8] In another instance, Shirazi resisted wearing English clothes

---

[6] Shirazi, *Safarnameh*, p. 316.

[7] Ibid, pp. 316-17.

[8] Mojtaba Minovi, "Avvalin Karevan-e Ma'refat," *Yaghma*, vol. 6, no. 5 (1953), p. 406.

as requested by Colonel D'Arcy. In the *Safarnameh*, Shirazi explained that he saw no reason to change clothes, and that 'Abbas Mirza had specifically instructed the students not to.[9] Shirazi, therefore, did not perceive his mission to England as including the acquisition of English culture, and nowhere suggested that the English were culturally or socially "superior." Although he eventually did wear English clothes from time to time, he did so only for practical considerations and to prevent drawing unwanted attention to himself, not because he wanted to adopt English customs or because he felt the clothes were an improvement over his own.[10]

While Shirazi refrained from outlining specifically which elements found in Europe would be beneficial for Iran to adopt, he did provide some indications concerning his views. His emphasis on European education and its importance as a prerequisite to strong military power indicates a belief in the value of European technology and science for Iran. Shirazi also recognized the importance of education in the preparation of government elites who could thus guide the country onto the path of progress. The belief in the need for Iran's leaders to be versed in the new world political and technological situation is also attested to by Shirazi's importation of a printing press to Iran, and his subsequent publication of Iran's first newspaper which will be discussed below.

Mirza Mostafa Afshar

Mirza Mostafa Afshar, like Mirza Saleh Shirazi before him, was conscious of his purpose in recording events and the current situation in Russia. Like Shirazi's *Safarnameh*, Afshar's account was predicated on the perception of Iranian "deficiency." As a member of 'Abbas Mirza's court, he was doubtlessly well informed about the *Nezam-e Jadid* reforms instituted by the crown prince in Azarbayjan.[11] In addition, the recent defeat of Iran by Russia in the second Russo-Persian War, and

---

[9] Shirazi, *Safarnameh*, p. 169.

[10] Ibid, pp. 169, 171, 345. For example, Shirazi mentioned that he changed into European clothes in order to work at the printing workshop. This may have been due to the danger of operating the machinery while wearing loose Iranian-style clothing.

[11] Mirza Mostafa Afshar was the assistant of Mirza Mas'ud, 'Abbas Mirza's personal secretary who served as official secretary of Prince Khosrow Mirza's mission to Russia.

the resulting indemnity imposed on Iran in the Treaty of Turkmanchay of 1828, reinforced contemporary awareness of Iranian military inferiority vis-à-vis the West. Afshar, in his *Safarnameh-ye Khosrow Mirza beh Petersburg* written in 1829, went much further than Shirazi in both diagnosing and prescribing a remedy for Iran's "deficiency." In his account of nearly ten months in Russia, Afshar openly compared and contrasted Russia and Iran. The conclusions he drew, moreover, were neither veiled nor apologetic.

Afshar clearly identified three elements as the cause of Russian strength: a strong military, education, and a powerful centralized government. While he did not delve into Russian history, Afshar attributed credit for Russia's current strength on the reforms initiated by Peter the Great. According to Afshar, Peter the Great laid the foundations for the creation of a stable and prosperous state:

> Apart from the promotion and management of affairs of the monarchy and the regulation of the military, the results and ideas of which are the abundant causes of the power and stability of the monarchy and the splendor of the affairs of the Russian government today, [Peter the Great] was also accomplished in a great number of the foreign sciences and novel arts and industries.[12]

Inherent in Afshar's notion of progress and modernization is his conception of the beginning of a new era. He wrote that by means of knowledge, Russia was brought into line with "the current world situation," or *"asr-e jadid."*[13] Like Mirza Saleh Shirazi some fifteen years previously, Afshar was convinced that the world had entered a new stage that was characterized by the internationalization of the political and commercial arenas and the onset of "progress." In order not to be left behind, countries must necessarily undergo the process of modernization.

Afshar repeatedly emphasized the connection between Russian "progress," and Peter the Great's importation of Western European sciences and arts. Progress was equated with modernization that in turn was founded on European sciences and technology. European-style education thus emerged for the first time as an agent of change.

---

[12] Mirza Mostafa Afshar, *Safarnameh-ye Khosrow Mirza beh Petersburg* (ed) Mohammad Gulbun (Tehran: Ketabkhaneh-ye Mostowfi, 1349/1971), p. 236.
[13] Ibid, pp. 235-36.

According to Afshar, with Russia's conversion to Christianity, she developed a desire for sciences. Peter the Great recruited teachers from France and Austria and established schools to propagate Western technological arts.[14] The system of education established by Peter the Great was hailed by Afshar as having prepared the foundation for the development of a strong military and central government.

European education served two related functions. First, it was necessary for the training of a modern, standing army. Second, a European education was identified as a prerequisite for the creation of effective government cadres. In Russia, Afshar admired the fact that education in preparation for government service constituted a defining characteristic of the eighteenth-century nobility.[15] Afshar wrote that:

> The nobility, until they have entered service and have served for a period in the employ of the government, have no merit or value, and since they must enter service in the bloom of youth, it is a rare person who in those years has not completed studies in the practical and scientific arts ["*fonun-e amaliyeh va 'ilmiyeh*"].[16]

The nobility thus become educated for government service through a European-style curriculum of "practical and scientific arts." The establishment of educational requirements for government service is indicative of the importance placed not only on technology, but on effective government leadership. Government officials must be qualified to operate in the new age of world politics and diplomacy. Afshar also noted that the nobility, to better prepare themselves for state service in the new "world situation," kept abreast of world politics and developments by reading newspapers.[17]

By providing the precedent of Russian reform, Afshar deliberately furnished Iran with an example of both the benefits and the routes to reform. In particular, he vehemently advocated the adoption of Western sciences and schools in Iran. The following passage contains

---

[14] Ibid, p. 329.

[15] For an exposition of the relationship between Russian nobility and government service, and the emergence of the Russian intelligentsia, see Marc Raeff, *Origins of the Russian Intelligentsia: The Eighteenth-Century Nobility* (New York: Harcourt Brace Yovanovich, 1966).

[16] Afshar, *Safarnameh*, p. 352.

[17] Ibid, p. 357.

the crux of Afshar's ideas concerning European-style education as a vehicle of modernization and "progress."

> *The establishment of such [European-style] schools in the kingdom of Iran would be extremely simple and easy.* A few masters of Western sciences could be brought to Iran, and one of the schools for the children of the nobility of the land could be selected and they could be gathered together there and several people of high moral conduct could be selected to supervise them. [The students] would learn both Iranian sciences from Iranian teachers (*moddaresin*) as well as Western sciences from Western instructors (*mo alemin*) . . . In this way, whether from amongst the military or the men of the pen, *accomplished and capable servants will be obtained for the government who will be informed of the world situation* and the complicated ways of the world. *The military will be ordered and trained like the military of the rest of the governments, affairs of the kingdom would be organized like the rest of the kingdoms.* From this best management, the splendor and improvement of the kingdom would increase daily.[18] (Emphasis added.)

It is clear from the passage cited above that Afshar was unaware of the cultural and historical context of Western sciences and schools. He did not realize the implications of adopting sciences and institutions that emerged and developed in different historical and cultural conditions. Rather, he believed that the establishment of schools similar to those in Russia in order to teach Western sciences would be "extremely simple and easy."

By suggesting the transferability of Western sciences and institutions to Iran, Afshar also underestimated the practical difficulties involved. At the time of his writing, Iran lacked any kind of appropriate support system for the establishment of European-style schools on the Russian model; namely, secondary schools, adequate preparation of students at the primary level, the recruitment of European teachers, and the translation into Persian of appropriate texts for instruction. Afshar also failed to perceive the cultural implications of Western sciences and institutions. He assumed that the adoption of Western sciences did not involve the simultaneous transmission of Western culture or beliefs. If Russia has been successful, Afshar implied, there was no reason to believe Iran incapable of undertaking similar reform measures.

---

[18] Ibid, pp. 236-37.

According to Afshar's educational proposal, Iranian nobility would receive European-style training to better prepare them in both military and administrative positions. Only in this way will Iran's elite be able to compete in the new world situation. Afshar upheld the educational qualifications for government service in Russia as a model for Iran.

Despite the radical nature of Afshar's proposal, his conception of the benefits of European education remained limited in scope. For example, only the elite were targeted beneficiaries of the new, European-style schools. Afshar viewed the nobility as the key to effecting change in Iran— as military leaders and government officials, and in their role as potential supporters or opponents of reform measures. In his *Safarnameh* he attempted to convince court officials and members of the Qajar ruling family of the advantages which would accrue to them if Iran pursued a plan of reform similar to that of Russia. He argued that:

> The nobility in Iran . . . are always unbelievers in riches . . . [this is due to] lack of information about the situation and state of other kingdoms, and their sciences [because it has not been] possible to travel or to become informed through reading history. If the government, either sent the nobles of the kingdom on trips, or by studying made them aware of the customs, sciences and histories of other countries, it is surely likely that the nobles of the kingdom would transmit this awareness to the general population, and the reproachful and complaining talk would be replaced by praise and virtues [of the country], and attachment to the king would establish itself in the hearts [of the people], and for this reason, the government would find continuity and stability.[19]

Afshar's educational proposal was also limited in that he conceived of the European-style training schools as purely supplementary. They were in no way intended to replace the existing educational system, and thus would not constitute a threat to the educational prerogatives exercised by the ulama. The ulama would retain control of the educational system, and over the inculcation of values.

---

[19] Afshar, *Safarnameh*, p. 374.

Conclusion

Iranian travel literature written during the period of Crown Prince 'Abbas Mirza's *Nezam-e Jadid* reform program illustrates the gradual emergence of a spectrum of belief concerning change and reform in Iran. There was, however, no concensus on either the causes of or solution to Iran's weak-ness vis-à-vis Europe. The few other travel accounts to Europe from the 'Abbas Mirza period do not evidence the need for substantive change, but rather suggest that there is very little inbalance that effective leadership could not redress. For example, Mirza Abu al-Hasan Khan Shirazi "Ilchi" described Europe's curiosities and wonders, yet for him Europe remained essentially "irrelevant" to Iran.[20]

Mirza Saleh Shirazi and Mirza Mostafa Afshar, on the other hand, clearly perceived of "deficiency" in comparative terms. It is only when compared with European countries, that Iran appears weak. No fault is attributed to Iranian social institutions. In neither of their accounts is there any sense of Iranian social "inferiority" vis-à-vis the West. At this time "deficiency" had not reached the level of "backwardness" that it would by mid century. Mirza Saleh Shirazi and Mirza Mostafa Afshar saw Iranian "deficiency" principally in relation to Europe's advances. However, they both read substantially more into the reasons behind the "secret of European strength" than simply technological advances, also identifying European government organization and a strong military as the cause of European power.

The key to Shirazi and Afshar's perception of Iranian "deficiency" lay in the concept of "progress." They believed that the world had entered a new epoch. It was essential, they argued, for Iran to undergo a program of modernization in order to effect "progress." Modernization, in turn, was identified with "Westernization" in the sense that progress was first achieved in Europe. Shirazi and Afshar urged the Iranian government to jump on the bandwagon of modernization in order to rise to the new challenges of what they term "the new world situation." Their insistence on this point testifies to an awareness of the

---

[20] 'Abd al-Hasan Khan Shirazi, *A Persian at the Court of King George 1809-10: The Journal of Mirza Abul Hasan Khan* (trans) Margaret Moris Cloake (London: Barie & Jenkins, 1988).

internationalization of Iran's political arena. It also indicates a conception of modernization as involving the adoption of specific constitutive elements. Implicitly, therefore, they understood there to exist one path to "progress." At the same time, neither Shirazi nor Afshar were aware of the cultural implications of adopting European institutions and education and instead argued for the "ease and simplicity" of transferring European-style education into Iran.

Shirazi and Afshar's belief in the onset of an era of progress dramatically altered the concept of change and reform in Iran. For the first time, reform took on chronological direction. In the past, reformers did not advocate the adoption of anything *fundamentally* novel. Rather, reform connoted the restoration or reinstatement of a system or institution that was *perceived* at least, to have existed previously. Shirazi and Afshar's prescriptions for reform involve the adoption of entirely different and (by definition) new institutions and technology. They did not attempt to legitimize their reform proposals based on past models. They did not portray necessary reform as in fact constituting the readoption of Iranian or Islamic institutions. Instead, they equated reform with modernization.

Shirazi and Afshar also depart from previous discourses of reform in that they enjoin the government to take responsibility for spheres of activity not previously in its domain. Education and social services, previously largely the preserve if not the prerogative of the religious establishment, were now assigned to the government. Shirazi and Afshar display far-reaching notions of government responsibility that are clearly heavily influenced by their travels in Europe.

Mirza Saleh Shirazi and Mirza Mostafa Afshar's travel accounts are significant for the depth and breadth of reform they recommend. They are also remarkable for their conception of a "new world situation" defined by "progress" and modernization. In so doing, both accounts exhibit indications of a shifting conception of justice. They are in direct contrast with traditional Iranian conceptions of the "just king." Rather than focusing on the qualities of the individual ruler and his promotion of social equilibrium and agricultural prosperity, Shirazi and Afshar emphasize the functioning of the government. Thus, the qualities of the ruler are overshadowed by the ordering of the governmental institutions and the capabilities of the government officials. In the new age of politics (*siyasat*), justice becomes a function of the government's active promotion of "progress." It is in this context that Shirazi and Afshar attributed so much importance to governmental organization, and on the training of qualified government cadres.

Mirza Saleh Shirazi and Mirza Mostafa Afshar's discussions of education established the parameters of educational discourse that continued to characterize the educational reform agenda well into the 1860s. State responsibility for educational reform, the emphasis on providing European-style education to elite government cadres in order to prepare them to lead Iran in the "new world situation," and the importance of European science and technology, all persisted as fundamental issues in educational reform. The inherent conflicts and tensions in their arguments for the adoption of elements of European-style educational also remained unresolved. In particular, the transferability of European-style education into the Iranian socio-cultural and historical context remained largely unaddressed in reform circles until the late nineteenth century. It is not surprising, therefore, that the next major educational reform initiative—the establishment of the first Iranian European-style secondary school (the *Dar al Fonun*) in 1851—essentially reflected the educational proposals expressed by Mirza Mostafa Afshar in 1829.

CHAPTER III

THE *DAR AL FONUN*, 1851-71

The establishment of the *Dar al Fonun* (The Academy of Applied Sciences) in 1851 constituted a significant turning point in the history of education in Iran. As the first state-sponsored European-style educational institution in Iran, it represented the growing perception of the need for educational reform as a component of larger reforms. Moreover, it constituted a qualitative and quantitative leap in the introduction of European-style education to Iran. The *Dar al Fonun* also marked the deepening of the political and cultural chasms which existed between proponents and opponents of European-style education and modernization in Iran.

The first few years of Naser al-Din Shah's reign (1848-96) were remarkable for a series of far-reaching reforms effected by his prime minister, Mirza Taqi Khan Farahani, better known as Amir Kabir. Amir Kabir's primary objectives were twofold. First, he aimed to regularize and centralize the government. To this end he attempted to increase administrative accountability and efficiency and reduce the ulama's juridical prerogatives. He was also instrumental in putting down the Babi resurrections that he considered a challenge to the shah's authority. Second, as a corollary to his centralization policies, Amir Kabir sought to limit foreign interference in Iran's domestic affairs and increase Iran's self-sufficiency with regard to Europe. At this time, European interference in Iranian affairs had reached huge proportions. As described by Robert Grant Watson, a European in Iran at the time,

> Before this period it had been customary in Persia to concede an unusual degree of deference to the opinions and wishes of the foreign representatives accredited to the Persian court . . . The Ameer-i Nizam [Amir Kabir] did not fail to perceive that it was unbecoming that a government should not regulate the affairs of its own subjects, and he accordingly determined for the future to set himself against foreign interference in maters that only concerned Persia.[1]

Watson then described Amir Kabir's goal as endeavoring "to erect his country into a powerful and firmly-established monarchy upon the

---

[1]Robert Grant Watson, *A History of Persia from the Beginning of the Nineteenth Century to the Year 1858* (London: Smith, Elder & Co., 1866), pp. 381-82.

basis of law and justice."[2] A British government representative, Colonel Rawlinson, agreed with Watson's assessment of Amir Kabir's policy regarding European governments. He wrote that, "there can be no doubt that at this period the interference of the European missions at Teheran in the domestic affairs of the country was carried beyond all reasonable limit," and that Amir Kabir's "most difficult achievement . . . and [that] which he believed, perhaps with reason, to be of paramount importance to the interests of the Government—lay in his firm but consistent and impartial opposition to European pressure."[3]

Amir Kabir's plans to augment the authority of the central government, both domestically and internationally, and to increase the effectiveness of the administration were intimately connected to his educational objectives. He believed that the success of his political and administrative reforms necessitated a more informed government bureaucracy and better trained and equipped troops. He was conscious of the need to adopt certain elements of European technology and know-how. Nor did he ignore the importance of Iran's ability to participate in the international diplomatic arena. Amir Kabir was familiar with similar processes of the selective adoption of European education and technology in the Ottoman Empire and Egypt. He was therefore conscious that Iran was not alone in the need to reform and to adopt European technological advances. The fact that other Muslim countries were undertaking similar measures established a precedent and undoubtably contributed to both his acceptance of the *necessity* to reform, and of the *legitimacy* of such measures.[4]

Accordingly, one of the first actions Amir Kabir took upon becoming prime minister was the reorganization of the Ministry of Foreign Affairs, and the establishment of permanent embassies in London and St. Petersburg, and consulates in Bombay, the Ottoman Empire, and in the Caucasus.[5] In order to increase government

---

[2]Ibid.

[3]Henry Creswicke Rawlinson, *England and Russia in the East* (London: John Murray, 1875), pp. 82-86.

[4]See Feridun Adamiyat, *Amir Kabir va Iran* (Tehran: Amir Kabir, 1955), p. 158 for a similar emphasis on the legitimation of reform in Iran due to parallel processes in other Muslim countries. For an exposition of the influence of Ottoman reforms on Iran, see Anja Pistor-Hatam, *Iran und die Reformbewegung im Osmanischen Reich* (Berlin: Klausschwartz Verlag, 1992).

[5]Adamiyat, *Amir Kabir va Iran*, pp. 207-11.

officials' awareness of international developments, in 1851 Amir Kabir established the first official newspaper in Iran, the *Ruznameh-ye Vaqaye'-e Ettefaqiyyeh*. The stated purpose of this newspaper closely resembled that of the *Kaghaz-e Akhbar* printed by Mirza Saleh Shirazi from 1837-1839.[6] The eighth edition of the newspaper announced that:

> The royal ambition of His Majesty the Shah is the instruction of the people and the dignitaries and the subjects and the merchants and tradesmen of the state, so as to increase their knowledge and insight and to inform them of domestic and foreign events. To this end, [the shah] has ordered the printing and publication of newspapers and it is hoped that by means of the publication of these newspapers, the people of this exalted country will become more informed, aware and insightful.[7]

Amir Kabir also clearly intended for the *Ruznameh-ye Vaqaye'-e Ettefaqiyyeh* to serve as the mouthpiece for his reforms.[8] He hoped that greater knowledge of his reform program would result in political support amongst government officials. In order to ensure readership, Amir Kabir made subscriptions to the newspaper obligatory for all government officials earning over 200 tomans salary yearly.[9] In addition to subscribers, the *Ruznameh-ye Vaqaye'-e Ettefaqiyyeh* enjoyed circulation due to its being read aloud to those unable to read or purchase the newspaper.[10]

The content of the *Ruznameh-ye Vaqaye'-e Ettefaqiyyeh* included domestic news extracted from reports of governors and provincial administrators, foreign news, promotions, and articles on science. Officials stationed abroad were required to send news of their commissions for inclusion. In addition, Amir Kabir employed a translation bureau headed by the Englishman Edward Burgess to translate

---

[6]See chapter I, above.

[7]*Ruznameh-ye Vaqaye'-e Ettefaqiyyeh*, no. 8 as quoted in Feridun Adamiyat, *Fekr-e Azadi va Moqademeh-ye Nahzat-e Mashrutiyat dar Iran* (Tehran, 1340), p. 45.

[8]Issue 42 stated that the newspaper should be considered the "official government mouthpiece." See Peter Avery, "Printing, the Press, and Literature in Qajar Iran," *Cambridge History of Iran*, vol. 7, p. 826.

[9]Adamiyat, *Amir Kabir va Iran*, p. 373.

[10]The reading aloud of newspapers is a function of a society with a large percentage of illiteracy. For this reason, in censorship regulations in this period, both readers and listeners were targeted. See Avery, "Printing," p. 829.

articles from European, Ottoman, Egyptian and Indian newspapers.[11] According to Lady Sheil, the wife of the British ambassador to Iran at the time, Amir Kabir wrote many of the articles himself, which were "chiefly in praise of the Shah's government." She also explained that in addition to the "Gazette for the public [*Ruznameh-ye Vaqaye'-e Ettefaqiyyeh*], he [Burgess] had the superintendence of another newspaper, designed only for the eye of the Shah and his minister. The latter journal contained all the European political intelligence deemed unsuitable for the Persian public, besides details of gossip and scandal likely to give amuzement [sic] to the Shah."[12] The *Ruznameh-ye Vaqaye'-e Ettefaqiyyeh* enjoyed regular, continuous publication until 1860-61 when the name was changed to *Ruznameh-ye Dowlat-e Aliyeh-ye Iran* (The Journal of the Exalted State of Iran).

The *Dar al Fonun*

The cornerstone of Amir Kabir's educational reform agenda was the establishment of the *Dar al Fonun*. The school was intended to produce educated government cadres capable of implementing administrative reforms and of meeting the new diplomatic challenges posed by increased contacts with Europe. Amir Kabir's decision to establish the school was prompted both by domestic educational needs, and by his perception of the advantages to be gained by not sending students abroad. Amir Kabir believed that the policy followed by 'Abbas Mirza and Mohammad Shah of recruiting foreign military advisors and of dispatching select groups of students abroad was insufficient to train the large number of students required to implement substantive reform measures.[13] He moreover preferred not to be dependent on foreign advisors sent to Iran.[14] He calculated that a greater number of students could be educated at an Iranian institution at a lower cost than could be

---

[11] Husayn Mahbubi-Ardakani, *Tarikh-e Mo'assesat-e Tamaddoni-ye Jadid dar Iran* 2 vols. (Tehran: Tehran University Press, 1975), p. 251. For a listing of all subjects covered by the newspaper in the course of a year, see Adamiyat, *Fekr-e Azadi*, p. 46.

[12] Lady Leonora Mary Sheil, *Glimpses of Life and Manners in Persia* (New York: Arno Press, 1973), pp. 200-1.

[13] Adamiyat, *Amir Kabir va Iran*, p. 211.

[14] Mahbubi-Ardakani, *Tarikh-e Mo'assesat*, vol. I, p. 255.

achieved by further student dispatches to Europe.[15] He was also concerned about the dangerous political and perhaps cultural impact that study in Europe had on students sent abroad. As recorded by the Conte de Gobineau, Amir Kabir, "did not look favorably on Europeans, and desirous of keeping them at a distance, he wanted, on the other hand, to borrow from them military knowledge, and some of their industrial skills."[16] Jakob Polak, the medical instructor at the *Dar al Fonun*, observed that "despite bitter experiences and the most decided aversion against any foreign influence, [Amir Kabir] became convinced that the goal could not be reached without bringing in European teachers."[17]

In a letter to Naser al-Din Shah, Amir Kabir explained the importance of establishing a European-style educational institution in Iran. He wrote: "In the matter of the school, great precision is necessary. It requires very reasonable and dignified men who are skilled in everything European and Iranian."[18] The *Ruznameh-ye Vaqaye'-e Ettefaqiyyeh* described the establishment of the *Dar al Fonun* as promoting the "awareness and instruction and welfare and benefit of the people (*khalq*)."[19]

Amir Kabir's dilemma of how to establish a European-style educational institution while minimizing foreign diplomatic influence was partially resolved by his decision to recruit Austrian teachers to staff the *Dar al Fonun*.[20] Austrian teachers were selected for two reasons. First, Austria was not politically involved in Iran at the time. Amir Kabir thus successfully minimized the potential diplomatic complications which would result from having selected French, Russian

---

[15]Ibid.

[16]Joseph Arthur de Gobineau, *Trois ans en Asie* (Paris, 1859), p. 240. A Prussian minister is recorded as having had the same impression. See Adamiyat, *Amir Kabir va Iran*, p. 191.

[17]Jakob Eduard Polak, *Persien: das Land und seine Bewohner* 2 vols. (1858, repr. New York, 1976), vol. I, pp. 297-98.

[18]Quoted in Adamiyat, *Amir Kabir va Iran*, p. 190.

[19]*Ruznameh-ye Vaqaye'-e Ettefaqiyyeh*, no. 26 quoted in Adamiyat, *Amir Kabir va Iran*, p. 213.

[20]The British minister in Iran was upset about the recruitment of Austrian teachers and argued that the Austrians were under Russian influence. See Adamiyat, *Amir Kabir va Iran*, p. 356.

or British instructors. Second, Austria was renowned both for her scientific and military achievements.[21]

Negotiations were carried out in Austria on behalf of Amir Kabir by Jan Davud, a member of the Ministry of Foreign Affairs, and an official translator. The six instructors initially requested were for infantry, artillery, geometry, mining, medicine and cavalry. Before negotiations had been completed, however, Amir Kabir added a request for an instructor in pharmacology, and two persons to work in a mine.[22] Two of the instructors recruited were Italian. The Austrian government wanted to avoid a diplomatic presence in Iran that might jeopardize her relations with Russia and Great Britain. Accordingly, the instructors were informed that their engagements with the Iranian government would be considered private.[23] The Austrian government's hesitation to consider the instructors as constituting a diplomatic mission is reminiscent of the French government's similar fears concerning the contingent of military officers recruited "privately" during Mohammad Shah's reign.

Amir Kabir made his position concerning political involvement clear to the Austrian instructors. In the contract signed between the instructors and the Iranian government on August 10, 1851, the instructors agreed not to interfere in government business. Article three of the contract stipulated that when an instructor had a complaint, he would "proceed directly and without other mediation to the trustees of the exalted state of Iran to present [his] problem."[24] In other words, he would not involve the European diplomatic representatives in Tehran

---

[21]Mahbubi-Ardakani, *Tarikh-e Mo'assesat*, vol. I, p. 258. Russia was not considered to be as advanced technologically as were other Western European countries. This attitude toward Russia was also evident in Mirza Saleh Shirazi and Mostafa Khan Afshar's travel accounts discussed in chapter II, above.

[22]For the names and subjects taught by each instructor, see Mahbubi-Ardakani, *Tarikh-e Mo'assesat*, vol. I, p. 261; and Adamiyat, *Amir Kabir va Iran*, p. 360. For a complete listing of the instructors, their subjects, and their tenure in Iran, see Mariam Ekhtiar, "The Dar al Fonun: Educational Reform and Cultural Development in Qajar Iran," (Ph.D. diss. New York University, 1994), pp. 147-60. See also John Gurney and Negin Nabavi, "Dar al Fonun," *Encyclopaedia Iranica*, vol. 6 (1993), pp. 662-68.

[23]Polak, *Persien*, vol. 1, p. 298. See also Helmut Slaby, *Bindenschild und Sonnenlöwe: Die Geschichter der Österreichischen-Iranischen Beziehungen bis zur Gegenwart* (Graz, 1982), pp. 69-70.

[24]For the text of the contract, see Adamiyat, *Amir Kabir va Iran*, pp. 358-59.

in their business. Polak wrote in his memoirs that the instructors were told to limit their activities to teaching, and to refrain from any political involvement. He wrote that "it was [Amir Kabir's] intention to have the teachers . . . isolated from the politics of the country so that they would devote themselves to their teaching duties with undivided attention."[25]

The contract signed between the Austrian instructors and the Iranian government provided for a tenure of five years in Iran. In addition to the first group of European instructors, Amir Kabir employed translators from amongst Europeans living in Iran, as well as from among Iranians who had traveled and/or studied abroad.[26] Three of the five students dispatched by Mohammad Shah to study abroad were employed by the *Dar al Fonun* as translators and assistants.[27] The site chosen for the *Dar al Fonun* was an area previously used for military exercises in the royal citadel. The building of the *Dar al Fonun* was designed by Mirza Reza Mohandes, a member of the student mission to England in 1815, after the Royal British military college of Woolwich.[28]

An announcement was placed by the minister of foreign affairs in the *Ruznameh-ye Vaqaye'-e Ettefaqiyyeh* that the *Dar al Fonun* would be accepting thirty students for enrollment. The announcement read:

> Friends! With kindness and affection! According to the order of His Majesty The Omnipotent, His Highness, may our souls be sacrificed for him, it has been decided that thirty children between fourteen and sixteen years of age, from amongst the landowners (*khawanin*) and dignitaries (*a'yan*) and nobles (*ashraf*) [will be admitted to] the *Dar al Fonun* of the capital and be occupied with studying the Western sciences enumerated as philosophical sciences, geometry, mining, military arts, and others. Of course those kind friends should inform and persuade and excite everyone. Everyone [of you] who has the desire, come here so that together we can go to his Imperial Majesty, so that person will be appointed to the proper position and to the study of the sciences. Written on the 24th of Muharram al-Haram, 1268.[29]

---

[25]Polak, *Persien*, vol. I, pp. 297-98.

[26]Adamiyat, *Amir Kabir va Iran*, p. 362.

[27]Mahmud Mohit Tabataba'i, "Dar al Fonun va Amir Kabir," in (ed) *Iraj Afshar Amir Kabir va Dar al Fonun: Majmu'eh-ye Ketabha-ye Iradshodeh dar Ketabkhaneh-ye Markazi va Markaz-e Esnad-e Daneshgah-e Tehran*, p. 192.

[28]Iqbal Yaghma'i, "Bana-ye Dar al Fonun," in (ed) Afshar, *Amir Kabir va Dar al Fonun*, p. 69.

[29]Quoted in Adamiyat, *Amir Kabir va Iran*, p. 363.

The announcement indicates that the *Dar al Fonun* was designed to train selective administrative and military cadres for government service. The students selected were from elite social groups. Contrary to expectations, the demand for admission was so high that instead of the anticipated thirty students, 105 students were admitted in the first year.[30]

Amir Kabir was dismissed from office even before the *Dar al Fonun* opened. In his attempts at government regularization and centralization, he naturally came into conflict with established powers and the existing system of privileges and prerogatives. His opponents included government functionaries, courtiers, provincial administrators, and the Queen Mother.[31] The religious establishment also resented Amir Kabir's attempts to limit their influence in political affairs.[32] Only a few days before the inauguration of the *Dar al Fonun* in 1851, Naser al-Din Shah submitted to the opposition to Amir Kabir led by the Queen Mother and agreed to dismiss him from the office of prime minister. Following Amir Kabir's removal from office and his subsequent murder, the *Dar al Fonun* lost its primary promoter.[33]

The Austrian and Italian instructors arrived two days after Amir Kabir had been dismissed from office. Although military exercises had begun eight months previously, the official inauguration of the *Dar al Fonun* was on December 29, 1851. The ceremony was organized by the

---

[30]Gurney, "Dar al Fonun," p. 664. Hedayat cites the number of entering students as 100. See Mehdi Qoli Khan Hedayat, *Khaterat va Khatarat: Tushe'i az Shesh Padeshah va Gusha'i az Dowreh-ye Zendegi-ye Man* , p. 61.

[31]On opponents of Amir Kabir, see Abbas Amanat, "The Downfall of Mirza Taqi Khan Amir Kabir and the Problem of Ministerial Authority in Qajar Iran," *International Journal of Middle East Studies*, vol. 23, no. 4 (1991), pp. 577-99; and Adamiyat, *Amir Kabir va Iran*, pp. 211, 221; Adamiyat, *Fekr-e Azadi*, pp. 50-57; and Gobineau, *Trois ans en Asie*, pp. 241-42.

[32]In a letter to the British consul in Tabriz, Amir Kabir explained that the ulama needed to be restricted from engaging in political activity if reform measures were to succeed. He compared the situation with that of the Ottoman Empire: "it was only when the Ottoman government destroyed the dominance of the mollahs that it was able to revive its importance." See a letter by British Consul Stevens dated June 15, 1849 in the British foreign archives, as quoted in Adamiyat, *Fekr-e Azadi*, p. 50.

[33]Amir Kabir was dismissed from the office of prime minister on November 16, 1851. Five days later he was shorn of all responsibilities and titles. On January 10, 1852 he was killed on orders of Naser al-Din Shah.

minister of foreign affairs and attended by Naser al-Din Shah and a number of notables and courtiers.[34]

Curriculum

The course of study at the *Dar al Fonun* mirrored the specialties of the first group of Austrian and Italian instructors and was predominantly military in nature. Students specialized in one of the following seven areas: infantry (30 students), artillery (26 students), cavalry (5 students), geometry (12 students), mining (5 students), medicine and surgery (20 students), and physics and pharmacology (7 students). In terms of the total number of students, 58% specialized in military sciences, 5% in mining, 18% in mathematics and physics, and 19% in medicine. In addition to courses in their specialty, students attended classes in other appropriate fields, as well as history, and geography. Persian and Arabic languages were also taught.[35]

All the students began at the same level of instruction. Polak records that in general, the students could read and write Persian and had some knowledge of Persian literature.[36] As the students advanced, they were eventually divided into three groups according to their progress and how they performed on their exams. Advanced students would often assist in the teaching of the more elementary students. Exams were given three times per year, and prizes were awarded to those students who excelled. All students were provided with two sets of uniforms, one for winter and one for summer, which identified their branch of study. For the first class that enrolled at the *Dar al Fonun*, time to graduation was approximately eight years. It later was reduced to four or five years, although students often remained for an additional four years to assist in teaching.[37]

Language was initially a problem. The Austrian instructors did not know Persian, nor were there enough translators available who knew German. As a result, French was adopted as the language of instruction at the *Dar al Fonun*. French classes were taught by Richard Khan, a

---

[34]For a description of the event, see *Ruznameh-ye Vaqaye'-e Ettefaqiyyeh*, no. 44 (10 Safar 1268), as quoted in Mahbubi-Ardakani, *Tarikh-e Mo'assesat*, vol. I, p. 263.

[35]Mahbubi-Ardakani, *Tarikh-e Mo'assesat*, vol. I, pp. 294-96.

[36]Polak, *Persien*, vol. I, p. 303.

[37]Mahbubi-Ardakani, *Tarikh-e Mo'assesat*, vol. I, p. 297.

French convert to Islam living in Tehran. A large number of students took French language classes, although only until they reached a level of proficiency to allow them to pursue their other courses. Due to its early importance, French remained the predominant European language at the *Dar al Fonun* throughout its history. The lack of available course materials in Persian prompted the Austrian instructors to translate many of their course materials into Persian. A number of translations and new books by the European and Iranian instructors were published by the Royal Department of Publications located at the *Dar al Fonun*.[38]

In addition to their academic duties, the instructors at the *Dar al Fonun* performed a variety of functions. They held military drills in the compound, which were available to non-students as well. More importantly, the instructors supervised the establishment of a number of workshops at the *Dar al Fonun*. There were workshops in candle making, gunpowder making, and paper making. Additionally, a photography studio, a pharmacy, and a physics and chemistry laboratory were established by the first group of instructors.[39] Mr. Krziz, the Austrian artillery instructor, also taught geometry and geography and is credited with determining the height of Mt. Damavand and with establishing a telegraph line reaching from the *Dar al Fonun* to the royal palace. Dr. Polak encouraged his medical students to work actively among the sick. He took them to a leper colony, and allowed them to perform duties at the government military hospital, which he had established in 1854.

Governance

The *Dar al Fonun* was essentially a court institution. As such, it was controlled primarily by the court and the shah, who had the authority to make any and all decisions. As with other court institutions, the budget for the *Dar al Fonun* was overseen by the Revenue Office

---

[38]For a list of textbooks and books translated by European and Iranian instruc-tors at the *Dar al Fonun*, see Ekhtiar, "Dar al Fonun," appendix A, pp. 311-316. For a list of translations of European books, see indem, pp. 317-19. On medical works, see Hossein Ziai (ed) "19th Century Persian Medical Manuscripts: A Description," microfilms at the bio-medial library, University of California, Los Angeles.

[39]Fochettie accompanied Farrokh Khan to Paris in 1857 where he purchased a laboratory.

(*Edareh-ye Estifa*).[40] Although Naser al-Din Shah maintained the school in the face of early opposition, the *Dar al Fonun* suffered from its lack of autonomy. Directors and teachers' recommendations as well as educational aims were subordinated to court interests. According to Polak, despite the instructors' best efforts, the government only fulfilled its obligations towards them "pro forma." As a result, Polak wrote that, "our achievements fell far behind our intentions." Polak concluded that "little could be hoped for from the school under the conditions in Iran."[41]

Before his dismissal from office, Amir Kabir chose Mirza Mohammad 'Ali Khan Shirazi, the minister of foreign affairs, to be the superintendent of the *Dar al Fonun*. From its inception, the *Dar al Fonun* was associated with the Ministry of Foreign Affairs. This connection was due primarily to the fact that the recruitment of foreign instructors was considered a matter of foreign policy and was conducted by a representative of the Ministry of Foreign Affairs.[42] Shirazi was in charge of the inauguration ceremonies, but died shortly thereafter.

The subsequent two superintendents were both military officers. Following the death of Shirazi, Aziz Khan Mokri Ajudanbashi was selected as superintendent. He remained in this position for several months, until Mohammad Khan Amir Tuman was chosen to replace him.[43] Although Amir Tuman was superintendent of the *Dar al Fonun* until 1857, he had little impact on the administration of the school. He did, however, establish strict military discipline amongst the students, who at first tended to be unruly.[44] The fact that, with the exception of Shirazi's month-long tenure, the direction of the *Dar al Fonun* was in

---

[40]Ekhtiar, "Dar al Fonun," p. 133.

[41]Polak, *Persien*, vol. I, pp. 316-18.

[42]Hedayat, *Khaterat*, p. 63. See also Tabataba'i, "Dar al Fonun va Amir Kabir," p. 190.

[43]Gurney, "Dar al Fonun," p. 663. Mahbubi-Ardakani lists 'Abd al-Hosayn Khan as having been director of the *Dar al Fonun* following Aziz Khan Mokri and prior to Mirza Mohammad Khan, *Tarikh-e Mo'assesat*, vol. I, p. 263.

[44]Naser al-Din Shah ordered physical punishment of unruly students. See Yahya Dowlatabadi, *Tarikh-e Mo'aser ya Hayat-e Yahya Dowlatabadi* 4 vols. (Tehran: Ferdowsi, 1362) vol. I, p. 327. See also Iqbal Yaghma'i, "Madraseh-ye Dar al Fonun," *Yaghma*, vol. 22 (1969-70) and vol. 23 (1970-71), p. 223; and Mirza Mehdi Khan Momtahen al-Dowleh, *Khaterat-e Momtahen al-Dowleh* (Tehran: Amir Kabir, 1362), p. 70.

the hands of military officers for the first six years, certainly indicates the importance given to military instruction in the early years.

In addition to the position of superintendent, the administration of the *Dar al Fonun* comprised a managing director (*nazem*), a librarian (*ketabdar*), a manager (*mobasher*), an accountant (*mostoufi*), an overseer (*nazer*), a caller to prayer (*mo'azin*), and a number of guards and servants. Naser al-Din Shah selected Reza Qoli Khan Hedayat to serve as director.[45] Reza Qoli Khan maintained this critical position until 1860, when he was succeeded by his son, Ja'far Qoli Khan Hedayat. The predominance of the Hedayat family as high level administrators of the *Dar al Fonun* continued until the outbreak of the Constitutional Revolution in 1906.[46]

The First Graduating Class of 1858

The first phase of the *Dar al Fonun* ended in 1858, when the first group of students took their final examinations, and when the contracts of the first group of instructors expired. Already by this time, a number of the original instructors had died or had left Iran, and had been replaced by other instructors.[47] The final examinations of the first group of students to graduate from the *Dar al Fonun* were reported in the *Ruznameh-ye Vaqaye'e Ettefaqiyyeh*.[48] The information recorded concerning the field of study, illustrates the educational goals of the *Dar al Fonun* in the period 1851-58. Eighty-five students took final examinations in 1858. It is impossible to ascertain how many of these were among the entering class of 1851. In addition to students dropping out of the school, the newspaper reports that 21 of the 85 graduating students enrolled later

---

[45]Naser al-Din Shah selected Reza Qoli Khan Hedayat from a list of candidates prepared by Prime Minister Nuri. See Yaghma'i, "Dar al Fonun," p. 223.

[46]Ja'far Qoli Khan Hedayat was succeeded in the position of director in 1895-6 by his son Reza Qoli Hedayat. He remained in this position until 1906. See Gurney, "Dar al Fonun," p. 666. The Hedayat's prominence as a respected learned family extended well into the Pahlavi period.

[47]On the subsequent fate of the Austrian and Italian instructors, see Gurney, "Dar al Fonun," p. 665.

[48]*Ruznameh-ye Vaqaye'e Ettefaqiyyeh*, no. 394 (9 Muharram 1275/August 19, 1858). Quoted in Mahbubi-Ardakani, *Tarikh-e Mo'assesat*, vol. I, pp. 300-5.

at the *Dar al Fonun*— some as recently as several months before the final exams. Advancement depended on individual progress and not only on the number of years enrolled. In addition to the 85 graduating students, 39 students are mentioned as currently enrolled. This suggests a total student body of 125 prior to the graduation of the first class in 1858.

According to the report, 29 students majored in artillery, 12 in infantry, 6 in cavalry, 20 in mathematics/engineering, 17 in medicine, and 4 in natural sciences and pharmacy. Of the total number of students whose majors are enumerated in the report (including students who were not graduating in 1858), nearly 44% studied military sciences. This figure rises as high as 62.5% if the large number of students majoring in mathematics/engineering (19%) (which often had direct military applications) is included. The fact that medicine (including those in science/pharmacology) attracted 15% of the student body indicates the importance attributed to European-style medicine as an element in the improvement of the armed forces. Although courses in history, Arabic and Persian were offered, these were considered to be supplemental and not major fields of study, despite the fact that the report mentions two students majoring in Persian.

European languages also had an important place in the curriculum at the *Dar al Fonun*. As mentioned earlier, due to the language barriers between students and instructors, as well as the dearth of course materials available in Persian, French was the *lingua franca* at the *Dar al Fonun* throughout its existence. This was particularly true in the first period of 1851-58 when the instructors were almost exclusively European, and before many of the texts had been translated into Persian. It was therefore important for students to have a working knowledge of French. Indeed, as many as 34 of the 85 graduating students (40%) took a French exam in addition to exams in their major field of study. Students majoring in mathematics/engineering made up the largest group (13), with students in medicine (6) and military (5) also participating. Eleven of the students not graduating in 1858 took the French exam, which suggests that they may have majored in French. Six others are recorded as majoring in foreign [European] languages. The teaching of European languages at the *Dar al Fonun* confirmed the school's role in training diplomats, officials at the Ministry of Foreign Affairs, as well as official translators.

Final Examinations of the Graduating Class of 1858

Major Field	1858 Grads	French Exam	Late-comers	# Students Still Enrolled	Total # of Students	% of Total Students
Artillery	29	3	10	3	32	25.5%
Infantry	11	2	1	5	16	13%
Cavalry	4	0	1	2 $^\Omega$	6	5%
Math/ Engineering	20	13	2	4	24	19%
Medicine	17	3	7	1	18	14%
Science/ Pharma-cology	4	3	0	1	5	4%
Foreign Languages	0	0	0	6	6 $^\Psi$	5%
Persian	0	0	0	2	2	1.5%
Unknown	0	11	0	16	16	12.5%
Total	85	35	21	39 $^\Sigma$	125	99.5% $^\Delta$

Ω One student is recorded as having made no progress; the other was recommended for expulsion.

Ψ The total number may also include 11 of the students with no noted major who took the French exam.

Σ This takes into account that one cavalry student was expelled.

Δ This .5% discrepancy is caused by rounding off.

Available prosopographical material on 19 of the students who took exams in 1858 clarifies the social and professional role of the *Dar al Fonun* in this early stage.[49] Although information is available for only a small percentage of the total group, it is nonetheless informative. It is significant that the data were extracted from a variety of prosopographical works, including government documents, newspaper reports, and statesmen's memoirs. It must therefore be noted that those individuals who are recorded in such documents were considered important, and additionally, had positions which gained them public exposure. As governmental positions in Tehran would have given the individuals the most chance to be noted in these documents, it is not surprising that the majority of the individuals were connected to the *Dar al Fonun* and/or to the central government in Tehran in some way. Individuals who graduated from the *Dar al Fonun* and subsequently entered military service are less likely to be mentioned in Tehran government documents. Keeping the natural selection of these 19 individuals in mind, the following general conclusions may be drawn.

First, the students at the *Dar al Fonun* came from prominent families, many of whom had court connections. This is attested to by personal memoirs of students who attended the school.[50] Although it is difficult to ascertain, the report in the *Ruznameh-ye Vaqaye'-e Ettefaqiyyeh* discussed above suggests that 11 students of the graduating class (all but one of whom majored in military sciences) were from cities other than Tehran. It is impossible to determine how much of the student body as a whole was drawn from the provinces.

Second, graduates of the *Dar al Fonun*, like their fathers, were employed in prominent positions in the government and court. As many as 11 students in the graduating class of 1858 went on to play a role in the *Dar al Fonun*. It is likely that this number includes all of those who did so from this group, as others would most likely have been noted in the prosopographical sources had they been involved with the school. It is also evident that the school constituted a channel for advanced study abroad in Europe, and that graduates of the *Dar al Fonun* were called upon to serve in diplomatic assignments at home and

---

[49]Ekhtiar compiled this information based on a variety of prosopographical sources in "Dar al Fonun," pp. 179-82.

[50]Reza Qoli Khan Hedayat, *Khaterat*, pp. 85-86; Dowlatabadi, *Hayat-e Yahya* vol. I, p. 327.

abroad. Graduation from the *Dar al Fonun* confirmed the students' already high social status, and no doubt facilitated job placement in high positions. In particular, the students' familiarity with European sciences and languages was regarded as a valuable commodity. However, at this time, family standing and court connections remained the principal vehicle for advancement in government careers.

The 1858-71 Period

The second period of the *Dar al Fonun* coincides with the tenure of 'Ali Qoli Mirza E'tezad al-Saltaneh as superintendent from December 1857 until his death in 1880. Already in 1858, E'tezad al-Saltaneh had been named minister of sciences (*Vazir-e 'Olum*), although the ministry itself was not formally established until 1860. His government appointments, in addition to the fact that he was a son of Fath 'Ali Shah and enjoyed the support of the Queen Mother, enabled E'tezad al-Saltaneh to exercise substantial power. He was thus in a position to effect changes at the *Dar al Fonun*. For example, he supplemented the budget of the *Dar al Fonun* with revenues from two provinces of which he was governor.[51] E'tezad al-Saltaneh is credited with having consistently attempted to further the educational interests of the *Dar al Fonun*.[52]

E'tezad al-Saltaneh met regularly with both the European and Iranian instructors in order to evaluate the needs of the students.[53] In 1863, E'tezad al-Saltaneh founded a library at the *Dar al Fonun*. He also supervised a number of newspapers, including the *Ruznameh-ye Elmi-ye Dowlat-e 'Aliyeh-ye Iran* (The Scientific Journal of the Exalted Government of Iran), which began publication in January 1868 and which he used to promote new, European scientific theories and discoveries.[54]

A serious problem that confronted the *Dar al Fonun* during E'tezad al-Saltaneh's tenure as supervisor was the shortage of qualified instructors. Shortly prior to his appointment, in April 1857, Prime Minister Nuri ordered the Iranian envoy to Paris, Farrokh Khan, to

---

[51]Ekhtiar, "Dar al Fonun," p. 134.
[52]Yaghma'i, "Dar al Fonun," pp. 222-23, 517-18; Gurney, "Dar al Fonun," pp. 665-66.
[53]Yaghma'i, "Dar al Fonun," p. 517.
[54]Avery, "Printing," p. 826.

petition that as many as fourteen instructors be dispatched to Iran. Farrokh Khan requested that instructors be designated in the following areas: 5 for infantry training, 2 for geometry, 3 for artillery, 1 to work in an arsenal, and one each for physics, mining and sugar refining. Nuri was careful to specify that the instructors should be skilled and that they should be prepared to remain in Iran for a lengthy period of time. He also urged Farrokh Khan to make sure that the instructors devoted their time to training, rather than to scientific exploration as had some of the Austrian instructors. Nuri wrote:

> It should be requested of the worthy French government that the instructors be chosen from among trustworthy and honorable people and . . . they shall be instructed that their intentions be really the instruction of troops and the [training] of Iranian officers, and that they not come to Iran for one or two years, travel about, earn money, and return.[55]

In this letter, Nuri expresses dissatisfaction with individuals from among the first group of Austrian instructors. However, although the French dispatched a few teachers in November 1858, this group did not have nearly as much success as had the first group of instructors from Austria.[56]

Subsequently, as a result of the poor performance of European instructors recruited through diplomatic channels, E'tezad al-Saltaneh resorted to hiring instructors from among European residents of Tehran.[57] This policy resulted in the reversal of Amir Kabir's attempt to isolate European instructors at the *Dar al Fonun* from diplomatic involvement, since the European instructors simultaneously retained diplomatic positions with their own governments. However, after the departure of the majority of the first group of Austrian and Italian instructors, Iranians educated at the *Dar al Fonun* and/or abroad in Europe increasingly constituted the majority of instructors at the college.[58]

---

[55]Letter from Nuri to Farrokh Khan quoted in Yaghma'i, "Dar al Fonun," pp. 519-20.

[56]Polak reported that the French officers achieved no results and left shortly after their arrival in Iran. Polak, *Persien*, vol. I, p. 318.

[57]After 1861, no formal request was made to any European government for non-military instructors. Ekhtiar, "Dar al Fonun," p. 166.

[58]For lists of European and Iranian instructors see Mahbubi-Ardakani, *Tarikh-e Mo'assesat*, vol. I, pp. 271-92, Ekhtiar, "Dar al Fonun," pp. 146-77.

Educational Reforms

Following the graduation from the *Dar al Fonun* of the first group of students in 1858 and the official dispatch of students to France a year later, E'tezad al-Saltaneh attempted to initiate educational reforms at the *Dar al Fonun*. As the official mouthpiece, the *Ruznameh-ye Vaqaye'-e Ettefaqiyyeh* announced these changes in January, 1860.[59] This announcement constitutes a "manifesto of intent" concerning the government's goals for the *Dar al Fonun* as envisioned by E'tezad al-Saltaneh.[60] The manifesto clearly indicates that the court recognizes the important role of the *Dar al Fonun* in training government cadres and in serving as a channel for the adoption of European sciences and technology. The opening statement emphasizes the *Dar al Fonun*'s promotion of progress in Iran:

> The means of progress of every state have always been primarily the spreading of useful sciences and new industries . . . It was [therefore] decided to bring in from Europe knowledgeable instructors and qualified teachers in all the sciences and industries and build the blessed school *Dar al Fonun*.[61]

In the manifesto, E'tezad al-Saltaneh outlines his plans to expand the role of the *Dar al Fonun* as the focal point for the adoption of European sciences and technology. In order to accomplish this, he proposed to expand the role of the workshops, attract additional students, and institute general curricular requirements. The manifesto called on a variety of students to apply to the *Dar al Fonun*:

> All Iranians from [amongst] the royalty, ministers, holders of government office in the administration and military, large merchants, and tradesmen/artisans must not leave their sons uneducated, [but rather] occupy them with these sciences.[62]

Specifically, the inclusion of "tradesmen/artisans" constitutes a marked difference from the *Ruznameh-ye Vaqaye'-e Ettefaqiyyeh*'s 1851

---

[59]*Ruznameh-ye Vaqaye'-e Ettefaqiyyeh*, no. 458 (19 Jumadi al-Thani 1276/January 13, 1860), quoted in Mahbubi-Ardakani, *Tarikh-e Mo'assesat*, vol. I, pp. 311-14. All subsequent quotes refer to this citation.

[60]Mahbubi-Ardakani termed it a "manifesto of the Naseri government." *Tarikh-e Mo'assesat*, vol. I, p. 311.

[61]*Ruznameh-ye Vaqaye'-e Ettefaqiyyeh*, no. 458.

[62]Ibid.

invitation for children "from amongst the landowners and dignitaries and nobles" to enter the *Dar al Fonun*. The manifesto also urged students from the provinces to apply, and outlined the administrative procedures for doing so. According to the manifesto, the *Dar al Fonun* was in urgent need of new students to replace the graduating class of 1858.

E'tezad al-Saltaneh's intentions were twofold. First, he hoped to attract sons of "tradesmen and artisans" to the workshops at the school. Second, he intended to prepare larger numbers of students for a variety of government employment, both in Tehran and the provinces. In order to attract students to the *Dar al Fonun*, E'tezad al-Saltaneh offered a variety of inducements. All students were promised lunch, clothes and a stipend. He also assured the students that, depending on the field studied, graduation could be as rapid as one or two years:

> It must not be imagined that in all of the fields of study students require five or more years to graduate, but rather this process depends on [the students'] intelligence and understanding, and on the degree of difficulty of that field [of study]. Sometimes it is possible to graduate in one or two years, and sometimes it requires a particularly lengthy period [of study].[63]

Students were also promised government employment, in accordance with their field of study. The following occupations were specifically cited: military officer, physician, officer in the government, translator in the Ministry of Foreign Affairs and positions in domestic affairs. These promises indicate that lengthy study and the resulting opportunity costs were considered prohibitive to study at the *Dar al Fonun*. It also assured prospective students of future renumeration. The mention of potentially short period of study in some fields was intended to encourage socially elite students to attend the *Dar al Fonun* who might otherwise choose to enter government directly service without pursuing additional education.

As part of the 1860 reforms outlined in the *Ruznameh-ye Vaqaye'-e Ettefaqiyyeh*, E'tezad al-Saltaneh addressed the continuing problem of the variance and/or lack of prior education of incoming students. Some of the students had received a good deal of prior education. In fact,

---

[63]Ibid. It is not clear from this announcement whether E'tezad al-Saltaneh intended to reduce the time to graduation, or whether he was simply stating that some students advanced more rapidly than others.

amongst the first graduating class of 1858, 21 of the students (25%) had enrolled between two months and three years previously. Furthermore, six of these students graduated in the field of medicine after only two years of attendance at the *Dar al Fonun* and one student after only 2 months.[64] Many of the students admitted had received some prior training in French and occasionally in sciences. At the other end of the spectrum, however, were those students who, "due to their young age were not conversant in Persian and Arabic and lacked appropriate training in literature." Even graduates of the *Dar al Fonun* who later traveled to France for advanced study were required to undergo as many as two years of French language training before they were allowed to matriculate into French schools.[65]

E'tezad al-Saltaneh sought to establish a core curriculum in order to remedy the problem of insufficient levels of preparation prior to enrollment. Depending on the subject studied, the first two or three years were designated for general subjects. The subsequent five or six years would then be devoted to specialized training in the field of the students' choice. In addition, Persian and Arabic language courses would be offered to incoming students determined to have had little prior education.

In addition to the establishment of a fixed curriculum, the manifesto described the system of certification in place at the school. In the traditional educational system, a student's advancement and competence was marked by certificates of satisfactory completion (*ijazeh*). The *ijazeh* consisted of a writ of "permission" to teach a given text by a specific instructor. The *ijazeh* system therefore was based on a chain of transmission (*isnad*) from teacher to student. A student's advancement in his studies was marked by the accumulation of *ijazeh*s. Although the terminology was retained, E'tezad al-Saltaneh attempted to establish a more complex system of advancement and certification based on the student's performance on general exams relative to the rest of his class. The manifesto explains the different awards bestowed on different levels of achievement in exams. By replacing the institution of the *ijazeh*

[64]*Ruznameh-ye Vaqaye'e Ettefaqiyyeh* no. 394 (9 Muharram 1275/August 19, 1858). Quoted in Mahbubi-Ardakani, *Tarikh-e Mo'assesat*, vol. I, pp. 300-5. See the discussion of the first graduating class, above.

[65]Mahbubi-Ardakani, *Tarikh-e Mo'assesat*, vol. I, p. 339. See section on students abroad, below.

with a system of class levels and general exams on the European model, E'tezad al-Saltaneh regularized and simplified different levels of advancement and achievement, and facilitated the individual student's evaluation based on academic achievement and merit.

E'tezad al-Saltaneh's proposal to shape the *Dar al Fonun* into a preparatory school for increasing numbers of government officials reveals an additional, more radical underlying objective. In essence, he wanted to institute educational standards for government officials. Moreover, theoretically the *Dar al Fonun* promoted advancement on the basis of merit, rather than on family connections, although in practice, personal connections remained the dominant route of access to government office. The educational reforms proposed by E'tezad al-Saltaneh in the *Ruznameh-ye Vaqaye'-e Ettefaqiyyeh* were radical and threatened the political, professional, cultural and religious status quo in many ways which will be discussed in detail below. As a result, these reforms were never realized. In addition to opposition from a wide spectrum of socioeconomic groups, the initial encouragement and support afforded the *Dar al Fonun* by Naser al-Din Shah gave way in this period to suspicion and neglect. The result was a general decline in the quality of education at the *Dar al Fonun*, and its increasingly decorative function as a court institution.[66]

The *Dar al Fonun* of Tabriz

Shortly after the first group of students graduated from the *Dar al Fonun* in 1858, a similar polytechnic school, also named the *Dar al Fonun* (or sometimes the *Dar al-Saltaneh*), was established in Tabriz by Crown Prince Mozaffar al-Din Mirza.[67] The majority of the teachers

---

[66]Mahbubi-Ardakani asserts that both teachers and students came increasingly from certain upper class families, and that the *Dar al Fonun* became essentially a court institution for the creation of literate servants. See his discussion of the decline of the school, in *Tarikh-e Mo'assesat*, vol. I, pp. 310-16.

[67]The *Dar al Fonun* in Tabriz was established in 1859. See Mahbubi-Ardakani, *Tarikh-e Mo'assesat*, vol. I, p. 366. Omid mistakenly records the opening as in 1875 or 1876, some twenty years after the establishment of the *Dar al Fonun* in Tehran. See Hosayn Omid, *Tarikh-e Farhang-e Azarbayjan* (Tabriz: Farhang, 1332), vol. I, p. 29.

were graduates of the *Dar al Fonun* in Tehran.[68] The curriculum consisted of French, medicine, geometry, infantry, artillery and Persian.[69] Like the *Dar al Fonun* in Tehran, the student body was predominantly composed of sons of top government officials and courtiers. In the 458th issue of the *Ruznameh-ye Vaqaye'-e Ettefaqiyyeh* discussed above, the process of enrollment was explained in order to make access more readily available. However, E'tezad al-Saltaneh's goal of broadening access to the school was not realized in this period. It is known that after a number of years, the student body increased from 40 to 50 students, approximately half of whom paid tuition, while the other half attended free of charge. The basis of admission, however, was some prior education, including the study of specified texts.[70] This criterion may have, in effect, served to eliminate boys from non-elite backgrounds who had not received adequate preparation from attending the school.

Students Abroad

The period 1851-71 witnessed the largest number of Iranian students dispatched abroad to Europe prior to the Constitutional Revolution of 1906-11. The period was also remarkable both for the number of missions dispatched, and for the variety of fields of study pursued by the students.

The first dispatch of students in the Naser al-Din Shah period occurred in 1851. At this time, Amir Kabir selected six artisans to travel to Russia to learn a variety of trades.[71] This group of students was accompanied to Russia by a Tabriz merchant who supervised the students. After a period of three years, the group returned to Tehran with the necessary equipment to establish factories in paper milling and sugar refining. During his tenure as prime minister, Amir Kabir also

---

[68]For a list of directors, staff, and teachers at the *Dar al Fonun* in Tabriz, see Omid, *Tarikh-e Azarbayjan*, vol. I, p. 31.

[69]Ibid.

[70]Ibid, pp. 33-34.

[71]Mohammad Farhad Atai, "The Sending of Iranian Students to Europe, 1811-1906" (Ph.D. diss., University of California, Berkeley, 1992), pp. 76-77. Mahbubi-Ardakani only lists 5 students on this mission, in *Tarikh-e Mo'assesat*, vol. I, p. 196.

dispatched two rug weavers from Kashan to Istanbul to learn silk preparation.[72] These two dispatches represent a continuation of the established governmental policy of sending students to Europe to learn new technology and techniques.

It is also the case that in the period 1851-71 an increasing number of parents sent their sons abroad to Europe to study at their own expense. Often, if a diplomat traveled to Europe on an official mission, he would bring along a family member to study in Europe.[73] This practice amongst upperclass families became increasingly frequent after 1867 when Naser al-Din Shah imposed a travel ban. Paradoxically, although there were no more official dispatches of students, elite families were able to receive special permission to send their sons abroad. This trend enhanced the prestige associated with study in Europe. For example, in late 1856 Farrokh Khan Amin al-Molk, in the position of minister plenipotentiary, traveled to Europe to resolve the conflict with Great Britain over Herat.[74] Farrokh Khan brought two students along on his mission who proceeded to study in France: Mirza Reza and Mirza Hosayn. These two individuals were the first Iranians to receive medical degrees in France. Upon completion of their studies in 1861, the two returned to Iran where they taught medicine at the *Dar al Fonun*. Farrokh Khan's first deputy, Mirza 'Ali Naqi, who had previously studied medicine at the *Dar al Fonun*, also studied medicine in Paris, while simultaneously retaining his official position. He subsequently participated in the student mission to France in 1859.[75] There is no evidence of official sanction for the dispatch of these three medical students. Atai surmises that Mirza Reza and Mirza Hosayn's expenses were paid for by the Iranian government. It is more likely, however, that they accompanied Farrokh Khan as a result of family connections, and that their expenses were thus assumed by their families. This hypothesis is substantiated by the fact that Mirza 'Ali

---

[72]Mahbubi-Ardakani, *Tarikh-e Mo'assesat*, vol. I, p. 196; Atai, "Iranian Students," p. 77.

[73]Mahbubi-Ardakani mentions 13 students who were sent abroad, either in association with an official mission or independently, in the 1851-71 period. See his *Tarikh-e Mo'assesat*, vol. I, pp. 339, 352-53. There were surely others.

[74]Negotiations under French mediation resulted in the Treaty of Paris of 1857.

[75]Atai, "Iranian Students," pp. 82-83.

Naqi, a medical student, apparently accepted a diplomatic appointment in order to study medicine in France.

The most significant dispatch of students to Europe was the Garrusi mission of 1859. The first group of students graduated from the *Dar al Fonun* in 1858. Polak, who was primarily interested in his own medical students receiving additional education in France, broached the subject of an official student mission with E'tezad al-Saltaneh.[76] The minister of sciences and superintendent of *Dar al Fonun* then presented the idea to Naser al-Din Shah, who agreed to allow the formation of a student mission to Europe.

France was chosen as the destination of the student mission for a variety of reasons. Iran enjoyed significantly better diplomatic relations with France than with other Western European countries at the time. Iran had only just resumed friendly diplomatic relations with Great Britain as a result of Farrokh Khan's mission of 1856-57. In addition, although Russia was often the destination of artisans seeking to learn new techniques, at the time Russia was not perceived to be as advanced in higher learning and in military sciences as were Western European countries. In contrast, France was renowned for her military schools.[77] France had also been the principal destination of student missions since the Mohammad Shah period. When Farrokh Khan returned from France in 1859, he reported the success of his mission, and his favorable impressions of France in general.[78] France also offered certain practical advantages. The primary foreign language studied at the *Dar al Fonun* was French. The students, therefore, would be better prepared to study in France than elsewhere. Furthermore, students from Egypt and the Ottoman Empire had been dispatched to France since 1826.[79] At the time of the Iranian mission of 1859, Ottoman students were currently studying in Paris. France therefore had the advantage of offering the facilities and experience of hosting a relatively large number of foreign students.

---

[76]Polak, *Persien*, vol. I, p. 318.

[77]French military schools such as St. Cyr and the Ecole Polytechnique were considered the best in Europe until 1871 when the Prussian army defeated the French. After this time, Prussian military schools were commonly believed to be superior.

[78]Atai, "Iranian Students," p. 86.

[79]See Alain Silvera, "The First Egyptian Student Mission to France under Muhammad 'Ali," *Middle Eastern Studies*, vol. 16, no. 2 (1980), pp. 1-22.

Naser al-Din Shah charged Farrokh Khan with selecting 100 students from amongst the nobility to participate in the mission. However, after a period of negotiation, only 56 families agreed to allow their sons to participate. According to Atai, this was because some families were concerned about the possible negative cultural impact of study abroad.[80] Eventually, Farrokh Khan selected 42 students to take part in the mission. Of this group, at least 17 were either students at the *Dar al Fonun*, or recent graduates. Information on the educational background of the remaining group is not available. Given the high social status of the group of students, it can be surmised that the students had received education comparable to students entering the *Dar al Fonun*, and may have additionally studied on their own.

In addition to the 42 students, the mission included diplomatic staff and a number of relatives of members of the staff. One of the students, 'Abd al-Rasul Khan, was selected as the student leader. Hasan 'Ali Khan Amir Nezam Garrusi was appointed by Naser al-Din Shah to replace Farrokh Khan in the position of resident minister plenipotentiary to the courts of Europe. In this capacity he was also in charge of the student mission. On April 1, 1859 the students received an audience by the shah before departing for France.

In France, Garrusi entrusted responsibility for the students' academic studies to Aleksander Chodzko, a professor of Slavic studies at the Collège de France.[81] Chodzko had participated in diplomatic missions to Iran on behalf of the Russian government, and therefore spoke Persian.[82] All the students were provided with French language courses upon their arrival, as their French was not sufficient to enter French educational institutions.[83] The students were divided according to level of preparation. Those younger students requiring secondary education were placed in appropriate institutions. Advanced students were sent to colleges in accordance with their field of study. The 42 students specialized in the following fields:

---

[80]Atai, "Iranian Students," pp. 84-85.

[81]Momtahen al-Dowleh, *Khaterat*, p. 74.

[82]Chodzko was also the first to compile and translate the Iranian passion play, or "*ta'ziyeh*." See Aleksander Edmund Boreyko Chodzko, *Théatre Persan: Choix de Téaziés* (Paris: Ernest Leroux, 1878).

[83]Mahbubi-Ardakani, *Tarikh-e Mo'assesat*, vol. I, p. 339.

Military Sciences:	11
Medicine:	4
Mathematics/Engineering:	4
Literature/Politics/Law:	3
Pharmacology:	1
Optics:	1
Astronomy:	1
Painting:	1
Technical Fields and Crafts:	16

In addition to the 42 designated students, four other members of the mission (diplomatic staff and relatives of diplomats) studied military sciences, medicine, geography, and history.

Three years after their arrival in France, the majority of the students were engaged in specialized study or were prepared to do so. Already by this time, some of the advanced military students and those who had studied technical skills and crafts had completed their studies and were preparing to return to Iran.[84] Details of the students' progress were reported regularly by Chodzko to Amir Nezam Garrusi.

The experience of the students who participated in the Garrusi mission of 1859 is in sharp contrast to that of previous student missions. The large number of participants meant that the students were never isolated physically from one another. Most students studied together at different colleges in groups. Nor were the students isolated culturally. Arrangements were made for students to perform religious duties while in France.[85]

The Garrusi mission students also benefitted from appropriate guidance. Unlike Mirza Saleh Shirazi's account of being left to his own devices while in England in 1815-19, the students on the Garrusi mission were provided for at all levels. Their accommodations and food were furnished. In addition, Chozdzko facilitated their enrollment in appropriate French colleges. Amir Nezam Garrusi was resident in

---

[84]Atai, "Iranian Students," p. 100.

[85]Garrusi also held Persian New Year (*nowruz*) celebrations which European diplomats attended. See Momtahen al-Dowleh, *Khaterat*, pp. 75, 116-17.

France for the length of their studies. His position as official Iranian diplomat in France, and his close personal relationship with Napoleon III undoubtably contributed to the success of the student mission.[86]

The majority of the students completed their studies and were prepared to return to Iran in 1863. Amir Nezam Garrusi accompanied the students back to Iran. After this time, students returned to Iran individually or in small groups as they completed their studies. In 1867, the last group of students left France.[87]

Data concerning the subsequent careers of the Garrusi mission students reveal the changing nature of European-style education in Iran.[88] Of the 12 individuals who studied military sciences in France, 7 entered military positions, 1 was employed by the Ministry of Foreign Affairs, and 2 had governmental positions. No data was available for 2 students. Military skills continued to provide a means of government advancement, whether in civil or military positions. Of the 5 students who pursued medical degrees in France, all practiced medicine upon their return to Iran. One taught medicine at the *Dar al Fonun*, and 4 attained prominent positions as court physicians. European medical degrees almost always led to prestigious appointments as royal physicians. Indeed, since the 'Abbas Mirza period, court physicians were increasingly Europeans or European-educated Iranians. Of the students who learned technical trades, all were employed in positions that made use of their area of expertise. The students who pursued mathematics (2), optics (1), and engineering (2), however, were not all subsequently employed in positions requiring their specific skills. Apart from one individual who taught mathematics at the *Dar al Fonun*, the other 4 were either idle, or assumed duties that had no bearing on their newly-acquired skills.[89]

Amir Nezam Garrusi recognized the obstacles confronting these students. Before returning to Iran in 1863, he took measures to provide

---

[86]Garrusi dined with Napoleon III twice a month. In addition, Napoleon III desired for him to become foreign minister in Tehran. See Momtahen al-Dowleh, *Khaterat*, p. 90.

[87]Atai, "Iranian Students," p. 111.

[88]These data have been extracted from biographies of the 42 students and an additional 3 members of the Garrusi mission who studied in France which are provided in Atai, "Iranian Students," pp. 115-36.

[89]Momtahen al-Dowleh, for example, was forced to undertake manual work in order to support himself.

the necessary technical equipment for students returning to Iran. However, the Iranian government had no system for benefiting from the new skills. In sharp contrast to the Ottoman and Egyptian governments, the Iranian government made no attempt to benefit from the skills acquired in Europe. Instead, the students were employed largely on the basis of family connections. The under-utilization of the students' skills led to frustration amongst them concerning government initiative, particularly regarding educational reform. The situation only worsened when, in 1867, Naser al-Din Shah issued a ban on student travel abroad. After this time, study abroad became the sole prerogative of boys whose families enjoyed court connections and could obtain special permission from the shah, or who could accompany family members on diplomatic assignments abroad.[90]

It is noteworthy that three of the students who participated in the Garrusi mission of 1859 studied European law (2) and European literature and political science (1). On their return, the 2 law students were employed by the Ministry of Foreign Affairs. One of them even attained a diplomatic position. No data are available on the career of the political science student. These three students represent the first attempt to acquire European education outside the parameters of technical fields. These are the first students to study fields that are intimately connected to European society and culture. Previously, Iranians perceived of European technology (military and artisinal) as devoid of cultural content.[91] The choice of law and political science indicates a recognition of the need to be informed of the European political and legal systems. The fact that these students were subsequently employed by the Ministry of Foreign Affairs illustrates the growing need for educated cadres to staff the ministry.

Opposition to the *Dar al Fonun*

Ever since Amir Kabir first proposed the idea of the *Dar al Fonun*, rival courtiers opposed it. Political posturing and personality conflicts often expressed themselves as opposition to or support for specific govern-

---

[90]See Momtahen al-Dowleh, *Khaterat*, pp. 107-8; and Dowlatabadi, *Hayat-e Yahya*, vol. I, p. 298.
[91]For a discussion of this perception, see chapter II, above.

ment actions. The *Dar al Fonun*, inasmuch as it was identified with Amir Kabir's reforms, did not find favor amongst his political rivals. Amir Kabir's successor in the office of prime minister, Mirza Aqa Khan Nuri, showed particular animosity towards the college and favored its closure, along with a general reversal of many of Amir Kabir's unpopular reforms. According to Dr. Polak, Nuri wanted to pay the instructors off and send them home. He also succeeded in preventing them from receiving ceremonial robes (*khal'at*) as well as the housing and food usually accorded European guests.[92] Nuri's opposition was seconded by the British representative in Iran at the time. Colonel Sheil was concerned about the potential political ramifications of the fact that of all the European instructors at the *Dar al Fonun*, none were British. In an attempt to convince Naser al-Din Shah to follow Nuri's recommendation and close the school, Sheil advised the shah that it was not in his royal interest to maintain such an institution.[93]

Despite such warnings, and the high level of opposition to Amir Kabir's reforms that had prompted his dismissal, Naser al-Din Shah did not close the *Dar al Fonun* down. Yahya Dowlatabadi, a contemporary of Naser al-Din Shah, suggests that this was due in part to the shah's concern not to cause diplomatic friction with Austria. According to Dowlatabadi, Naser al-Din Shah was pressured by nobles and courtiers to keep the *Dar al Fonun* open because they believed that their sons would receive better instruction there than that afforded by private tutors.[94] Regardless of the foreign or domestic pressures, it is true that Naser al-Din Shah exhibited genuine interest in the *Dar al Fonun*. Indeed, in the first few years of its operation, he took an active interest in the school. He frequently went to inspect it and ordered that the *Ruznameh-ye Vaqaye'e Ettefaqiyyeh* report regularly on the progress of the institution and the students.[95] In addition, Naser al-Din Shah personally

---

[92]Polak, *Persien*, vol. I, p. 301. Ceremonial robes were traditionally bestowed on foreign diplomats and sometimes foreign merchants as a mark of esteem and honor by the shah.

[93]Yaghma'i, "Dar al Fonun," p. 147. Polak reported that Sheil supported Nuri's attempts to close the school. See *Persien*, vol. I, p. 301.

[94]Dowlatabadi, *Hayat-e Yahya*, vol. I, p. 338.

[95]Yahma'i, "Dar al Fonun," p. 404.

awarded medals and honors to students and teachers at the final examinations.[96]

Gradually, however, the initial encouragement and support that Naser al-Din Shah afforded the *Dar al Fonun* gave way to suspicion and neglect. The change in the shah's attitude stemmed from his association of the school with dangerous European political ideas. His suspicions concerning the hazards of European ideas in Iran came to a head during the *Faramushkhaneh* episode in 1861. Two years previously, Mirza Malkom Khan, an Armenian convert to Islam educated in France and a teacher at the *Dar al Fonun*, had established a pseudo-Masonic club called the *Faramushkhaneh* (House of Forgetfulness). Students and instructors at the *Dar al Fonun* comprised the majority of the secret organization's members.[97] Although Naser al-Din Shah initially viewed the *Faramushkhaneh* with approbation, courtiers succeeded in convincing Naser al-Din Shah of its anti-monarchical nature.[98] Mirza Malkom Khan was accused of Babi sympathies and of propagating "republicanism." In obvious reference to France's political system, "republicanism" at this time was synonymous not only with anti-monarchical convictions, but with radical, anti-religious ideas.[99]

---

[96]Sources differ as to the frequency of the shah's visits. Bozorg Omid reports that in the first few years of its establishment, Naser al-Din Shah visited the *Dar al Fonun* several times a year, in *Az Mast keh bar Mast* (Tehran: Donya-ye Ketab, 1363), p. 30. Yaghma'i asserts that in the first two years, the shah visited the school once or twice a week, in "Dar al Fonun," p. 223. Momtahen al-Dowleh, a student at the *Dar al Fonun* in the years 1857-59, relates that Naser al-Din Shah attended exams at that time. See his *Khaterat*, p. 70.

[97]For a list of some prominent members, see Hamid Algar, *Mirza Malkum Khan: A Study in the History of Iranian Modernism* (Berkeley: University of California Press, 1973), pp. 49-50. Amanat believes that the total membership did not exceed 500, despite Malkom Khan's claims to a membership of 3,000. See Abbas Amanat, *Pivot of the Universe: Nasir al-Din Shah Qajar and the Iranian Monarchy 1831-1896* (Berkeley: University of California Press, 1997), pp. 362-63.

[98]The *Faramushkhaneh* may initially have received royal sanction. See Joseph Arthur de Gobineau, *Les religions et les philosophies dans l'Asie Centrale* (Paris, 1865), p. 305; Amanat, *Pivot*, p. 363; Shaul Bakhash, *Iran: Monarchy, Bureaucracy and Reform under the Qajars, 1858-1896* (London: Ithaca,1978), p. 17.

[99]Naser al-Din Shah was particularly fearful of Babis since their attempted assassination of him in 1852. On the nature of opposition to Mirza Malkom Khan and the *Faramushkhaneh*, as well as Malkom Khan's refutation of the accusations, see Algar, *Mirza Malkom Khan*, pp. 31-42, 46-48.

When Naser al-Din Shah turned to members of the ulama and his personal physician, Dr. Tholozon for advice, they all confirmed the subversive nature of the *Faramushkhaneh*.[100] Accordingly, in 1861 Naser al-Din Shah ordered the closure of the *Faramushkhaneh* and exiled Mirza Malkom Khan.[101] In order to further stem the influx of dangerous European political ideas into Iran, Naser al-Din Shah banned all travel abroad in 1867 after the return of the students from the Garrusi mission.

Despite the censorship and political oppression that increasingly characterized Naser al-Din Shah's reign, the shah never closed the *Dar al Fonun*. This was partly due to Naser al-Din Shah's deep concern with how Europeans viewed Iran. The closure of the *Dar al Fonun* would signal Iran's "backwardness." It was also true that the *Dar al Fonun* did fulfill its function of producing educated government officials. As discussed above, many of the schools' graduates served in important government positions. The shah was, therefore, aware of the benefits of the *Dar al Fonun*. He was also conscious of these graduates' stake in the school, and their certain opposition to its closure. For the remainder of his reign, Naser al-Din Shah maintained an ambivalent attitude towards the school. Although he forbore closing it, he made certain that the school was kept on a tight leash. The educational reforms proposed by E'tezad al-Saltaneh in 1860 were not implemented, and the teachers enjoyed little academic freedom.

Naser al-Din Shah was not alone in associating the *Dar al Fonun* with European political influence. The nature of the school as a link to Europe, both intellectually and politically, was recognized from the outset, both by its advocates and adversaries. The *Faramushkhaneh* highlighted the connection between the *Dar al Fonun* and the growing reform impetus. This connection was reinforced over time as reform-minded individuals, many of them diplomats abroad, urged the shah to implement European-style reforms in Iran. Fears of growing European influence in Iranian affairs turned to alarm as many reformers called for European sponsorship in Iranian industrial and commercial development. Debate over reform was rife in the government bureau-

---

[100] Algar, *Mirza Malkom Khan*, p. 48.

[101] The *Faramushkhaneh* was ordered closed on October 18, 1861. Its dissolution was announced in the *Ruznameh-ye Vaqaye'-e Ettefaqiyyeh*. See Algar, *Mirza Malkom Khan*, pp. 48-49 for the citation.

cracy. Just as Naser al-Din Shah banned student travel to Europe, opponents of European-style reform attempted to thwart knowledge of and comparison with Europe.[102] In one instance, Prime Minister Nuri forbade the publication of Farrokh Khan's travel account of Europe.

The *Dar al Fonun*, inasmuch as it was associated with prestigious government positions, denoted a shift in the social status paradigm. At the same time, it theoretically, if not in practice, challenged the existing system of career advancement. Beginning with 'Abbas Mirza's first student dispatch in 1811, individuals who had studied in Europe often were awarded with important government posts. In addition to their expertise in various military, medical and engineering fields, these students were valued for their familiarity with Europe and their knowledge of European languages. Graduates of the *Dar al Fonun* embodied the emergence of European science and technology as a basis of status acquisition. This status shift is evidenced by the increasing number of parents who sent their sons abroad at this time, even after the travel ban was imposed in 1867.

This was further reinforced by the emphasis on merit. As illustrated in E'tezad al-Saltaneh's educational reform manifesto, the *Dar al Fonun* was organized around the principle of academic and career advancement based on achievement and merit. This constituted a direct challenge to the existing system that emphasized proximity to the court, and client-patron relations. It is no coincidence that one of the ten guiding principals of the *Faramushkhaneh* was advancement based on merit.[103] Not surprisingly therefore, the *Dar al Fonun* was the focus of general resentment in the government bureaucracy. As observed by Robert Watson, *Dar al Fonun* graduates and those who studied abroad "are looked on with an eye of distrust by the majority of their less instructed countrymen, who take care to do all in their power to prevent them from having the opportunity of putting in practice anything they may have learned, and thereby throwing others into the shade."[104]

Of all the opponents of the *Dar al Fonun*, however, none were as vociferous as members of the ulama and the medical community. These two groups were directly threatened— intellectually, culturally,

---

[102]Bakhash, *Iran*, p. 31.
[103]Ibid, p. 19.
[104]Watson, *History*, p. 20.

and professionally—by the European-style curriculum in place at the *Dar al Fonun*.

Medicine at the *Dar al Fonun*: A Case Study in Opposition

As a "traditional" science, Iranian medicine embodied cultural mores and legitimacy. Doctors were held in high esteem and the position of court doctor (*hakimbashi*) was a coveted one. Medicine was unique in that it was the only discipline taught at the *Dar al Fonun* both in accordance with current European medical practice and according to traditional Iranian methods and doctrine (after 1860).[105] The *Dar al Fonun* was thus the center of competition between the two schools of medicine.

European medicine had not always caused so much turmoil in Iran. European doctors had traveled to Iran as part of diplomatic missions throughout the Safavid period.[106] Nader Shah employed European physicians in his service.[107] It was not until the Qajar period that European medicine began to attract substantial attention.

Just as in Egypt and the Ottoman Empire, the adoption of European medical knowledge formed an important component of the defensive military reforms initiated by Crown Prince 'Abbas Mirza. As part of the *Nezam-e Jadid* reforms, 'Abbas Mirza employed British physicians, both to care for his own person, and to instruct students in European medical advances. It is notable that of the two individuals first to be dispatched to England for schooling, one of them was instructed by 'Abbas Mirza to learn medicine. Hajji Baba Afshar accordingly completed his medical degree and returned to Iran to become 'Abbas Mirza's, and subsequently Mohammad Shah's personal physician.[108] 'Abbas Mirza also ordered the translation and printing of

---

[105]The term "anatomo-clinical" is perhaps the most accurate, if not widely used, term for the contemporary European medical theory/practice. See Hormoz Ebrahimnejad, "Introduction de la médecine européenne en Iran au XIXè siècle," *Sciences Sociales et Santé*, vol. 16 (4 décembre 1998), pp. 69-96.

[106]Cyril Elgood, *A Medical History of Persia and the Eastern Caliphate from the Earliest times Until the Year A.D. 1932* (Cambridge: University of Cambridge Press, 1951), pp. 393-436.

[107]Ibid, p. 368.

[108]For a discussion of the dispatch of students abroad as a component of 'Abbas Mirza's *Nezam-e Jadid* reform program, see chapter I, above.

European medical treatises.[109] While there was no significant objection to 'Abbas Mirza's dispatch of students to Europe to study, the introduction of elements of his *Nezam-e Jadid* that were perceived to be foreign in provenance did arouse resentment. Thus there did exist some cultural resentment against the practice of European medicine. This is attested to by the fact that 'Abbas Mirza commissioned a book that sought to justify European "anatomo-clinical" medical practice. Completed in 1833, the book argued that European medicine was equally as valuable as Iranian medicine.[110] The book clearly addressed cultural concerns of people in contact with European doctors who resisted European medical prescriptions and/or methods as foreign and Christian.

'Abbas Mirza was not the only one to recognize the value of European medical advances. Many Qajar princes employed European doctors. The rulers themselves were no exception. Fath 'Ali Shah employed a European as his personal physician; and in the Mohammad Shah period many of the court physicians were either Europeans, or Iranians who had studied medicine in Europe. Naser al-Din Shah, too, employed a series of European doctors as his personal physicians. At the same time, he, like his predecessors, did not eliminate the traditional position of *hakimbashi* held by an Iranian doctor. Rather, the positions of Iranian and European court doctors existed simultaneously, side-by-side. Unlike the situation in other Middle Eastern countries (Egypt and Syria for example), the Iranian *hakimbashi* was supplemented, but not displaced in the Qajar period. The European court doctor and Iranian *hakimbashi* cared for the person of the shah alternately, concurrently, or even in some instances, in collaborative efforts.[111]

Prior to the establishment of the *Dar al Fonun*, Naser al-Din Shah ordered his royal court physician, Dr. Cloquet, to train a number of Iranians in European medicine.[112] However, this initiative, like the

---

[109]Browne gives the date of the earliest medical work printed in Iran as 1825, whereas Najmabadi writes that it was in 1830. See Edward Granville Browne, *Arabian Medicine* (Cambridge: Cambridge University Press, 1962), p. 94, and Mahmud Najmabadi, "Tebb-e Dar al Fonun va Kotob-e Darsi-ye an," in (ed) Iraj Afshar *Amir Kabir va Dar al Fonun*, p. 203.

[110]Mohammad ibn 'Abd al-Sabbar, *Jame' al-Hikmatayn va Majma' al-Tibbayn*, located at the Biblioteque Nationale, supplément persan, no. 870.

[111]Ebrahimnejad, "la médecine européenne en Iran," pp. 70-71.

[112]Najmabadi, "Tebb-e Dar al Fonun," pp. 202, 204.

previous dispatch of small numbers of students abroad for medical study did not arouse much negative attention. The establishment of the *Dar al Fonun*, however, signaled a qualitative and quantitative shift in the status of European medicine in Iran. The teaching of European medicine as a field of study led to a confrontation with the Iranian medical community. According to Najmabadi, doctors trained in traditional medicine openly quarreled with those trained in European medicine.[113] Opposition to European medicine at the *Dar al Fonun* undoubtably contained a strong element of a defense of social status and technical qualifications against threats from European-trained doctors. Traditional Iranian medicine was under siege from multiple fronts.

First, relatively large numbers of students were being trained in European medicine at the *Dar al Fonun*. Of the first graduating class in 1858, as many as 18 students majored in medicine. Medicine continued to be a popular field of study at the *Dar al Fonun* throughout its existence. For the first time therefore, European-trained doctors were being produced in Iran in sufficient numbers to compete with traditionally-trained doctors for jobs and court appointments. In practice, the appointment of *Dar al Fonun* graduates to prestigious positions was facilitated by the government itself, which promised (implicitly, and then explicitly after 1860) government employment.

Second, the system of exams and certification, culminating in the *Dar al Fonun* diploma, directly challenged the traditional system of professional qualifications. These new requirements and standards threatened to marginalize doctors who did not receive *Dar al Fonun* diplomas.

Third, the marginalization of the traditional medical profession was reinforced by the growing divergence of the two medical terminologies. The traditional medical vocabulary lacked adequate terms. Dr. Polak, the first European medical instructor at the *Dar al Fonun*, recounts that he read the existing Iranian medical treatises and attempted to create Persian words to correspond to new medical terminology. In the absence of sufficient Persian terms, however, Polak employed French

---

[113]Ibid, p. 204. Opposition to European medi-cine and its instruction at the *Dar al Fonun* was spearheaded by Hajj Mirza Baba Shirazi, Malek al-Atebba who wrote a treatise refuting Western medicine entitled "Jowhariyeh." A copy of this treatise could not be located for access at this time.

words. The subsequent publication of many of his works into Persian and their use as textbooks at the school perpetuated the use of much French terminology in the Iranian medical vocabulary. The differentiation between the traditional and the new medical vocabularies not only contributed to the growing separation between new, European techniques and knowledge and the more traditional body of medicine, but it made the deficiencies of traditional medicine increasingly apparent.[114]

Fourth, in addition to fears of professional marginalization, traditionally-trained doctors exhibited cultural resistance to some aspects of European medicine. Although texts written by opponents of European medicine at the *Dar al Fonun* are unavailable, the records of European doctors in Iran at the time reveal the nature of this opposition. The principal cultural objection to European medical practice at the *Dar al Fonun* concerned the performance of autopsies as a method of medical instruction. Polak recorded that, "existing religious prejudice did not enable me to perform autopsies, not even of criminals."[115] The ban on autopsies restricted Polak's teaching methods. As described by Dr. Feuvrier, Naser al-Din Shah's French physician from 1889-91, medical instructors at the *Dar al Fonun* could not overcome Iranian religious sensibilities concerning autopsy and were therefore unable to engage in practical instruction.[116] Polak wrote that, "Once during the Babi massacres, I was approached with the suggestion that I could perform it [autopsy] on the cadavers of executed persons so that they might be shamed even after death. I did not like the idea of serving as a tool of revenge."[117] Because corpses were considered unclean (*najis*) according to religious law, autopsies were viewed with such aversion that they were considered to "shame" the dead.

By 1860 the conflict between the two schools of medicine was in full swing. After nearly a decade of the exclusive instruction of European medicine at the *Dar al Fonun*, traditional medicine was incorporated into the curriculum. This event was reluctantly announced as part of E'tezad al-Saltaneh's 1860 educational reforms outlined in

---

[114]Tabataba'i, "Dar al Fonun va Amir Kabir," pp. 192-94.
[115]Polak, *Persien*, vol. I, p. 306.
[116]Joannes Feuvrier, *Trois ans à la cour de Perse* (Paris: F. Juven, 1899), p. 80.
[117]Polak, *Persien*, vol. I, p. 306.

the *Ruznameh-ye Vaqaye'e Ettefaqiyyeh*. The newspaper explained that, despite the fact that traditional Iranian medicine had effectively been superseded, it would be admitted into the curriculum at the *Dar al Fonun*:

> Since some of the people of Iran are not yet convinced of European medical practice, in order to inform medical students of the prevailing Iranian medical practice, Mirza Ahmad Hakimbashi Kashani, who, both in terms of practice and knowledge is the best of the Iranian doctors, was assigned to teach Iranian medicine in the blessed school.[118]

This clearly illustrates the existence of popular inhibitions of following European medical prescriptions. It is also evidence of the continued clout of the existing medical profession, and their attempt to defend their status. However, this announcement leaves no doubt as to the preeminence of European medicine— as an academic discipline if not yet in practice— at this time.

In Defense of Islamic Cosmology

The nature of ulama opposition to the *Dar al Fonun* was both more complicated, and more religiously charged than that of the traditional medical establishment. The *Dar al Fonun* did not present an *explicit* institutional challenge to the existing educational system as controlled by the ulama. As a specialized secondary school it was not oriented towards mass primary education and therefore was not intended to replace, or even to supersede the traditional educational system. Its function was limited to the training of a small, elite government cadre, as well as tradesmen in the workshops. Nor did the curriculum at the *Dar al Fonun* duplicate that of the *madraseh*. With the exception of Persian and Arabic, which were considered largely supplemental, the curriculum at the *Dar al Fonun* was entirely different from that of the *madraseh* system. Philosophy, jurisprudence, and theology all remained the domain of the *madraseh*. The *Dar al Fonun* did not aim to educate future religious scholars. Moreover, sons of members of the religious establishment were not highly represented at the *Dar al Fonun*. This was not because they were not qualified for admission, but because the *Dar*

---

[118]*Ruznameh-ye Vaqaye'e Ettefaqiyyeh*, no. 458 (19 Jumadi al-Thani 1276/ January 13, 1860), as quoted in Mahbubi-Ardakani, *Tarikh-e Mo'assesat*, vol. I, p. 313.

al Fonun served as a channel for entrance into government service, and therefore mainly attracted government elites. The *madraseh* continued to attract those students interested in academic disciplines (with the exception of medicine noted above). The *Dar al Fonun*, therefore, did not divert talent from the *madrasehs* in any significant way.

The absence of a direct professional threat notwithstanding, the teaching of European sciences at the *Dar al Fonun* was condemned by some ulama. As pointed out by Arjomand, some European scientific theories were held to be incompatible with Islamic cosmology.[119] Members of the ulama, alarmed at what they considered to be the propagation of anti-religious ideas, opposed the instruction of "new" sciences at the *Dar al Fonun*. Religious scholars were concerned that modern science would lead to materialism and atheism. In particular, European heliocentric astronomical theory became the focus of many attempts at refutation. According to Arjomand, the conflict centered on the question of the earth's movement versus stasis. Religious scholars were determined to preserve the geocentric vision of the universe which they believed was attested to in the Qur'an and the Hadith.[120] As the head of the *Dar al Fonun* and Minister of Sciences, E'tezad al-Saltaneh took the offensive against traditional sciences (including astrology) and published a number of books which promoted new, European scientific theories. The growing influence of European science and the mutual reinforcement of the social prestige associated with the *Dar al Fonun* led some religious scholars to feel a loss of social preeminence and intellectual standing. Mohammad Karim Khan Kermani, in an essay criticizing the teaching of European sciences at the *Dar al Fonun*, complained that whereas Europeans enjoyed great intellectual and social prestige, people were no longer willing to listen to the ulama [on scientific matters].[121] Arjomand also notes that the absence of adequate terminology for new scientific discoveries

---

[119]See the ground-breaking study on the conflicts surrounding the introduction of European sciences into Iran by Kamran Arjomand, "The Emergence of Scientific Modernity in Iran: Controversies Surrounding Astrology and Modern Astronomy in the Mid-Nineteenth Century," *Iranian Studies*, vol. 30, nos. 1-2 (1997), pp. 5-24.

[120]Ibid.

[121]Ibid, pp. 18-19.

contributed to a "communication breakdown" between scholars trained in the modern versus the traditional sciences.[122]

The institutionalization of the adoption of European science into Iran as manifested in the *Dar al Fonun* threatened the very foundations of the religious establishment in Iran. The *Dar al Fonun* offered an alternative body of knowledge from that of the *madraseh*. Modern sciences, medicine, and European languages taught at the *Dar al Fonun* were all subjects outside the purview of the *madraseh* system. The *Dar al Fonun* presented an alternative means of acquiring status on the basis of European education and texts. The *Dar al Fonun* emerged as a purveyor of cultural and intellectual capital— formerly the sole prerogative of the *madraseh* system. The *Dar al Fonun* also challenged the heretofore existent monopoly on education and the existing body of knowledge of the *madraseh*. For the first time, there emerged a differentiation between "useful," European-style education, and the traditional body of scholastic knowledge transmitted in the *madraseh*. This dichotomy was reinforced by the marginalization of the traditional medical profession and the ulama's defense of untenable scientific theories. However, this dichotomy remained latent, if not largely invisible, before 1870.

Conclusion: Educational Change 1851-1871

The *Dar al Fonun* was the first government-sponsored European-style educational institution founded in Iran. As such it had a momentous impact on the introduction of European-style education into Iran, and on the relationship between education and the developing reform agenda. Its inauguration established the government as the initiator of reform and the promoter of European-style education in Iran. This was a result of the top-down reform impetus. However, in the absence of strong centralized government and supporting institutions, the potential of the *Dar al Fonun* remained unrealized. As a court institution, the *Dar al Fonun* enjoyed only limited autonomy. It was dependent on court appointed administrators and vulnerable to both political change and the vagaries of royal approbation. The educational goals of the *Dar*

---

[122]Ibid, p. 19.

al Fonun were frustrated by lack of royal commitment which in practice limited the ability of the teachers and staff to effect necessary changes. One of the greatest educational obstacles confronting the *Dar al Fonun* of Tehran and the *Dar al Fonun* of Tabriz resulted from their being, with the exception of a few missionary schools, the only institutions of European-style learning in Iran. There were no other supporting institutions at the primary or secondary levels to prepare students for entry to the *Dar al Fonun* in Tehran or Tabriz. Instructors had to take into account the need to provide remedial education to a student body of diverse levels of preparation. In addition, limited funds and qualified teaching staff prevented the *Dar al Fonun* from becoming an institution of higher learning. In order to attain advanced degrees, students specializing in medicine and sciences traveled to Europe.[123]

The government was also the primary consumer of the products of this new education. The majority of graduates in the 1851-71 period entered government service where many became high administrative and military officials. The government also benefited from the European-educated doctors and Iranians skilled in sciences and new technology that were trained at the *Dar al Fonun*. In line with the goal of training government cadres, the student body of the *Dar al Fonun* was highly select. Although admission was theoretically open to all, in practice the students who attended the *Dar al Fonun* were by and large sons of courtiers, princes and high ranking government officials. These students often received tutorial training at home, and would have been candidates for government service in any event. The *Dar al Fonun* served as a means of legitimizing these students' already high status. It served to preserve privilege by providing further bases of legitimacy in the forms of academic merit and accomplishment.

The association of the *Dar al Fonun* with Western learning and culture also extended into the realm of political ideas. As demonstrated by Naser al-Din Shah's alarm concerning the *Faramushkhaneh*, the *Dar al Fonun* represented European political ideals and presented the specter of reform in Iran. The *Dar al Fonun* constituted the physical locus of European-style education and established an intellectual bond among those graduates and others who believed in the importance of

---

[123]Polak concluded that he could only provide a basic grounding in medicine and natural sciences, and that his medical students would need further education in Europe or on their own. Polak, *Persien*, vol. I, p. 305.

continued reform in Iran. It served as the symbol that aligned those who favored reform against those who opposed it.

As evidenced in the case of traditionally-educated doctors and members of the ulama, opposition to the *Dar al Fonun* was based both on professional as well as intellectual and cultural concerns. In a manner reminiscent of the opposition to the *Nezam-e Jadid*, the school was attacked as anti-Islamic and accused of serving as a venue for European political and cultural incursions. However, unlike the absence of concern over the early student dispatches under 'Abbas Mirza and Mohammad Shah, the students at the *Dar al Fonun*, and especially those who traveled abroad, were the focus of much antipathy. Iranian students were for the first time perceived to be bearers of European culture back to Iran. Even proponents of European-style education and its role in the reform process found the European cultural affectations and mannerisms of some students offensive.

The *Dar al Fonun* embodied the fundamental reform dilemma in Iran which first emerged as a result of 'Abbas Mirza's *Nezam-e Jadid* reform program. Amir Kabir's intention in establishing the European-style school was to train a government cadre to assist in increasing royal and state power, and in so doing, to strengthen Iran and protect her from foreign incursions. Amir Kabir believed that the *Dar al Fonun* would increase Iran's independence vis-à-vis Europe, and reduce the influx to Iran of European culture and political ideas. He failed to recognize the long-term implications for the adoption of European-style education. Amir Kabir dismissed Naser al-Din Shah's fears of ulama opposition to the establishment of the *Dar al Fonun* as groundless. The ulama, he assured the shah, would be amongst the first to send their sons to the school.[124] In fact, however, the school itself emerged as a primary conduit for European culture and political ideas. For this reason, it was also actively opposed by many ulama. Moreover, in the absence of centralizing and bureaucratizing reforms in the 1851-71 period, European political influence in Iranian affairs only increased.

Iran's tenuous political situation was exacerbated by the behavior of the monarch himself. Naser al-Din Shah wavered in his commitment to reform. Unlike the Mohammad Shah period, the impetus to change

---

[124]This letter is paraphrased in Mahbubi-Ardakani, *Tarikh-e Mo'assesat*, vol. I, p. 255.

passed from the monarch to his prime minister. However, Naser al-Din Shah failed to adequately support Amir Kabir against his opponents. While the shah was conscious of the advantages to be gained by centralization and reform, he was also aware of the disadvantages. He found himself unsure how to harness reform for his benefit, without at the same time, loosing control over its effects. Faced with the dangers of reform, Naser al-Din Shah opted for security. For the remainder of the 1851-71 period, no serious attempts at educational reform were undertaken.

CHAPTER IV

MISSIONARY AND FOREIGN SCHOOLS

IN IRAN, 1830-1906

Even before the establishment of the *Dar al Fonun* in 1851, European-style schools had been founded in Iran by European and American missionaries. Although there were only a few missionary schools in the first half of the century, their numbers swelled rapidly beginning in the 1870s. Two European societies, the *Alliance Française* and the *Alliance Israélite Universelle*, also established schools in Iran at this time. As they received their impetus from abroad, missionary and foreign schools embodied the political, religious and cultural objectives of their European sponsors, founders and teachers. They differed radically in their goals from the *Dar al Fonun* and other schools established later in the century by Iranian educational activists. Nonetheless, these schools were not completely divorced from the process of educational reform in Iran. Missionary and foreign schools served as an important channel for the introduction of European education in Iran— particularly amongst Iranian religious minorities. These schools were also the first European-style schools for women. Most importantly, the increasing popularity of missionary and foreign schools was a function of the growing appeal of European education in Iran amongst an expanding spectrum of socioeconomic and religious groups. Monarchical policy towards these schools indicates perceptions of the benefits and dangers of European education, and the ongoing conflict between educational reform and fear of European political and cultural incursions.

Western religious figures have traveled to Iran for centuries. At least as early as the eleventh century, European priests journeyed to and resided in Iran. In the Safavid period, various religious orders established bases in Iran, and were accorded royal protection. Indeed, religious figures served as official representatives of various European powers. In the mid seventeenth century, the king of France wrote to the shah that "the Augustinians are at Isfahan as ambassadors of the king of Spain; the Carmelites as guests sent by the Pope; the Capuchins sent by the king of France."[1] Most European missionaries left Iran

---

[1] *A Chronicle of the Carmelites in Persia* 2 vols. (London: Eyre & Spottiswoode, 1939), vol. I, p. 284.

following the invasion of Iran by the Afghans and the subsequent collapse of the Safavid monarchy in 1722. With the return to stability and the concomitant renewal of European interest in Iran in the Qajar period, Western missionaries began to return to Iran in greater numbers.

Early Missionary Activity, 1830-1860

Missionary activity in the Qajar period was quantitatively and qualitatively different from that of the past. European and American churches established permanent missions in Iran in large cities as well as in remote villages. For the first time, missionaries were actively engaged in educational and medical work. There is some evidence that several German missionaries opened schools for Christians in about 1830 in Tabriz and Shisheh, although these schools did not last more than a few years.[2] The British Church Missionary Society reportedly established a mission in Iran in 1839 and opened a small school.[3] The most significant activity in the 1830-71 period, however, belonged to the American and French missions.

The American Mission

In 1829, American Protestant missionaries Smith and Dwight arrived in Iran to investigate the situation of Christians in Azarbayjan. The report on their findings prompted the American Board of the Presbyterian Church to dispatch Reverend Justin Perkins to Iran in order to establish a permanent mission among the Nestorians in northeastern Iran.[4]

---

[2]Curzon refers to these early German attempts in George Curzon, *Persia and the Persian Question* (London, 1892), p. 506. Boré notes that a German pastor opened a school in Tabriz at this time which closed three years later due to scarcity of students, in Eugène Boré, *Correspondance et mémoires d'un voyageur en Orient* 2 vols. (Paris: Olivier-Fulgenie, 1840), vol. II, pp. 347-48. No mention of these schools in made in Perkins' own account. See Justin Perkins, *Historical Sketch of the Mission to the Nestorians* (Boston: American Board of Commissioners for Foreign Missions, 1866).

[3]James Bassett, *Persia: the Land of the Imams* (London, 1887), p. 157.

[4]Board of Foreign Missions of the Presbyterian Church in the U.S.A., *A Century of Mission Work in Iran, 1834-1934* (Beirut: The American Press, 1936). See also Iqbal Yaghma'i, "Dastani az Moballeghayn-e 'Isavi dar Iran," *Yadegar* nos.6-7, pp. 60-66.

The American Mission established by Reverend Perkins in Urumia in 1835 attempted to convert the large Nestorian Christian community that lived in northern Iran to Protestantism.[5] Once this goal had been accomplished, the Americans believed that the Nestorians would assist in the conversion of Muslims as well. Indeed, the goal of the Mission was no less than the spiritual regeneration of the Middle East. According to the account of American Presbyterian Church activity in Iran, the purpose of their Mission was "to enable the Nestorian Church, through the grace of God, to exert a commanding influence on the spiritual regeneration of Asia."[6] As described by Reverend Perkins himself, the first goal of the Mission was to work towards the "amelioration and salvation" of the Nestorians, whom he viewed as "those fallen Christians."[7] In his account of his work in Iran, Perkins explained that:

> Interesting as is the reformation in progress among the Nestorians, it should still be regarded more as a means than as an end. Exceedingly encouraging in itself, it looks to an *ulterior and far broader object— the conversion of the missions of Mohammedans*, among whom Providence has placed and preserved them, we trust for such an end. (Emphasis added.)[8]

However, this "ulterior object" remained just that due to the fact that the proselytization of Muslims was strictly forbidden.[9]

---

[5]Watson, writing in 1858, records the Nestorian population in the Urumia plain as approximately 25,000 and adds that there were also 5,000 Nestorian mountain-dwellers nearby. Robert Grant Watson, *A History of Persia from the Beginning of the Nineteenth Century to the Year 1858* (London: Smith, Elder and Co., 1866), p. 202.

[6]Board, *Century*, pp. 1-2.

[7]Perkins, *Mission*, pp. 8-10.

[8]Ibid, p. 26.

[9]European missionaries abandoned attempts to convert Muslims during the Mongol period. From this time forward, their attention focused on the conversion of Armenian and Nestorian Christians to Catholicism. In 1710 Shah Sultan Hosayn issued a *farman* forbidding European Catholics from forcing Armenian children into their churches. See M. K. Sadre, *Relations de l'Iran avec l'Europe* (Paris, 1937), pp. 71, 177-78. Mohammad Shah issued a similar *farman* forbidding proselytization amongst all segments of the Iranian population, including Muslims as well as other Christian groups. However, while missionaries made no attempt to convert Muslims in this period, they ignored this restriction concerning Iranian Christians. See Homa Nateq, *Karnameh-ye Farhangi-ye Farangi dar Iran* (Tehran: Khavaran, 1375), pp. 154-55.

Activities of the American Mission included education, medicine, preaching and the establishment of a printing press. Education in particular was regarded as a means of religious propagation.[10] The first mission school was established in Urumia in January 1836 and had seven male students. By the end of Mohammad Shah's reign in 1848, the number of students had grown to approximately 50. The school was essentially a theological seminary, and students who enrolled were expected to convert to Protestantism. For this reason, the curriculum in the schools was largely religious. However, students were taught the Syriac alphabet, and "graduated with very respectable attainments in literature and science."[11] Some of the more advanced students were also taught English. In addition, the school reportedly instructed students in carpet weaving and iron smithing.[12] From its establishment until 1879, Perkins' boys school produced 122 graduates.[13]

The American Mission believed it necessary to educate girls in their schools as well, although they encountered some resistance. According to Perkins, "for females in general to read, was an idea so alien to the people, that when we proposed that a few little girls should assemble for the purpose of learning, they laughed boisterously, and inquired whether we would make priests of the girls?"[14] Despite local objections, a girls' school was established in Urumia in 1838 with four Nestorian students. In addition to religious studies, the girls were taught household skills.[15] The Mission also established three primary schools in nearby villages in 1836 where students were taught basic reading and religious instruction. The number of village schools increased steadily throughout the Mohammad Shah period. Between 1837-47 the average number of schools existent was 24, and the average total number of students was approximately 530.[16] In 1840 the Mission established a printing press. Materials were printed for use in the schools, and a number of books were translated and printed in Syriac. The press also

---

[10]American missionaries in other parts of the Middle East also believed education was a means of religious propagation. See Adnan Abu-Ghazaleh, *American Missions in Syria* (Brattleboro: Amana Books, 1990), p. 32.

[11]Perkins, *Mission*, p. 10.

[12]Yaghma'i, "Dastani az Moballeghayn," p. 60.

[13]Board, *Century*, pp. 75-76.

[14]Perkins, *Mission*, pp. 10-11.

[15]Board, *Century*, p. 76; Perkins, *Mission*, p. 11.

[16]Board, *Century*, pp. 76-77.

printed a monthly periodical, *Rays of Light* that included articles on "religion, education, science, juvenile matter, miscellany, and poetry."[17]

Medical treatment and instruction was an integral part of the American Mission's work from the outset. Dr. Grant, at the specific request of some Muslims, conducted medical classes. In 1840 he established a medical school where 7 Muslims attended for a period of 2-3 years.[18] The Mission also provided relief work during the cholera epidemics in 1846 and 1847.[19]

The Boré Mission

The French, too, returned to Iran in the Mohammad Shah period. As news of the success of American Protestant missionary work in Iran came to the attention of the Pope, he resolved to send Catholic missionaries to Iran.[20] French Lazarist Catholics, meanwhile, decided to dispatch their own mission. Accordingly, a priest by the name of Eugène Boré arrived in Tabriz on November 6, 1838 with the intention of effecting an educational and religious revolution in Iran. In his memoirs and letters, Boré explained his civilizing mission, and the causal connection between modern science, the French language, and the eventual triumph of Catholicism over Islam. Boré argued that:

> Mohammadanism, which must necessarily perish as an anti-natural and antisocial religion, can not be attacked but by the weapons of science. Knowledge will necessarily establish doubt in the souls that we will instruct; and that will be sufficient. Time will accomplish the rest.[21]

The French language, as the "vehicle of science and . . . ideas of liberty," thus served to hasten the triumph of Catholicism in Iran.[22] Although primarily motivated by religious concerns, Boré was also

---

[17]Perkins, *Mission*, pp. 12-13.

[18]Perkins, *Mission*, p. 94; and Thomas Laurie, *Dr. Grant and the Mountain Nestorians* (Boston: Gould and Lincoln, 1853), pp. 64, 75.

[19]Ibid, p. 64.

[20]Yaghma'i asserts that French Minister of Foreign Affairs, Mr. Guizot, suggested that Boré accompany the French scientific and diplomatic mission that was due to travel to Iran. However, Boré arrived over a year prior to this mission. See Yaghma'i, "Dastani az Moballeghayn," p. 62.

[21]Boré, *Correspondance*, vol. II, p. 109.

[22]Ibid, vol. I, p. 166.

aware of the practical advantages which would accrue to France from enhanced cultural and political connections with Iran.[23]

In 1839, Boré opened a school in Tabriz, the *Dar al-'Ilm Shenasa'i-ye Melal* with 14 students— three of them Armenian and the rest Muslim.[24] In direct opposition to the American Protestant Mission schools, Boré deliberately excluded religious instruction from the school's objectives.[25] The curriculum, designed to approximate that of a French school, consisted of French language and literature, philosophy and European sciences.[26] Boré's efforts were reportedly so successful that Crown Prince Naser al-Din Mirza's mother sent him to Boré's school to learn French.[27] Later in the year, Boré established five smaller schools in the area.[28]

Despite the evident popularity of Boré's schools, they were the object of much opposition. Boré faced intense competition from the schools run by the American Protestant Mission. He believed that his ultimate success depended on routing the Protestants from Iran. He denounced the Americans for allegedly paying students to attend their schools. Boré repeatedly requested reinforcements from France to "fight the influence of the American schools."[29] He also complained that alone in Iran, he was left to counter "Russian defiance, English jealousy, American rivalry, Armenian intrigues, and coldness on the part of some Persian authorities."[30] In a letter to a French associate, Boré complained that the Iranian government had not gone far enough in supporting his schools:

> The government is satisfied with according the tolerance of its protection, without adding to this any direct and manifest encouragement. I thus find myself alone, obliged to fight against a silent opposition, which comes from the Muslim clergy, and always fearful of offending another power,

---

[23]Ibid, vol. II, pp. 121, 439.
[24]Ibid, vol. II, pp. 108, 122, 294, 311. See also Nateq, *Kamaneh*, pp. 161-62.
[25]Boré, *Correspondance*, vol. II, p. 369.
[26]Ibid, vol. II, pp. 121-22.
[27]Ibid, vol. II, p. 308. Atai reports that 20 members of the court studied French at Boré's school. See Mohammad Farhad Atai, "The Sending of Iranian Students to Europe, 1811-1906," (Ph.D. diss. University of California, Berkeley, 1992), p. 50.
[28]Boré, *Correspondance*, vol. II, pp. 363-64, 434.
[29]Ibid, vol. II, pp. 312, 327-28, 331, 364-67.
[30]Ibid, vol. II, p. 308.

[which is] little disposed in favor of all that which could diminish its own authority.[31]

Boré does not specify the nature of the ulama's "silent" opposition. However, he suggests that the ulama were concerned about government protection of foreign and Christian activity in Iran and may have been wary of attempts at proselytization amongst the Muslim community.

In Tabriz, Boré prided himself on the fact that he had been able to attract Armenian students whereas the American schools had not. He recorded that an Armenian delegation visited him before his school was established to request that Armenian students be allowed to attend. The school opened with three Armenian students, two of whose fathers were khans.[32] However, in 1840 when he established a similar school in Isfahan, Boré was confronted with intense opposition from the Armenian Church.[33] Thirty-one students enrolled in the school— five of them Muslims and the rest Armenians.[34] Despite Boré's insistence on the purely cultural nature of his schools, he encountered severe opposition from the Armenian religious authorities, who perceived his educational activities as attempts at religious proselytization.[35] Fearing for his safety, Boré departed for Tabriz. Along the way he received notification of his appointment as French Consul in Jerusalem and therefore was unable to continue his educational activities in Iran. Years later, after Boré had left Iran and was the principal of a school outside of Istanbul, he confided to an Iranian visitor the broad nature of opposition against him while in Iran. He complained to Hajj Sayyah, self-proclaimed dervish, reform advocate and author of an important travel book to Europe, that he had been unjustly accused of attempts at proselytism:

> I went to Isfahan in Iran and opened a school there. The people prevented me from keeping my school. God knows that I had nothing in mind but serving people. The Armenians said that I wanted to convert their children to Catholicism, and the Muslims said that I wanted to convert their

---

[31]Ibid, vol. II, p. 434.

[32]Ibid, vol. II, pp. 310, 311.

[33]Ibid.

[34]Nateq, *Kamaneh*, pp. 162-63. Yaghma'i believes that Boré never actually established a school in Isfahan. See Yaghma'i, "Dastani as Moballeghin."

[35]Boré, *Correspondance*, vol. II, p. 369.

children to Christianity, and they caused trouble. The government supported me, but I felt affection could not be produced with force. There was no remedy and no hope. I had to close the school. At the time the same people came to me and discussed religion with me. I told them: "I have nothing to do with your religion and customs. I just want you to come and get an education. Your lodging, clothing, and living expense will be free." However, I could not make them understand my aim. A few who understood did not dare express their ideas. If anyone showed eagerness to come and study, the clergy would curse him, and he would be subject to sarcasm and persecution.[36]

After Boré's departure from Iran, his school in Tabriz closed down. Another French missionary (who had been the director of the school) established a second school called *Madraseh-ye Urumiyeh*. However, this school closed soon also due to competition from the American schools in the area.

Boré, although the most notable Lazarist activist in Iran in the early part of the century, was not the only one. In 1840, Fathers Cluzel and Darnis established a boys school in the Urumia region. According to Nateq's data, by the end of Mohammad Shah's reing in 1848, the Lazarists were operating as many as 26 boys' schools with a total of 400 students, and six girls' schools in the Urumia region.[37]

Government Policy Towards Missionary Schools

The Iranian government's reaction to and treatment of the American and French missions in Iran was a complex one. It reflected contemporary attitudes concerning the benefits of European education. At the same time, Mohammad Shah and other government officials were not unaware of the missionaries' ulterior religious motivations. Nor were they blind to the diplomatic ramifications involved.

American and French missionary schools received protection and encouragement from local government officials as well as from the shah. Mohammad Shah conceived of the schools as furthering his aim

---

[36]Haj Sayyah, *An Iranian in Nineteenth Century Europe: The Travel Diaries of Haj Sayyah 1859-1877*, (trans) Mehrbanoo Naser Deyhim (Bethesda: Ibex, 1998), p. 60.
[37]Nateq, *Kamaneh*, pp. 163, 171.

of adopting European languages, sciences and technology into Iran. Support for the missionary schools complemented his dispatch of students abroad, his attempts to obtain French assistance in training his military, and his invitation for European artisans and technicians to settle in Iran.

The American Mission was assisted by the governor of Urumia, Malek Qasem, who was known for his support of foreign schools.[38] Perkins records having given him English lessons. Malek Qasem requested that the American Mission establish a school to teach English that would not include religious instruction, a request the Americans refused.[39] Nonetheless, on Perkins' behalf, Malek Qasem asked for Mohammad Shah's protection of the American Mission. Accordingly, in 1838 Mohammad Shah issued a writ declaring government protection of the American Mission. The writ also commended the Mission's work in education. Mohammad Shah specifically encouraged the teaching of history, geography and mathematics:

> With enthusiasm and interest [Perkins] established a school in the Urumia region and with extreme effort and precision is engaged in teaching and instructing youths and spreading knowledge . . . [concerning] the education and refinement (*takmil*) of youths, he has brought more than the usual amount of efforts and endeavors to teaching history, geography, geometry, arithmetic.[40]

Boré too received official approbation. He repeatedly mentioned receiving support from a number of high-ranking officials, as well as of Mohammad Shah. For example, Prince Kamran Mirza assisted in the selection of the first group of students enrolled at Boré's school.[41] The governor of Azarbayjan, Prince Qahraman Mirza, strongly encouraged Boré's educational work, as did Prince Hasan Mirza.[42] In 1839, Mohammad Shah's uncle, Mansur Mirza, issued an edict officially

---

[38]Many European travelers to the area attest to Malek Qasem's interest and encouragement of European education. See Homa Nateq, *Iran dar Rahyabi-ye Farhangi* (Tehran: Khavaran, 1990), pp. 105-6.

[39]Nateq, *Kamaneh*, p. 165.

[40]A copy of the writ is reproduced in Yaghma'i, "Dastani az Moballeghayn," p. 61.

[41]Boré mentions this is passing only once, see *Correspondance*, vol. II, p. 122.

[42]Ibid, vol. II, pp. 121, 363-64.

authorizing Boré to establish additional schools in the province.[43] Boré also recorded that Prince Qasem Mirza was ordered by Mohammad Shah to encourage the development of sciences and industries in Azar- bayjan. Europeans were encouraged to settle in Azarbayjan and establish workshops and factories. They were assured government protection, as well as an exemption from all taxes for fifteen years. In accordance with these aims, Boré was awarded a *farman* encouraging his educational activities.[44] In 1840, Mohammad Shah issued a similar *farman* which specifically commended the teaching of European sciences and French language in Boré's schools. The *farman* reads:

> It has been decided that the honorable M. Eugène Boré, of recognized knowledge and capability, and one of the pillars of the Catholic Church, having made himself known to the ministers of the victorious kingdom that he has come to the orient to spread instruction, and that, to this end, he has settled in Tabriz, regarding his request of teaching the Iranian youth the French language and instructing the sciences of history, geography, philosophy, physics, geometry and medicine, without demanding any recompense from the sublime empire, we order our very powerful brother [Qahraman Mirza], given the advantages of all sorts resulting from the education of the youth and from the attainment of these sciences, to accord respect, protection and encouragement to the honorable afore- mentioned M. Eugène Boré.[45]

Mohammad Shah's active support of the missionary schools was also driven in part by foreign policy considerations. He was acutely aware of European interest and support for the missions. The American Mission, for example, enjoyed the protection of the British Consul in Tabriz.[46] European powers were willing to take diplomatic action to protect European and American missions in Iran. Perkins recorded in his journal that the British ambassador, Sir John McNeil, requested that the shah protect the American Mission. Both of the

---

[43]Boré, provides a translation of this edict in his *Correspondance*, vol. II, pp. 362-63.

[44]Ibid, vol. II, pp. 423-24.

[45]A translation of the farman is provided by Boré in *Correspondance*, vol. II, pp. 431-32.

[46]According to Dr. Grant, the British Consul, Sir Henry Ellis provided Rev. Perkins and himself with British passports. Following the British departure from the area, Dr. Grant secured protection from the Russians. See Laurie, *Dr. Grant*, pp. 44-45, 101.

French ambassadors to visit Iran also urged the shah to support the French Lazarist missions.[47]

Mohammad Shah also knew that European governments had declared protection over religious minorities in the Ottoman Empire, thereby essentially usurping some of the Ottoman government's authority. Nor would he have forgotten that under Fath 'Ali Shah, Christian Georgia had successfully disassociated herself from Iran by declaring herself a protectorate of Russia. At the very least, a failure to champion religious minorities in Iran clearly could have dangerous political repercussions. It might even serve as an excuse for foreign intervention.

In extending protection to the missionaries, Mohammad Shah did not encounter serious opposition from government ministers and courtiers, landowners, or the ulama— the three traditional sources of power.[48] Indeed, missionary activity was by and large considered to be a religious minority issue. The American schools, as they were religious in nature, only targeted Nestorian Christians. Boré's schools attracted Muslim students, but were avowedly secular. None of the schools therefore constituted a religious threat to the Muslim community in general, or to the existing educational establishment and the ulama in particular. In fact, both the Americans and the French considered the other to be their greatest rival.[49] It was however the case that missionary schools, especially the Boré schools, encountered resistance from Iranian Christians, especially the Armenian Church.[50] Mohammad Shah, in order to further his educational and diplomatic goals, extended protection to European missionary activity despite strong objections on the part of indigenous Iranian Christians. As a result, Mohammad Shah wavered on the issue of conversion.

---

[47]Iranian Armenians, too, benefitted from foreign protection on occasion. For example, when Naser al-Din Mirza departed Tabriz for Tehran on the death of Mohammad Shah, the English consul in Tabriz was requested to take the local Armenians under his official protection. See Watson, *A History*, pp. 381-82.

[48]Nateq, *Kamaneh*, p. 178. Boré mentions the "silent opposition" of the ulama, in *Correspondance*, vol. II, p. 434.

[49]Perkins, *Mission*, p. 15.

[50] The conflict betweenn the Armenian Church and Catholic missionaries in Iran dates to the late 17th century. See Vazken Ghougassian, *The Emergence of the Armenian Diocese of New Julfa in the Seventeenth Century* (Atlanta, 1998), pp. 125-156.

In 1840, a French diplomatic embassy arrived in Iran, and championed the cause of the Catholic Church. The French ambassador, the Comte de Sercy, asked Mohammad Shah for the protection of Catholic activities in Iran, including the Catholic Church in Julfa. Mohammad Shah agreed, and issued an order that French Catholics were free to continue their religious activities. Through the royal order, Mohammad Shah guaranteed the rights of Catholics to pursue religious activities, including the building of churches, the observance of religious ceremonies and the pursuance of religious rules governing marriage, inheritance, etc., and the establishment of schools. The royal order was written in Persian, Armenian, and French, and read aloud to a gathering of Christians in a church in Julfa, Isfahan.[51] Shortly thereafter, when Boré established a school in Isfahan which attracted many Armenian students, he aroused the enmity of the Armenian Church, and as a result, was forced to leave town.

Armenian opposition to French (and American) missionary activity reached such proportions that in 1841, Mohammad Shah issued a *farman* prohibiting proselytization among Christian minorities in Iran:

> We order and make it a regulation that from now on different religions and nationalities who live in this exalted country of ours and in our territories shall not change religions. *If priests, be they Armenian or Catholic, invite the other [religious group] to convert, they will be called to account and subject to harsh policies.* Anybody who does this and by preaching and advising makes another people convert to their own faith, will be fired from their jobs, punished, and fined if they are citizens of this exalted government. If they belong to a different country, they will be expelled from the country [Iran].[52] (Emphasis added.)

The inherent conflict between diplomatic relations and the issue of European missionary activity amongst Iranian Christians continued unabated. In fact, one of the main goals of the second French diplomatic mission to Iran under the Comte de Sartiges in 1844 was to ensure Iranian governmental protection of the French Catholic

---

[51]Mohammad Shah's *farman* is reproduced in Yaghma'i, "Dastani az Moballeghayn," p. 65.
[52]Nateq, *Karnameh*, p. 167. See also pp. 154-55.

missionaries who had been run out of the Urumia area in part as a result of local Orthodox Armenian agitation.[53]

Royal policy towards missionary activity in Iran was further complicated by the shah's ambivalent attitude towards European powers. Although Mohammad Shah, like his father 'Abbas Mirza, was convinced of the importance of adopting new technology from Europe, he was not enthusiastic about importing European culture. For example, Mohammad Shah specifically warned the students that he sent to Europe against loss of faith. However, as long as the missionary schools did not seek to proselytize Muslims, their advantages generally outweighed the anger they aroused amongst Iranian Christian communities. They did not present a cultural threat in the eyes of the shah.

This equation began to shift in the early Naser al-Din Shah period. The growing political clout of European powers in Iran caused much resentment. This was accompanied by an increasing concern about the negative effects of European cultural contact. These two trends combined to impact the monarchical relationship with the missionaries. According to Perkins, a general cooling off of relations with the Iranian government led the American Mission to forestall plans to expand their activities. In his journal he wrote:

> For a score of years, our missionary operations in Persia were not only tolerated by the government, but received from it positive encouragement, even being favored with strong *firmans* for its protection. But in 1853 the government having become jealous of all foreign influence, naturally ranged our mission with other Europeans, and it sent an agent to Oroomiah, [sic] to restrict our labors, particularly our schools and the preaching of the Gospel . . . [Persecution] raged most . . . during the war between England and Persia [in 1856-57].[54]

The association of missionary schools with European political power and cultural incursions deepened in the course of the Naser al-Din Shah period. Moreover, the expansion of these schools highlighted the growing conflict over and connection between education and reform in Iran.

---

[53]Yaghma'i, "Dastani az Moballeghayn," p. 63. The Armenians were apparently British and Russians, a fact that further illustrates the diplomatic jostling common at the time. See also Nateq, *Rahyabi*, pp. 128-29 on the Sartiges mission to Iran.

[54]Perkins, *Mission*, p. 23.

Missionary, Foreign, and Minority Schools, 1860-1906

Beginning in the 1860s, and particularly after 1870, there was a dramatic increase in the number of schools established by European and American missionaries in Iran. Missionary schools were opened in Tehran and many other major cities, and were no longer confined to predominantly rural locations among minority religious populations. European countries, desirous of furthering their political and commercial interests in Iran, actively supported missionary activities. Their increasing political clout enabled them to assure government protection of the missionary schools. The establishment in Iran of schools by the French cultural society, the *Alliance Française*, and by the international Paris-based *Alliance Israélite Universelle* in the 1890s further cemented the connection between European-style schools and the advancement of European political objectives.

Although the missionary and foreign schools received their impetus from abroad, Iranians were not simply passive bystanders of these political and educational initiatives. Rather, the expansion of these new schools was also due in part to the growing popularity of European-style education in Iran. The history of the missionary and foreign schools thus also chronicles the increasing connection of education to the larger reform agenda.

In the 1834-70 period, American and European missionaries were active primarily in the province of Azarbayjan in the vicinity of Urumia and Salmas. Beginning in the 1870s, American missionaries increased the level of activity in Azarbayjan and for the first time opened new missions throughout major cities in Iran. The American Mission continued to emphasize religious instruction, a fact that doubtlessly contributed to the lack of interest in the schools amongst Muslims.

In addition to continuing its educational activity in Urumia, the Presbyterian Board established a mission in Tabriz in 1873. The same year the Mission opened two girls schools for Armenians with an initial enrollment of 20 (13 Armenians, 1 Nestorian, 4 French, 2 Muslims). In 1879 the schools merged to form The Boarding and Day School for Armenian and Muslim Girls, which by the end of the year had 10 boarding students (7 Armenian, 1 Nestorian, 2 Muslim). By 1883 the number of students had grown to 42 (including 4 Muslims), although during the period 1884-96 the school attracted exclusively Iranian Christians.[55] A boys school was opened in 1880. The first American missionary school in Tabriz to attract more than a handful of Muslims, in addition to Jews and Christians, was the *Ma'refat* school in Urumia established in 1906.[56]

In 1872 the American Board founded a Tehran mission. Unlike the Tabriz mission, whose operations were conducted in the Turkish and Armenian languages, the Tehran mission adopted Persian in order to appeal to Muslims as well as Christian and other minorities.[57] A boys elementary school was opened the same year which by 1900 had attracted 22 Muslim students.[58] At the request of some Armenians, the mission opened a school for Armenians in 1873. A school for Jews was opened, also by request, in 1875, although the school closed in 1880-81 due to lack of funds.[59]

In 1874 a day school for girls, *Iran Bethel*, was established with 12 students. A year later, the school opened a boarding option and had a total of 9 students. Ten years later the school moved to the American Mission headquarters and enjoyed an immediate increase in attendance to 40 students. Although Mozaffar al-Din Shah visited the school and promised a yearly contribution of 100 *tomans*, most payments were not made. For the first time in 1888 Zoroastrian and Muslim girls applied for admission to the school, although in small numbers. In 1896 18 Muslims applied for admission. The school was modified into a day school in 1898 and had a total student body of 63, including 7 Muslims. In 1903 Mozaffar al-Din Shah issued an order that parents must withdraw their daughters from the "foreign" school on the grounds that they "were being taught to wear high shoes and long skirts." Parents immediately took their daughters out of school, although within a month nearly all the students had resumed attendance.[60] By 1905 the total enrollment was 95, of which 24 were Muslims.

---

[55]Board, *Century*, pp. 9, 88-89.

[56]Hosayn Omid, *Tarikh-e Farhang-e Azarbayjan* 2 vols. (Tabriz: Farhang, 1332), vol. I, p. 92. Unfortunately, no statistics are provided concerning the actual number of Muslim students at the school.

[57]Board, *Century*, p. 5.

[58]Board, *Century*, p. 7. This school was later expanded into a high school and renamed Alborz College.

[59]Board, *Century*, p. 85.

[60]Ibid, pp. 87-88.

Medical work was begun in 1881 for men, and in 1889 a clinic for women was opened. The American Mission also opened missions in Hamadan (1880), Rasht (1906), and Qazvin (1906) where it founded schools and engaged in medical work.

Apart from the American Presbyterian Mission, the French Lazarists were the most active foreign missionaries in Iran. Like the Americans, the French greatly expanded their educational operations beginning in the 1860s, both in the Urumia region, as well as in Tabriz, Tehran and Isfahan. In Urumia and neighboring Salmas, girls' schools were established by the Catholic order of the Sisters of St. Vincent de Paul. By 1867, the *St. Vincent de Paul* girls' school in Urumia had 150 students in attendance.[61] The region experienced a famine in 1873-74 that was followed by pillaging by Kurdish tribes. The devastation and destruction also led to the closure of many missionary schools. By 1875, however, the Lazarist mission had established or re-established 26 boys' schools in the Urumia region with a total of 400 students, 10 girls' schools with 418 students, and more than 700 students combined in schools located in the surrounding countryside. Nateq notes that by 1882, the Lazarists were running 74 elementary schools and two schools explicitly designated for orphans in the Urumia region.[62] In 1896 there were 8 Lazarist boys' schools with 420 students and 8 Lazarist girls' schools with 303 students in the vicinity of Urumia. [63]On the eve of the Constitutional Revolution the Lazarists were operating 3 schools in Urumia proper (with 290 students) and had 49 schools in the surrounding villages (with a total of 965 students).[64]

It is very difficult to draw any conclusions from the incomplete and often sporadic data available on these Lazarist schools, and on missionary schools in general. However, it appears that the number of Lazarist *schools* in Urumia proper declined between the 1875-1896 period, while retaining approximately the same number of total *students*. This is probably the result of a consolidation of the schools and may additionally include dropout rates, as well as the gradual addition of different grade levels at the schools. The 1905 figure of only three

---

[61]Nateq, *Karnameh*, pp. 181-82.
[62]Nateq, *Karnameh*, pp. 183, 190, 197. See also Djavad Hadidi, "French Schools in Persia" *Encyclopaedia Iranica*, vol. 10, pp. 178-181.
[63]Nateq, *Karnameh*, p. 205.
[64]Hadidi, "French Schools," p. 179.

Lazarist schools with 290 students suggests that these schools, like many of their American counterparts and the *Alliance* schools, suffered from anti-foreigner agitation on the eve of the Constitutional Revolution. The number of students recorded in the village schools, however, continued to rise throughout the 1875-1905 period and it is likely that these schools were primarily devoted to basic literacy and may have additionally included instruction in some crafts/trades.

In Tabriz and Isfahan too, the Lazarists increased their activities, opening many schools for both girls and boys. At least three boys' schools were established in Tabriz: one in 1863, the *St. Vincent* in 1884, and another in 1901 by Father Auguste Malaval that had 95 students by 1904.[65] Girls' schools were also established in Tabriz by the order of Saint Vincent de Paul (1863) and by the Daughters of Charity (1865).[66] Lazarist missionaries and Roman Catholics established three girls' schools in Isfahan (1863, 1875, and 1904) and two boys' schools (1875, 1904). The boys' school curriculum consisted of French, Persian, history, geography, arithmetic and some sciences in addition to religion. The governor of Isfahan, Prince Zell al-Soltan, supported both the boys and the girls' school (as well as a medical clinic) that were founded in 1875, and awarded the boys' school a yearly stipend of 150 *tomans*.[67]

Gradually the focus of the Lazarists educational efforts shifted to Tehran. The Tehran mission had been established as early as 1861 and had opened a number of schools there. One of the most important schools, particularly after the Constitutional Revolution, was the *St. Louis* school, which was founded by French Catholic missionaries in 1862 with the express encouragement of Gobineau, then the French minister to the Persian court. The school opened with 15 students, nearly half of whom were Muslims.[68] By 1909 the school enjoyed a student body of 90. In addition to French language and literature, the curriculum comprised Persian language, world history and geography,

---

[65]On the St. Vincent school see Omid, *Tarikh-e Azarbayjan*, vol. I, p. 190.

[66]See Hadidi "French Schools in Persia" and Nateq, *Kamameh*, pp. 203-4, 215-18 and A. Ghaffari, *Tarikh-e Ravabet-e Iran va Faranseh az Teror-e Naser al-Din Shah ta Jang-e Jahani-ye Avval* (Tehran: 1368/1989), pp. 154.

[67]Nateq, *Kamameh*, p. 191-92.

[68]Nateq records the date of opening as March 10, 1862 in *Kamameh*, p. 180. Mahbubi-Ardakani notes that the school opened in 1861, in *Tarikh-e Mo'assesat-e Tammaduni-ye Jadid dar Iran* 2 vols. (Tehran: Tehran University Press, 1975), vol. I, p. 367.

Persian history and geography, arithmetic, calligraphy and painting.[69] The Muslim students attended classes in Islamic instruction outside the school's auspices. At the successful completion of a five-year program, students received a certificate equivalent to French elementary schooling.[70]

In 1875 the sisters of St. Vincent-de-Paul established the *St. Joseph* girls' school. The curriculum consisted of reading, writing, sewing, ironing and housekeeping. French, and some history and geography were also taught. Naser al-Din Shah provided the school with 1,500 French franks yearly. According to a French woman resident in Tehran in 1881,

> It has been several years now since the sisters established a church and a school in Tehran, and in this manner, are occupied with the children of several European families living in Tehran. A large number of Armenian girls also attend the school, and a very small number of Muslims also have entrusted their children to the supervision of the sisters under the condition that their beliefs and religion not be interfered with.[71]

The Lazarists also opened the school in 1881 that after nine years of operation had educated over 200 boys and girls. In 1890 the school had 60 girls and 40 boys in attendance. Three additional schools were established in 1894, with a total of 150 students. The first school for higher education, the *Ecole Supérieure* (*Madraseh-ye 'Ali*) was founded in 1896. The curriculum, largely indicative of the Christian student body, consisted of Syriac, Armenian, Persian, French, Latin, history, geography and sciences, in addition to religious instruction.[72]

The British Church Missionary Society

British Anglican missionary activity was largely centered in the southern cities of Isfahan, Kerman, Yazd and Shiraz. Activities intensified after 1862 with the arrival in New Julfa, Isfahan of Robert Bruce, a missionary and educational activist. In 1872 he took over the *George Joseph* School in Julfa— reputedly established by Armenians— on behalf of the British Church Missionary Society (CMS). A year later, this

---

[69]Nateq, *Kamaneh*, pp. 179-81.
[70]Ibid, pp. 180-81.
[71]Mahbubi-Ardakani, *Tarikh-e Mo'assesat*, vol. I, p. 367.
[72]Nateq, *Kamaneh*, pp. 201, 203, 205.

school absorbed the Armenian *Batavian* school. Despite ongoing quarrels between the CMS, the Armenian Church, and the ulama hierarchy over the issue of curriculum and evangelization, by 1875 the CMS school had 135 students of a variety of backgrounds, including Catholics, Armenians and as many as 30 Muslim boys.[73] Zell al-Soltan supported the school and lent it official protection. As a symbolic gesture of defiance of the ranking religious figures in Isfahan, he is recorded as having ordered some of his courtiers to send their sons to the school. He also occasionally visited the school and deliberately expressed his approbation and general promotion of European-style education by giving the school the honorific title of "*Mas'udieh*" after his own name: Mas'ud.[74] Only a decade later, the CMS boys and girls school together boasted of 300 students.[75]

As the century progressed, more schools were established by the CMS, some in the city's Jewish quarter, but most of them in Julfa amongst the Armenian community. For this reason, the schools aroused the ire of the Armenian Church, with whom they directly competed for students. The schools were also repeatedly closed down by powerful ulama in Isfahan, sometimes at the instigation of or at least with the tacit cooperation of Armenian priests. Despite some success in attracting Muslim students, the CMS schools' location in Julfa rather than in Isfahan (per order of the ulama according to the *shari'a*) as well as ulama opposition and the inclusion of Bible studies in the curriculum, meant that the CMS schools, like their American and French counterparts, mainly taught religious minority students.

Armenian Schools

The Iranian Armenian community promoted the foundation of Armenian schools in the 1870-1906 period in reaction to the American Protestant and French Catholic missionary schools. The Armenian educational effort was spearheaded by Armenian nationalists concerned

---

[73]Bruce to Taylour Thomson, 11 December 1875 and Taylor Thomson to Bruce in a telegram dated 8 January 1876, IO L/P&S/9/178 quoted in Heidi Wachler, "In the Shadow of the King: Politics and Society in Qajar Iran, 1874-1907" (Ph.D. diss. Yale University, 2000).

[74]Bruce to Gray, no. 11, July 14, 1879; CMS C PE-O 1/62 as cited in Walcher, "Isfahan."

[75]Bruce to Legation; 24 June 1886; FO 248/437 as cited in Wachler, "Isfahan."

over a possible loss of religious and/or cultural identity as a result of Armenian attendance of Western missionary schools. According to an Armenian educational activist in the 1870s, "the existence of those [missionary] schools . . . is not only unnecessary but also harmful. It is necessary to expand the national schools and to try to neutralize the missionaries."[76] It is not surprising therefore that the impetus for the establishment of "new" Armenian schools came from church leaders.

The establishment of European-style schools by the Armenian Church is evidence of the growing popularity of a European-style curriculum with its emphasis on (European) languages, and sciences. Prior to the establishment of "new" European-style schools, Armenian schools were essentially similar to the traditional Iranian *maktabkhanehs* and taught basic literacy, religion and Armenian language. They were usually attached to Armenian churches. The Armenian school in Tabriz which was newly reestablished in 1875 provided instruction in Armenian, Persian, French, Russian, Armenian history, religion, geography, and mathematics.[77] Teachers were recruited from the Caucasus, particularly Tiflis, and from Ottoman Armenia. Naser al-Din Shah provided the school with an annual stipend of 250 *tomans*, as did Mozaffar al-Din Shah on occasion.

Many Armenian elementary schools and a few middle schools were established elsewhere in Azarbayjan and in Isfahan— towns which both boasted of large Armenian communities. Tehran and Hamadan also had elementary schools. The first Armenian girls' school was opened in Tabriz in 1879 with 45 students. Armenian women were active in the educational reform effort. In Tabriz the Armenian Women's Benevolent Society established in 1890-91 not only promoted the establishment of girls' schools in the area, but also provided the students with the necessary tuition, clothing and supplies. Similar women's associations were established in New Julfa, Isfahan in 1892 and in Tabriz in 1895. It has been estimated that up to 6,000 Armenian girls and boys attended school in Azarbayjan in the 1904-5 period.[78]

---

[76]Yervand Frangian, *Atrpatakan*, quoted in Houri Berberian, "Armenian Partici-pation in the Constitutional Revolution," (Ph.D. diss., University of California, Los Angeles, 1997), p. 19.

[77]Berberian, "Armenians," pp. 20-22.

[78]Berberian, "Armenians," pp. 22, 25-27.

The *Alliance Française*

The *Alliance Française* was founded in Paris in 1884 as a "national association for the propagation of the French language in the [French] colonies and abroad."[79] The society proposed to achieve this primarily through the establishment of French schools abroad and by supporting those schools already operating which taught French. The *Alliance Française* was avowedly non-partisan, and denied any political, religious or ideological leanings. Despite this claim, the *Alliance Française* was an intensely political organization. The spreading of French language served the explicit purpose of enhancing France's international political and commercial interests. According to the *Bulletin* published by the society, their goal was "to establish links with expatriate French, and to keep alive the national language amongst them, and amongst all lovers of French language and culture, from any race and from any nationality." The *Bulletin* further explained that "the spreading of the French language abroad is an effective tool for expanding relations, in facilitating commerce, and therefore for increasing national sentiments."[80] In another issue it was blatantly asserted that "every client of the French language will become a client of French products."[81] The *Alliance Française* took up the crusade to spread modern [read French] civilization throughout the world.

The *Alliance Française* hoped to counter the overwhelming political influence of the British and Russians in Iran. The society embarked on an ambitious, organized, and well-funded campaign to spread the teaching of French in Iran. This led to fierce opposition to the *Alliance Française* on the part of British and Russian diplomats in Iran. The first mention of the *Alliance Française* in Iran appeared in the *Bulletin* in 1889. According to this account, there were two branches of the *Alliance Française* in Tehran and one in Shiraz.[82] The Alliance opened its first school in Tehran in 1890 with five students in a rented room in the

---

[79]Maurice Bruézière, *L'Alliance française: histoire d'une institution* (Paris: Hachette, 1983), p. 11.

[80]*Bulletin de l'Alliance Française*, cited in Nateq, *Kamaneh*, p. 83.

[81]*Bulletin de l'Alliance Française*, cited in Bruézière, *L'Alliance*, p. 29.

[82]Nateq, *Kamaneh*, p. 84.

home of the French minister plenipotentiary.[83] The *Alliance* chose Naser al-Din Shah's French physician, Dr. Feuvrier, to head the school since he had close court connections and was also on good terms with the British diplomatic representatives in Iran at the time.[84]

Many of the French diplomats and educators in Iran became active members of the *Alliance*. The explicit political (and commercial) agenda also explained the *Alliance Française*'s eagerness to work in concert with the Iranian government and to involve high-ranking Iranian officials in the society. The *Alliance* also invited European doctors, diplomats, and missionaries in an attempt to neutralize potential opposition, and to create profitable political connections.[85] Notably, Rev. Justin Perkins (head of the American Mission), and Lazarist missionaries in Tehran and Urumia were invited to join. The *Bulletin* listed founding members of the *Alliance*, associated members, and members elected on a yearly basis. Iranian founding members of the *Alliance Française* included 'Ali Asghar Khan Amin al-Soltan, Amin al-Dowleh, Kamran Mirza Nayeb al-Saltaneh, and Ja'far Qoli Khan Nayyer al-Molk (director of the *Dar al Fonun*). An additional six prominent Iranian officials and doctors figure among the associate members. French diplomats, educators and doctors constituted the remaining 37 odd members of the *Alliance*.[86] Throughout its existence in Iran, the *Alliance* received financial contributions from many Iranian government officials and notables.[87]

The shah did not initially oppose the establishment of the *Alliance Française* nor of the *Alliance* school. However, Naser al-Din Shah was concerned about the possible spread of revolutionary ideas associated with the French Revolution of 1789. In 1890, concerned that the *Alliance* was a dangerous secret society similar to Freemasonry, Naser al-Din Shah ordered all foreign schools closed. According to a British official, "the shah is inclined for the time being that all foreign schools in Iran be closed. He looks upon them with suspicion and is afraid that

---

[83]Homa Nateq, "A Short History of the Alliance Française and Alliance Israelite in Iran," in (ed) Homa Sarshar, *Yahudian-e Irani dar Tarikh-e Mo'aser* (Beverly Hills: Markaz-e Tarikh-e Shafahi-ye Yahudian-e Irani, 1997), p. 61.

[84]Joannes Feuvrier, *Trois ans à la cour de Perse* (Paris, F. Juven, 1899), pp. 268-69. Nateq records the date of establishment as a year later in 1891, and the royal physician as having been Dr. Tholozon. See Nateq, *Kamaneh*, p. 92.

[85]Nateq, "A Short History," p. 59.

[86]Nateq, *Kamaneh*, pp. 84, 86.

[87]Ibid, pp. 84, 91.

they nurture revolutionary ideas."[88] The French Minister Plenipotentiary promised the shah that the *Alliance* was not "an enemy of religion and state" and had nothing to do with either religion or politics. Rather, its sole purpose was to spread the French language. He further suggested that the shah himself become the honorary head of the *Alliance Française* in Iran. With these reassurances, Naser al-Din Shah rescinded his order to close the schools and issued a *farman* in permitting them to reopen. The *farman* read:

> Given that our exalted person has and does always aspire for the progress and welfare of the subjects of the country and given that the *Alliance Française* has set up a committee for the propagation of the French language in the capital, now our positive perspective and royal view, for the encouragement and progress of the *Alliance*, it has been decided to place this society under the shadow of our exalted governance and pursing that, we order our ministers to support this society and give the needed place in public schools to it.[89]

The *Alliance Française* school provided instruction from the elementary through the high school level— equivalent to the French baccalaureate. The director hoped that the school would serve as a channel for Iranian students to pursue advanced studies in France. To this end, the *Alliance* repeatedly requested that the French government recognize the school's diploma as the equivalent of the baccalaureate, to facilitate the students' integration into the French university system after graduation. However, the French government continued to insist that Iranian graduates of the *Alliance* school successfully pass a series of qualifying exams before being admitted to university in France.[90]

The schools' primary emphasis was on teaching French language and literature. The texts used were similar to those employed in France. They were available to students either in French, or in Persian translation at a number of bookstores in Iran.[91] After the opening of the

[88]Feuvrier, *Trois ans à la cour de Perse*, pp. 269-70. Nateq records this incident as having occurred in 1891 and that the shah's actions had been in fact encouraged by the British, in *Kamaneh*, p. 89.

[89]Nateq believes that this was issued in 1891, in *Kamaneh*, pp. 91-92. Feuvrier records only that *he* assured the shah that the *Alliance* was not concerned with political or religious issues, in *Trois ans à la cour de Perse*, p. 269.

[90]Nateq, *Kamaneh*, pp. 94-96.

[91]The Tarbiyat, Khorshid and Sharafat bookstores carried French books. For a list of the novels used at the school, see Nateq, *Kamaneh*, p. 102.

school's library in 1902, many of the texts were available at the school itself. Basic arithmetic, history, geography and philosophy were also offered. Religious instruction was provided outside of school hours and in 1904 Persian and Arabic courses were taught for the first time.[92]

By 1902 the number of students had increased to 80. Only a year later there were 100 students, and in 1904 this number increased to 130. At this time the school had a yearly budget of 12,000 French francs. Mozaffar al-Din Shah pledged an additional 10,000 French francs the same year.[93] The school witnessed a decline in student attendance after 1905, when the student population at the *Alliance* dropped from 130 to 95. Much of this loss can be attributed to the transfer of students from the *Alliance Française* school to the *Dar al Fonun*, which had recently undergone improvements and had recruited new teachers. Moreover, with the outbreak of disturbances surrounding the Constitutional Revolution in 1906-11, many students stopped attending the *Alliance Française* school out of concern for anti-foreign sentiments. Iranian donations to the school dropped off dramatically in this same period. In order to forestall the loss of students and income, the French minister plenipotentiary and the head of the *Alliance* school declared that the school had no political aims and should only be regarded as a cultural institution.[94] Despite concerns surrounding anti-foreign sentiments, according to the *Alliance*, French was being taught in 24 schools in Iran in 1905 and there were more than 300 students learning French in Tabriz alone.[95]

In addition to the school in Tehran, the *Alliance Française* established schools in Rasht (1897), Borujerd (1901), Shiraz (date unknown), and Tabriz (1902) where the *Alliance* merged its school with the *Loqmaniyyeh*. The *Alliance Française* also established close working relations with many missionary and Iranian schools which taught French, providing financial subsidies as well as educational supplies.[96] In addition to its relationship with the *Loqmaniyyeh* in Tabriz (with 100 students), the *Alliance* also contributed to the *Roshdiyyeh* in Tabriz (15 students), a

---

[92]Nateq, *Karnameh*, p. 96.
[93]Ibid, pp. 95-96.
[94]Ibid, pp. 94-98.
[95]*Bulletin*, no. 100, April 15, 1905, p. 228; and *Bulletin*, no. 102, October 15, 1905, p. 286, as quoted in Nateq, *Karnameh*, pp. 106 and 97, respectively.
[96]Bruézière, *L'Alliance*, p. 26.

Lazarist school in Tabriz (116 students), a Lazarist girls school in Khosrowabad (60 students), the Suzanian school in Urumia (35 students), and two recently established Armenian schools in the area. Each of these schools was given 500 *qerans* of financial aid and occasionally textbooks.[97]

The *Alliance Israélite Universelle*

An international Jewish cultural society, the *Alliance Israélite Universelle*, was also active in opening schools in Iran in the late nineteenth century. Established in 1860 in Paris, France, the *Alliance Israélite Universelle* aimed improve the intellectual, moral, social and legal situation of Jews around the world.[98] Education was believed to constitute the principal means of emancipation, moral regeneration, and spiritual renaissance of Jewish communities.[99] The *Alliance Israélite*, like the *Alliance Française*, believed in its civilizing mission, and emphasized the teaching of French in this context. The *Central Committee Report* of 1873 published a number of guiding principles regarding the establishment of schools. The first principal emphasized the urgency of establishing schools in the Middle East. The fifth principal discusses the status of the French language:

> The *Alliance Israélite* being universal [in nature], its schools will not have an exclusively French character . . . Besides the language of the country, foreign languages considered to be the most commonly in use amongst the population will be taught there . . . but . . . the French language, which has done the most for liberty of conscience, and whose soundest liberal tendencies are personified in the *Alliance Israélite*, will be preferred in the schools.[100]

---

[97]Nateq, *Kamaneh*, p. 106.

[98]See Georges Olivier, *L'Alliance Israélite Universelle 1866-1960* (Paris: Librarie Française, 1959), pp 13-16; and Habib Levy, *Tarikh-e Jame'eh-ye Yahudian-e Iran* (Beverly Hills: Cultural Foundation of Habib Levy, 1997), p. 437.

[99]André Chouraqui, *L'Alliance Israélite Universelle et la Renaissance Juive Contemporaine, 1860-1960* (Paris: Presses Universitaires de France, 1965), p. 151.

[100]Report of the Central Committee in 1873, as quoted in Chouraqui, *L'Alliance*, p. 157.

Despite the special place reserved for French, the *Alliance Israélite Universelle* was much more international in scope and purpose than the *Alliance Française*. Although headquartered in Paris, the organization did not itself seek to promote French commercial or political interests. Not surprisingly, it did not receive the same degree of support and encouragement for its activities, either on the part of the French or Iranian governments. For this reason, it took nearly three decades of efforts before the first *Alliance Israélite* school was established in Iran.

The first medical instructor at the *Dar al Fonun*, Jakob Eduard Polak, is credited with having proposed that the *Alliance Israélite Universelle* establish schools in Iran.[101] More than a decade later, representatives of the *Alliance Israélite* approached Naser al-Din Shah while he was in Europe in 1873 concerning their desire to establish a school for Jews in Iran.[102] After having been promised the shah's support, the head of the *Alliance Israelite* wrote a letter to Mirza Hosayn Khan Sepahsalar during his tenure as prime minister requesting official, royal protection for the school, to which he agreed.[103] Discussions concerning the protection of Jews and the establishment of an *Alliance Israélite* school continued throughout Naser al-Din Shah's reign. With the ascension to the throne of Mozaffar al-Din Shah, both the *Alliance Israélite Universelle* and the English Jewish Society requested that the new shah improve the situation of Jews in Iran.[104] In 1898, with royal support assured by the prime minister, the first *Alliance Israelite* school, the *Madraseh-ye Ettehad*, opened in Tehran with an entering class of 100 students.[105]

In addition to two Hebrew instructors, six Muslims were recruited to teach Persian and Arabic. All books and teaching materials were sent

---

[101]Polak resided in Iran from 1851 until 1860. See Levy, *Tarikh-e Yahudian*, p. 438. See also "Polak" in *Judaica* 13: 708.

[102]The central committee of the *Alliance Israélite Universelle* estimated that the total Iranian Jewish population in 1873 was 40,000. Tehran was believed to be home to 3,000 Jews. See Nateq, *Kamaneh*, p. 117.

[103]Aniseh Shaykh Reza'i, "Madares-e Faransavi," *Ganjineh*, vol. 2, nos. 7-8 (Spring/Summer 1371), p. 98.

[104]Naser al-Din Shah was asked in person again in Europe in 1889 to permit the establishment of *Alliance Israélite* schools. For the chronology of these early attempts, see Levy, *Tarikh-e Yahudian*, pp. 438-451; and Chouraqui, *L'Alliance*, pp. 107-8.

[105]Nateq, *Kamaneh*, p. 132. Levy believes that the number of entering students was as high as 300 and that 421 attended the second year. See Levy, *Tarikh-e Yahudian*, pp. 456-57.

from France.[106] Shortly thereafter the *Alliance Israelite* opened a girls school with 150 students in attendance. The Minister of Foreign Affairs wrote a letter of support to the *Alliance Israelite* and sent 500 French francs as a gift. Mozaffar al-Din Shah also pledged to provide the school with 200 *tomans* yearly and sent a letter praising the educational efforts of the *Alliance Israelite*. In his letter he wrote:

> I have been delightfully informed that a group of Jews would like their children to receive education that would not be available in other schools because the doors to those schools are closed to them. Therefore, they intend to collect financial support and establish an educational institution such that poor and orphaned children will learn there to celebrate my name based on the religion of Moses and pray for me and my country. I have always considered Jews my loyal subjects and *I consider this school, which they are building for the purpose of educating a segment of my subjects, useful to the entire country.*[107] (Emphasis added.)

The *Alliance Israelite* subsequently established schools for Jews in Hamadan (1900), Isfahan (1901), Shiraz (1904), Seneh (1904) and Kermanshah (1904).[108] The school in Isfahan attracted 220 students its first year. In 1902 the number had increased to 350; by 1904 the *Alliance Israelite* estimated that over 400 students were in attendance. A girls' school was also established in 1903 with 75 students and by 1904 boasted 270 students. The school in Hamadan opened with 350 boys and 250 girls. Some Muslims attended the school to learn French and were exempt from all religious instruction.[109]

The curriculum for boys differed from that offered the girls. Boys pursued their education from age 8 through age 22, and were taught Hebrew, religion, French language and literature, history, physical and natural sciences, mathematics and Persian. Advanced classes often included English instruction. Girls were primarily instructed in Hebrew, religion, reading and writing, French, personal hygiene and home-making skills such as sewing and embroidery. They usually finished

---

[106]Reza'i, "Madares-e Faransavi," p. 98.

[107]Nateq, *Kamaneh*, p. 132.

[108]The *Alliance Israelite Universelle* estimated that in 1873 the Jewish population in Hamadan was 3,000; in Isfahan 2,400; in Shiraz 3,000; and in Kermanshah 200. See Nateq, *Kamaneh*, p. 117. Levy dates the establishment of the Shiraz school as 1903. See Levy, *Tarikh-e Yahudian*, p. 452.

[109]Nateq, *Kamaneh*, pp. 138-40.

their schooling at age 14. The emphasis for girls was on improving their sense of dignity, and on preparing them for their future roles as mothers and wives.[110] The directors of the *Alliance Israélite* believed that schools for girls would directly contribute to the improvement of women's social conditions. It was argued that schools for girls were "decisive factors" in reducing the prevalence of child marriages, polygamy, and divorce, and conversely in according women their "traditional dignity as mistress of the home."[111]

Opposition

The French government, which actively supported the *Alliance Israélite*, in Iran, was nonetheless concerned about the competition their schools posed to the *Alliance Française* schools, particularly given the similarity of the names.[112] Foreign consuls of other European nations, too, promoted the missionary schools established by their compatriots and did not actively support the efforts of the *Alliance Israélite*. American missionary schools in particular had attracted many Jewish students and were therefore in competition with the *Alliance Israélite* for these students.

The *Alliance Israélite* schools encountered unanticipated foes amongst the Iranian Jewish communities themselves. Religious leaders and instructors often viewed the *Alliance Israélite* teachers with a mixture of jealousy and suspicion. Their traditional role as teachers and spiritual guides were threatened by the new schools. The conflict between the traditional and new teachers was also cultural in nature. The new *Alliance Israélite* teachers were Europeans who often did not speak Persian, and who had come to "civilize" and "socially regenerate" the Iranian Jewish community. This friction usually resolved itself in compromise. The director of the *Alliance Israélite* school oversaw the "profane" instruction of the students (sciences, mathematics, history and languages), while the traditional teachers continued to provide religious instruction.[113]

---

[110]Nateq, *Kamaneh*, pp. 134, 138; and Chouraqui, *L'Alliance*, pp. 190-93.
[111]Chouraqui, *L'Alliance*, p. 197.
[112]Nateq, *Kamaneh*, pp. 120-21.
[113]Chouraqui, *L'Alliance*, p. 157.

The *Alliance Israélite* encountered a stumbling block in the form of anti-Jewish sentiment amongst the general population, as well as the ulama. Members of the *Alliance Israélite Universelle* played quasi official roles as mediators between Iranian Jewish communities and the Iranian government. The *Alliance Israélite* sought to protect Iranian Jews from persecution, and improve their legal status. To this end, the *Alliance* frequently requested that the French government intercede on their behalf with the shah. The *Alliance Israélite* school in Tehran frequently served as a place of refuge for Jewish residents of the city.[114] Despite attempts by the shah and local governors to protect Jewish communities, the decentralized nature of the government meant that they were unable to prevent recurrences of anti-Jewish incidents.[115] For example, in January 1901 Shaykh Ibrahim incited riots in Tehran's Jewish quarter which resulted in serious damage done to the school. Mozaffar al-Din Shah took measures to end the disturbances and provided 1,000 *tomans* in reparations. Other instances centered on Muslim religious figures' insistence on the adherence to distinctive sartorial laws, and on their prohibition against Muslim students attending the *Alliance Israélite* schools.[116]

Conclusion: Opposition, Tolerance, Approbation

Throughout the 1830-1906 period, the missionary and foreign schools established in Iran reflected the political, commercial, religious and social objectives of their European founders. Education served as a vehicle of political ambitions and access to commercial markets, as well as the means of improving the standard of living and effecting a spiritual regeneration of the Middle East.

Foreign and missionary schools are also significant for the impetus they provided to women's education in the pre-constitutional period. Indeed, they should be credited as pioneers in women's education. Missionaries provided education to girls from the outset of their activities in Iran as part of their attempt to convert Iranian Christian groups. The Americans in particular viewed women's education as a

---

[114]Olivier, *L'Alliance*, p. 39.
[115]Nateq, *Kamaneh*, pp. 133-34.
[116]Chouraqui, *L'Alliance*, pp. 107-8.

means of improving general living standards. In addition to religious education, the American missionary schools often provided instruction in various sanitation and homemaking skills, whereas the traditional *maktabs* did not.

As the dominant forces behind the establishment of these schools, American and French missionaries and cultural societies were in direct conflict with each other. They competed for students, and by extension, for political and religious predominance. The fact that the some of the strongest opponents of the missionary schools consisted of their European and American counterparts illustrates the political nature of the competition between the Western powers in Iran. The American Protestant Mission targeted Christian minorities for conversion. Their emphasis on religion meant that the curriculum in the schools (with the exception of medical instruction where offered) was dominated by religious instruction. The schools therefore failed to attract many Muslim students in the nineteenth century, despite the incorporation of Persian into the curriculum of the Tehran school in 1872. While the Americans also established schools especially for Armenians (1873) and for Jews (1875), the American schools did not achieve the same popularity as the French Lazarist missionary schools.

From the establishment of the Boré school in 1839, the French Lazarists deliberately attempted to attract Muslims as well as Iranian Christians. The appeal of the French missionary schools stemmed from their emphasis on the teaching of the French language. A relatively large number of princes and courtiers received language instruction from the French missions.[117] This also accounts for the popularity of the *Alliance Israélite Universelle,* and especially of the *Alliance Française* schools. Indeed, the dominant characteristic of the French schools, both missionary and "secular," was their "Frenchness."[118] Particularly in the *Alliance Française* schools, which were neither Christian nor Jewish in orientation, the provision of sciences in addition to solid French preparation rendered them very popular. Not surprisingly, attendance

---

[117]Perkins records having given Malek Qasem English lessons, and Atai refers to 20 members of the Tabriz court who studied French at Boré's school. See Atai, "Iranian Students," p. 50.

[118]Michael Zirinsky, "Missionaries, Education and Social Change in Iran, 1834-1941," paper presented at the Middle East Studies Association Conference, 1996, p. 6.

at the *Alliance Française* school in Tehran soared after 1903 when the school began to offer Persian and Arabic as part of its standard curriculum. The *Alliance Française* schools also actively attracted Muslim students by exempting them from religious instruction. The schools awarded diplomas compatible with the French system in order to facilitate entrance into French universities. The provision of subsidies to other schools that taught French was also designed to enhance Iran's educational orientation towards France.

Diplomatic relationships between Western powers and Iran helped determine the shahs' behavior towards the missionary and foreign schools. Foreign diplomats in Iran actively supported the schools and pressured the shah and the government to extend protection and freedom of action with regard to the establishment of additional schools. While Mohammad Shah strongly encouraged both the American Protestant Mission schools and those established by Boré, his successors were more cautious in lending their support. As European political influence in Iran grew, particularly after the 1880s and the period of "concession mongering," so too did Iranian resentment. Fears of European political encroachment were exacerbated by apprehensions concerning European cultural incursions. The missionary and foreign schools were perceived to be cultural and political extensions of the Western powers.

Both Naser al-Din Shah and Mozaffar al-Din Shah were ambivalent concerning the schools' effects on Iranian society. On the one hand, they recognized the educational benefits that the schools provided. They offered protection, and in addition made financial contributions. On the other hand, the shahs occasionally viewed the schools as presenting a cultural and/or political threat. As long as the schools confined their activities to Iranian minority groups, the schools were considered to be beneficial. However, when the schools overstepped their boundaries and admitted Muslim students, they became threats to the cultural belief system, as well as to the existing educational institution controlled by the ulama.

Naser al-Din Shah and Mozaffar al-Din Shah repeatedly ordered foreign and missionary schools to close or limited their activities when they believed the schools were inculcating Muslim students with Christian and/or foreign beliefs, or when the monarchs wished to limit the influence of foreign powers in Iran. For example, in 1880, the minister of foreign affairs issued an order forbidding all missionaries to teach Muslims.[119] Two years later, as a result of pressure from members of the ulama, Naser al-Din Shah issued an edict forbidding the construction of new Christian churches.[120] He also ordered Muslims not to enroll in French Catholic schools. Again in 1889, in reaction to his concession to the British for opening the Karun River to navigation in 1888, he forbade the establishment of any additional European schools and cut off his financial aid to existing schools.[121] A similar order was also issued in 1890. Naser al-Din Shah regarded the teaching of French language as a vehicle for the spread of dangerous French political ideas. For example, in a personal letter to Kamran Mirza, he wrote that French language instruction should only be permitted in government schools such as the *Dar al Fonun*, "otherwise, the next day the Catholics and the Protestants will ask for the same thing [permission to teach French] in other schools [throughout Iran] . . . and this will lead to uprising among the people."[122] As mentioned previously, in 1903 Mozaffar al-Din Shah issued a proclamation forbidding Muslims from attending the American Presbyterian school in Tehran on the grounds that the girls were encouraged to "wear high shoes and long skirts."

The cultural threat posed by the missionary and foreign schools was also apparent in the reaction of the ulama, as well as of the Iranian Jewish and Armenian communities to the schools. Jewish community leaders resented the *Alliance Israélite Universelle*'s proclaimed "civilizing mission," and jealously guarded their role as spiritual leaders. The Armenian community also reacted against European and American missionary activity. The Armenian schools established in this period were an indigenous response to the perceived threat to Armenian identity presented by the proselytization of the missionary schools. The

---

[119]James Bassett, *Persia: the Land of the Imams* (London, 1887), p. 337.

[120]Angelo Piemontese, "An Italian Source for the History of Qagar Persia: the Reports of General Enrico Andreini (1871-1886)," *East and West*, vol. 19, no. 1 (1969), p. 161.

[121]Nateq, *Kamaneh*, pp. 197-201.

[122]Naser al-Din Shah in a letter addressed to his paternal uncle Kamran Mirza as quoted in Ehsan Yarshater, "Observations on Nasir al-Din Shah," in (eds) Edmond Bosworth and Carol Hilleband, *Qajar Iran: Political, Social and Cultural Change, 1800-1925* (Edinburgh: Edinburgh University Press, 1983), pp. 5-6.

Armenian Church provided an institutional structure and organizational framework for the mobilization of the community and the establishment of Armenian schools. The ulama believed that the teaching of European languages in Iran posed a cultural and political threat.[123] In 1906 a *fatwa* was issued from Najaf and Karbala concerning the teaching of foreign languages in Iran. The *fatwa* attempted to prohibit foreign language instruction in Iran, claiming that it led to the corruption of morals and a weakening of Islam. This *fatwa* targeted a variety of schools, including: a) Iranian schools that taught foreign languages such as the *Loqmaniyyeh* in Tabriz; b) missionary schools; c) the *Alliance Française* and the *Alliance Israelite Universelle*; and d) Armenian schools.

The political and cultural implications of the spread of foreign and missionary schools in Iran—and the opposition this engendered—demonstrates the complexity of the perceived benefits and dangers of European-style education. It also testifies to the intensification of the modernization dilemma in this period. The history of missionary and foreign schools in Iran also provides evidence of a shift in the political and intellectual climates. It illustrates the beginning of the process of the popularization of the educational arena.

Despite serious opposition to the missionary and foreign schools, they continued to expand throughout the nineteenth and early twentieth centuries. Expansion occurred in the student body, in the geographical location of the schools, and in the breadth of curricular offerings. Although Iranian Christians and Jews made up by far the largest segment of students at these schools, the percentage of Muslim students rose considerably, particularly at the French schools. The expansion of the foreign and missionary schools is partially attributable to the political power of the European powers in Iran. The relative political laxity of Mozaffar al-Din Shah (1896-1903) compared with that of his predecessor, Naser al-Din Shah (1848-1896), also contributed to the huge growth in school numbers and student attendance during his reign. However, the expansion of missionary and foreign schools could not have taken place solely on the basis of European determination and political opportunity. Rather, it was directly related to the increased

---

[123]Ibid, pp. 75-76.

demand for European-style education amongst segments of the Iranian populace.

Demand for European-style education was itself a result of the confluence of several factors. European education (and even travel to Europe) conferred social prestige and often high-ranking government employment, and nothing signaled a European education more than knowledge of French. French was the principal European language taught at the *Dar al Fonun*, and its predominance was further secured by the selection of France as the most common destination of students pursuing advanced degrees abroad.

On a practical level, the missionary and foreign schools offered something that the traditional schools (whether the *madrasehs*, or Armenian, Nestorian or Jewish schools) did not. Namely, a European-style curriculum with a focus on sciences, mathematics, and European languages, in addition to subjects such as history and geography. Students who were not interested in becoming members of the religious establishment were attracted by what they believed were more "practical" and therefore "useful" courses of study. Furthermore, a European-style education was established as a stepping-stone to prestigious government employ by the *Dar al Fonun* schools of Tehran and Tabriz. Although evidence is not available concerning the duration, specialty, or subsequent career of missionary and foreign school graduates, students may have anticipated that these schools would increase their marketability. For example, Mozaffar al-Din Shah, in an audience with students of the *Alliance Israélite Universelle* school in Tehran, promised to employ graduates of the school in the government.[124]

The continued, if not growing equation of modernization with Westernization also contributed to the support of the foreign and missionary schools by Iranian reform-minded individuals. In real terms, this translated into the support (both political and financial) of foreign and missionary schools— particularly of the *Alliance Française*— on the part of many Iranian officials.

Drawing from the fact that missionary schools were the first European-style schools established in Iran, it would be simple to

---

[124]Mozaffar al-Din Shah's promise was reported in a letter by Mr. Joseph Kazes to the Central Committee of the *Alliance Israélite Universelle* in Paris dated November 1898. See Levy, *Tarikh-e Yahudian*, p. 455.

conclude that they heavily influenced the establishment of European-style schools in the 1890-1906 period by Iranian educational activists. However, it would be a mistake to assume a causal connection between these two genres of schools. While their founders shared many of the same social concerns, the fundamental impetus and objectives of Iranian educational reformers in the pre-constitutional period differed dramatically from those of the founders of missionary and foreign schools. In fact, memoirs of Iranian educational activists make no mention whatsoever of missionary and foreign schools in Iran. Instead, schools in Europe, the Ottoman Empire and Japan served as models for the Iranian "New" schools. The popularity of the missionary and foreign schools, and the Iranian educational reform movement, were both separate results of a shift in the Iranian political and intellectual climate at that time.

CHAPTER V

THE "NEW" SCHOOL MOVEMENT,

1870-1906

Education became increasing central to the larger reform process in the last three decades of the nineteenth century. Whereas education had always been an important component of reforms aimed at increasing centralization and enhancing administrative efficiency, in practice educational initiatives had long remained limited to the adoption of military related technology and sciences, and the training of an elite military and administrative cadre. Educational goals changed dramatically in the 1870-1906 period when education emerged as a social and political panacea. Many reform-minded individuals saw education as a necessary prerequisite for larger social and political change. Educational goals shifted from a focus on training elite government cadres to achieving general literacy. The existence of a literate public was directly and causally connected to the strength and prosperity of the country. Consequently, the nation, rather than the government apparatus, became the focus of educational reform efforts. Education emerged as an *end* in and of itself, but also as a *means* of effecting broader change.

The belief that educational reform was a prerequisite of social and political reform was a result of the increased scope and nature of perceived Iranian "backwardness." Reformers became aware that Iran's problems were not a result of a passing failure to adhere to old methods of government, nor were they merely superficial in nature. No longer, therefore, would it suffice to import aspects of Western technology. Rather, reformers became convinced of the necessity of fundamentally reconstructing Iran's political institutions. Increasing contact with the West at all levels and the example of modernizing reforms taking place in the Ottoman Empire and Egypt led Iranian reform-minded individuals to become concerned at the slow pace of reform at home.[1] Europe, which had long been compared and contrasted to Iran, served as a model for modernization and reform. Moreover, with the worsening of Iran's finances and the simultaneous

---

[1]On Ottoman influences, see especially Anja Pistor-Hatam, *Iran und die Reformbewegung im Osmanischen Reich* (Berlin: Klausschwartz Verlag, 1992); Thierry Zarcone and Fariba Zarinebaf-shahr, (eds) *Les iraniens d'Istanbul* (Paris, 1993); and Feridun Adamiyat, *Amir Kabir va Iran* (Tehran: Amir Kabir, 1955).

push on the part of European powers to gain economic, commercial and political concessions in Iran (especially after 1888), reformers also viewed European powers as threats to Iran's territorial integrity and political autonomy. Reform became increasingly a matter of national survival. However, the absence of substantive reform under Naser al-Din Shah led to growing apprehension and frustration among those who favored change. The unexpected death of Naser al-Din Shah in 1896 and the accession of Crown Prince Mozaffar al-Din Mirza to the throne renewed reformers' hopes for monarchical support.

The Mozaffar al-Din Shah period witnessed the twin processes of politicalization and popularization of the reform process and its development into a bona fide movement. Increasing numbers of individuals from a broader socioeconomic spectrum recognized the need for change and were drawn into the reform effort. On their own initiative, educational reformers took steps to establish European-style schools in Tehran, Tabriz, and other major cities. In addition, a number of educational activists formed a society for the promulgation of education in Iran, the *Anjoman-e Ma'aref*, an event which marked a fundamental departure from the past reliance on government reform initiatives.

The "public" was drawn in to the reform debate on two fronts. First, as the *recipient* of educational reform measures, with the long-term goal of achieving general literacy. Second, as evidenced by the emergence of Iranian non-governmental journals published abroad in the late 1890s, the public for the first time was targeted as an *audience* and *source of mobilization* for reform proposals.

At the same time, receptivity towards European-style education increased dramatically. There occurred a shift in demand in both relative and absolute terms. For the first time, momentum for change was generated both from above by a widening spectrum of groups in addition to high level government officials, and for the first time, from below in the form of the increasing demand for European-style curriculum amongst segments of the urban population.

The popularity of the "New," European-style schools established in the 1890s greatly enhanced the threat to the existing educational system. Student enrollment at the New schools was significantly larger than the *Dar al Fonun*. Moreover, the emphasis on primary education and the incorporation of both traditional and European-style subjects into the curriculum meant that the New schools directly encroached upon prerogatives formerly maintained by the traditional educational system.

Naser al-Din Shah and Educational Stagnation, 1870-1896

Following the dismissal of Amir Kabir's successor, Mirza Aqa Khan Nuri, in 1858, Naser al-Din Shah ruled without a prime minister. After more than a decade, however, the shah displayed a renewed interest in implementing reform. He was impressed with the Iranian ambassador to the Porte, Mirza Hosayn Khan, who accompanied him on a visit to the shrine cities in Ottoman Iraq. In 1870, Naser al-Din Shah recalled him from this post, where he had been serving since 1858, and appointed him prime minister.

During his brief tenure as prime minister (December 1870-September 1873), Mirza Hosayn Khan attempted widescale reforms in numerous areas of political life. With the support of Naser al-Din Shah, he introduced reforms in the judicial, administrative, financial and military spheres of government, in addition to educational improvements.[2] His primary goal in undertaking the arduous task of reforming administrative frameworks and practices was to centralize state organs and increase the power of the shah. His reforms constituted attempts to correct abuses of the system and to rationalize the government apparatus.

Mirza Hosayn Khan conceived of educational reform as a component of his larger reform agenda. Already from Istanbul he had frequently written to the minister of foreign affairs and to the shah concerning the necessity of establishing schools along Ottoman lines, in order to make Iran competitive in the new international world of politics and diplomacy.[3] Only thus would Iran be able to effect increased centralization, administrative efficiency and renew her former

---

[2]For details on Mirza Hosayn, see Shaul Bakhash, *Iran: Monarchy, Bureaucracy and Reform Under the Qajars, 1858-96* (London: Ithaca Press, 1978), pp. 83-103. See also Guity Nashat, *The Origins of Modern Reform in Iran, 1870-80* (Urbana: University of Illinois Press, 1982).

[3]For more on Mirza Hosayn Khan's dispatches see chapter VII, below.

vigor. His educational agenda, however, remained essentially un-
changed from that of Amir Kabir some twenty years before, namely,
the training of elite military and administrative cadres. To this end, he
established several specialized secondary training schools.

Despite conflicting accounts, it is probable that Mirza Hosayn Khan
founded the *Maktab-e Moshiriyyeh* with the assistance of E'temad al-
Saltaneh sometime during his tenure as prime minister.[4] The school
taught history, geography, mathematics and European languages and
existed at least until 1897.[5] In 1872 Mirza Hosayn Khan established a
translation school, the *Dar al-Tarjomeh*, which taught the French,
English, Russian and Turkish languages. In the first year, 60 students
were enrolled, including 1 son of a low-level religious figure, 3 sons of
merchants, 1 son of an architect, and the son of a ranking military
officer.[6] The vast majority of the students thus hailed from the Tehran
court and government elite.

In 1875, in the capacity of minister of war, Mirza Hosayn Khan
founded a military training school, the *Madraseh-ye Nezami*, which was
placed under the supervision of the Ministry of War. In addition to
purely military subjects, the curriculum included military history,
physics, engineering and French.[7] The establishment of the *Madraseh-ye*

---

[4]According to Fakhr al-Din Roshdiyyeh, Mirza Hosayn Khan established
the school in collusion with Mohammad Hasan Khan Sani' al-Dowleh,
the minister of press and publications, in 1870. The school's curriculum
consisted of the Qur'an, *Golestan*, arithmetic, geography and medicine. He
further reports that the school was closed down by Naser al-Din Shah as a
result of complaints by members of the ulama. For this version of events, see
Fakhr al-Din Roshdiyyeh, *Zendeginameh-ye Pir-e Ma'aref-e Roshdiyyeh: Bonyangozar-e
Farhang-e Novvin-e Iran* (Tehran: Hirmand, 1370), pp. 224-25.

[5]There are few details concerning this school. Evidence suggests that it was
later known as the *Madraseh-ye Naseri*. See Hosayn Mahbubi-Ardakani, *Tarikh-e
Mo'assesat-e Tammadoni-ye Jadid dar Iran*, 2 vols. (Tehran: Tehran University
Press, 1975), vol. I, pp. 366-67; 'Abd al-Hosayn Khan Sepehr, *Mer'at
al-Vaqaye'-e Mozaffari va Yaddashtha-ye Malek al-Movarrekhayn*, (ed) 'Abd
al-Hosayn Nava'i (Tehran: Zarin, 1328), p. 119; Nashat, *Origins*, p. 148. See
also Mohammad Hasan Khan E'temad al-Saltaneh, *Al-Ma'asir va al-Asar*
(Tehran, 1306), pp. 277-78.

[6]Homa Nateq, *Kamameh-ye Farhangi-ye Farangi dar Iran* (Tehran: Khavaran,
1375), p. 44.

[7]Nateq, *Kamameh*, pp. 43-44. Nateq also believes that French Brigadier-
General Félix Vauvillier assisted Mirza Hosayn Khan in establishing the
school. Gurney places the date for the establishment of the school in 1885
with an initial enrollment of 150 students. See John Gurney and Negin Nabavi,

Nezami as a specialized military school probably contributed to the shift in focus of the *Dar al Fonun* in Tehran away from military subjects.

Mirza Hosayn Khan also attempted to improve the quality of the *Dar al Fonun* which had considerably deteriorated in the course of the past two decades. Newly established in his post in Tehran, Mirza Hosayn Khan reported to Naser al-Din Shah on the poor condition of the *Dar al Fonun*. He wrote: "The truth is that that which I expected and awaited was not that which I observed. First, the European teacher(s) that should be worthy of confidence, with the exception of Monsieur Richard and one other Englishman, were not."[8] Mirza Mahmud Khan Ehtesham al-Saltaneh in his memoirs of his studies at the *Dar al Fonun* from 1872 to 1879 provides a similarly disparaging view of the quality of the school. With the exception of the medical students, whose discipline was to be their livelihood and who would no doubt find suitable employment after graduation, Ehtesham al-Saltaneh recounts that the other students were poorly trained. He described his enrollment at the *Dar al Fonun* as a waste of time since the school did not provide much more than an elementary level of education.[9] Ehtesham al-Saltaneh complained that the entire life of the students was wasted, despite the fact that the purpose of the establishment of the *Dar al Fonun* was ostensibly the creation of educated individuals who would lead the country towards prosperity through the spread of sciences and technology.[10] He wrote,

> The unfortunate students were entrusted to stupid, uninformed and unconcerned teachers like revenue assignments (*tiyul*) and provisions, and nobody considered themselves responsible for looking after and preventing the waste of the valuable lives of the students and the waste of the sums that were spent on the management of the school.[11]

"Dar al Fonun," *Encyclopaedia Iranica*, vol. 6, p. 667-69. See also Feridun Adamiyat, *Andishehha-ye Taraqqi va Hokumat-e Qanun-e Asr-e Sepahsalar* (Tehran: Kharazmi, 1351), pp. 388, 429.

[8]Nateq, *Kamaneh*, p. 42.

[9]Mirza Mahmud Khan Ehtesham al-Saltaneh, *Khaterat-e Ehtesham al-Saltaneh*, ed. Sayyed Mohammad Mahdavi-Musavi, (Tehran: Zavar, 1366), pp. 25-30.

[10]According to Fakhr al-Din Roshdiyyeh, the *Dar al Fonun* was given by Naser al-Din Shah as a *tiyul* to Malijak. See Fakhr al-Din Roshdiyyeh, *Zendeginameh*, p. 81. I have come across no corroborative evidence of this.

[11]Ehtesham al-Saltaneh, *Khaterat*, p. 29.

Despite the relatively constant level of student attendance at the *Dar al Fonun* (between 200 and 250 in the period 1870 to 1890[12]), the school was not the subject of any long-lasting improvements. However, according to first-hand accounts, the emphasis on military disciplines so predominant in the 1850s and 1860s gave way to a focus on sciences, European languages and medicine. Whereas the number of students studying military disciplines was as high as 58% amongst the first class of students in 1851, in the 1880s this number had dropped to approximately 30%.[13] According to Ehtesham al-Saltaneh, between 1872 and 1879 the curriculum included mathematics, drawing, natural sciences, medicine, French, Russian, English, infantry and mining.[14] German was added to the curriculum in 1885.[15] The European visitor Edward Granville Browne recorded during his stay in Iran in 1887-88 that the curriculum consisted of English, French, Russian, mathematics and medicine, but makes no mention of other subjects, including military arts.[16] A court chronicler describing exams in 1898 list the curriculum as including mathematics, sciences, foreign languages, astronomy, drawing, geography and mining, but does not mention any military disciplines.[17] Since evidence of military disciplines at the *Dar al Fonun* becomes increasingly rare, it is very possible that the Military College (*Madraseh-ye Nezami*) established in 1875 supplanted military training at the *Dar al Fonun* in this period. Ehtesham al-Saltaneh's remark that the only serious field of study was medicine is further substantiated by the fact that the *Majles-e Sihat* (Medical Council) was established at the *Dar al Fonun* in 1887. This group was composed of 16 leading Iranian physicians who taught according to both the European and traditional Iranian methods, as well as a few European physicians in Tehran. The group met regularly to discuss local and national

---

[12]Ehtesham al-Saltaneh gives the approximate number of students when he was there (1872-1879) as 250, in *Khaterat*, p. 316; in 1889 British diplomat Curzon records the number of students as 225, in George Curzon, *Persia and the Persian Question* (London, 1892), p. 494.

[13]Gurney, "Dar al Fonun," p. 667.

[14]Ehtesham al-Saltaneh, *Khaterat*, pp. 26-27, 30.

[15]Gurney, "Dar al Fonun," p. 667.

[16]Edward Granville Browne, *A Year Amongst the Persians* (London: Adam and Charles Black, 1893), pp. 94-95.

[17]Sepehr, *Mer'at*, pp. 243-44.

medical issues.[18] In 1891 the *Dar al Fonun* was formally converted into a high school and, although it continued to attract a large number of students, its former predominance was increasingly challenged by the growing number of other new secondary and specialized training schools. Already in 1906, plans for the establishment of a separate medical college were underway.[19]

The *Dar al Fonun* in Tabriz, which never achieved the same level of academic standards as its counterpart in Tehran, continued to decline in the 1870s and 1880s. According to an entry in *Mer'at al-Boldan* (Mirror of Lands), in 1877 the curriculum was limited to French, medicine, geometry, infantry, artillery and Persian language.[20] An article appearing in 1882 in the newspaper *Akhtar* mentions that the school was in poor condition: "The situation of the *Dar al Fonun* of Tabriz has become so disorderly [that] there are no teachers and those that it has are incompetent (*naqes*). The food is inedible. The students at the school [spend their time in] amusements and games. Altogether [it is] completely disorderly."[21] Two years later, the student population had declined from 40 to 25, of which 20 were admitted free of charge.[22] In 1894 the school closed down briefly, but reopened shortly thereafter as the *Mozaffariyyeh* school with the assistance of Amir Nezam Garrusi, the steward (*pishkar*) of Azarbayjan. In his inauguration speech, Garrusi mentioned that the students were drawn from established Azarbayjani noble families who, upon completion of training by qualified instructors, would surely go on to serve state and country.[23] The newly reestablished school provided courses in Persian, Arabic, medicine, mathematics, geometry, arithmetic, geography, French and calligraphy. The Consul General of Iran in Tiflis sent books and drawings to be used in the school. Despite initial support, the *Dar al Fonun* of Tabriz closed down permanently only three years later in 1897 following the departure of both Garrusi and the school's director, Mirza Jahangir

---

[18]See a description in Browne, *A Year Amongst the Persians*, pp. 97-98.

[19]Gurney, "Dar al Fonun," p. 667.

[20]Quoted in Hosayn Omid, *Tarikh-e Farhang-e Azarbayjan*, 2 vols. (Tabriz: Farhang, 1332), vol. I, p. 30.

[21]*Akhtar* no. 36, yr. 8 (9 Ramazan 1299/1882) quoted in Omid, *Tarikh-e Azarbayjan*, vol. I, p. 34.

[22]Omid, *Tarikh-e Azarbayjan*, vol. I, p. 34.

[23]Quoted in Omid, *Tarikh-e Azarbayjan*, vol. I, pp. 37-38. Amir Nezam Garrusi served as steward of Azarbayjan from 1883-96.

Khan Nazem al-Molk, for Tehran.[24] The school was unable to survive in the absence of a powerful protector at the ministerial or court level.

Mirza Hosayn Khan had no lasting effect on either the *Dar al Fonun* in Tehran or that in Tabriz. His tenure as prime minister was brief due to the level of opposition that his administrative and centralizing reforms aroused. His attempts at securing British assistance in modernization and development efforts earned him the enmity of many groups with a vested interest in the status quo. He was accused, not unjustly, of facilitating foreign influence in Iran. As had repeatedly been the case in the Qajar era, opposition was articulated as defense of Islam and of Iranian honor. Mirza Hosayn Khan's enemies presented his reform programs as cultural intrusions and offenses against both state and religion. Opposition intensified around his proposed signing of the Reuter Concession with Great Britain. According to E'temad al-Saltaneh, it was rumored in the bazaar that Mirza Hosayn Khan intended to Christianize Iran. Mollah 'Ali Khani believed that the proposed new railroad would run directly through the middle of the *Shah 'Abd al-Azim* shrine. Another *mojtahed*, Aqa Sayyed Saleh Arab, declared Mirza Hosayn Khan an infidel.[25]

Following his return from Europe in 1873, Naser al-Din Shah gave in to the coalition of opposition to Mirza Hosayn Khan and dismissed him from the office of prime minister. Although Mirza Hosayn Khan continued in government service, his power to enact reforms was effectively curtailed. His dismissal and the failure of his reform efforts constitutes a turning point in the history of reform in Iran. Naser al-Din Shah, alarmed by the extent of resentment aroused amongst both officials and the ulama to centralizing reforms, was thereafter more circumspect in championing reform. His reign grew increasingly conservative and repressive. Those who questioned the government's actions were accused of being Babis or "Republicans," and of harboring malevolent intentions with regard to the monarchy. Although newspapers abroad discussed political problems in Iran, courtiers and

---

[24]Omid, *Tarikh-e Azarbayjan*, vol. I, p. 44. The last mention of the school appeared in the school newspaper, *Ruznameh-ye Naseri* in 1897.

[25]Mirza Hosayn Khan accused Mirza Sa'id Khan, then foreign minister, of distorting the translation of the concession and leading Mollah 'Ali Khani to believe that the railroad would destroy the shrine. On this and other criticisms of Mirza Hosayn Khan, see Bakhash, *Iran*, pp. 117-18.

nobles in Iran maintained silence with regard to the necessity of reform.[26]

Naser al-Din Shah was particularly alarmed at the potentially dangerous effect of European political ideas. He recognized that Iran lagged behind Europe in many ways, although he did his best to prevent Iranians from drawing the same conclusions. Amin al-Dowleh, Naser al-Din Shah's private secretary from 1873 until the shah's death in 1896, wrote in his memoirs that Naser al-Din Shah did not want either his own officials, or Iranians in general to see Europe or to be informed of European affairs because Iran was sure to compare unfavorably. According to Amin al-Dowleh, on many occasions the shah said: "My servants and the people of this country should not be informed of any other places except Iran and their own world . . . if they hear the word 'Paris' or 'Brussels' they should not know whether these two [things] are edible or wearable."[27] 'Abdollah Mostowfi described an environment of fear where "people did not dare to make statements concerning the social and political situations and arrangements of European nations and countries."[28]

Educational reform in particular was viewed as undesirable by the shah. Amin al-Dowleh repeatedly urged the shah to establish secondary and advanced schools in order to bring Iran into line with contemporary, "civilized" nations. Despite his appeals to the shah's honor and the place in history the shah would ensure for himself by promoting education, Amin al-Dowleh's pleas went unheeded.[29] According to Ehtesham al-Saltaneh, a leading educational activist of the period, Naser al-Din Shah was unwilling to promote European-style education in Iran because he believed that his kingship rested on the foundation of illiterate masses. For this reason, he wrote, Naser al-Din Shah refused to grant him permission to establish several public

---

[26]See Dowlatabadi's description of the mood at the time, in Yahya Dowlatabadi, *Tarikh-e Mo'aser ye Hayat-e Yahya Dowlatabadi* 4 vols. (Tehran: Ferdowsi, 1362), vol. I, p. 104.

[27]Mirza 'Ali Khan Amin al-Dowleh, *Khaterat-e Siyasi-ye Mirza 'Ali Khan Amin al-Dowleh*, (ed) Hafez Farman-Farmaian (Tehran: Ketabha-ye Iran, 1341), p. 131. See also p. 48.

[28]Abdollah Mostowfi, quoted in M. A. Sepanlu's introduction of Zayn al-'Abedin Maragheh'i, *Siyahatnameh-ye Ibrahim Beg* (Tehran: Nashr-e Asfar, 1364), p. iii.

[29]Amin al-Dowleh, *Khaterat*, p. 268.

schools in Zanjan.[30] In his attempt to maintain the delicate balance amongst competing sources of power, Naser al-Din Shah preferred not to challenge the ulama's prerogatives with regard to the educational system.[31]

In essence, Naser al-Din Shah viewed reform as a remedy for Iran's backwardness, but a remedy whose negative effects outweighed its potential benefits. He was concerned that he would be unable to control the momentum generated by reform, and feared that he might lose his throne. He felt an abiding need to appease entrenched powers: the Qajar aristocracy, bureaucrats and the ulama.[32] He preferred to prevaricate, play the Great Powers off against each other, and staunchly resist any attempts to limit his own authority. By 1890, the shah was too frightened at the potential negative repercussions of reform to take decisive action. His alarm only increased following the debacle of the Tobacco Concession in 1890-92. The last years of his rule witnessed a serious breakdown of central authority as the shah himself lapsed into indifference.[33] After the failure of any real reform by Mirza Hosayn Khan while he was prime minister, reform-minded individuals gradually lost hope in obtaining the shah's support. By the 1890s, reform-minded individuals concluded that reform in Iran would not be achieved under Naser al-Din Shah. Furthermore, after nearly two decades of attempting to secure British support for the Iranian reform effort, proponents of reform abandoned hopes of outside assistance. A mood of resignation was widespread in the bureaucracy.[34] No concrete governmental initiatives to reform the educational system or to establish new schools were undertaken for the remainder of Naser al-Din Shah's reign.

---

[30]Ehtesham al-Saltaneh, *Khaterat*, pp. 315-16.

[31]This interpretation is found in Abbas Amanat, *Pivot of the Universe: Nasir al-Din Shah Qajar and the Iranian Monarchy 1831-1896* (Berkeley: University of California Press, 1997), p. 414.

[32]Amanat, *Pivot*, p. 410.

[33]See Bakhash, *Iran*, especially pp. 234-39, 243, 261-70; and Amanat, *Pivot*, especially pp. 425, 429, 442.

[34]Bakhash, *Iran*, pp. 234-39.

The *Roshdiyyeh* Schools

Despite the stagnation and general inertia that characterized the reform effort under Naser al-Din Shah, momentum behind educational change was gradually developing. The establishment of a school in Tabriz by Mirza Hasan Roshdiyyeh illustrated the growing receptivity to educational change. It was also indicative of the shift of the reform impetus away from the official level to the level of private citizens. What began as an individual's effort to teach basic literacy using new methods developed into a preliminary curricular model for the New school movement nearly a decade later.

Mirza Hasan "Roshdiyyeh," the son of a high-ranking religious scholar in Tabriz, received a traditional elementary education. After an additional 11 years of religious training, he intended to travel to Najaf in Iraq to continue his religious education. However, apparently after becoming aware of the difference in literacy rates between Iran and European countries from an article in the newspaper *Sorayya*, he became convinced that the cause was the poor teaching methods employed in Iran. Mirza Hasan decided to study teacher training in Beirut where the French had established a teacher preparation school.[35]

In 1883 Mirza Hasan left Beirut after two years of instruction and returned to Iran via Istanbul where he visited newly established Ottoman schools called *rüsdiye*.[36] The same year, Roshdiyyeh established an elementary school in Erevan in Russian Armenia that taught the alphabet aurally according to new methods. In conscious imitation of similar elementary schools in the Ottoman Empire, the school was named *Roshdiyyeh*.[37] The school enjoyed much popularity amongst the Iranian community in Erevan, which due to its location in Russia and

---

[35]On Mirza Hasan Roshdiyyeh's early education and childhood, see Fakhr al-Din Roshdiyyeh, *Zendeginameh*, pp. 17-20; and Shams al-Din Roshdiyyeh, *Savaneh-ye Omr* (Tehran: Nashr-e Tarikh-e Iran, 1362), pp. 17-23.

[36]Fakhr al-Din Roshdiyyeh and Shams al-Din Roshdiyyeh both record Mirza Hasan's tenure in Beirut as two years, see op. cit., above. Mahbubi-Ardakani, however, believes he studied in Beirut for three years. See *Tarikh-e Mo'assesat*, vol. I, p. 376. On the Ottoman *rüsdiye* schools, see Carter Findley, *Ottoman Civil Officialdom* (Princeton: Princeton University Press, 1989), pp. 134-35.

[37]Although Mirza Hasan borrowed the name from the Ottoman schools, coincidentally in Persian "*roshd*" means growth, development.

proximity to the Ottoman Empire, was more receptive to change and innovation. In 1887 Naser al-Din Shah reportedly visited the school and invited Mirza Hasan to open a similar school in Tehran. Mirza Hasan left the school in the care of his brother and accompanied the shah back to Iran. Along the way, however, courtiers convinced Naser al-Din Shah of the inadvisability of permitting the establishment of such a school in Tabriz, arguing that Mirza Hasan's intention was to spread European ideas and laws which were dangerous to the monarchy. Naser al-Din Shah withdrew his offer of support for Mirza Hasan and forbade him to open a school in Tehran.[38]

Undeterred however, Mirza Hasan proceeded to Tabriz where in 1888 he founded a *Roshdiyyeh* school.[39] The school soon came to the attention of ulama in Tabriz who accused Mirza Hasan of heresy, forcing the school to close and Mirza Hasan to flee for safety to Mashhad. There, Mirza Hasan attempted to establish another *Roshdiyyeh* school. Seminary students, *tollab*, however, had heard of Mirza Hasan's school and its novel teaching methods, and soon destroyed the school, forcing Mirza Hasan out of town. Several months later, he returned to Tabriz and reestablished the school in the bazaar area. The school reportedly had over three hundred students.[40] Over the following five years, the *Roshdiyyeh* school was repeatedly closed down and Mirza Hasan run out of town, only to return once again to reestablish the school. Sources indicate that the *Roshdiyyeh* school was reopened at least three additional times during this period, and enjoyed a high student attendance of between 370 and 480 students each time, although this figure may be inflated.[41] Mirza Hasan's principal opponents each time were local ulama and *tollab*. Specifically, the *tollab* at the *Madraseh-ye Sadeqiyeh* and other traditional *maktab* schools were threatened by the success of the *Roshdiyyeh* in teaching reading and writing. Some high-

---

[38]Fakhr al-Din Roshdiyyeh, *Zendeginameh*, pp. 21-22; Mahbubi-Ardakani, *Tarikh-e Mo'assesat*, vol. I, p. 376.

[39]Fakhr al-Din Roshdiyyeh, *Zendeginameh*, p. 28; Shams al-Din Roshdiyyeh, *Omr*, p. 31. Mahbubi-Ardakani records the opening of the first Roshdiyyeh school in Tabriz as one year later, in 1889. See *Tarikh-e Mo'assesat*, vol. I, p. 376.

[40]Shams al-Din Roshdiyyeh, *Omr*, p. 31.

[41]Mahbubi-Ardakani reports that the Roshdiyyeh school was opened five times total in Tabriz, *Tarikh-e Mo'assesat*, vol. I, pp. 336-37. Fakhr al-Din Roshdiyyeh records eight different openings of the Roshdiyyeh school, *Zendeginameh*, pp. 28-34. Shams al-Din Roshdiyyeh concurs with eight openings, *Omr*, pp. 31-34.

ranking ulama supported the *tollab* in their opposition. On one occasion, Ra'is al-Sa'dat issued a *fatwa* accusing Mirza Hasan of heresy. In another instance, some ulama approached Mirza Hasan's father and asked him to request that the school close down. Students from the religious seminaries are known to have physically attacked and destroyed the *Roshdiyyeh* school on a number of different occasions, once even killing one of the school's students.

Despite fierce and often violent opposition, Mirza Hasan's school and new approach were welcomed by many. At least twice the school was opened in the bazaar area of Tabriz where it was well attended by local students. When, in 1894, Mirza Hasan reestablished the school once again, it remained open for three years. In order to protect the school, Mirza Hasan requested permission from ulama in Najaf to purchase space in the *Shaykh al-Islam* mosque located near the *Dar al Fonun* of Tabriz. Both Crown Prince Mozaffar al-Din Mirza and the steward of Azarbayjan at the time, Amir Nezam Garrusi, visited the school, thereby conferring their approbation.[42] Parents who had been afraid for the welfare of their children at the *Roshdiyyeh* school felt renewed confidence with the apparent protection lent the school by the crown prince.[43]

A newspaper article in 1895 concerning the exams given at the end of the first year is the first concrete evidence of the curriculum at the *Roshdiyyeh*. According to the report published in *Naseri*, students between the ages of 25 and 40 were successfully taught how to read and write in approximately 90 hours. In addition, courses in Arabic, Persian and French were offered. *Naseri* also reported that some teachers and the head of the *Dar al Fonun* of Tabriz, as well as some local nobles, attended the exam ceremony.[44] Reports indicate that 'Abd al-Rahim Talebof, an intellectual living in the Caucasus, donated 200 books on physics to the *Roshdiyyeh* school in 1894; however, there is no mention of physics being taught at the *Roshdiyyeh* at this time.[45]

---

[42]Fakhr al-Din Roshdiyyeh, *Zendeginameh*, p. 32.

[43]Shams al-Din Roshdiyyeh, *Omr*, p. 34.

[44]*Naseri*, no. 11, yr. 1 (Rabi' al-Awwal 1312/1895) quoted in Omid, *Tarikh-e Azarbayjan*, vol. I, p. 37. See also Fakhr al-Din Roshdiyyeh, *Zendeginameh*, p. 31.

[45]Talebof's book donation is recorded in *Naseri*, no. 5, yr. 1 (Zu' al-Hujja 1311/1894). For a quotation of the article, see Fakhr al-Din Roshdiyyeh, *Zendeginameh*, p. 33.

Despite the fact that the *Roshdiyyeh* enjoyed the favor of Crown Prince Mozaffar al-Din Mirza and was located in a mosque, the school was again the subject of attack. When the crown prince was away in Tehran, Sayyed 'Ali Aqa Yazdi, in a sermon at a mosque, accused the *Roshdiyyeh* school of being anti-Islamic. A crowd from the mosque proceeded to attack and destroy the *Roshdiyyeh*.

Shortly after the reestablishment of the *Roshdiyyeh* in 1897, Mirza 'Ali Khan, Amin al-Dowleh was appointed to the court in Azarbayjan as steward (*pishkar*).[46] During his brief tenure in this position, Amin al-Dowleh actively supported the *Roshdiyyeh* school, and secured official support from the crown prince. Amin al-Dowleh assisted the school financially as well, personally funding 100 needy students and providing them with food, clothing and supplies.[47] Opponents of the *Roshdiyyeh* accused Mirza Hasan of being a Babi and of atheism (*bi dini*). The school was purported to promote antagonism towards Islam and Islamic law. However, opponents did not dare engage in open confrontation with the school as long as Amin al-Dowleh remained in Azarbayjan. Following the death of Naser al-Din Shah and Mozaffar al-Din Mirza's assumption of the throne in Tehran, Amin al-Dowleh was called to Tehran in 1897.[48] After Amin al-Dowleh's departure, opponents of the *Roshdiyyeh* resumed their propaganda against the school and students gradually dropped out as their parents feared once again for their safety. Finally, when Mirza Hasan was invited by Amin al-Dowleh to establish a *Roshdiyyeh* school in Tehran and departed from Tabriz, the school succumbed to its opponents and was closed.

The significance of the *Roshdiyyeh* school(s) in Tabriz lies in its position as a watershed in the educational reform movement in Iran. It signaled a fundamental shift in the political reform objectives and their expression in the educational reform agenda. The *Roshdiyyeh* school heralded the emphasis on general, primary education and the explosion of reform momentum in the New schools movement of the 1890s.

Mirza Hasan's intention in establishing the *Roshdiyyeh* schools was to introduce new methods for the teaching of basic reading and writing

---

[46]Amin al-Dowleh remained in Azarbayjan for a few months in 1897. See Nateq, *Kamameh*, p. 66.

[47]Omid, *Tarikh-e Azarbayjan*, vol. I, pp. 47-48; Fakr al-Din Roshdiyyeh, *Zendeginameh*, p. 34.

[48]Sepehr, *Mer'at*, pp. 122-23.

skills and thereby to combat illiteracy. By teaching the alphabet phonetically, he was able to impart a functional literacy to his students. This was in direct contrast to the traditional *maktabs*, which taught students to read specific religious texts, but which often did not produce students able to read texts that they had not studied, or to write.[49] Unlike the *Dar al Fonun* schools in Tehran and Tabriz, the *Roshdiyyeh* were not geared towards the training of elite governmental administrative cadres. The fact that the schools offered general primary education which consisted of a synthesis of the traditional school curriculum *and* the inclusion of European languages (notably French) and sciences generated a degree of opposition not experienced by the *Dar al Fonun*. By targeting all school age children, the *Roshdiyyeh* schools posed a threat to the existing, traditional schools— particularly given their evident success and resultant popularity. Traditional teachers who were not schooled in new teaching methods were understandably threatened. Moreover, *tollab* were incensed at the loss of jobs as private tutors (which constituted a major source of income) to children who began to attend the *Roshdiyyeh* schools.

Opposition to the *Roshdiyyeh* was also due to the novelty of the teaching methods, and the inclusion of European-style subjects in the curriculum. Mirza Hasan was accused of perverting the Arabic alphabet, thereby committing an act of disrespect to Islamic teachings and directly undermining the *shari'a*. The fact that French was added to the curriculum, at least by 1895, further linked the new teaching method with Christian and foreign knowledge, and fueled general anxiety concerning foreign influence in Iran at the time.

The "New" Schools Movement

The assassination of Naser al-Din Shah in 1896 and the accession to the throne of Mozaffar al-Din Shah provided a major impetus to educational reform in Iran. Naser al-Din Shah's successor, Mozaffar al-Din Shah, did not maintain the same degree of control over the new

---

[49]While allowing for a variable quality amongst *maktabs*, Iranian *maktabs* did not differ greatly from their Central Asian counterparts. See Adeeb Khalid, *The Politics of Muslim Cultural Reform: Jadidism in Central Asia* (University of California Press, Berkeley, 1998), pp. 24-25.

administration as had his father, and was initially receptive to educational reform efforts, unlike his father. While he was crown prince and governor of Azarbayjan, Mozaffar al-Din Mirza accorded protection to Mirza Hasan Roshdiyyeh's new schools and was generally perceived as open to reform measures. However, not all the reformers' hopes for progress were due to Mozaffar al-Din Shah's active support of reform. According to contemporaries, it was primarily his laxity that permitted a flourishing of ideas and actions. Bozorg Omid wrote that "Mozaffar al-Din Shah, contrary to [his] father, was not opposed to the spread of education. Or rather, I should say that during the reign of Mozaffar al-Din Shah everybody did whatever they pleased."[50]

More so than the shah's own commitment to change, educational reform was given new stimulus in the person of Mozaffar al-Din Shah's new prime minister, Mirza 'Ali Khan Amin al-Dowleh. During his relatively brief tenure as prime minister, from March 1897 until early 1898, Amin al-Dowleh actively promoted educational reform.[51] During this time, at least nine New schools were established.

For the first time, in November 1897, reform-minded individuals met privately to discuss plans for the advancement of new education.[52] Seven prominent individuals, including Prince 'Emad al-Dowleh, Mirza Mahmud Khan Ehtesham al-Saltaneh, Mirza Yahya Khan Dowlatabadi, and Mirza Hasan Roshdiyyeh, together with members of the Ministry of Foreign Affairs and other government officials, decided at the meeting to establish a new school for orphans.[53] Shortly thereafter, one of the attendees of this meeting, Mirza Karim Khan Montazam al-

---

[50]Abu al-Hasan Bozorg Omid, *Az Mast keh bar Mast* (Tehran: Donya-ye Ketab, 1363), p. 95.

[51]Many differing dates are recorded for Amin al-Dowleh's appointment as prime minister. Ehtesham al-Saltaneh records it as having been in February, 1897 in *Khaterat*, p. 283. Algar agrees, in Hamid Algar, *Religion and State in Iran* (Berkeley: University of California Press, 1969), p. 223. Mozaffar al-Din Shah's court chronicler records his ascension to the post in April, 1897, as does Dowlatabadi. See Sepehr, *Mer'at*, p. 156; and Dowlatabadi, *Hayat-e Yahya*, vol. I, p. 178, respectively. March 1897 is the date given by Hafez Farmayan in "Amin al-Dowleh," *Encyclopaedia Iranica*, vol. 1, p. 994.

[52]Dowlatabadi records the meeting as having taken place in early Rajab 1315, *Hayat-e Yahya*, vol. I, p. 186. According to Sepehr, however, *Khayriyyeh*, the New school which resulted from this meeting, opened as early as September 1897, *Mer'at*, p. 156.

[53]Dowlatabadi, *Hayat-e Yahya*, vol. I, p. 186.

Dowleh Sardar-e Mokaram-e Firuzkuhi provided funds to establish the *Khayriyyeh* school.[54] He paid the teachers' salaries and provided lunch and dinner, clothes and books for the students.[55] Mirza Karim Khan also established a *vaqf* (endowment) for the school.[56] Initially the school accepted 20 students, although the number soon rose to 30.[57] The curriculum consisted of reading and writing of Persian, elements and principles of religion, history, geography, and arithmetic. In order to provide sources of livelihood for the students upon graduation, the school also taught various crafts, including shoe making, paper making and carpet weaving, among others.[58]

Soon after the establishment of the *Khayriyyeh* school, Mirza Hasan Roshdiyyeh, who had been invited to Tehran by Amin al-Dowleh, established a school of his own. Amin al-Dowleh, as part of his attempt to encourage progressive elements in the country to engage in reform efforts, assisted Mirza Hasan Roshdiyyeh in establishing an elementary school. Both Amin al-Dowleh and Mirza Hasan himself both hoped the school, which had already enjoyed a certain amount of success in Tabriz, would serve as a model for the subsequent establishment of other, similar schools.[59] In January 1898 the *Roshdiyyeh* school opened.[60] An account of the school's inauguration was published in *Tarbiyat* on January 27, 1898.[61] The school was enthusiastically received by parents who believed that it was more effective than both private tutoring or the traditional *maktabkhaneh* schools.[62] Capital for the schools was provided by Amin al-Dowleh (12,000 *tomans*) and by Mozaffar al-Din

---

[54]Mirza Karim Khan was head of the arsenal and of the *Madraseh-ye Nezami*. See Mahbubi-Ardakani, *Tarikh-e Mo'assesat*, vol. I, p. 382.

[55]Sepehr, *Mer'at*, p. 156; Mahbubi-Ardakani, *Tarikh-e Mo'assesat*, vol. I, p. 382.

[56]Sepehr, *Mer'at*, p. 156.

[57]Sepehr records 20 students admitted initially, *Mer'at*, p. 156. Mahbubi-Ardakani writes that 30 orphans boarded at the school although no specific date is given, in *Tarikh-e Mo'assesat*, vol. I, p. 382.

[58]Sepehr, *Mer'at*, p. 156.

[59]Dowlatabadi, *Hayat-e Yahya*, vol. I, pp. 182-83.

[60]Fakr al-Din Roshdiyyeh, *Zendeginameh*, p. 39. Nateq and Omid concur, see *Kamameh*, p. 64; and *Tarikh-e Azarbayjan*, vol. I, p. 49, respectively. Sepehr records the date as November/December 1897 in *Mer'at*, p. 194.

[61]See Omid, *Tarikh-e Azarbayjan*, vol. I, p. 40.

[62]Fakhr al-Din Roshdiyyeh, *Zendeginameh*, p. 40.

Shah (2,000 *tomans*). Other notables also contributed funds.[63] A few individuals, including Hajj Shaykh Hadi Najmabadi and Entezam al-Saltaneh, personally sponsored poor students.[64] In addition, Amin al-Dowleh established an official budget for the school from government funds.[65]

Initially the school admitted 20 students.[66] By the end of the year this number had risen to 50, of which half were accepted free of charge.[67] The student body eventually reached 400. According to Dowlatabadi, 250 of these students were from amongst the nobility, 100 were from families with average incomes, and 50 were from needy families and accepted free of charge. Wealthy children were charged 3 *tomans* entrance fee, 3 *tomans* per month, and 3 *tomans* every three months to pay for lunch. The rest of the paying students were charged 3 *tomans* in entrance fee, anywhere from 2 *tomans* to 15 *qerans* per month, and 3 *tomans* every three months for lunch. An additional 25 *qerans* were charged for any student who wished to receive a certificate of graduation from the school.[68]

The school was divided into two sections: an elementary and a more advanced, scientific section. From the outset until the school's change in location to Amin al-Dowleh's residence in 1903/4 the school comprised 6 grades. The first three grades had two classes each, and the three advanced grades one class, which meant that the school had nine classes in total. The curriculum consisted of: Persian (reading and writing), Qur'an, *fiqh*, *shari'a*, mathematics, prosody and style (*badi va ma'ani bayan*), Arabic language and literature, Russian, French, drawing and calligraphy.[69]

---

[63]Sepehr, *Mer'at*, pp. 154, 194.

[64]Hajj Shaykh Hadi Najmabadi paid the monthly fee of three *tomans* on behalf of 60 students. Mashhadi Kazem sponsored 10 and Entezam al-Saltaneh 5; see Shams al-Din Roshdiyyeh, *Omr*, p. 47.

[65]Mahbubi-Ardakani,*Tarikh-e Mo'assesat*, vol. I, p. 377.

[66]Ehtesham al-Saltaneh, *Khaterat*, p. 324.

[67]Sepehr, *Mer'at*, pp. 154, 194.

[68]Dowlatabadi as quoted in Fakhr al-Din Roshdiyyeh, *Zendeginameh*, pp. 40-43.

[69]For a list of subjects taught and texts used in the 1898-1903/4 period, see Shams al-Din Roshdiyyeh, *Omr*, pp. 66-67. Sepehr only records classes in Persian, calligraphy, geography, astronomy, arithmetic and other sciences, *Mer'at*, pp. 154, 194. Either he is generalizing, or additional courses in foreign languages were added subsequent to the school's establishment.

Schools Established by the *Anjoman-e Ma'aref*

The establishment of the *Anjoman-e Ma'aref* (The Society for Education) in February/March 1898 provided an enormous boost to educational reform. The *anjoman*, composed of a number of educational activists and sympathizers, took concrete measures to establish New schools. Although many schools were also established independently of the *anjoman*, their founders were often members of the *Anjoman-e Ma'aref*. In the year following the establishment of the *Roshdiyyeh* school in Tehran, five additional schools based on the same model were founded. Only a month after the opening of the *Roshdiyyeh* school, educational activists Ehtesham al-Saltaneh and 'Ali Khan Nazem al-'Olum established the *Elmiyyeh* school in the Lalezar district of Tehran in April/May 1898. The director of the school was 'Ali Khan Nazem al-'Olum, who was then followed by Hajj Mokhber al-Saltaneh Hedayat.

Like the *Roshdiyyeh*, the *Elmiyyeh* too comprised both an elementary and an advanced/scientific section. The elementary section provided the last two years of elementary education, and the advanced section provided the first three years of middle school.[70] According to Dowlatabadi, upper-class students attended the advanced, scientific branch of the school, while lower-class students with limited incomes made up the elementary grades. Parents of both socioeconomic classes of students were pleased with the school. Wealthy parents believed that the school provided more qualified teachers in more subjects than they could provide by employing private tutors, and at a lower cost. Parents with more limited means believed that their children learned more than they would have in traditional *maktabs*.[71] The curriculum of the school was essentially the same as at the *Roshdiyyeh* school, with an emphasis on reading and writing, and some Arabic at the elementary level, and mathematics, sciences and foreign languages at the advanced level.[72] In addition, exercise and military maneuvers were part of the *Elmiyyeh* curriculum, and the school had a small library.[73] Financially, although the elementary branch accepted students with limited incomes, the

---

[70]Mahbubi-Ardakani, *Tarikh-e Mo'assesat*, vol. I, pp. 379, 384.

[71]Dowlatabadi, *Hayat-e Yahya*, vol. I, p. 194.

[72]For a list of teachers at the school, see Mahbubi-Ardakani, *Tarikh-e Mo'assesat*, vol. I, p. 396; and Dowlatabadi, *Hayat-e Yahya*, vol. I, p. 195.

[73]Mahbubi-Ardakani, *Tarikh-e Mo'assesat*, vol. I, p. 384.

school maintained solvency because wealthy students paid a monthly fee.[74] The school retained this form until November 1902 when the High State Consultative Council of Education (*Majles-e Showra-ye 'Ali-ye Dowlati-ye Ma'aref*) decided to eliminate the elementary sections and transform the *Elmiyyeh* into a middle school.[75]

As a result of the enormous demand of poor students for admission to the *Elmiyyeh* school, the *Anjoman-e Ma'aref* decided to establish a separate school for needy children.[76] Accordingly, in August/September 1898 the *Anjoman-e Ma'aref* opened the *Sharaf* school in the Shemiran district of Tehran under the directorship of Mirza 'Ali Akbar Khan Nazem al-Attiba Kermani, and subsequently Hosayn 'Ali Khan Nazem al-'Olum.[77] Two hundred students were admitted free of charge.[78] The school survived intact until the end of March 1903 when the Committee for School Reform found that the school had deviated from its original purpose of providing free education to the poor and had been admitting wealthy students. The school then merged with the *Mozaffariyyeh* school to form a new middle school, the *Sharaf-e Mozaffariyyeh*.[79]

Between September 1898 and the end of the year, three additional New schools based on the model of the *Roshdiyyeh* school were established directly by the *Anjoman-e Ma'aref*, or with the assistance of its leading members. In September/October 1898, using funds provided by the *Anjoman-e Ma'aref*, Mirza Mahmud Khan Meftah al-Molk established the *Eftetahiyyeh* school in the Sanglaj district of Tehran.[80]

---

[74]Dowlatabad, *Hayat-e Yahya*, vol. I, pp. 194, 196.

[75]Ibid, vol. I, pp. 302-3.

[76]Dowlatabadi, *Hayat-e Yahya*, vol. I, p. 215; and Mahbubi-Ardakani, *Tarikh-e Mo'assesat*, vol. I, pp. 386-87.

[77]Mahbubi-Ardakani, *Tarikh-e Mo'assesat*, vol. I, pp. 380, 386-87.

[78]Dowlatabadi, *Hayat-e Yahya*, vol. I, p. 215; Mahbubi-Ardakani, *Tarikh-e Mo'assesat*, vol. I, pp. 386-87.

[79]Dowlatabadi, *Hayat-e Yahya*, vol. I, p. 310. Mahbubi-Ardakani, *Tarikh-e Mo'assesat*, vol. I, pp. 386-87 writes that the school was closed and the students transferred.

[80]Sepehr records the opening of the school in August/September of 1899, in *Mer'at*, pp. 279-81.

A court chronicler provides a detailed account of the rules governing the school.[81] According to the directives, all expenses of the school, including teacher salaries, rent and work materials were paid for by the *Anjoman-e Ma'aref*. Any books that were received as donations to the school library were lent to the students for their studies. The students themselves were charged one *toman* monthly, although they were expected to provide for their own lunches, and to purchase all necessary books and materials. According to the rules established for the administration of the school, for every 100 paying students admitted, the school would accept 25 needy and/or orphaned children free of charge. It was believed that in this manner, the paying students would subsidize the education of needy students.

It is interesting to note that the regulations of the school stipulated that all students were subject to the same rules regardless of family background, including the wearing of uniforms as determined by the head of the school. However, as an exception, the school did allow children of the ulama to continue to wear their customary attire. This exception suggests an attempt by the director of the school to accommodate ulama religious and cultural sensibilities. Moreover, it therefore indicates that for the first time, children of the ulama, who would otherwise be schooled in traditional *maktabs*, were attracted to the *Eftetahiyyeh*.

This New school was reportedly able to accommodate 500 students between the ages of 7 and 12, although the actual number of students who attended is not known.[82] The *Eftetahiyyeh* consisted of 5 years of elementary schooling. The curriculum, like other schools funded by the *Anjoman-e Ma'aref*, included: Persian (reading and writing), principles of religion, religious beliefs, morals, *shari'a*, introduction to Arabic and history, and some arithmetic, geometry and other new sciences.[83] The *Eftetahiyyeh* school lasted until November 1902 when the High State

---

[81]See Sepehr, *Mer'at*, pp. 279-81 for a list of directives concerning the establishment of the school.

[82]Sepehr, *Mer'at*, pp. 279-81.

[83]Sepehr does not specify what, if any, additional sciences were actually taught. See *Mer'at*, pp. 279-81.

Consultative Council of Education decided to combine the *Eftetahiyyeh* and *Islam* schools and change them into a middle (*moteuaset*) school.[84]

Approximately one month after the inauguration of the *Eftetahiyyeh* school, the *Anjoman-e Ma'aref* sponsored the establishment of another New school, the *Mozaffariyyeh*.[85] The sixth school established directly by the *Anjoman-e Ma'aref* or one of the society's principal members, the *Mozaffariyyeh* was modeled on the *Roshdiyyeh* school. Two hundred students between the ages of 8 and 12 years old were admitted for a monthly fee of one *toman*. Although details are unavailable, Dowlatabadi records that in March 1903 the Committee for School Reform was not pleased with the progress of the *Mozaffariyyeh* school. According to Dowlatabadi, the Committee (of which he was a member), found that the school had only 60 students in attendance and was not providing a curriculum deemed appropriate. The Committee decided to merge the *Mozaffariyyeh* school with the *Sharaf* school and make the resulting *Sharaf-e Mozaffariyyeh* school into a middle school subject to government oversight.[86]

The *Madraseh-ye Danesh* and the *Dabestan-e Danesh*, both established in 1898, were important New schools. The *Madraseh-ye Danesh* was founded by Mirza Mohammad Khan Namjavani, a graduate of the *Dar al Fonun* of Tehran who had previously taught at the *Roshdiyyeh* school.[87] The school followed the guidelines established by the *Anjoman-e Ma'aref* and permitted oversight by the *anjoman*. During the period of his prime ministership, Amin al-Dowleh awarded land titles and other funds to the school.[88] In 1903 the school was merged with the *Adab* school to form the *Seruat* middle school.[89]

---

[84]Dowlatabadi, *Hayat-e Yahya*, vol. I, pp. 302-3. Mahbubi-Ardakani reports that the school did not last long due to problems with the *Anjoman-e Ma'aref*, in *Tarikh-e Mo'assesat*, vol. I, p. 386.

[85]The *Mozaffariyyeh* opened in October 1898 according to Sepehr, in *Mer'at*, p. 322.

[86]Dowlatabadi, *Hayat-e Yahya*, vol. I, p. 310.

[87]Mahbubi-Ardakani asserts that the school was established in April/May 1900. This is contrary to Dowlatabadi's account of the relative order of establishment of new schools. See Mahbubi-Ardakani, *Tarikh-e Mo'assesat*, vol. I, p. 386; and Dowlatabadi, *Hayat-e Yahya*, vol. I, p. 241.

[88]Dowlatabadi, *Hayat-e Yahya*, vol. I, p. 241.

[89]Ibid, vol. I, p. 310.

Although not funded by the *Anjoman-e Ma'aref*, leading members of the *anjoman*, Mirza Mahmud Khan Meftah al-Molk and Dowlatabadi both served as directors of the *Dabestan-e Danesh* school.[90] The school was financed by Mirza Reza Khan Tabrizi, "Prins Arfa' Danesh," who was the Iranian ambassador to St. Petersburg. Initially the school consisted of a section of the *Eftetahiyyeh* school that was separately funded by Mirza Reza Khan Tabrizi. On a trip to Tehran from Russia, he visited the school and not pleased with the progress, separated the school from the *Eftetahiyyeh*, where it had been under the direction of Meftah al-Molk, and placed it under the direction of Dowlatabadi instead.[91] Hajj Mohammad Hasan Amin al-Zarb, the wealthy reform-minded merchant and director of the royal mint, provided space for the school.[92] Although the exact curriculum of the school is not known, it most likely resembled that of the other New schools established in this period. In addition, several rooms were specifically designated at the school for teaching artisanal trades to children with no financial means such as weaving, carpentry, and shoe making.[93]

After 1898 the *Anjoman-e Ma'aref* was beset with difficulties and entered a period of rapid internal transition. For this reason, the initiative for the establishment of schools proceeded from individuals rather than the *anjoman* itself. In 1899 six New schools were founded by educational activists. The next school to be established after the *Dabestan-e Danesh* was the *Sadat* school in April/May 1899. Dowlat-abadi, together with Sayyed Morteza, founded the *Sadat* school in the Shahabad district of Tehran in the home of Amir Khan Sardar.[94] Supervision of the school was undertaken by Hajj Mir Mohammad Ali Larijani and Aqa Sayyed Nasrollah Akhavi. The director was Sayyed Jalil Khalkhali. According to Dowlatabadi, the school was founded

---

[90]Ibid, vol. I, p. 291.

[91]For an account of the establishment of the school, see Dowlatabadi, *Hayat-e Yahya*, vol. I, pp. 283, 291; and Mahbubi-Ardakani, *Tarikh-e Mo'assesat*, vol. I, pp. 380, 388. Also see Mirza Reza Khan Tabrizi, *Sharh-e Hal-e Prins 'Erfa Danesh*, (ed) Mohammad Javad Hushmand; and Mirza Mahmud Khan Meftah al-Molk, *Ramz-e Mahmudi*.

[92]On Mohammad Hasan Amin al-Zarb, see his biography by Shireen Mahdavi, *For God, Mammon, and Country: A Nineteenth-Century Persian Merchant, Hajj Muhammad Hasan Amin al-Zarb* (Boulder: Westview Press, 1999).

[93]Mahbubi-Ardakani, *Tarikh-e Mo'assesat*, vol. I, p. 389.

[94]Dowlatabadi, *Hayat-e Yahya*, vol. I, p. 245; and Mahbubi-Ardakani, *Tarikh-e Mo'assesat*, vol. I, p. 389.

exclusively to provide free education for impoverished children of *sayyeds* (descendants of the Prophet Mohammad). Dowlatabadi, in order not to be forced to follow educational guidelines established by the *Anjoman-e Ma'aref*, took up a collection for funds to support the school. Many merchants contributed to the school, including Amin al-Zarb, and the school prospered.[95]

In the same month, Mirza Shokrollah Tafrashi Motarjam al-Dowleh, with the assistance of Dowlatabadi, established the *Adab* school in the Chaleh Maydan district of Tehran. Two hundred students were admitted to the school's elementary and middle sections. The school enjoyed particular success, which was partly attributed to the quality of the teachers.[96] In November 1902 the High State Consultative Council of Education eliminated the elementary classes, making the *Adab* a middle school.[97] Shortly thereafter, in February/March 1903 the *Adab* became a state (*dowlati*) school and thus eligible for government money. It was further decided to merge the school with the *Madraseh-ye Danesh* to become the *Servat* school. At the time, there were 200 students in attendance in eight grades.[98]

Four additional New schools established in 1898-99 were the *Aqadasiyyeh*, the *Ebteda'iyyeh*, the *Tarbiyat* and the *Kherad* schools. Apart from the date of establishment and the directors, little information exists concerning these schools. It is known, however, that the *Aqadasiyyeh*, *Ebteda'iyyeh* and *Kherad* schools were essentially private (*melli*), although through compliance with directives established by the *Anjoman-e Ma'aref*, they received some government money.[99] The *Tarbiyat* school, established by Mirza Forughi Isfahani Zoka al-Molk, taught arithmetic, algebra, geometry and foreign languages including French.[100] The curricula of the other three schools are unknown, although since the *Ebteda'iyyeh* school's exams in September/October

---

[95]Dowlatabadi, *Hayat-e Yahya*, vol. I, pp. 245, 250.

[96]For a list of some of the teachers, see Mahbubi-Ardakani, *Tarikh-e Mo'assesat*, vol. I, p. 396.

[97]Dowlatabadi, *Hayat-e Yahya*, vol. I, pp. 302-3.

[98]Ibid, vol. I, p. 310.

[99]Ibid, vol. I, p. 311.

[100]Nateq, *Karnameh*, p. 48.

1898 were administered by the *Anjoman-e Ma'aref*, it is likely that the curricula resembled those of other New schools discussed above.[101]

Three other schools were established in the 1898-1901 period that were not "New" schools in the form of the *Roshdiyyeh* per se. These were the *Ehsani, Akaber* and *Islam* schools. The *Maktab-e Ehsani* was founded in Tehran in July/August 1898 by Prince Mirza Movasseq al-Dowleh Khansalar at the urging of Hajj Mohammad Hosayn Shariatmadar-e Tabrizi. All expenses for establishing and running the school were provided by Movasseq al-Dowleh. The *Maktab-e Ehsani*, as its name suggests, was essentially a traditional *maktab* elementary school, with the exception that it, too, taught arithmetic and astronomy in addition to elementary Arabic and principles of the *shari'a*.[102]

The *Akaber* school was opened by the *Anjoman-e Ma'aref* in 1898. Under the directorship of Adib Kashani, the *Akaber* provided two separate classes exclusively for adults. The first class provided literacy training for adults. The second class, also for adults, provided additional instruction in French and Persian literature for those students who had mastered basic literacy skills and who desired additional education.[103] The *Akaber* depended solely on the *Anjoman-e Ma'aref* for funding and was forced to close down only months after it was opened in late 1898, when the *anjoman* underwent a dramatic downsizing of its activities.[104]

The *Islam* school was founded in April/May 1900 by Sayyed Mohammad Tabataba'i.[105] It was directed by Mirza Mohammad Kermani. Although the school received some funds from the government, it refused to abide by the educational guidelines established by the *Anjoman-e Ma'aref*. However, in November 1902, the High Council on Education enforced the merging of the *Islam* school with the *Eftetahiyyeh*.[106]

---

[101]These exams were for four schools: the *Elmiyyeh, Ebteda'iyyeh, Eftetahiyyeh* and *Sharaf*. A total of 400 students participated. See Sepehr, *Mer'at*, p. 276.

[102]The only reference to this school is in Sepehr, *Mer'at*, p. 266.

[103]Doctor Morel was the French language instructor; Mirza 'Abd al-Motalleb Kashani taught Persian literature; see Ehtesham al-Saltaneh, *Khaterat*, pp. 327-8.

[104]Dowlatabadi, *Hayat-e Yahya*, vol. I, pp. 222, 240.

[105]Shams al-Din Roshdiyyeh, *Omr*, p. 53.

[106]Dowlatabadi, *Hayat-e Yahya*, vol. I, pp. 302-3.

Between 1899-1900 several additional new schools were established under private initiative. These included the *Sa'adat* school founded as a free school by Motarjem al-Dowleh in 1899-1900;[107] the *Madraseh-ye Falahat-e Mozaffari* agricultural school established with the assistance of the Belgian government in 1900-1;[108] the *Kamaliyyeh*, and the *Madraseh-ye 'Olum-e Siyasi*. The *Kamaliyyeh* school was established jointly by Dowlatabadi and Morteza Khan Kamaliyyeh, a high-level court servant (*pishkhedmat*) in September 1900.[109] Under the direction of Morteza Khan, the school employed at least eleven teachers. Apart from the fact that French was included in the curriculum and that the school contained both elementary and middle school classes, no other detailed information is available. After two years, the school suffered from competition. The Committee for School Reform urged Dowlatabadi to make the school exclusively a primary school. He agreed, and accepted the curricular guidelines of the Ministry of Education.[110]

The *Madraseh-ye 'Olum-e Siyasi*

The *Madraseh-ye 'Olum-e Siyasi* was one of the few specialized schools of higher education established in the pre-constitutional period. It was founded in 1899 for the explicit purpose of training future diplomats to serve in the Ministry of Foreign Affairs. Mirza Hasan Khan Moshir al-Molk, having recently received a law degree in Europe, believed that Iranian diplomats were not respected in European due to their lack of adequate training. Together with his father, Mirza Nasrollah Khan Moshir al-Dowleh (a member of the Ministry of Foreign Affairs), he approached Mozaffar al-Din Shah and the prime minister, Amin

---

[107]See Mahbubi-Ardakani, *Tarikh-e Mo'assesat*, vol. I, p. 375; and Dowlatabadi, *Hayat-e Yahya*, vol. I, p. 260.

[108]Nateq asserts that it was established in 1889. For information on this school, see Nateq, *Kamaneh*, pp. 44-5; and Mahbubi-Ardakani, *Tarikh-e Mo'assesat*, vol. I, p. 406.

[109]See Nateq, *Kamaneh*, p. 45; and Mahbubi-Ardakani, *Tarikh-e Mo'assesat*, vol. I, p. 391.

[110]Mahbubi-Ardakani, *Tarikh-e Mo'assesat*, vol. I, p. 391.

al-Soltan, with the proposal to establish the school. The shah consented and agreed to pay 4,000 *tomans* yearly for the school's expenses.[111]

Like the *Dar al Fonun*, the *Madraseh-ye 'Olum-e Siyasi*'s stated purpose was to train students for government service. The *Madraseh-ye 'Olum-e Siyasi* provided a curriculum designed specifically around the needs of the Ministry of Foreign Affairs. Unlike the *Dar al Fonun*, no military sciences or training were offered. Prior to this time, only two students are known to have studied European law and political science. These two were members of the Garrusi student mission of 1859-67. The establishment of the *Madraseh-ye 'Olum-e Siyasi* indicates a broadening and deepening of the perceived need for change. Mastery of European and international law and diplomacy were now considered essential to permit Iran's diplomats to function in the widening international arena. It was natural, therefore, that the Ministry of Foreign Affairs enjoyed direct oversight of the school, and that all graduates were subsequently employed by that ministry.[112]

The school went through continuous expansion and development prior to the Constitutional Revolution. Mirza Hasan Khan drew up the school's program of study and organization along European lines. Both European and Iranian teachers were employed at the school, including Joseph Hanbeck, a Belgian advisor on law to the Ministry of Foreign Affairs and a member of the *Anjoman-e Ma'aref* at the time.[113] The school also published translations of a number of books concerning economics, political science, and international law undertaken by various instructors at the school.[114]

Less than twenty students were enrolled in the first class.[115] In order to be admitted to the school, candidates were required to pass an entrance examination in Arabic syntax and grammar, arithmetic, calligraphy, and writing of essays (*ensha va enla*). Students in the first

---

[111]Profits from a turquoise mine in Khorasan for the amount of 4,000 tomans were designated for the school's funding. Changiz Pahlavan, *Hoquq-e Asasi: Ya'ni Adab-e Mashrutiyat-e Dowl*, (Tehran, 1268), p. 332.

[112]Nateq, *Karnameh*, p. 44.

[113]Hanbeck also headed the *Alliance Française* in Iran for a time.

[114]See Mahbubi-Ardakani, *Tarikh-e Mo'assesat*, vol. I, p. 403 for a list of translators.

[115]Mostowfi, a member of the first class, lists twelve students by name and notes that there were "a few others" in this group. Abdollah Mostowfi, *Sharh-e Zendegi-ye Man* (Tehran: Ketabforushi-ye Zavvar, 1360), vol. 2, p. 71.

entering class had received prior elementary education at the *Dar al Fonun*, *Elmiyyeh*, *Eftetahiyyeh* and *Kherad* schools. Some also had been instructed by private tutors, or had attended traditional *maktab* schools.[116] Initially, these examinations were largely perfunctory and primarily designed to eliminate students who had received no prior education. Later, under the directorship of Mohammad 'Ali Forughi (1907-1912) examinations for entrance and advancement into the advanced grades were revised and made more challenging.

The school opened with only one class of students, although as they progressed and others were admitted, the classes expanded. The curriculum initially consisted of courses in history, geography, French, international law, and *fiqh*. The inclusion of *fiqh* was contentious. Mirza Hasan Khan included a course on Islamic law in the curriculum so that students would be knowledgeable concerning Islamic law, in addition to the primary focus of the school on European and international law. The ulama, however, strongly condemned the inclusion of *fiqh* in a European school, arguing that it was an inseparable part of religious sciences and could not be taught independently of a thorough religious education. They also objected to *fiqh* being taught in a school with European teachers, tables and chairs. Mirza Hasan Khan assured them that his only intention was to ground the students in the principles of Islamic law in order to better prepare them to withstand the allure of European laws and customs. He did not aim to train qualified practitioners of Islamic law.[117] According to Mohammad 'Ali Forughi (later a director of the school), it was only due to the power of the Ministry of Foreign Affairs that the ulama eventually conceded and allowed *fiqh* to be taught at the school, and abandoned their threat to promulgate a *fatva* against the school.[118] An uneasy agreement was reached whereby Mirza Habibollah and later, Shaykh Mohammad Taqi E'temad al-Islam were employed to teach the course.

In 1901 and 1902 additional grades were added. Persian and Arabic literature, and Greek history courses were also begun at this time. A year later, the first graduation exams were given and seven students

---

[116]Pahlavan, "Madraseh-ye 'Olum-e Siyasi," p. 334.

[117]For the controversy over the inclusion of fiqh, see Mahbubi-Ardakani, *Tarikh-e Mo'assesat*, vol. I, pp. 402-3; and Pahlavan, "Madraseh-ye 'Olum-e Siyasi," pp. 337-38.

[118]Pahlavan, "Madraseh-ye 'Olum-e Siyasi," pp. 337-38.

received a diploma after a four-year period of study. In 1905, Hosayn Pirnia assumed the directorship of the school and added courses on ancient Egyptian and Iranian history. Two years later, when Mohammad 'Ali Forughi took over the direction of the school, the curriculum was again expanded and comprised the following subjects: economics, law and accounting, *fiqh*, Persian and Arabic literature, French, mathematics, geography, Iranian and European history, political science, and international law.[119] Six students graduated from the school that year. The school suffered from lack of attendance during the Constitutional Revolution when no students enrolled for several years. After the revolution, however, attendance increased, and the school was reformed and underwent a period of growth.

"New" Schools in Azarbayjan

Tehran was not the only place in the 1897-1906 period to witness the flourishing of New schools. Azarbayjan in particular was in the forefront of the educational reform movement for a number of reasons. Azarbayjan was the most populous as well as the wealthiest province in Iran at the time. The capital of the province, Tabriz, was the customary seat of the crown prince.[120] In addition, Azarbayjan had many Christian minorities— a fact that had led, since the reign of Mohammad Shah, to much foreign missionary educational activity. Most importantly, Azarbayjan's proximity to Russia and the Caucasus provided political, social and commercial influence and contacts between Iran and her neighbors in this area to a greater extent than any other province.[121] It is not surprising, therefore, that Azarbayjan played a leading role in educational reform in this period, just as it would in the Constitutional Revolution only a short while later.

Following Mirza Hasan Roshdiyyeh's departure for Tehran in 1897, a number of former teachers at the Tabriz *Roshdiyyeh* school opened

---

[119]Nateq, *Kamaneh*, p. 44; and Mahbubi-Ardakani, *Tarikh-e Mo'assesat*, vol. I, pp. 402-3; and Pahlavan, "Madraseh-ye 'Olum-e Siyasi," pp. 340-41.

[120]This tradition was begun with the appointment of Crown Prince 'Abbas Mirza to the governorship of Azarbayjan by Fath 'Ali Shah in 1804. Although it continued in practice from this time, Tabriz was not officially established as the residence of the crown prince until 1839.

[121]The fact that the Turkish language was shared by Azarbayjanis and their Ottoman and Caucasian neighbors further facilitated mutual influence and contacts.

their own schools where they employed his new teaching methods. Of the four schools known to have been founded by former teachers of the *Roshdiyyeh*, two of them were essentially similar in curriculum to the traditional *maktab* schools, and two additionally included subjects such as foreign languages and elementary sciences that were not found in the *maktab* curriculum.[122]

Due to fierce opposition to the New schools on the part of local *tollab* and ulama which led to the destruction and closure of schools on a number of occasions, many schools in Tabriz retained similar forms to the traditional *maktab*. Although they employed new teaching methods, the curriculum at these elementary schools was limited to teaching the Qur'an, grammar, Persian and Arabic. Of the 19 new schools known to have been established in Tabriz in the 1898-1906 period, 8 of them took the traditional *maktab* form, 3 were new middle schools, and 8 were New schools that also included sciences and foreign languages in their curriculum. Although scarce information prevents distinguishing these types of schools conclusively, often the schools in the form of *maktabs* but employing new teaching methods retained the appellation "*maktab*." In contradistinction to the traditional *maktab* schools, the schools with European-style curriculum were differentiated by the appellation "*madraseh*" and should thus be considered New schools similar to their Tehran counterparts.

The most important schools established in Tabriz during the 1898-1906 period were the *Tarbiyat, Loqmaniyyeh*, and *Sa'adat madrasehs*, and the *Dabestan-e Nowbar*. The *Madraseh-ye Tarbiyat* was established in 1899 by a group of educational activists, including noted author and political leader Sayyed Hasan Taqizadeh.[123] As the only New school in existence at the time (the *Roshdiyyeh* having been closed down), the *Tarbiyat* school became the target of opposition. Only months after the school's inauguration, Hajj Sayyed Mohammad Yazdi "Taleb-e Haqq" gave a sermon in a Tabriz mosque denouncing the school. Yazdi declared that the founders were infidels and atheists (*bi dini*). He issued a *fatwa* that anyone who sent their children to the school was liable to be punished by death and would no longer be considered Muslims. As a result,

---

[122]See Fakhr al-Din Roshdiyyeh, *Zendeginameh*, p. 49.
[123]Other founding members included Sayyed Hosayn Khan "Edalat," and Mirza Mohammad 'Ali Khan Tarbiyat. See Omid, *Tarikh-e Azarbayjan*, vol. I, p. 52.

parents withdrew their children from the school out of fear for their safety and the school was forced to close.[124] Persian-language newspapers published abroad reported this event. From an account in *Sorayya*, it is evident that the curriculum at the *Tarbiyat* school included geography, Italian and French.[125]

The second New school established in Tabriz was the *Madraseh-ye Loqmaniyyeh*. In November 1899 Mirza Zayn al-'Abedin Khan Loqman al-Mamalek, a graduate of the *Dar al Fonun* of Tehran who had recently completed a medical degree in Paris, founded the *Loqmaniyyeh* school.[126] Loqman al-Mamalek was assisted financially by a number of benefactors in Azarbayjan, including the French consulate in Tabriz.[127] The school employed a number of Iranian and European teachers, including two of the founders and instructors of the closed *Tarbiyat* school: Sayyed Hasan Taqizadeh and Mirza Mohammad 'Ali Khan Tarbiyat. French and Egyptian newspapers wrote about the school. The *Bulletin* of the French educational and cultural association in Iran, the *Alliance Française*, published an announcement of the inauguration: "Doctor Loqman al-Mamalek, personal physician to the crown prince, graduate from the Paris academy and friend of the French, has opened a school in Tabriz."[128] The *Alliance Française* also arranged for French textbooks to be sent to the school from France via Tiflis. The predominance of French influence at the school was further illustrated by the fact that the directorship was given to Henri Renard, one of the French instructors, in 1899.[129]

In 1899 the *Loqmaniyyeh* formally established a program of study along European lines. According to this program, the school offered a seven-year course of study geared towards preparing to take an equivalency exam for a French secondary school diploma. The curriculum of the *Loqmaniyyeh* closely resembled that of a French secondary

---

[124]Yazdi's sermon was delivered in the month of Muharram 1317. See Omid, *Tarikh-e Azarbayjan*, vol. I, pp. 55-56.

[125]*Sorayya*, no. 36, yr. 1, (22 Safar 1317/June-July 1899) as quoted in Omid, *Tarikh-e Azarbayjan*, vol. I, pp. 55-56. Nateq also finds evidence that French was part of the curriculum in *Kamaneh*, p. 51.

[126]On Loqman al-Mamalek, see Omid, *Tarikh-e Azarbayjan*, vol. I, p. 63; and Nateq, *Kamaneh*, p. 67.

[127]Omid, *Tarikh-e Azarbayjan*, vol. I, p. 63; and Nateq, *Kamaneh*, p. 68.

[128]Quoted in Nateq, *Kamaneh*, p. 68.

[129]Ibid, p. 69.

school. It had a broad curriculum which consisted of: French (mandatory), Persian, Arabic grammar, calligraphy, arithmetic, algebra, astronomy, physics, chemistry, surgery, biology, physiology, pharmacology, anatomy, optometry, sanitation, medicine, photography, dentistry, history and geography. Both the British and Russian governments contributed funds to the school so that English and Russian language courses would be offered, since neither government had yet established schools of their own in Iran.[130] According to newspaper accounts of the period, there were approximately 150 students at the *Loqmaniyyeh* between the ages of 7 and 20.[131]

In 1900-1 the *Loqmaniyyeh* school established an educational society and newspaper. Like the *Anjoman-e Ma'aref* in Tehran, its purpose was to discuss and propagate ideas concerning education. Names of the benefactors of the school were published along with a monthly financial report. The school also had a library that lent books not only to students, but to all other interested individuals.[132]

In 1903 the New schools in Tabriz were subject to restrictions imposed by some local *mujtaheds*. In reaction to Loqman al-Mamalek's attempt to establish a hospital, they insisted that the *Loqmaniyyeh* and other New schools announce their intention to include religious courses in the curriculum. It was also stipulated that students must participate in daily prayers, and that only Muslims be admitted to the school.[133] In an effort to appease this opposition, religious sciences were offered by the school.[134]

Shortly after this episode, after four years of operation, the *Loqmaniyyeh* school was destroyed. Hajj Sayyed Mohammad Yazdi, a fierce opponent of New schools in Tabriz, gave a sermon in which he labeled them "anti-Islamic." By successfully connecting antagonism concerning the activities of a Belgian customs official in Tabriz and the

---

[130]Ibid, p. 70.
[131]See *Etela'* (8 Muharram 1318/May 1900), published in Tehran; and *Sorayya*, no. 35, yr. 2, (Jumadi al-Awwal 1318/October 1900), as quoted in Omid, *Tarikh-e Azarbayjan*, vol. I, pp. 58 and 61, respectively.
[132]Nateq, *Kamaneh*, p. 70. For more on the educational society, see below, chapter VI.
[133]Nateq, *Kamaneh*, pp. 72-73.
[134]According to Omid, religious sciences (*'olum-e dini*) were part of the curriculum; *Tarikh-e Azarbayjan*, vol. I, p. 61. Nateq mentions that religious studies were available in the afternoons; *Kamaneh*, p. 71.

existence of Armenian wine shops with the growth of New schools, Yazdi was able to incite a mob which rampaged through Tabriz, destroying wine shops, as well as three of the New schools, including the *Loqmaniyyeh*.[135]

Two years later, in 1905, with the financial assistance of the French foreign minister, the *Loqmaniyyeh* was reestablished, albeit in modified form. The new school explicitly announced that its purpose was to prepare students for further education in Europe: "The school of advanced studies, Madraseh-ye Loqmaniyyeh. Established in 1899. Full preparation for European universities. Complete instruction in French and Russian languages."[136] While the school concentrated on European languages, Persian and Arabic continued to be taught. However, after the departure of Loqman al-Mamalek for Tehran in 1906, the school ceased teaching sciences, Persian and Arabic literature, and became essentially a French language school with only French teachers. After this transformation the school lasted until 1908 when it was forced to close due to the disturbances in Tabriz associated with the Constitutional Revolution.[137]

The importance of French language instruction and the influence of the French government in Iranian education was also evident in the *Sa'adat* school which was established in 1904. Like the *Loqmaniyyeh*, the *Sa'adat* received financial assistance from the French Consul in Tabriz as well as from the *Alliance Française*. The curriculum consisted of French, arithmetic, natural sciences and history. The school was destroyed by Russian soldiers in 1911.[138]

By the 1890s, New schools began to be established in cities besides Tehran and Tabriz. Between 1903-5, more than 14 New schools were established in cities in Azarbayjan apart from Tabriz.[139] Although many of the schools did not last long, they represented the growing

---

[135]For an account of the disturbances, see Nateq, *Karnameh*, pp. 72-73; and Omid, *Tarikh-e Azarbayjan*, vol. I, pp. 64-65.

[136]This appeared in French as: "Ecole Supérieure Loghmaniyé. Fondation en 1899, préparation aux facultés d'Europe. Enseignement complet des langues française et russe." See Nateq, *Karnameh*, p. 74.

[137]Omid, *Tarikh-e Azarbayjan*, vol. I, p. 63. Nateq believes the school continued operation until the death of Loqman al-Mamalek in 1919, see *Karnameh*, p. 77.

[138]Nateq, *Karnameh*, p. 77.

[139]Omid, *Tarikh-e Azarbayjan*, vol. I, pp. 131-41.

movement towards educational reform in Iran. A few New schools were also established in this period in Rasht, Isfahan and Mashhad.[140] For example, the reformist cleric, Mirza Nasrullah Beheshti Malek al-Motekallemin founded a school in Isfahan which included European-style subjects in the curriculum. The school did not last long, however, as it was forcibly closed by a gang of *tollab*. Malek al-Motekallemin himself was decried as a Babi heretic and driven out of town. Some years later he returned, and together with like-minded reformists Jamal al-Din Va'ez and Majd al-Islam Kermani, opened a similar New school. This school managed to survive briefly, but only because the teachers publicly promoted the *Sherkat-e Islam*— a holding company owned by powerful religious, commercial and administrative figures in Isfahan.[141]

Conclusion

In conclusion, the period 1870-1906 was particularly fertile with regards to education in Iran. However, the dearth of data on the New schools with regard to the numbers of students involved, the socioeconomic status of the students and founders, as well as the exact curriculum followed at each school, renders any conclusions tentative. The problem is further exacerbated by the often conflicting chronological accounts of the establishment of the schools. A critical reading of both secondary and primary accounts of this period suggests that there were 23 New schools established in Tehran in the 1890-1906 period. During the same time period, there were at least 20 New schools established in Tabriz, and at least 16 in other cities and towns. Evidence concerning the numbers of students attending the New schools in Tehran indicates that in 1898, after 8 New schools had been founded, the number of students was approximately 1,300. Corroborative data suggest that by 1900, the number of students in New schools in Tehran could easily

---

[140]Information on new schools established outside of Tehran and Tabriz is particularly scarce. See Omid, *Tarikh-e Azarbayjan*, vol. I, pp. 131-41; Sepehr, *Mer'at*, p. 163; and Mahbubi-Ardakani, *Tarikh-e Mo'assesat*, vol. I, pp. 380-82, for available data.

[141]See Heidi Walcher, "In the Shadow of the King: Politics and Society in Qajar Isfahan, 1874-1907" (Ph.D. diss. Yale University, 2000).

have exceeded 2,000.[142] The number of students was lower in Tabriz and doubtless substantially lower elsewhere in Iran as there were fewer schools which satisfactorily met the criteria for New schools.

The New Schools and Reform

The New schools represented the fruition of political and intellectual trends which first became visible with the emergence of the *Roshdiyyeh* schools, and which had been gaining momentum ever since. Educational objectives kept pace with the politicization and popularization of the reform movement. The New schools thus signaled the development of a bona fide educational reform movement. Educational reform became an alternate route to political change.

The New schools movement was characterized by two factors: a shift in reform impetus, and the growth in demand for European-style education. Like the missionaries and French cultural societies, Iranian educational activists benefited from a relaxation in the political climate during Mozaffar al-Din Shah's reign. As discussed previously, Mozaffar al-Din Shah allowed a great deal of latitude towards educational reform efforts. His predecessor, Naser al-Din Shah, was suspicious, if not openly hostile, towards reforms, particularly those which he identified as the adoption of Western ideas and institutions. However, despite Mozaffar al-Din Shah's political leniency, he failed to commit himself to substantive change. The promise that his new reign spelled to reformers gradually gave way to feelings of frustration and anger at the shah's lack of support.

The absence of educational initiatives on the part of the shah or the government, combined with a growing sense of the need for reform, led to a shift in reform impetus. Before 1890, educational reform efforts came primarily, if not exclusively, from prime ministers with the authority to impose reform from the top. An important testimony to the growing sense of the urgency of implementing reform was the growth not only in numbers of educational activists and supporters, but in their social and occupational diversity. The 1890-1906 period

---

[142]Available data suggest that the number of students per school was anywhere between 130 and 160. This would result in a total student body by 1900 of 2,340-2,880. However, this estimate must be tempered by the lack of sufficient accounting practices, the variance of popularity of the schools, and by the tendency of those involved to exaggerate.

witnessed the growing participation of merchants, members of the ulama, and other members of the community in the success of the New schools. Activists established the New schools on their own initiative. Private organizations were established for the promotion of European-style education—the *Anjoman-e Ma'aref* in Tehran and the *Anjoman-e Loqmaniyyeh* in Tabriz. Founders of the New schools in Tehran and Tabriz came from five major groups: staff of the Ministry of Foreign Affairs and those who had been stationed abroad (Mirza Reza Khan Tabrizi, "Prins Arfa' Danesh", Mohammad Khan Meftah al-Molk, and Ehtesham al-Saltaneh); former students of the *Dar al Fonun* and/or those who had studied abroad (Loqman al-Mamalek, Ehtesham al-Saltaneh, Mirza Reza Parvaresh, the founders of the *Madraseh-ye Danesh* and *Adab* schools); ulama (Yahya Dowlatabadi, Mirza Hasan Roshdiyyeh, Sayyed Mohammad Tabataba'i, Shaykh Hadi Najmabadi, Sayyed Jamal al-Din Va'ez, Malek al-Motekallemin, and the founder of the *Aqadasiyyeh* school); and merchants (Amin al-Zarb, his son, and the group of merchants who founded the *Dabestan-e Nowbar*). Additionally, members of the community provided financial assistance to a number of schools, and educational societies.[143]

In Tehran, educational activists benefited from the concentration of reform-minded individuals. As the seat of the central government, Tehran was home to government officials who had traveled abroad and/or worked in the Ministry of Foreign Affairs, as well as graduates and teachers of the *Dar al Fonun*.[144] Moreover, as it had with the establishment of the *Dar al Fonun* in 1851, the Ministry of Foreign Affairs played a major supporting role in the foundation and operation of the *Madraseh-ye 'Olum-e Siyasi*. Powerful benefactors and reformers such as Amin al-Dowleh resided in Tehran, along with a larger concentration of high-level ministers and reform-minded individuals than anywhere else in Iran. Reformers in Tehran therefore benefited from a greater basis of support, both ideological and financial, than did those in Tabriz or elsewhere. Reform in Tehran, however, was

---

[143]See the subsequent discussion of membership and financial contributions to educational societies in chapter VI.

[144]Dowlatabadi refers to diplomats and those Iranians educated abroad as the primary advocates of educational reform. For the specific names he gives, see *Hayat-e Yahya*, vol. I, p. 184.

tempered by problems of governmental prerogative, conflictual power arrangements, and the informal nature of ministerial responsibilities.

In Tabriz, educational reform was achieved entirely by private individuals, with virtually no assistance from or interference by the government. The presence of the crown prince (Mozaffar al-Din Mirza until 1896 and then Mohammad 'Ali Mirza until 1906), sometimes lent tacit support to the attempt to establish New schools, although more often than not, the crown prince repeatedly succumbed to opponents of the New schools. Relative to Tehran, Tabriz had a smaller concentration of high-level government officials and reform-minded individuals. However, Tabriz's proximity to the Caucasus exposed it to influences not only from the Ottoman Empire and Russia, but from expatriate Iranian communities in Istanbul and Tiflis. These contacts, along with the greater concentration of European and American missionary activity in the area, distinguished Tabriz as the second most reform-oriented city in Iran after Tehran. Even so, the New schools established in Tabriz suffered from lack of protection by high government figures, and were more often closed down by their opponents than were the New schools in Tehran. Even individual opponents, such as Yazdi, repeatedly succeeded in closing down the New schools in Tabriz. Outside of Tehran and Tabriz, the lack of financial backing and ideological support meant that the schools established were to a greater extent dependent on the support and approbation of the local populace. Not surprisingly, these schools were more modest in their aims and more closely resembled the traditional *maktab* schools.

Literacy and Leadership

The New schools were a radical response to the perceived need to implement reform in Iran. Activists understood that substantive political reform, in the absence of royal initiative and commitment, would not be forthcoming, However, they believed that educational reform was an alternative means of effecting change. The New schools would themselves lead to changes; they were believed to be "catalysts" to political and social reform. The establishment of New schools was thus intimately connected to larger social and political reform goals. This is manifested in the educational goals embodied in the New schools. The New schools were conceived of as replacements for the existing educational system, not supplementary. They embodied the two principal goals of literacy and leadership.

The founders of the New schools recognized the importance of literacy as a prerequisite of constitutional government. The New schools employed new methods of teaching literacy first used by Mirza Hasan Roshdiyyeh in his schools in Tabriz. The emphasis on primary education found at the New school, in marked distinction with the *Dar al Fonun* and other elite preparatory schools, should be seen in this light. The importance of literacy is also evident in the establishment of the *Akaber* school, which sought to redress the problem of adult illiteracy.

However, educational activists certainly recognized that general literacy must necessarily remain a long-term objective. The more immediate goal was furthering the prospects for reform and modernization. To this end, the New schools had two related goals: First, the founders of the New schools strongly believed in the need to create a new leadership cadre which would spearhead the reform effort. The New schools thus were also intended to provide sufficient preparation for continued study at the advanced level. They attempted redress the problem of insufficient middle school preparation that had first surfaced at the *Dar al Fonun*. The decision by the Committee for School Reform in 1903 to increase the number of middle schools should be seen in this light. At this time, four schools were turned from primary-middle into exclusively middle schools, whereas only one became exclusively primary.

Second, the New schools attempted to create a new socioeconomic group which would support reform. Such a group was notably lacking in Iran where the reform effort continued to be exclusively dependent on the will of the monarch, and had little institutional backing. The relatively small numbers of graduates of the *Dar al Fonun* and other European-style secondary schools, coupled with their elite background, meant that there was no substantial group that both depended upon and supported political change. To redress this, the New schools sought to educate a large number of students. They also deliberately sought to attract students from a wider variety of socioeconomic backgrounds. A serious effort was made to accommodate poor students in the New schools who otherwise could not afford to attend. In fact, several schools, such as the *Khayriyyeh*, *Sharaf* and *Sadat*, were established for the express purpose of educating poor students. In

1903, the Committee for School Reform criticized the *Sharaf* school for deviating from its purpose of providing education to poor students. In addition, attention to the special needs of poor students is evident in the provision of instruction in trades at the *Khayriyyeh* and *Dabestan-e Danesh* schools to prepare students for future employment.[145]

The tensions inherent in the socioeconomic makeup of the student body resulted in a de facto division of the New schools along class lines. For example, many of the schools had both elementary sections attended by poor students and advanced, middle school sections attended by wealthier students. This division existed partially as a result of prior education, or lack thereof, amongst the different social classes of students. There is little record of the poorer students continuing their education to the middle school level, whereas the wealthier students anticipated continuing their education as a means of attaining government or other employment.

The tendency of the New schools to cater to the needs of wealthier students was also partially a result of financial necessity. The schools were generally under funded, or privately funded, and often struggled to maintain financial solvency. For these reasons, wealthier students often increased their representation at the schools. For example, in its first year of operation, a full half of the students at the *Roshdiyyeh* school in Tehran were designated as poor, and thus admitted free of charge. A number of years later, when the student body reached 400, only 50 (or 12.5%) of the students were considered poor, and as many as 250 (62.5%) of the student body consisted of children of the nobility.

The New Schools as a Threat

The New schools represent a deliberate break with the past. They were *not* believed by their founders to constitute modified versions of traditional schools. Indeed, the New schools constituted a bid to replace the existing educational system. In conscious distinction to the traditional *maktab* elementary schools, the New schools were called "*madraseh*" or "new" (*jadid*) by their founders. The names given to the

---

[145]The inclusion of practical training in a variety of trades was prevalent in the American Protestant missionary schools in the Urumia area prior to the 1870s. See chapter IV, above.

schools were programmatic of their European orientation (e.g. Knowledge, Honor, Wealth, Education).

The New schools differed from the existing schools in three ways. First, many of them employed the new teaching method that centered on the instruction of the alphabet phonetically. This method was successful in promoting functional literacy, unlike many *maktabs* where students could only read the specific texts that they had studied. Second, the formal institutionalization of the New schools differed dramatically from the informal organization of the traditional schools. Entrance requirements, exams, a uniform curriculum, the division of students into classes, advancement as a result of mastery of the curriculum, and diplomas upon graduation were in direct contrast to the traditional schools where progress was a function of proof of sufficient understanding of individual texts, and students proceeded from text to text as they chose, with no formal graduation or termination of course of study.

Third, the New schools introduced subjects into the curriculum which were not found in traditional schools, namely sciences, history, geography, and European languages. The curriculum at the New schools was a combination of European-style subjects, as well as some core subjects taught in traditional Iranian schools such as religious principles, Arabic and Persian language. The New schools, thus, were a uniquely Iranian synthesis, or "translation" of key elements of both European and traditional Iranian schools. European organization and subjects were adopted which were believed to be needed for the modernization and "progress" of Iran, while traditional subjects were retained which were believed to constitute core elements of Iranian cultural and religious identity. Although the *Anjoman-e Ma'aref* attempted to control the curriculum and organization of the New schools, its guidelines and directives were never binding. The New schools thus display a range of "translations" of elements of European education to Iran's needs. On one end of the spectrum was the *Madraseh-ye 'Olum-e Siyasi*. This was the most fully European-style school at the time.

At the other end of the spectrum were those schools whose directors/founders refused to abide by *Anjoman-e Ma'aref* curricular guidelines. Dowlatabadi, who both founded and directed schools that did adhere to *Anjoman-e Ma'aref* guidelines, also founded the *Sadat* school that did not. This school was established for the express purpose of educating children of poor *sayyeds*. The *Islam* school, founded by Sayyed Mohammad Tabataba'i and directed by Mirza Mohammad Kermani Nazem al-Islam, also refused to adhere to *anjoman* curricular guidelines. Although the reasons for this are not explicitly stated, it is possible that the student body in both schools was made up primarily by sons of the ulama, who were attracted to the schools' promise of literacy, but who were not interested in learning European sciences or languages. This hypothesis is supported by the fact that the Committee for School Reform merged the *Islam* school with the *Eftetahiyyeh* school, which made special accommodations to appeal to sons of the ulama by exempting them from the dress code.

The successful synthesis of Iranian and European subjects in the New schools constituted their greatest threat to the traditional educational system and the religious establishment. Their incorporation of both modern, "useful" subjects, along with traditional subjects which constituted the basis of moral and cultural traditions made them an increasingly popular alternative to the traditional schools. The New schools constituted a bid to replace the traditional system by rendering it obsolete. Their increasing popularity and their deliberate attempt to attract sons of the ulama made them a viable substitute and threatened to marginalize the religious establishment's hold on the educational system.

CHAPTER VI

THE *ANJOMAN-E MA'AREF*

The *Anjoman-e Ma'aref* (The Society of Education) was the first organized, non-governmental attempt to promote educational reform in Iran. Its establishment is indicative of the increasing politicization of the 1890s period, as well as of the general willingness of Mozaffar al-Din Shah to allow private initiative in the reform process. The *Anjoman-e Ma'aref* also clearly indicates the growing sense of urgency felt by a widening group of reform-minded individuals in effecting modernization, and their determination to provide the initiative and funding to promote it. Despite the *anjoman*'s founding of many New schools in the last decade of the nineteenth century, it did not succeed in overcoming the barriers to reform, and after a number of metamorphoses, was finally dissolved after six years of operation. Throughout its existence, the *anjoman* was plagued by internal rivalry and factionalism. It also was confronted with the twin problems of negotiating change within a governmental structure which lacked clear institutional lines of authority, in the absence of strong monarchical support. The history of the *Anjoman-e Ma'aref* thus illustrates both the energy and the obstacles which characterized modernization in Qajar Iran.

There are conflicting accounts of the initial impetus behind the formation of the *Anjoman-e Ma'aref*. According to Dowlatabadi, Mirza Karim Khan Savadkuhi Montazem al-Dowleh (later Sardar Mokarram) gathered a group of individuals together in order to found an orphanage and school, the *Khayriyyeh*, in November 1897. This group then proceeded to establish itself as an *anjoman*.[1] Ehtesham al-Saltaneh records that he and Sayyed Karim Khan Firuzkuhi brought a group of 50-60 men together to discuss how best to promote education in Iran. Together, they decided to form an *anjoman*. Ehtesham al-Saltaneh then wrote a letter to this effect to Amin al-Dowleh who pledged his support.[2] Among secondary sources, Fakhr al-Din Roshdiyyeh asserts that Mirza Hasan Roshdiyyeh was the founder of the *anjoman*, while Anwar records that Amin al-Dowleh ordered the formation of the

---

[1]Yahya Dowlatabadi, *Tarikh-e Mo'aser ya Hayat-e Yahya Dowlatabadi*, 4 vols. (Tehran: Ferdowsi, 1362), vol. I, pp. 186-88.

[2]Mirza Mahmud Khan Ehtesham al-Saltaneh, *Khaterat-e Ehtesham al-Saltaneh*, (ed.) Sayyed Mohammad Mahdavi-Musavi (Tehran: Zavvar, 1366), pp. 316-18.

anjoman and requested that Ehtesham al-Saltaneh prepare a list of potential members.[3]

In any case, the *Anjoman-e Ma'aref* was established in February/ March 1898 and enjoyed the full support of Amin al-Dowleh, who had ascended to the position of prime minister in March 1897. The first official meeting took place in March 1898 at the *Roshdiyyeh* school (established in January/February 1898). At this meeting, the name *Anjoman-e Ta'sis-e Makateb-e Melli-ye Iran* (The Society for the Establishment National Elementary Schools in Iran) or *Anjoman-e Ma'aref* (The Society of Education), as it was more commonly called, was chosen.[4] An announcement of the establishment of the *anjoman* was published as follows:

> The meetings will take place on Sundays and Wednesdays, from four in the afternoon until nightfall. The above society will convene in order to [effect] necessary organization, reform and establishment of additional elementary (*maktab*) and middle (*madraseh*) schools. Funds that are received for these schools will in their entirety be used for the schools' expenses, and for the particular benefit of the society . . . All of the promissory notes are guaranteed by the seal of the great Ministry of Sciences and the special seal of the society will be in the hands of Meftah al-Molk. The accounts of this [society] and its funds will be recorded in the special book of the society under the supervision of the same [Meftah al-Molk] . . . At the end of every three months, the receipts and disbursements and funds of the schools will be recorded in this special book and will be available for review by the members of the society who will have access whenever they desire . . . Anyone desirous of participating in the work on the society is invited to do so.[5]

According to Dowlatabadi, the initial members consisted of himself, Mahmud Khan Ehtesham al-Saltaneh, Ja'far Qoli Khan Nayyer al-Molk (minister of sciences and principal of the *Dar al-Fonun*), Mahmud Khan

---

[3]Fakhr al-Din Roshdiyyeh, *Zendeginameh-ye Pir-e Ma'aref-e Roshdiyyeh: Bonyangozar-e Farhang-e Novvin-e Iran* (Tehran: Hirmand, 1370), p. 43; and A. Anwar, "Anjoman-e Ma'aref," *Encyclopaedia Iranica*, vol. 2, p. 87, respectively.

[4]See Ehtesham al-Saltaneh, *Khaterat*, p. 325. Fakhr al-Din Roshdiyyeh believes that the name was initially "*Anjoman-e Omana-ye Madraseh-ye Roshdiyyeh va Ta'asis-e Makateb*" which is in keeping with his assertion that the *anjoman* was founded by Mirza Hasan Roshdiyyeh; see *Zendeginameh*, p. 43.

[5]Abd al-Hosayn Khan Sepehr, *Mer'at al-Vaqaye'-e Mozaffari va Yaddashtha-ye Malek al-Movarekhayn*, ed. 'Abd al-Hosayn Nava'i (Tehran: Zarin, 1328), pp. 264-65.

Meftah al-Molk, Mehdi Khan Momtahen al-Dowleh, 'Ali Khan Nazem al-'Olum, and Mohandes al-Mamalek.[6] Ehtesham al-Saltaneh records Mirza Hasan Roshdiyyeh as having also been present, and omits mention of Nayyer al-Molk.[7] According to Dowlatabadi, Ehtesham al-Saltaneh attempted to exclude the minister of sciences as a member, hoping thereby to keep the *anjoman* away from direct control by the government, although Amin al-Dowleh insisted that he be included.[8] The number of members rose rapidly in the first few weekly meetings and by the fall of 1898 comprised about thirty individuals.[9] Already at the second meeting of the *anjoman*, Mirza 'Ali Khan Moshir al-Dowleh Kashani (editor of the *Iran* newspaper), Shaykh Mehdi 'Abd al-Robabadi Shams al-Ulama, and Mohammad Hosayn Khan Adib al-Dowleh (director of the *Dar al Fonun*) joined the *Anjoman-e Ma'aref*.[10] Many of the members were employed in the Ministry of Foreign Affairs. Others included doctors, merchants (Hajj Mohammad Hasan Amin al-Zarb and his son Hajj Hosayn Aqa joined at the sixth meeting), and others interested in furthering educational reform in Iran.

Ehtesham al-Saltaneh was made the chairman of the *anjoman*, although Nayyer al-Molk was the *ex officio* head (*ra'is*) in his position as minister of sciences. At the sixth meeting, Ehtesham al-Saltaneh gave Meftah al-Molk the position of treasurer in order to placate his concerns over Ehtesham al-Saltaneh's predominance.[11] In February/March 1899, after Ehtesham al-Saltaneh resigned from the *anjoman*, Mirza Mehdi Khan Momtahen al-Dowleh was elected superintendent.[12]

Immediately after its establishment, members of the *anjoman* concentrated on raising funds. Ehtesham al-Saltaneh, as directed by Amin al-Dowleh, collected donations. Amin al-Dowleh himself

---

[6]Dowlatabadi, *Hayat-e Yahya*, vol. I, pp. 188-89.

[7]Ehtesham al-Saltaneh, *Khaterat*, p. 325. Anwar records the initial membership as consisting of Ehtesham al-Saltaneh, Dowlatabadi, Nayyer al-Molk, Meftah al-Molk, Nazem al-'Olum, Momtahen al-Dowleh and 'Abbas Khan Mohandesbashi; see Anwar, " Anjoman-e Ma'aref," p. 87.

[8]Dowlatabadi, *Hayat-e Yahya*, vol. I, p. 188.

[9]Ibid, vol. I, p. 223. For the names of members, see Dowlatabadi; and Husayn Mahbubi-Ardakani, *Tarikh-e Mo'assesat-e Tamaddoni-ye Jadid dar Iran* 2 vols. (Tehran: Tehran University Press, 1975), vol. I, p. 370.

[10]Dowlatabadi, *Hayat-e Yahya*, vol. I, p. 190.

[11]Ibid, p. 192.

[12]Sepehr, *Mer'at*, p. 328.

contributed 12,000 *tomans*. Mozaffar al-Din Shah pledged 2,000 *tomans*. Ehtesham al-Saltaneh then requested donations from various ministers, wealthy princes, merchants and other prominent individuals. Ehtesham al-Saltaneh records that nearly everyone who was approached pledged an amount to the *anjoman*, and that even members of the ulama promised 10 or 15 *tomans*.[13]

As the champion of the New schools, the *anjoman* had a twofold agenda. First, to establish and regularize a universal system of education. This new system was to be entirely independent of the traditional system and was to comprise all levels of education, from primary to advanced. This system of New schools, despite its organizational and educational shortcomings, constituted a direct bid to replace the existing *maktab-madraseh* system. No attempt was made by the educational activists to reform the traditional system, or even to effect a limited integration of the two systems at any level. As discussed in chapter V, the synthesis of the traditional and European-style curriculums implicitly marginalized the traditional system. Although the number of students at the New schools remained limited compared with those at traditional *maktabs*, the ultimate aim of the *Anjoman-e Ma'aref* was to provide for universal, compulsory education.

The second component in the *Anjoman-e Ma'aref*'s agenda was the direct oversight of all European-style schools. The *anjoman* attempted, albeit with limited success, to control the organization, administration, and funding of the New schools. It also intended to impose educational guidelines concerning the curriculum and texts used in the schools. The *Anjoman-e Ma'aref*, as conceived by many educational reformers, was to serve as a foundation on which to build the larger reform movement.[14]

---

[13]On initial donations to the *anjoman*, see Ehtesham al-Saltaneh, *Khaterat*, pp. 325-26; Fakhr al-Din Roshdiyyeh, *Zendeginameh*, p. 44; and Dowlatabadi, *Hayat-e Yahya*, vol. I, p. 189.

[14]In their memoirs, two central figures in the *Anjoman-e Ma'aref*, Yahya Dowlatabadi and Ehtesham al-Saltaneh, repeatedly emphasize this as a primary goal. See *Hayat-e Yahya*, vol. I, pp. 198, 221, 338; and Ehtesham al-Saltaneh, *Khaterat*, p. 330, respectively.

The Establishment of Perimeters

During its existence, the *Anjoman-e Ma'aref* went through a number of different periods of activity and leadership. The first period roughly coincides with Amin al-Dowleh's tenure as prime minister. During this time, he provided active support for the *anjoman* and for educational reform in general. He called for wide cooperation in furthering New education and attempted to solicit the participation of a larger segment of the population in supporting reform than had previously been the case. He also frequently reminded Mozaffar al-Din Shah of the importance of education, the freedom of the press, and other reform measures designed to increase the efficiency and power of the central government.[15]

This period witnessed the attempt of the *anjoman* to establish the perimeters of its activity. A daily newspaper, *Kholasat al-Havades*, was published by the *Anjoman-e Ma'aref* in order to promote the goals of the *anjoman* amongst the reading public. Members of the court and the government, particularly the minister of sciences, were displeased about its publication. They were unable to prohibit it, however, because, according to Ehtesham al-Saltaneh, it was distributed daily by students of the New schools on their way home. In addition, the paper enjoyed the support of the British minister, who ensured that daily news received by telegraph from Europe was published in the paper. Despite its popularity, the *Kholasat al-Havades* ceased publication after a short while.[16]

In the same period, a publication house, the *Sherkat-e Tab'*, was set up in order to compose, translate, and print school textbooks and other works. Because the *anjoman* was unable to reach an agreement over the management and operations of the the *Sherkat-e Tab'*, it was established

---

[15]On Amin al-Dowleh's aims with regard to educational reform, see Mirza 'Ali Khan Amin al-Dowleh, *Khaterat-e Siyasi-ye Mirza 'Ali Khan Amin al-Dowleh*, (ed) Hafez Farman-Farmaian (Ketabha-ye Iran, 1341), p. 268; and Dowlatabadi, *Hayat-e Yahya*, vol. I, pp. 182-83. On Amin al-Dowleh's reform program, see Shaul Bakhash, *Iran: Monarchy, Bureaucracy and Reform Under the Qajars, 1858-96* (London: Ithaca Press, 1978), pp. 211-22, 233.

[16]The only mention of the *Kholasat al-Havades* is in Ehtesham al-Saltaneh, *Khaterat*, pp. 328-9. No mention is made again later in his memoirs and it can be assumed that the paper ceased publication by the time Ehtesham al-Saltaneh resigned from the *Anjoman-e Ma'aref* in November/December 1898.

outside the auspices of the *Anjoman-e Ma'aref*, although it was run by members of the *anjoman*. Proponents of the publishing house included Dowlatabadi and Hajj Mohammad Hasan Amin al-Zarb. During the several years that the *Sherkat-e Tab'* maintained operations, it published books on European history, science and literature, in addition to many textbooks for use in Iran.[17] During the premiership of Amin al-Dowleh plans were made to establish a national library and 1000 volumes were collected, although the formal establishment of the library was not accomplished until after Amin al-Dowleh's dismissal from office.[18] The *Anjoman-e Ma'aref* was also successful in founding a school for adults, the *Akaber*, at this time.

An attempt was also made to expand the activities of the *Anjoman-e Ma'aref* into the provinces. A company was established, the proceeds from which were intended to go toward the promotion of education outside of Tehran. Ehtesham al-Saltaneh, the main sponsor behind this company, hoped that the *Anjoman-e Ma'aref* would thereby be able to create a financial and organizational power base to support educational reform. However, the company was soon disbanded due to lack of governmental support.[19]

Many of the problems which eventually led to the dissolution of the *Anjoman-e Ma'aref* were present from the outset. Rivalry, both personal and professional, was prevalent among the most active members of the *anjoman*. Problems of this nature first emerged with regard to Mirza Hasan Roshdiyyeh. Amin al-Dowleh, having invited Mirza Hasan Roshdiyyeh to Tehran to establish a school there, arranged for the school to be partially financed by the government, in addition to *Anjoman-e Ma'aref* funds. Mirza Hasan himself was paid a government salary. At the first official meeting of the *Anjoman-e Ma'aref*, the huge expense of the *Roshdiyyeh* school was discussed. Ehtesham al-Saltaneh and others at the *anjoman* were concerned about the school's spending and requested that Mirza Hasan reduce the school's budget and stop providing free lunches to the students and teachers. Mirza Hasan's

---

[17]Dowlatabadi, *Hayat-e Yahya*, vol. I, p. 201; and Fakhr al-Din Roshdiyyeh, *Zendeginameh*, p. 47.

[18]Ehtesham al-Saltaneh, *Khaterat*, pp. 327 and 239; and Dowlatabadi, *Hayat-e Yahya*, vol. I, p. 222.

[19]On the "*sherkat*" and Ehtesham al-Saltaneh's ambitions, see his *Khaterat*, pp. 329-30. See also Dowlatabadi, *Hayat-e Yahya*, vol. I, p. 203.

refusal to accede to these requests led to his ouster from the *anjoman*. At the fifth meeting it was decided that in order not to alienate Amin al-Dowleh, who supported Mirza Hasan, *anjoman* funds would be used to establish additional schools. In this way, the *Roshdiyyeh* school would not be the sole beneficiary of *anjoman* support, and the *anjoman* would have more influence in the management of other New schools.[20] At the eighth meeting of the *Anjoman-e Ma'aref*, Mirza Hasan was accepted back into the organization. Shortly thereafter, the *anjoman* assisted with the establishment of the *Elmiyyeh* school.

Ehtesham al-Saltaneh's authority as chairman of the *anjoman* was challenged by Nayyer al-Molk, in his position as minister of sciences. In May 1898, Nayyer al-Molk announced that anyone wanting to place an advertisement in the official newspaper regarding the establishment of schools must first obtain his signature.[21] This announcement, coming only days after the inauguration of Ehtesham al-Saltaneh's school, the *Elmiyyeh*, was a clear bid for control over any educational initiatives— whether by members of the *anjoman* or by non-affiliated individuals. However, due to his position as prime minister and the personal interest he took in the activities of the *anjoman*, Amin al-Dowleh remained the most influential governmental figure during his tenure in office.

Amin al-Dowleh and the reforms he sponsored engendered serious opposition amongst a number of important groups. In particular, government and military officials, courtiers and some members of the ulama coalesced in opposition to Amin al-Dowleh.[22] Alarmed at his attempts to restrict the traditional system of paybacks and the purchase of offices, opponents represented Amin al-Dowleh to Mozaffar al-Din Shah as an enemy of the state and the country. Many opponents also pointed to Amin al-Dowleh's projected loan from the British as essentially a step towards selling control of the country to foreigners.

---

[20]Mahbubi-Ardakani, *Tarikh-e Mo'assesat*, vol. I, p. 38; and Dowlatabadi, *Hayat-e Yahya*, vol. I, pp. 189-91.

[21]Sepehr, *Mer'at*, p. 239.

[22]A contemporary historian and court chronicler cites these groups as constituting the most vocal opposition to Amin al-Dowleh. See Sepehr, *Mer'at*, p. 237. According to Bakhash, court intrigue against Amin al-Dowleh was led by 'Abd al-Hosayn Mirza Farmanfarma and amongst the ulama by Mirza Hasan Ashtiyani. See Shaul Bakhash, "Evolution of Qajar Bureaucracy: 1779-1879," *Middle Eastern Studies*, vol. 7 (1971), pp. 139-68.

Hajj Shaykh Mohsen Khan Moshir al-Dowleh informed the shah that if Amin al-Dowleh were permitted to remain in his position as prime minister, he would surely bring down the Qajar monarchy. Opponents also presented Amin al-Dowleh's support of educational reform and the establishment of New schools as an attempt to enlighten the populace and make them aware of European principles of thought concerning freedom. The New schools, they argued, promoted civil law and constitutionalism and would eventually upset the foundations of the Iranian monarchy.[23]

According to Dowlatabadi, the ulama opposed Amin al-Dowleh because he tried to limit their power vis-à-vis the government. It was also the case that a number of religious seminary students (*tollab*) were put out of work as private tutors by the establishment of New schools. Some ulama were further incensed by the friction amongst themselves that resulted from Amin al-Dowleh's collaboration in the educational arena with such other ulama as Shaykh Hadi Najmabadi.[24]

Ulama opposition to Amin al-Dowleh was articulated in terms of the protection of Islam, although it certainly had as much to do with the ulama's vested interests in the educational system and status quo. Mirza Hasan Ashtiyani, one of the most prominent religious figures in Tehran, believed that the New schools would introduce irreligion (*la mazhabi*) and would lead to the corruption of religious beliefs.[25] In February 1898 a number of ulama in Tabriz preached against Amin al-Dowleh. They maintained that he would destroy Islam and would implement European law in Iran that they claimed was incompatible with the system of life pensions (*mostamarri*).[26] Clearly the ulama opposition equated the disruption of established governmental and social institutions with an attack on Islam. By presenting themselves as the guarantors of religion, the ulama also established themselves as the defenders of the social and political status quo. In June/July 1898 Mozaffar al-Din Shah, disappointed with Amin al-Dowleh's inability to obtain a foreign loan guarantee, removed him from office.

---

[23]Fakhr al-Din Roshdiyyeh, *Zendeginameh*, pp. 56-57.
[24]Dowlatabadi, *Hayat-e Yahya*, vol. I, p. 207.
[25]Fakhr al-Din Roshdiyyeh, *Zendeginameh*, p. 56.
[26]Sepehr, *Mer'at*, p. 224.

Loss of Autonomy

The second period of the *Anjoman-e Ma'aref* begins with the granting of the position of prime minister to Amin al-Soltan following Amin al-Dowleh's dismissal. Educational reformers, concerned at the downfall of their ardent supporter, were not sure of his successors' level of commitment to educational reform. The *Anjoman-e Ma'aref*'s membership declined. Once Amin al-Soltan showed himself to be amenable to the *anjoman*'s educational efforts, however, plans to establish additional New schools proceeded.[27] Indeed, this period witnessed the founding of five New schools (*Sharaf, Eftetahiyyeh, Mozaffariyyeh, Madraseh-ye Danesh, Dabestan-e Danesh*).

Soon after Amin al-Soltan's appointment as prime minister, the *Anjoman-e Ma'aref* drew up internal regulations in an attempt to stem the rising level of internal dispute.[28] Factionalism, however, intensified in the *Anjoman-e Ma'aref* in this period. With the dismissal of Amin al-Dowleh, his supporters rallied around Mirza Hasan Roshdiyyeh and the *Roshdiyyeh* school against Amin al-Soltan. Pamphlets (*shabnameh*) criticizing Amin al-Soltan were distributed in Tehran and left in the palace for the shah to read. In addition to calling for the dismissal of Amin al-Soltan, the *shabnamehs* demanded the establishment of a national consultative council (*majles-e showra-ye melli*). For fear of retribution on the part of Amin al-Soltan, parents withdrew their children from the *Roshdiyyeh* school. From a position of exile in Qom, Mirza Hasan Roshdiyyeh requested that Mozaffar al-Din Shah allow *Roshdiyyeh* school graduation certificates to be awarded on his behalf by Amin al-Soltan. Amin al-Soltan's forced appearance at the ceremony reassured parents, who then sent their sons back to the school.[29] Despite the tentative truce, however, the *Roshdiyyeh* school remained the center of the Amin al-Dowleh faction which opposed Amin al-Soltan, thereby increasing tensions within the *anjoman*.

Rivalry between Ehtesham al-Saltaneh, then deputy general (*mo'aven-e koll*) of the Ministry of Foreign Affairs, and two of his subordinates at the ministry, Meftah al-Molk and Momtahen al-Dowleh, was played out

---

[27]Dowlatabadi, *Hayat-e Yahya*, vol. I, pp. 214, 221-22.
[28]Ibid, p. 222.
[29]Fakhr al-Din Roshdiyyeh, *Zendeginameh*, pp. 90-91, 94-97.

in the arena of the *anjoman*. Following Ehtesham al-Saltaneh's sponsorship of the establishment of the *Elmiyyeh* school in April/May 1898, the
Anjoman-e Ma'aref moved its headquarters there. In September/October
of the same year, Meftah al-Molk, with the assistance of Momtahen
al-Dowleh, sponsored the establishment of the *Eftetahiyyeh* school and
attempted to have the *anjoman* meet at his school. Competition between
Ehtesham al-Saltaneh and Meftah al-Molk was further enhanced by the
fact that Meftah al-Molk refused to follow *anjoman* guidelines in the
operation of the *Eftetahiyyeh*.[30] The *Anjoman-e Ma'aref* split into two rival
camps surrounding Ehtesham al-Saltaneh and Meftah al-Molk, with
each camp supporting their candidate for leadership of the *anjoman*.[31]

Ehtesham al-Saltaneh's conflict with Nayyer al-Molk also assumed
greater proportions as Amin al-Soltan and Meftah al-Molk's faction
within the *anjoman* allied with Nayyer al-Molk against him. On one level,
the friction was that of personalities. However, at the root of their
conflict was a dispute over the authority of the *anjoman* versus that of
government officials: the prime minister and the minister of sciences.

The conflict intensified when Ehtesham al-Saltaneh requested that
the *Dar al Fonun* be placed under the purview of the *Anjoman-e Ma'aref*.
As Minister of Sciences and head of the *Dar al Fonun*, Nayyer al-Molk
considered this as an attempt to usurp his prerogatives with regard to
education. Opponents of Ehtesham al-Saltaneh, both in the *Anjoman-e
Ma'aref* and the Ministry of Foreign Affairs, cooperated in an attempt to
oust him from control of the *anjoman*. Nayyer al-Molk, in collusion with
Meftah al-Molk and Momtahen al-Dowleh, wrote to the shah charging
that the *anjoman* under Ehtesham al-Saltaneh had overstepped its
authority. Opponents of Ehtesham al-Saltaneh's at the Ministry of
Foreign Affairs reported to the shah that Ehtesham al-Saltaneh was
planning to lead a revolt against the monarchy and establish a
republic.[32] Attempts to discredit political opponents often took the
form of accusations of anti-monarchical sentiments. Nonetheless, any

---

[30]Dowlatabadi, *Hayat-e Yahya*, vol. I, pp. 197-98; and Mahbubi-Ardakani, *Tarikh-e Mo'assesat*, vol. I, pp. 370-71.
[31]Supporters of Ehtesham al-Saltaneh included: E'temad al-Saltaneh, Nazem al-Attiba, Mohammad Isma'il Khan Ajudanbashi, Hajj Shaykh Mehdi Sharif Kashani, and Dowlatabadi. Supporters of Meftah al-Molk included: Momtahen al-Dowleh, Shaykh Mehdi Shams al-Ulama, and Mo'tamen al-Attiba. See Dowlatabadi, *Hayat-e Yahya*, vol. I, p. 216.
[32]Ehtesham al-Saltaneh, *Khaterat*, p. 333.

challenge to the authority of a minister, by extension, represented a challenge to that of the shah himself. As the ultimate arbiter of all disputes, in November/December 1898 Mozaffar al-Din Shah issued a royal edict resolving the conflict in favor of the minister of sciences:

> Nayyer al-Molk, Minister of Sciences and Education, as he has established national elementary and middle schools and a national library to the glory of God and [has provided] the best supervision and [he] and the *Anjoman-e Ma'aref* have achieved many advances, and have been the cause of our pleasure, and I hope that God willing [the situation] will become better and more perfect day by day. On my behalf this matter must be given supervision and special attention. In truth, the head of this administration and council is the special right of ourselves, the sovereign. Because of this, you [Nayyer al-Molk], who are a supremely experienced person and a statesman (*dowlatkhah*) without personal motives and who is fully aware of the domestic and foreign situation . . . I give you the particular position . . . of total control in the organization of the schools and the *Anjoman-e Ma'aref* and the finances of the society and the maintenance of respect of the members of it in their works . . . the prime minister, without delay, will be informed of the workings of the society.[33]

With the placement of the *Anjoman-e Ma'aref* under the aegis of the minister of sciences, the *anjoman* as a spontaneous, independent body ceased to exist. In its place was established a quasi-governmental organization. In addition, all the New schools established up to this point were placed under the auspices of the minister of sciences, thereby formally ending their nominal independence. According to Ehtesham al-Saltaneh, Nayyer al-Molk privately promised Mozaffar al-Din Shah to gradually dismantle the *anjoman*, the schools, and all the other projects which he considered to be a cause of strife.[34]

Nayyer al-Molk, exercising his new prerogatives, insisted that the *Anjoman-e Ma'aref* now served no purpose and should be dissolved. However, given that Ehtesham al-Saltaneh resigned from the *anjoman* and departed from Tehran, Nayyer al-Molk agreed to reconstitute the *anjoman* at his own home in December 1898.[35]

---

[33]Sepehr, *Mer'at*, p. 329.

[34]Ehtesham al-Saltaneh, *Khaterat*, p. 338.

[35]Dowlatabadi, *Hayat-e Yahya*, vol. I, pp. 232-33, 237. On plots to kill Ehtesham al-Saltaneh and his de facto exile in Kordestan, see Ehtesham al-Saltaneh, *Khaterat*, pp. 207, 336-37, 340, 344-45.

The ouster of Ehtesham al-Saltaneh as chairman of the *Anjoman-e Ma'aref* signified the demarcation of the perimeters of activity of the *anjoman*. A number of the *anjoman*'s projects collapsed after Ehtesham al-Saltaneh's departure. The library and adult school (the *Akaber*) both closed and the translation center was taken over by the publication society run by Dowlatabadi and others.[36] After Ehtesham al-Saltaneh, no other leader of the *Anjoman-e Ma'aref* was as ambitious with regard to spreading the *anjoman*'s activities to other areas of Iran. Most important, the royal *farman* placing the *anjoman* under the control of the Ministry of Sciences marked the delimitation of the *anjoman* within the boundaries of governmental control and subjected it to the initiative and goals of both the minister of sciences and the monarch himself.

Dissolution

The reestablishment of the *Anjoman-e Ma'aref* in December 1898 marks the beginning of the third phase of its existence. With the exception of two or three individuals, the new *anjoman* enjoyed a similar membership as its predecessor.[37] Ehtesham al-Saltaneh's rival, Meftah al-Molk, with the backing of Amin al-Soltan, was made chairman of the new *anjoman*. The first few meetings were held at different schools. Subsequently, the *anjoman* met at Nayyer al-Molk's house.

In order to raise sufficient funds to establish additional New schools, Meftah al-Molk organized a benefit party for the *anjoman* in the garden of the *Eftetahiyyeh* school in March/April 1899. The "garden party" (*garden parti*), as it became known, generated funds to permit the establishment of many New schools. In April/May of the same year, two New schools were founded with the assistance of *anjoman* funds: the *Adab* and *Ebteda'iyyeh*. In addition, two other schools were established by members of the *anjoman*, but without the benefit of *anjoman* funds: the *Sadat* and *Aqadasiyyeh*. The *Madraseh-ye Danesh* was established in this period by Mirza Mohammad Khan Namjavani, who agreed to abide by *Anjoman-e Ma'aref* guidelines.[38] Before the end of the

---

[36]Dowlatabadi, *Hayat-e Yahya*, vol. I, pp. 239-40.

[37]Ibid, p. 240.

[38]Dowlatabadi, *Hayat-e Yahya*, vol, I, p. 241; and Mahbubi-Ardakani, *Tarikh-e Mo'assesat*, vol. I, p. 386.

year, the *Tarbiyat*, *Kherad*, *Sa'adat* and *Dabestan-e Danesh* schools were also founded, some with financial assistance from the *Anjoman-e Ma'aref*.

The "garden party" aroused the furor of opponents of the New schools, who pointed to the European-style party as indicative of the anti-Iranian nature of the schools themselves.[39] At the same time, the reputation of the *Anjoman-e Ma'aref* was tarnished by newspaper reports concerning the misuse of *anjoman* funds by Meftah al-Molk.[40] By July 1900, the *anjoman* existed in name only.

Interregnum

The following spring, Nayyer al-Molk agreed to reconstitute the *anjoman* with those members who had previously supported him. The first session of the new *Anjoman-e Ma'aref* met on May 1, 1901 at Nayyer al-Molk's home.[41] In addition to the minister of sciences, who presided as the head of the *anjoman*, other members included his son Reza Qoli Khan Mokhbar al-Saltaneh, Moshir al-Molk and Dowlatabadi. At the second meeting of the new *anjoman*, a proposal was made by Dowlatabadi to eliminate the distinction between state and private schools and place them all under the oversight of the *Anjoman-e Ma'aref*. It was agreed that the four state schools (*Elmiyyeh*, *Eftetahiyyeh*, *Sharaf*, *Mozaffariyyeh*) and the four that Dowlatabadi himself was in charge of (*Adab*, *Kamaliyyeh*, *Dabestan-e Danesh*, *Sa'adat*) would be placed under the control of the *Anjoman-e Ma'aref*. Other schools that operated outside the purview of the *anjoman* were invited to place themselves under the control of the *anjoman*, although the *anjoman* had no means of forcing compliance.[42] Apart from this attempt to establish universal guidelines for the New schools, no other reforms were undertaken at this time.

---

[39]'Abu al-Hasan Bozorg Omid, *Az Mast keh bar Mast* (Tehran: Donya-ye Ketab, 1363, p. 95; Dowlatabadi, *Hayat-e Yahya*, vol. I, p. 242.

[40]Mahbubi-Ardakani, *Tarikh-e Mo'assesat*, vol. I, p. 373; Dowlatabadi, *Hayat-e Yahya*, vol. I, pp. 243-44.

[41]According to Mahbubi-Ardakani, the *anjoman* was reconstituted on May 9, 1901; see *Tarikh-e Mo'assesat*, vol. I, p. 374.

[42]Dowlatabadi, *Hayat-e Yahya*, vol. I, pp. 286-88.

Structural Reform

In October 1901, Amin al-Soltan took over control of the *anjoman*, thereby inaugurating the fifth and final phase of the *Anjoman-e Ma'aref*. Amin al-Soltan called together a meeting of approximately thirty ministers and other individuals. At the "*Majles-e Park*," named because of the outdoor meeting place, the prime minister criticized Nayyer al-Molk's direction of the Ministry of Sciences. He also announced that the situation of education in Iran was in need of reform. As a solution, Amin al-Soltan proposed two goals. First, he called for a Ministry of Sciences (*'Olum*) with an attached consultative council (*majles-e mash-verat*). Second, the Ministry of Education should be constituted like its European counterparts. To this end, a European code of regulations (*nezamnameh*) should be translated and adopted for use in Iran.[43]

Shortly thereafter, the shah signed the regulations prepared by the minister of sciences. The Ministry of Education was combined with the Ministry of Sciences to form a new, expanded ministry (*Vezarat-e 'Olum va Ma'aref*). According to these new stipulations, all New schools, with the exception of three, were placed under the control of the new Ministry of Sciences and Education. The exceptions were: 1) the *Madraseh-ye 'Olum-e Siyasi*, which remained under the control of the Ministry of Foreign Affairs headed by Moshir al-Dowleh; 2) the *Madraseh-ye Nezami*, which was overseen by the Ministry of War under Vajiehollah Mirza Sepahsalar; and 3) the recently established *Madraseh-ye Falahat*, which was considered the domain of the governor of Tehran, Ayn al-Dowleh.[44] The three schools that were not placed under the auspices of the Ministry of Sciences and Education were all secondary and/or specialized training schools. It is also significant that control of two of the schools, the *Madraseh-ye Nezami* and the *Madraseh-ye Falahat*, remained the prerogative of Amin al-Soltan's greatest political adversaries.

In December 1901, Amin al-Soltan created the High State Consultative Council of Education (*Majles-e Showra-ye 'Ali-ye Ma'aref*) for

---

[43]Dr. Schneider, the French court physician and ranking member of the *Alliance Française*, assisted in the translation of the European regulations. The only account of the "*Majles-e Park*" is found in Dowlatabadi, *Hayat-e Yahya*, vol. I, pp. 298-99.

[44]Ibid, vol. I, p. 299.

the purpose of making recommendations concerning primary, secondary and higher education in Iran. The members of this council were personally recommended by Nayyer al-Molk and confirmed for inclusion by Amin al-Soltan. Iranian members included: Nayyer al-Molk, Mokhbar al-Saltaneh, Mirza Karim Khan Sardar Mokaram, Mirza Mehdi Khan Za'im al-Dowleh (editor of the Cairene *Hekmat* newspaper who was briefly in Tehran), several administrators and teachers from the *Dar al Fonun* and the *Madraseh-ye 'Olum-e Siyasi*, and Dowlatabadi. European members included: Doctor Schneider (the shah's French personal physician), Joseph Hanbeck (the Belgian advisor to the Ministry of Justice), and Monsieur Washer (the Belgian head of the *Madraseh-ye Falahat*).[45] Nayyer al-Molk, as the minister of sciences and education, was placed in charge of the council.

As a result of concern among some council members concerning the inclusion of Europeans in the Consultative Council, it was decided to subdivide the council into two parts. The general council would consist of all members, and the European members would be considered honorary. A smaller, governing council was also established whose members were to be selected from among Iranian general council members only. The regulations for the council, following their ratification, were published in both Persian and French.

The Consultative Council on Education was responsible for wide-reaching educational reforms. Problems addressed included the preponderance of elementary schools relative to middle schools, government funding for education, the dearth of textbooks, and the lack of established official guidelines regulating the establishment of new schools.

The first measures instituted by the Council involved a restructuring of the schools in an attempt to develop a comprehensive educational system comprising all levels of schooling. In order to achieve this, the Council determined that four of the new elementary schools should be transformed into middle (*motevasseteh*) schools. Accordingly, the elementary sections of the *Elmiyyeh* and *Adab* schools were eliminated and the middle sections enhanced. The *Islam* and *Eftetahiyyeh* schools were combined and made into a middle school, and the *Kherad* school was merged with one of the European schools and also made into a

---

[45]Ibid, p. 301.

middle school. The *Kamaliyyeh* school, on the other hand, was made exclusively into a primary school.

Following these structural changes, the Council enjoyed the oversight of eight elementary and four middle schools. The annual educational allowance received from the government was 6,000 *tomans*, which the Council found insufficient. Dowlatabadi reported that many students who were unable to pay school fees were subsidized by himself and other individuals, but that nonetheless the schools were consistently under funded.[46]

The Council also took measures to regulate the establishment and operations of new schools. In December 1901 the general membership of the Council decided that the Ministry of Sciences and Education would thereafter be responsible for determining the right to establish new schools. It also would have the duty to determine the nature of courses and regulations of both state (*doulati*) and private (*melli*) schools. Members of the Council hoped that the Ministry of Sciences and Education would fulfill its responsibility in this regard and enact laws determining the establishment and operation of all schools, thereby ending the chaos (*harj va marj*) which prevailed. The minister of sciences and education, Nayyer al-Molk, never succeeded in accomplishing this task.[47]

The Council also established subcommittees for the purpose of writing needed textbooks. Special groups of experts in geometry, mathematics, Arabic, and Persian literature were formed in order to write textbooks for use in middle and advanced schools.[48]

Despite the structural reforms and the attempts at creating an organized educational system, guidelines regulating the establishment and operation of schools still had not been completed a year later. According to Dowlatabadi, chaos reigned in the schools.[49] All reform measures were on hold pending Mozaffar al-Din Shah's return from Europe. Educational activists hoped that the shah, having been exposed to European government and social advances, would return to champion the cause of educational reform. Students from the New schools were sent to greet Mozaffar al-Din Shah on his return to

---

[46]Ibid, p. 303.
[47]Ibid, pp. 303-4, 306.
[48]Ibid, p. 304.
[49]Ibid, p. 306.

Tehran in early November 1902. It became obvious to all, however, that neither the court nor the shah were committed to reform in Iran. Many educational activists were frustrated by lack of monarchical support and dismayed at the continuing confusion that persisted in the New schools.[50]

In late March 1903, the Council made a renewed attempt at improving and regularizing the New schools. A small committee was formed to resolve issues which were first undertaken with the establishment of the Council on Education in 1901, but which continued to plague the New schools— namely, the distinction between state and private schools, revenues, and the jurisdiction of the Ministry of Sciences and Education over the New schools. This committee consisted of Yahya Dowlatabadi, Nayyer al-Molk, his son, and Mirza Hasan Khan Moshir al-Molk.

Despite previous attempts by the *Anjoman-e Ma'aref* and the Council on Education to unify all New schools under the direction of the Ministry of Sciences and Education, the schools remained divided according to supervision, funding, and the extent of control exerted by the government. At this time, the four schools directly under the supervision of the Ministry of Sciences and Education (*Elmiyyeh, Eftetahiyyeh, Sharaf, Mozaffariyyeh*) received no government funding, and were in worse condition than many private (*melli*) schools (such as *Kamaliyyeh, Islam,* and *Roshdiyyeh*). It was decided to end the distinction between state and private schools and place them all under the governance of the Ministry of Sciences and Education. All schools would be required to adhere to the educational guidelines established by the Ministry. To this end, the committee undertook to finalize work on the code of regulations (*nezamnameh*) which had remained incomplete since first begun in 1901.

The ministry would also be responsible for determining the necessary revenues for each school based on the number of students in attendance and the number of paying versus free students enrolled. In order to encourage the private schools to agree to these terms, the

---

[50]According to Dowlatabadi, Hajj Mohammad Hasan Amin al-Zarb asked whether he was not tired of pursuing educational work and achieving such limited results, and Mokhbar al-Saltaneh returned from Europe convinced that it was hopeless to pursue educational reform. See *Hayat-e Yahya*, vol. I., pp. 307-8.

Council stipulated that only those schools under the control of the Ministry of Sciences and Education would receive funds from the government and/or the Council of Education. Those schools which remained independent would receive no financial assistance, nor would they be considered New, "*madraseh*" schools, but rather would fall under the rubric of traditional, "*maktab*" schools.[51] However, this attempt at reform was handicapped by the fact that the ministry did not take measures to enforce compliance, and by the fact that the Council on Education did not agree to institute central control over the revenues. Individual school revenues therefore remained outside the control of the Council on Education, thereby frustrating any attempt to centralize and regulate the schools' finances.[52]

The committee proceeded to visit each school and recommend structural and financial reforms. As a result, the majority of private schools agreed to submit to Council reforms and to place themselves under the control of the Ministry of Sciences and Education, thereby remaining eligible for receiving government funding. However, the directors of the *Kherad, Aqadasiyyeh* and *Islam* schools refused to accept reforms suggested by the Council on Education. With the exception of the *Islam* school, directed by Mirza Sayyed Mohammad Tabataba'i, none of these schools received a government stipend.[53]

By August/September 1903 the success of the reform effort resulted in increased prestige for the Council on Education. Membership grew so much that the Council moved from the home of Nayyer al-Molk and established offices in the old library of the *Dar al Fonun*. The Council began to articulate additional concerns related to educational reform in general. For example, Dowlatabadi records that at the meetings, problems associated with absolutist government and the resulting lack of ministerial responsibility were discussed. It was at this time that the Council also deliberated on the necessity of establishing girls' schools.[54] Shortly thereafter, however, in September 1903, Amin al-Soltan was replaced by Ayn al-Dowleh in the position of

---

[51]Dowlatabadi, *Hayat-e Yahya*, vol. I, p. 311.

[52]The members of the Council on Education and Nayyer al-Molk were opposed to central control of school revenues, according to Dowlatabadi. See *Hayat-e Yahya*, vol. I, p. 312.

[53]Ibid, pp. 308-12.

[54]News concerning the Council of Education appeared in the newspaper *Tarbiyat*. See also Dowlatabadi, *Hayat-e Yahya*, vol. I, pp. 331-32.

prime minister and the Council on Education dissolved for the last time.

Conclusion

Despite its brief existence, the *Anjoman-e Ma'aref* and its successor, the High State Consultative Council of Education, represented a major turning point in the history of Iranian educational reform. The mere fact of the *Anjoman-e Ma'aref* having been established demonstrates a shift in reform initiative away from prime ministers and the court and towards the growing involvement of individuals from a broader socioeconomic spectrum. The goals and achievements of the *anjoman* are further testimony to the change in the educational reform agenda in the post-1890 period. Unlike earlier attempts to train a limited number of elites for government service, as illustrated by the establishment of the *Dar al Fonun* in Tehran and Tabriz, the *Anjoman-e Ma'aref* embodied the significantly broader educational and political goals of literacy and leadership.

Throughout its existence, the *anjoman* was beset with internal rivalry. This rivalry, particularly among the *anjoman*'s leadership, permeated the *anjoman* to such an extent that at times it disabled the *anjoman* completely. However, the problem of rivalries went beyond a clash of personalities. The problem was essentially the failure to resolve the boundaries of governmental authority. The *Anjoman-e Ma'aref* began as a private society which was not beholden to the government. Gradually, however, the *anjoman* became subsumed under the Ministry of Sciences and Education. This was due partly to the *anjoman*'s need for governmental funding, and partly because of the lack of established lines of authority with regard to the government. Competition between Ehtesham al-Saltaneh (as the head of the *anjoman*), and Nayyer al-Molk (the minister of sciences), was essentially the conflict between a private society (and therefore private initiative) and the state. This manifested itself again as the conflict between the *anjoman* leadership and Prime Minister Amin al-Soltan. This conflict was only resolved in November/ December 1898 when Mozaffar al-Din Shah himself decreed that the *Anjoman-e Ma'aref* was thereafter subject to the control of the minister of sciences. As a result, the *anjoman* lost its ability to make independent decisions. Its initiative was thereafter tied to that of the government.

The source of the problem lay in the nature of the Iranian administrative and governmental system. In the absence of clear lines of authority and ministerial responsibility, all actions and attempts at reform were subject to factionalism and uncertainty. All decisions ultimately depended on the will of the monarch in his capacity as the final arbiter. This resulted in the inability of the *anjoman*, or even of the minister of sciences and education, to establish and enforce boundaries of authority. As discussed above, both the *Anjoman-e Ma'aref* and the Council on Education repeatedly urged the New schools to submit to their directives. However, the *anjoman* never enjoyed the authority to enforce compliance.

At the heart of the matter was the question of monarchical commitment to reform. In a political climate of factionalism and informal government offices, the *anjoman* remained dependent on monarchical approbation. Even when supported by a reform-minded prime minister such as Amin al-Dowleh, the *anjoman* relied ultimately on Mozaffar al-Din Shah's willingness to comply with the prime minister's reform agenda. Amin al-Dowleh's fall from grace only served to confirm the fragility of governmental institutions vis-à-vis the shah. Reformers persisted in hoping for Mozaffar al-Din Shah's support, if not sponsorship for reform, but their hopes proved to be misplaced. The shah's lukewarm commitment to reform brought to the fore the structural weaknesses in the Iranian political system. No substantive change could occur without the full backing of the monarch. And the monarch was himself, after all, tremendously vested in the system and feared risking change. The ultimate failure of the *Anjoman-e Ma'aref* thus uncovered the weakness of the "catalyst" approach to reform, as it became obvious that educational change was insufficient to herald real social and political change. Piecemeal reform was discredited as a solution and by the end of the century, reformers realized that modernization could not proceed in the absence of an overall reform of governmental institutions and administration.

CHAPTER VII

MODERNIZATION, CULTURAL INTEGRITY AND
THE BATTLE FOR IRAN, 1860-1906

Ever since Crown Prince 'Abbas Mirza's *Nezam-e Jadid* reforms and the first dispatch of students abroad, the adoption of some form of European education had been acknowledged as an important means of achieving reform. Although limited at that time to the adoption of elements of technology and know-how, the awareness of the benefits of European-style education continued to increase amongst reform-minded individuals. The establishment of the *Dar al Fonun* in mid century highlighted many of the dangers and threats inherent in the adoption of European education to the cultural, social, intellectual, and political status quo. As a result, reformers were forced to defend the continued adoption of European-style education as the principal element of educational reform. With the establishment of the New schools in the latter part of the century, and the associated politicization and popularization of the reform movement, the conflict over modernization erupted into crisis. The modernization dilemma was recognized as such, and issues of cultural integrity, sources of knowledge, and the foundations of authority entered the arena of debate. Education was at the center of contestation over culture, identity and social leadership. As a result, both proponents and opponents of educational reform and modernization were forced to defend their positions. This process led to the clarification and articulation of positions and their ramifications that had previously been less than fully conscious and/or explicit. This chapter presents the debates surrounding educational reform in the 1860-1906 period in order to chart the shift in the reformers' educational objectives, and their connection to the larger reform agenda. The arguments used to legitimate educational reform, the solutions proposed to the modern-ization dilemma and the maintenance of cultural integrity, along with their weaknesses, will be revealed. This chapter will also discuss the cultural, social and intellectual ramifications of this debate, and the shifting boundaries of identity, knowledge and political legitimacy that resulted.

Reform from the Center

In practice, educational reform initiatives from the 1850s up until the establishment of the New schools in the Mozaffar al-Din period largely resembled those first undertaken by Amir Kabir at the outset of Naser al-Din Shah's reign. Apart from the establishment of the *Dar al Fonun*, educational reforms remained limited to those sponsored by Mirza Hosayn Khan: namely, the establishment of a number of secondary schools designed to better train future government administrators and diplomats to lead the nation in the increasingly internationalized political arena. Mirza Hosayn Khan believed in the necessity of reforming and revitalizing existing governmental institutions, and in establishing a centralized and smooth-running administration. He did not propose radical reform. However, the sense of urgency felt by reform-minded individuals in the 1870s was much stronger than that felt in Amir Kabir's day. Moreover, unlike Amir Kabir, Mirza Hosayn Khan reserved an important role for Europe in promoting reform in Iran. Although he recognized that European-style education was an important component of "progress" and "civilization," his conception of educational reform remained essentially elitist and thus limited to the training of governmental administrators.

Mirza Hosayn Khan's most important writings on reform were the diplomatic dispatches that he wrote during his diplomatic appointment in Istanbul from 1858 to 1870, prior to his tenure as prime minister. At that time, he witnessed first-hand the Ottoman reform movement in the *Tanzimat* period. He also established close personal acquaintances with leading Ottoman reformers. In his dispatches to Naser al-Din Shah and to the Ministry of Foreign Affairs, Mirza Hosayn Khan emphasized the urgency of implementing reform in Iran. He was aware of the danger threatening Iran in the form of European intervention and believed that only through a program of restrengthening could Iran hope to maintain her independence. Iran's present state of disorder and weakness, he thought, could serve as an excuse for foreign intervention.[1] In a letter to the minister of foreign affairs, he lamented

---

[1]Feridun Adamiyat, *Fekr-e Azadi va Moqademeh-ye Nehzat-e Mashrutiyat dar Iran* (Tehran, 1340), pp. 69-70.

the failure of the shah and the government to recognize the seriousness of Iran's situation:

> The reason for my sadness is that, not only have we made no effort in this direction [to carry out reforms], but we do not even believe there is anything wrong with our state or that our affairs need improvement. To the contrary, we believe that we have reached the highest degree of progress and have nothing to worry about.[2]

While other countries were advancing daily, Iran was languishing and would increasingly find herself left behind. Mirza Hosayn Khan complained: "for how long must we observe the progress of others" while Iran remains in her present condition.[3]

Mirza Hosayn Khan believed that the European-style reforms implemented in the Ottoman Empire should serve as a model for Iran. "Whatever is beneficial for the Ottoman Empire should without delay be adopted in Iran," he insisted.[4] The Ottoman Empire indicated the viability as well as the possibility of implementing European-style institutional reforms in an Islamic country. He also noted that European countries had done much to promote reform in the Ottoman Empire, and encouraged Iran to adopt a similar patron-client relationship with European powers in order to implement reform at home.[5]

Specifically, Mirza Hosayn identified the establishment of the rule of law and the end of arbitrary government as a prerequisite of modern "civilized" states. He also believed that Iran must develop its industry and commerce in order to become competitive with Europe.[6] In a diplomatic dispatch, Mirza Hosayn Khan enumerated the key reforms undertaken by the Ottomans:

> The development of the bases of education and sciences, the augmentation of the number of public schools, the Naval Academy, and the condition of the State Consultative Assembly that in the terminology of the French is

---

[2]Mirza Hosayn Khan to Foreign Minister Mirza Sa'id Khan, 24 Rabi' al-Awwal 1286 (July 5, 1869), quoted in Guity Nashat, *The Origins of Modern Reform in Iran, 1870-80* (Urbana: University of Illinois Press, 1982), p. 137.

[3]Quoted in Adamiyat, *Fekr-e Azadi*, p. 71.

[4]Adamiyat, *Fekr-e Azadi*, p. 68.

[5]Hamid Algar, *Mirza Malkum Khan: A Study in the History of Iranian Modernism* (Berkeley: University of California Press, 1973), p. 67; Adamiyat, *Fekr-e Azadi*, pp. 58-75, 113-4.

[6]Adamiyat, *Fekr-e Azadi*, pp. 59, 69.

called the "Conseil d'Etat" . . . these reforms are the cause of their good and well-being and will be the means of progress of the nation and state.[7]

This statement makes clear the great importance he placed on the effects of education. He urged Naser al-Din Shah to institute educational reform measures similar to those implemented in the Ottoman Empire. In addition to the above-mentioned "augmentation of the number of public schools," he advocated a better understanding and awareness of international affairs through the publication of newspapers.[8]

Mirza Hosayn Khan's view of the benefits of European-style education was limited. Despite his calls for a more informed populace and the spread of literacy and newspapers, his focus remained on the education of the governmental and administrative elite. He clearly believed that Iran's primary problem was her leadership. The focus of Mirza Hosayn Khan's proposed advances in education, therefore, was the training of qualified government cadres. He believed that the training of administrators and diplomats was the key to progress, without which all other measures would be wasted. In his opinion, government leaders were like doctors and the populace was their patient.[9] Mirza Hosayn Khan wrote that "what Iran needs more than anything else today are men with experience and know-how." He went on to elaborate that:

> A governor cannot know about his duties without education, a knowledge of world affairs, and study of the history of all states, so that he can learn from these pursuits the ways of those governments that have attained progress, have become important nations, have build great cities, and have transformed themselves into much better nations. In short, *individuals can with prudence transform a small nation into a strong and great nation.*[10] (Emphasis added.)

---

[7]Mirza Hosayn Khan, diplomatic dispatch dated 1 Safar 1284, quoted in Adamiyat, *Fekr-e Azadi*, p. 61.

[8]Adamiyat, *Fekr-e Azadi*, p. 69.

[9]The doctor-patient metaphor was common in reform circles in the Middle East and Central Asia and illustrates the conception of progress and just government as emanating from the quality of leadership, not the capabilities of the populace.

[10]Mirza Hosayn Khan dispatch to the Minister of Foreign Affairs, Mirza Sa'id Khan, 23 Rabi' al-Awwal 1283 (August 6, 1866), quoted in Nashat, *Origins*, p. 145.

In his view, Iran needed to develop a government elite that would lead the country to strength, prosperity, and "progress." As he himself proclaimed:

> The indicators of progress and education and aptitude of a country in the views of the European nations is limited to four matters: newspapers and the degree of information on domestic and foreign affairs; the level and quality of industries and commerce; *the dispatch of educated and informed diplomatic representatives [abroad] and their knowledge of international affairs*; and the capabilities of a modern army.[11] (Emphasis added.)

Mirza Hosayn Khan provided a specific example of the type of training for government officials that he had in mind. In describing a royal school in Istanbul established along the lines of a French lycée, he wrote:

> Until the men of the pen there [in the Ottoman Empire] have [learned] grammar and syntax, logic, literature, general history, history of the Ottoman Empire, writing (*tahrir*), arithmetic, politics (*politik*), and geography, their skills are not sufficient, they do not receive certification, and they are not able to fill any government position.[12]

He then proceeded to declare that those thus educated would certainly be the "cause of knowledge and arts and vision of a nation, and shortly skillful men will be created for the benefit of the state."[13] In order for Iran to participate in the new international order, Iranian diplomats and officials needed to be more informed of world affairs and experienced in new diplomatic skills. To this end, they needed to master subjects such as literature, history, arithmetic, geography, and most importantly, politics.[14] Mirza Hosayn Khan's conviction concerning the need for trained officials was manifested in his establishment of both a translation and a military school to prepare students for government service, as well as in his attempts to redress the decline of the *Dar al Fonun*.

---

[11]Mirza Hosayn Khan dispatch, quoted in Adamiyat, *Fekr-e Azadi*, p. 68.

[12]Mirza Hosayn Khan dispatch, 1283, quoted in Adamiyat, *Fekr-e Azadi*, p. 62.

[13]Mirza Hosayn Khan dispatch, 25 Ramazan 1284, quoted in Adamiyat, *Fekr-e Azadi*, p. 62.

[14]Some literature and arithmetic was sometimes taught in *maktabs*. In addition, literature was often studied by *madraseh* students informally *outside* of the *madraseh* itself.

211

His view of European-style education was ambivalent with regard to its benefits for women. On the one hand, he praised the efforts in the Ottoman Empire to educate women in new, European-style subjects. The first Ottoman schools established for this purpose, he wrote, enrolled 100 women between 15 and 35 years old. The curriculum consisted of ethics, history, geometry and French. On the other hand, Mirza Hosayn Khan believed that such education for women was inherently dangerous and threatened cultural mores since girls who received a European-style education would refuse to wear a veil.[15] In short, he was unsure of the long-term advantages of European-style education for women, given the obvious cultural repercussions.

Mirza Hosayn Khan's heavy emphasis on elite leadership as constituting the key to progress is within the bounds of traditional theories of kingship and justice. The benefits of European-style education, in his view, were not connected to social or political reform. Even his recognition of the benefits of the rule of law was not tied to the need for educational reform. His understanding of reform was also superficial in the sense that he perceived of it as the acquisition of elements of European civilization. Education was a symbol of progress towards modern (read European) "civilization."

In promoting European-style education, Mirza Hosayn Khan also assumed its separation from its historical and cultural contexts and thus its easy transferability to Iran. He was unaware of any potential problems of adaptation apart from the possible effects on women's self-identity. This is illustrated in his recommendations to Naser al-Din Shah that he visit Europe. Mirza Hosayn Khan hoped that if the shah traveled to Europe and witnessed the advancements there first-hand, he would understand the seriousness of the growing disparity between Europe and Iran. In the official newspaper *Iran*, Mirza Hosayn Khan explained that the shah's visit to Europe would:

> enable His Majesty to lead the country to the path of European progress and bestow upon the people those advantages of which the peoples of the East have been deprived for so long. His Majesty will be able to witness personally all those beneficial means used by European governments to ensure the welfare of their people and to protect their rights and prosperity. Observing these means, which are the basis of Europe's

---

[15] Adamiyat, *Fekr-e Azadi*, p. 62.

fantastic advancement, will assist His Majesty to *provide immediate solutions* for the prosperity of his own people.[16] (Emphasis added.)

In a letter to Naser al-Din Shah, Mirza Hosayn Khan wrote that upon the shah's return from Europe, "we can claim that Iran has entered the company of civilized states. In short, today Iran's future depends on this trip to Europe, and without a doubt it will bring about a thousand major benefits for Iran; nay, it will be the means of saving this land."[17] Mirza Hosayn Khan was principally concerned with conveying the urgency of reform. At issue was the progress of Iran and her reentry into the ranks of civilized countries. He did not address opposition to reform on a theoretical level, since despite the use of the language of Islam to discredit reform initiatives, he believed that this was tactical and primarily derived from the political, not cultural, effects of reform on the political status quo.

Education as a Panacea

The 1860-1906 period witnessed more radical educational reform proposals than those put forward by Mirza Hosayn Khan. In the form of essays, newspaper articles, and novels, reform-minded individuals discussed the benefits of European-style education, and attempted to resolve the problems of importing foreign institutions into Iran. The twin processes of politicization and popularization were echoed in the educational reform literature. As reform circles broadened to include government officials (particularly those associated with the Ministry of Foreign Affairs or who had traveled abroad) as well as merchants and members of the religious establishment, so too did the authors of reform texts. Moreover, these individuals evidenced more latitude in expressing opinions than did Mirza Hosayn Khan. This is partly due to their often ambivalent relationship to the government, and was certainly enhanced due to the relative laxity in censorship under Mozaffar al-Din Shah after 1896.

---

[16]Mirza Hosayn Khan, *Iran*, 15 Ramazan 1289 (December 17, 1872), quoted in Nashat, *Origins*, p. 138. Emphasis added.

[17]Mirza Hosayn Khan to Naser al-Din Shah, Ramazan 1289 (December 1872), Supplément Persan, Bibliotèque Nationale, Paris, quoted in Nashat, *Origins*, p. 140.

EDUCATION, RELIGION, AND THE DISCOURSE OF CULTURAL REFORM

European-style education was believed to have three principal benefits for Iran. First, new knowledge, sciences, and technology were deemed important in order to advance commerce and industry, and to effect general technological improvements such as the telegraph and engineering. Second, in order to effectively negotiate in the increasingly international arena, Iran needed statesmen and administrators trained in the new methods of politics and diplomacy, or the art of *siyasat*. Third, in the second half of the nineteenth century, general literacy was identified as a prerequisite for constitutional government. The emphasis on the development of a literate citizenry made educational reform a principal agent of change, and a general panacea for Iran's backwardness.

Another important feature of the reform literature in this period, particularly later in the century, is the attempt to address, if not resolve, the modernization dilemma. The problems of adopting foreign institutions (if not yet technology at this time) were recognized. Reformers proposed a variety of solutions, and increasingly asserted themselves as the guarantors of Iran's cultural traditions.

Mirza Malkom Khan

One of the most important theoreticians of reform was Mirza Malkom Khan. His many essays and journal articles, which spanned a period of forty years, contributed to the establishment of a reform agenda in pre-constitutional Iran. Mirza Malkom Khan served as a link between traditional reformers, such as Mirza Hosayn Khan, and those of the 1890s. While he displayed many of the rudimentary arguments concerning reform that typify the 1850-90 period, he also anticipated many ideas that emerged to characterize the post-1890 reform agenda. He was one of the first to address the modernization dilemma, and certainly the first to advocate the comprehensive adoption of European institutions into Iran. He also proposed the earliest plan for the establishment of a completely new, European-style educational system.

Mirza Malkom Khan was an early advocate of comprehensive reform. He promoted a broad definition of modernization, which included the large-scale adoption of European institutions, technology and education. This was a natural result of his inclusive conception of Iran's "backwardness." Previously, Iran's backwardness was believed to be essentially superficial in nature and due either to a failure to maintain

214

the traditional system, or to incidental historical events. Mirza Malkom Khan was one of the first to posit that Iran's backwardness was in fact due to a failure to develop a whole system of adequate institutions. The selective adoption of European technologies came to seem insufficient. In order for Iran to regain viability in the international arena, Malkom Khan believed that she must adopt the three primary components responsible for Europe's success: rule of law and efficient government organization; industry and commerce; and education.

Rule of law and governmental organization was given particular prominence as the root of European progress. In the third issue of his journal, *Qanun*, he wrote:

> I will say nothing regarding the English law and [that of] the rest of the countries because it is clear as the sun that all that amazing prosperity and general comfort and those endless conquests and those oceans of wealth that we witness in foreign countries—all of it is the result of the establishment of law.[18]

In addition, it was imperative for Iran to organize her government along European lines.[19] He urged the shah to initiate reform, arguing that if Iran failed to modernize, she would be left behind and become increasingly backward vis-à-vis other nations.[20] He also expressed concerns—universally shared by reformers since the Russo-Persian Wars earlier in the century had devasted the Iranian sense of superiority—that should Iran fail to modernize, she would forfit territory to stronger European states.[21] In short, Iran's survival depended on governmental reform:

> Profit from the example of the Ottoman Empire . . . Iran, faced with the onslaught of European conquest, is not in the least different from the

---

[18]Mirza Malkom Khan, *Qanun*, (ed) Homa Nateq (Tehran: Entesharat-e Amir Kabir, 1876-77), no. 3, Ramazan 1307, p. 3.

[19]Mirza Malkom Khan to Naser al-Din Shah, quoted in Adamiyat, *Fekr-e Azadi*, pp. 114-16.

[20]Mirza Malkom Khan to Naser al-Din Shah, quoted in Adamiyat, *Fekr-e Azadi*, p. 116.

[21]On the preoccupation with land, loss of land, and its consequences for the Iranian *Weltanschauung*, see Firoozeh Kashani-Sabet, *Frontier Fictions: Shaping the Iranian Nation, 1804-1946* (Princeton: Princeton University Press, 1999). On the pre-19th century Iranian world-view, see Rudi Matthee, "Between Aloofness and Fascination: Safavid Views of the West," *Iranian Studies*, vol. 31, no. 2 (Spring 1998), pp. 219-46.

Ottoman Empire . . . The essential point is that the surging power of Europe has rendered impossible the survival of barbarian states. Henceforth all governments in the world will have to be ordered [*munazzam*] like those of Europe, or be subjugated and conquered by European power.[22]

Malkom Khan blamed the government for Iran's weakness, and called for better leadership and administration. He wrote that Iran's state organization was 3,000 years old, and hopelessly irrelevant to contemporary needs. He argued that Iran must either adopt European state organization, or spend 3,000 years developing a similar system on her own.[23] He implicitly distinguished between types of knowledge. The distinction between "new" and "old" knowledge is in fact a claim that the contemporary situation is fundamentally different from previous periods, and requires different, heretofore nonexistent knowledge and skills. New knowledge, he explained, was not based on intelligence. For example, 2,000 of the smartest Iranians could not guess what a bank was.[24] New sciences and technology, as well as statecraft, were without precedent in Iran—they were entirely new. In the time of Shah Tahmasp [in the 16th century], he explained, government was run on the basis of natural talent and innate intelligence. Today, however, the foundation of modern countries is science and new skills. Iranians have no choice but to learn these new skills if they are to achieve progress.[25]

As a result of the importance of adopting new sciences, technology, leadership skills, and the rule of law, Mirza Malkom Khan laid great emphasis on the complete overhaul of the educational system. He was the first to advocate universal literacy. To this end, he believed that the Arabic alphabet used in Iran should be simplified, as its difficulty prevented the attainment of general literacy in Iran. The educational inferiority of Muslims in Iran (and, he believed, in the Ottoman Empire

---

[22]Mirza Malkom Khan, "Dastgah-e Divan," quoted in Hamid Algar, *Mirza Malkun Khan*, p. 70.

[23]Mirza Malkom Khan, "Ketabcheh-ye Ghaybi," in *Majmu'eh-ye Asar*, (ed) Mohammad Mohit Tabataba'i (Tehran: Elmi, 1327), pp. 12-13.

[24]Ibid, p. 9.

[25]Mirza Malkom Khan, "Osul-e Taraqqi," quoted in Adamiyat, *Fekr-e Azadi*, pp. 116-17.

as well) compared to Europeans was partially attributed to the "defectiveness" of the Arabic alphabet.[26]

As early as 1857-58 in an essay entitled *Ketabcheh-ye Ghaybi*, Malkom Khan presented a detailed blueprint for educational reform. According to his scenario, the system of education should consist of three levels: elementary (*tarbiyeh*), secondary (*fazliyeh*), and higher (*'aliyeh*). At the elementary level, students should be taught basic literacy, arithmetic, history, geography, and introductory geometry and natural sciences. Students at the secondary level would be instructed in philosophy (*hekmat*), mathematics, natural sciences, history, drawing and penmanship, and religious texts (*'olum al-sunna*). Higher education should consist of advanced training in any of five different fields: literature, law, higher education, medicine, or arts and industries. In addition to this general three-tiered system of education, Mirza Malkom Khan proposed specialized schools in the following disciplines: military, religious law, mining, teaching, industries, and drawing. According to Mirza Malkom Khan, provisions should be made for the establishment of this system of education not only in Tehran, but in all provinces of Iran.[27]

Mirza Malkom Khan's educational proposal constituted a direct challenge to the existing system of education as controlled by the religious establishment, both institutionally and culturally. He outlined an entire system of education from the primary through the higher level, including provisions for specialized training schools. He then placed this system under the control of the Ministry of Education, to which he assigned the responsibility for determining the curriculum and organization of all schools. The educational system would thus be completely removed from the control of the religious establishment. Even religious instruction was to be overseen by the government. This new, European-style educational system was not intended to exist parallel to or as a supplement to the traditional system— it was intended to replace it.

The challenge to the traditional educational system is further evident in the division of subjects of study. Significantly, at the primary level,

---

[26]For Mirza Malkom Khan's discussion of the need for alphabet reform, see his "Shaykh va Vazir" in Mirza Malkom Khan, *Kulliyat-e Malkom Khan* (ed) Hashem Rabi'zadeh (Tabriz, 1325), pp. 87-124.

[27]Mirza Malkom Khan, "Ketabcheh-ye Ghaybi," pp. 45-48.

no provision is made for instruction in subjects that formed the basis of the traditional curriculum; namely, Arabic, the Qur'an and principles of religion. At all levels, a European-style curriculum prevails. The instillation of basic values, morality and belief systems is therefore accomplished through a European-style curriculum, and firmly outside the purview of the religious establishment.

There is furthermore and important distinction made between subjects taught at the higher levels, and those that Malkom Khan believed should constitute specialty education outside of the normal three-tiered system. His placement of religious law in a group with military arts, mining and industries clearly suggests that it is less valuable than European law, which conversely is placed in the category of higher education, along with medicine, and arts and industries. By proposing that Islamic law be taught in specialized training schools, Malkom Khan marginalized not only traditional education, but also threatened the legal prerogatives of the religious establishment. Religious law would become an area of specialized, scholastic study. De facto, the realm of religious law, *shar'*, is reduced and the realm of customary law, *'urf*, is expanded, Europeanized and becomes the dominant law of the land.

It should also be noted that the marginalization of traditional education and law also meant that the traditional educational system lost ground to European-style education as a magnet for talent. The traditional system was effectively excluded from serving as a means of obtaining status and rank, or as a channel for prestigious government employment or the practice of law.

It is also significant that Malkom Khan included Iranian literature in the category of higher education. Literature was not a field of formal study at the advanced level in the traditional educational system, although it was certainly an important component of informal study. Malkom Khan's inclusion of it alongside of law and medicine attributes a great deal of value to the formal teaching of literature and may have been influenced by literature's prominent place in European university curriculums. The elevation of Iranian literature to the status of a field of formal higher study also implicitly emphasizes its role as an important pillar of Iranian identity— in contradistinction to the virtual absence of religious texts and instruction in his proposed educational system.

218

Mirza Malkom Khan's arguments and reform agenda are more sophisticated and certainly more far-reaching that those typical of the 1800-90 period. He was aware of the connection between education and social and political reform. Nonetheless, his advocacy of broadbased reform led him to maintain a paradoxical position concerning the transferability of European institutions to Iran. Earlier in the century, reform advocates such as Mirza Saleh Shirazi and Mirza Mostafa Afshar believed in the easy adoption of selective European technology and education into Iran. Afshar insisted that European-style schools that he visited in Russia could easily be imported into Iran. As evidenced in the problems that emerged concerning the *Dar al Fonun*, such a transfer was not without difficulties. Mirza Malkom Khan's conception of the transferability of European institutions to Iran was similarly simplistic.

Malkom Khan's equation of "civilization" with "modernization" and "Europeanization" meant that his reform proposals essentially consisted of the adoption of European institutions and technology. He firmly believed that European principles and organization of government could be imported as easily as European technology. He insisted that just as Iran was able to quickly and easily import the telegraph and install it in Tehran, so too could European organization and law be established in Iran. He assumes their similarity by joking that certainly Iranians would not be so simpleminded as to argue for the necessity of reinventing the telegraph, or European government organization, all over again.[28]

However, Malkom Khan was cognizant that a major basis of opposition to reforms and modernization was the belief that modernization was synonymous with Westernization, and that this necessarily involved the adoption of Christian (or at least culturally alien) institutions and culture. Given Malkom Khan's advocacy of comprehensive adoption of European institutions, he needed to differentiate between progress and modernization on the one hand, and Westernization on the other. In defense of his position, he used two related arguments to resolve this modernization dilemma.

First, he distinguished between new, scientific knowledge as developed in Europe, and traditional knowledge. In so doing, he hoped

---

[28]Mirza Malkom Khan, "Ketabcheh-ye Ghaybi," p. 13.

to demonstrate that Iran had no alternative to modernization if she were to regain her strength and her international viability and respect. Indeed, the key to Malkom Khan's attitude to reform was exactly this. Given the urgent need to restrengthen Iran, and given that modernization *cum* Westernization was the means, how could any group oppose it? In his first reform essay, he wrote that ulama were against European governmental organization, and cite conflict with the *shari'a* as the reason. However, he asked, how can the ulama maintain this position and not be criticized for preventing the strengthening and safeguarding of Iranian independence? How can the *shari'a* be opposed to a stronger Iran, he asked rhetorically.

Malkom Khan also employed the argument for the decontextualization of European institutions, in order to assuage the opposition. He argued that the essence, or underlying principles, of European institutions could be extracted from their socioeconomic, cultural, and historical contexts.[29] Modernization could thus be isolated from Westernization, and thereby freed of any Christian accretions. Modernization thus becomes "religiously innocuous" and universally relevant.[30] Progress is achievable by any country that adopted these "principles of civilization." To prove his point, Malkom Khan cited Egypt and the Ottoman Empire as examples of Muslim countries undergoing the process of modernization and restrengthening.[31] Malkom Khan did not succeed in resolving the inherent conflict between his view that new sciences, technology and organization/law developed in Europe, with his insistence that they somehow contained principles or essences which were distinct from their context, and thus reconcilable with Iranian traditions.

Although theoretically Malkom Khan's argument for the universality of progress leaves open the *possibility* of rigorous adaptation to indigenous contexts, he did not develop this line of thought. It is as if he himself only insisted on the possibility of decontextualization to appease the opposition, and was not himself convinced of any real

---

[29]Mirza Malkom Khan presented this argument in primitive form as early as 1877 in a letter to Mirza Hosayn Khan. See Adamiyat, *Fekr-e Azadi*, pp. 114-16 for excerpts of this letter.

[30]Algar, *Mirza Malkum Khan*, p. 29.

[31]On Egypt, see Adamiyat's discussion in *Fekr-e Azadi*, pp. 116-17; on the Ottoman Empire, see "Shayk va Vazir," cited in Algar, *Mirza Malkum Khan*, p. 70.

conflict. In a lecture given in Great Britain in 1891, Malkom Khan urged the British to present the "principles of civilization" as having Islamic origins in order to make them palatable:

> As to the principles which are found in Europe, which constitute the root of your civilization, we must get hold of them somehow, ho doubt; but instead of taking them from London or Paris, instead of saying that this comes from such an ambassador, or that it is advised by such a Government (which will never be accepted), it would be very easy to take the same principle, and to say that it comes from Islam, and that this can be soon proved.[32]

This (in)famous statement concerning his approach certainly makes Malkom Khan's claims for decontextualization seem purely tactical. Indeed, he himself explicitly acknowledged the need to *portray* reforms as adaptations or even rediscoveries of traditional institutions and modes of behavior. Just as 'Abbas Mirza had presented the *Nezam-e Jadid* as following in the footsteps of the Prophet's military feats, Malkom Khan was careful to trace significant European institutions to Islamic origins. There is no question that, particularly after 1890 and Malkom Khan's establishment of the newspaper *Qanun*, he consciously attempted to attract a wide spectrum of support for his reform proposals outside of the elite government bureaucracy.[33] Because he believed that only the ulama would be able to lead a popular movement in Iran, he deliberately coveted ulama approbation.[34]

The Changing Reform Agenda— The Indigenous Solution

The number of essays and letters advocating reform increased throughout the nineteenth century. Many of the concerns discussed by Mirza Malkom Khan were echoed by others. There were important differences, however. Increasingly, the parameters of the reform agenda

---

[32]Mirza Malkom Khan, "Persian Civilization," *Contemporary Review* 59 (February 1891) quoted in Algar, *Mirza Malkum Khan*, p. 13.

[33]*Qanun* enjoyed extraordinary popularity amongst politically oriented Iranians. See Algar, *Mirza Malkum Khan*, p. 192; and Homa Nateq (ed) *Qanun*, p. 1.

[34]See Shaul Bakhash, *Iran: Monarchy, Bureaucracy and Reform Under the Qajars, 1858-96* (London: Ithaca Press, 1978), p. 343.

came to include two features. First, reformers deepened their calls for change to include more than the revitalization of the government administration through reorganization along European lines and the establishment of ministerial accountability and responsibility. Rule of law became synonymous with the end to absolutism and arbitrary government. The idea of a constitution as a necessary instrument for the salvation of Iran surfaced.

The shifting definition entailed by rule of law, *qanun*, from a reordering of government to constitutional law was intimately tied to a change in the perceived benefits of European-style education. As the focus changed from the need to better train government administrators to the call for a literate citizenry, so too did proposals for the adoption of European-style education. The centrality of education in the reform debates in the latter part of the nineteenth century was primarily a result of the emergence of a causal connection between universal literacy and a constitutional government. Educational reform therefore became much more than a call for the training of a governmental elite to better lead the country. The establishment of a citizenry able to participate in establishing and maintaining a constitutional government was called for.

The causal connection between a literate citizenry and the ability to establish a constitutional government in Iran was conclusively made by Mirza Yusef Khan Mostashar al-Dowleh in 1871. His famous essay entitled *Yek Kalameh* ("One Word," i.e. *qanun*) made the connection explicit. It was the government's responsibility, and moreover a pre-condition of "civilization," to establish a system of universal education. Mirza Yusef Khan attempted to reconcile the French constitution with Islamic law by arguing that their intents (or "principles" to use the terminology developed by Mirza Malkom Khan), were compatible.[35] "Progress" and "civilization" were in no way antithetical to Islam and the *shari'a*.[36] *Yek Kalameh* is particularly important as it signaled the emergence of the notion of the political rights of individuals, and conversely state responsibility (and thus legitimacy) towards its citizens.

Second, reform literature began to seriously address the modernization dilemma and the associated threat to Iran's cultural

---

[35]Mirza Yusef Khan Mostashar al-Dowleh, *Yek Kalameh*, (ed) Sadeq Sajadi (Tehran: Nashr-e Tarikh-e Iran, 1364).

[36]Bakhash, *Iran*, p. 40.

traditions. The last two decades of the nineteenth century were affected by the trends towards politicization and popularization of the reform movement. Educational reform literature became increasingly focused on the educational requirements of a literate citizenry, and the implications of a citizenry on political change and legitimacy. At the same time, advocates of modernization evidenced a growing disaffection with the role of European powers in Iran, as well as with the cultural and religious implications of the adoption of foreign institutions. Unlike Mirza Malkom Khan, who saw the problem primarily from a tactical standpoint, reform-minded individuals accepted the validity of cultural and religious opposition. They addressed problems of cultural adaptation in an attempt to arrive at a viable synthesis— in effect an indigenous solution.

Abu Taleb Behbehani

The shifting educational agenda is aptly illustrated in a reform text written in 1877 by Abu Taleb Behbehani. As a government official, Behbehani had lived in Egypt and the Ottoman Empire and was familiar with some of the *Tanzimat* reform writings, as well as with the work of Mirza Malkom Khan. Throughout his essay, *Minhaj al-A'la* (The Lofty Way), Behbehani emphasizes the need for Iran to adopt a *qanun* like that found in Europe. He specifically states that absolutist government is inherently weak, and that it has thus far failed to uphold liberty, freedom, security, and justice in Iran. Moreover, the system of absolute monarchy promotes a government administration where "conspiracies and plotting" are more commonplace than capable and responsible individuals.[37] The solution was undoubtably consitutional monarchy.

Education was a critical component of Behbehani's vision of Iran's future. He described the type of education that all members of the consultative assembly (*majles*) should be required to have: literacy, reading and writing of Persian, French language and the ability to read

[37]Abu Taleb Behbehani, "*Minhaj al-A'la,*"as presented and quoted in Feridun Adamiyat and Homa Nateq, *Afkar-e Ejtema'i va Siyasi va Eqtesadi dar Asar-e Montasher Nashodeh-ye Dowran-e Qajar* (Saarbrücken: Nawid, 1989), pp. 99-114.

French books, information regarding current foreign affairs, and knowledge of religious law.[38]

At the same time, his focus was not entirely on the education of government officials. He outlined an entire system of universal national education, not unlike Mirza Malkom Khan's system formulated some twenty years previously. The system was comprised of primary (*madraseh-ye mobteda*), scientific (*madraseh-ye 'olum*) and advanced (*madraseh-ye ali*) schools. At the primary level, the curriculum consists of: Persian, introductory grammar, geometry, history, geography, and vocabulary. The curriculum at the scientific level included: rhetoric, logic, *fiqh* and principles of justice, *kalam*, mathematics and natural science. At the advanced level the curriculum consisted of a wide spectrum of subjects: foreign languages (including writing of), physics, natural sciences, practical wisdom, law, noble industries, ethics, principles of religion, principles of arithmetic, algebra, biology, agriculture and animal husbandry, medicine, mining, drawing, drafting/ engineering, military sciences (military engineering, artillery, infantry, cavalry), and geography. Behbehani also declared that all schools should be under the control of the Ministry of Science, members of which should be required to have attended between ten and twelve years of schooling in this system—thus effectively eliminating the possiblity of ulama control of the Ministry.

Behbehani excluded any traditional religious-oriented instruction from the primary curriculum. However, despite the overwhelming prominence of European-style subjects at the scientific and advanced levels, he does make provisions for traditional subjects such as *kalam*, *fiqh*, and ethics. Behbehani viewed this curriculum as a synthesis of the most valuable subjects in both European and Iranian school systems. Elsewhere in his essay he argues that *fiqh* has dominated other sciences to the long-term detriment of Islam, since without the fields of governance, astronomy, agriculture and commerce, industry and handicrafts, Iran will continue to decline and Islam will suffer as a result.[39]

No mention whatsoever is made of the religious establishment, or the traditional system of education. It is unclear, therefore, whether his proposed educational system is intended to replace, or merely

---

[38]Ibid, pp. 105-6.
[39]Ibid, p. 103.

supplement the existing system. His call for the establishment of a Ministry of Science to oversee a national educational system, however, at the very least infringes on the educational prerogatives of the religious establishment, and indicates the de facto marginalization of the traditional educational system. Moreover, like Mirza Malkom Khan's educational proposal, the inclusion of European and Islamic law in an essentially Europeanized school system threatened the ulama's monopoly on the interpretation of religious law. It served as a prelude to the reduction of their juridical prerogatives and the eventual expansion of *'urf* law at the expense of *shar'* law.

Behbehani essentially argued for the importance of modernization and the adoption of European-style law, sciences and an educational system in order to strengthen Iran, and by association, Islam. He, however, demonstrated a high degree of sensitivity in maintaining Iran's cultural and religious integrity. He maintained that any *qanun* adopted into Iran must conform to the principles of religious law (*shari'a*). He criticized those reformers who maintain that Iran must abandon religious law in order to fully adopt European law. He also disagreed with those who argued that the *shari'a* should be relegated to "otherworldly affairs" only.[40] A European-style *qanun* and the *shari'a* are entirely compatible, Behbehani insisted, as illustrated by the example of Egypt where European-style law has been established on the basis of religious law.[41] Indeed, the progress of Europe has nothing to do with Christianity, as there is no such thing as Christian law. Rather, the secret of European strength lies in the establishment of personal security, justice, and freedom as protected by the state.[42] Behbehani promised that the status of women and social customs would in no way be effected by the adoption of a European-style *qanun*, since it is limited to the political and administrative realm, and has no bearing on social or cultural traditions.[43]

Behbehani's essay evidences contradictory attitudes towards the role of the religious establishment. Although not stated explicitly, the

[40]See for example Mirza Sa'id Khan Ansari Mo'tamen al-Molk's essay composed in 1862 in (eds) Adamiyat and Nateq, *Afkar-e Ejtema'i*, pp. 120-29; and Masud Mirza Zell al-Soltan, *Safarnameh-ye Farangestan* (Tehran: Entesharat-e Asatir, 1368) for arguments of this sort.

[41]Ibid, pp. 103-4.

[42]Ibid, p. 108.

[43]Ibid, p. 107.

inclusion of *fiqh* in the European-style system of education, together with Behbehani's insistence that *Majles* deputies be schooled in European-style curricula, suggest that this role of adaptation of European constitution and education to the Iranian context be taken up by the government, rather than the religious establishment. However, this interpretation is somewhat contradicted by his specification that *Majles* deputies also be versed in religious law, his provision of one religious figure to oversee the drafting of the constitution in Iran, and his insistence on the adaptation of European law to Islamic *shari'a*.[44] Following traditional Islamic political theory, Behbehani declared his fealty to the notion that the most important duty of the government is to establish justice based on the principles of the *shari'a*.[45]

A much clearer and more significant role is reserved for the ulama in adapting a European-style constitution to Iran's needs in an anonymous reform essay written in 1875. The author begins his essay by insisting that Iran import European sciences, technology, and law. He then proceeds to refute various arguments against the adoption of European law. According to the author, opponents have voiced three principal objections: 1) European law is the law of infidels; 2) reform is being implemented hastily; and 3) rather than borrowing from Europe, Iran should look to its own traditions in reforming the political system, and spreading education. In response, the author insists that the adoption of European law would not require giving up any of Iran's customs. Furthermore, there is nothing in the *shari'a* which forbids borrowing from other countries. If Iran's traditional system of governmental organization and education, etc. are so wonderful demands the author, then why is Iran now in a state of weakness, poverty and illiteracy? At the same time, he freely concedes that blind imitation of Europe is undesirable and unnecessary. Iranian customs must be taken into account in the adoption of European institutions. Specifically, the author calls on the religious establishment to encourage progress and to begin work on adapting the European law to Iranian needs.[46]

---

[44] Ibid, p. 111.
[45] Ibid, p. 109.
[46] Ibid, pp. 112-16.

The notion of the ulama as the principle "translators" of a *qanun* in accordance with the *shari'a* and the acknowledgement of their social role is echoed in an article which appeared in *Akhtar* in 1890. In an editorial on the connection between education and reform, an anonymous author asserted that before law (*qanun*) can be established, "people are needed that know the rights under the law and [can staff] the courts [and serve as] judges. The first thing that we need in Iran is not the promulgation of law, but a spread of sciences and expertise . . . the ulama of the Islamic world more than anyone else are bound with the duty to adjust the course (*maslak*) and [to conceive of] a remedy."[47]

Siyahatnameh-ye Ibrahim Beg

The emerging centrality of the citizen and the importance of *adapting*, not just *adopting*, foreign institutions in Iran are evident in the hugely influential novel, *Siyahatnameh-ye Ibrahim Beg* (The Travel Account of Ibrahim Beg) by Hajj Zayn al-'Abedin Maragheh'i. This book, written sometime between 1888 and 1894, was widely read in Iran. *Siyasat-nameh-ye Ibrahim Beg* is a fictional account of the travels through Iran of an expatriate Iranian (Ibrahim Beg) who had grown up in Cairo. The novel presents a grim view of the social and political institutions in Iran. According to a contemporary historian, Nazem al-Islam Kermani, no other book contributed so much to the empowerment and political "awakening" of Iranians prior to the Constitutional Revolution of 1906-11.[48]

Throughout the book, European powers are described as presenting an imminent danger to Iran's territorial and political integrity. Only a strong Iran will be able to withstand the inevitable onslaught of

---

[47]Quoted by Nateq in the introduction to *Qanun* (ed) Nateq.

[48]According to Bakhash, the book was written during Naser al-Din Shah's lifetime, and probably sometime after 1888. According to the 1910 Calcutta edition, the book was written in 1880. It is not certain whether mention of events of 1889 and 1894 in the book are a result of additions to later editions or were part of the original. See Bakhash, *Iran*, p. 305, and footnote no. 2, p. 359. On the influence of the book, see Bakhash, *op cit*; and Hafez Farmanfarma'ian, "The Forces of Modernization in 19th Century Iran," in (eds) Polk and Chambers, *Beginnings of Modernization in the Middle East* (Chicago: University of Chicago Press, 1968), p. 142; and also see the introduction to Hajj Zayn al-'Abedin Maragheh'i, *Siyahatnameh-ye Ibrahim Beg* (Tehran: Asfar, 1364).

European nations.[49] Unfortunately, unlike the rest of the world that has been advancing, Iran has been in decline for the past thirty years.[50] The principal character in the novel laments that in Iran he saw no evidence of farm machinery, trains, "no state schools, hospitals . . . companies or banks that are signs of progress and civilization."[51]

Much emphasis is also placed on the underdevelopment of Iran's industrial and commercial capacities. Throughout his travels, Ibrahim Beg finds many European imports, but very few Iranian-made goods. He concludes that: "I then thought that the European devils, from the strength of knowledge and industry, every year take so much money out of this country."[52] The consequences of European commercial strength vis-à-vis Iran should not be underestimated, according to Ibrahim Beg, since the safety of the country depends directly on her wealth.

Maragheh'i , in the words of the principal character, Ibrahim Beg, declares that in order for Iran to ameliorate her situation and join the ranks of advanced, civilized nations, she must establish schools, and promulgate a basic constitution. Since it would be impossible to establish a constitution in a country with such a high level of illiteracy, education is a prerequisite for the establishment of rule of law and a precursor for Iran's strength and independence vis-à-vis Europe. "The first means of defense is knowledge and intelligence."[53] In Europe, according to Maragheh'i, governments consider themselves responsible for the upbringing of children. Europeans understand the direct relationship between the schooling of children, and increased prosperity.[54]

The type of education that Maragheh'i promotes in *Siyahatnameh-ye Ibrahim Beg*, while not specifically outlined, is clear from his explicit comparisons between Europe and Iran, and from his criticisms of traditional Iranian education. Maragheh'i describes the traditional

---

[49]In particular, Maragheh'i believed that Russia was by nature expansionist and posed the greatest danger to Iran in her quest to take over all of Asia. In contrast, he presented Great Britain as Russia's only feasible competitor and possible protector of Iran. See *Siyahatnameh*, pp. 199-202.

[50]Maragheh'i, *Siyahatnameh*, p. 359.

[51]Ibid, pp. 155-56.

[52]Ibid, p. 137.

[53]Ibid, pp. 293-95, 359.

[54]Ibid, p. 167.

educational system as backward and nonsensical. In one instance, Ibrahim Beg visits a *madraseh* where he witnesses two seminary students yelling and hitting each other, while a religious instructor performs ablutions in apparent disregard of the students. When asked why he permited such uncivil behavior, the religious instructor replied that such behavior was a necessary part of learning.[55] In another instance, Ibrahim Beg suggested that a *maktab* incorporate geography and geometry into its curriculum. The teacher replied that those subjects were unnecessary.[56]

Maragheh'i believed that *maktabs* should teach "useful" skills, such as how to use a telegraph. After all, he wrote, "it is knowledge that can light up a large town in the night in the space of a few seconds without oil."[57] Clearly Maragheh'i conceived of "New" schools with a European-style curriculum as the first measures that Iran should implement in order to begin to ameliorate her situation. Only then could Iran establish a constitution and begin to develop her commerce and industry.

Maragheh'i differs significantly from Mirza Malkom Khan in his treatment of the issue of the transferability of European institutions. He was sensitive to the problem of maintaining cultural integrity despite the importation of European institutions. He attempted to resolve this paradox in two ways. First, like Mirza Malkom Khan, he argues that modernization is distinct from and need not involve Westernization. Second, unlike Mirza Malkom Khan, he proposed careful and select adaptation of European social and political institutions.

Maragheh'i puts forward two related arguments for the possibility of establishing a European-style constitution in Iran. First, he argues that there is nothing inherently contradictory in a European-style constitution to Islam.[58] A constitution consists of principles of statehood, military organization, maintenance of finances, guarantees of peoples' rights and the pursuance of justice. How can it be dangerous to the *shari'a*, if the purpose of a constitution is the protection of the *shari'a* and the country.

---

[55]Ibid, pp. 99-100.
[56]Ibid, pp. 35-37.
[57]Ibid, pp. 165-66.
[58]Ibid, p. 299.

Second, Maragheh'i's argues that the fundamental principles of European-style constitutions originated in Islam. If one were to investigate all of Imam 'Ali's directives, he insisted, one would discover that they are the same as those that have since been adopted and translated by the Europeans and then employed for their own benefit. It is therefore shameful for Muslims to allow the Europeans to claim such principles as their own rather than realizing that they are in fact of Islamic provenance.[59]

Maragheh'i's Islamic modernist stance, in effect, is a claim for the transferability of European institutions into Iran. On several occasions, Maragheh'i insists that the establishment of a constitution in Iran would be a simple matter. No money is required, nor would it entail bloodshed. Moreover, since Europe has already gone through the trouble of working out the provisions of various constitutions, Iran's leaders could simply translate and adopt those measures which they find applicable to Iran's needs.[60]

Maragheh'i frequently upheld Japan as an example of the benefits of adopting European-style education and political institutions. As a wise man in the novel explains, the situation in Japan was worse than it is today in Iran. However, by promoting European-style education in sciences and industries, as well as civility, morals and literature, the Japanese government developed its industries and army. Japan now has 14 universities, 300 middle schools and 58,000 elementary schools. Certainly with this investment in education, Japan will soon have the upper-hand over European countries, declares the wise man.[61] Maragheh'i posits that Japan has entered the ranks of "civilization," and at the same time, suffered no threat to her religion and culture. In fact, the establishment of a constitution strengthened her religion and indigenous customs.[62]

Evidence of an emerging nationalism is present in *Siyahatnameh-ye Ibrahim Beg*. The main character is an avid lover of all things Iranian, who throughout his travels falls into despair at the social conditions he witnesses. Implicitly, this book urges readers to become involved in promoting progress. This is in part in response to Maragheh'i's clear

---

[59]Ibid, p. 298.
[60]Ibid, pp. 72, 301.
[61]Ibid, p. 293.
[62]Ibid, pp. 296-97, 299.

condemnation of Iran's political and social leaders for their failure to promote "progress" and uphold justice. Maragheh'i criticizes the lack of educational reform initiatives—both on the part of government ministers, and the ulama.[63] Maragheh'i's criticism of the ulama's myopic refusal to incorporate "useful" subjects into the *maktab* curriculum paradoxically indicates his belief in the importance of arriving at a synthesis of the traditional educational system with new, "useful" subjects. It also suggests that he recognized the social role of the ulama, and his hope that they will agree to champion the cause of reform in Iran.

'Abd al-Rahim Talebof

The "indigenous solution" was most fully articulated by 'Abd al-Rahim Talebof in a number of essays and books. His book *Ketab-e Ahmad* (Ahmad's Book) deals specifically with the issue of educational reform and its role in restrengthening and regenerating Iran. *Ketab-e Ahmad* was published c. 1894 in Istanbul and widely read in Iran. In fact, it was used as a text in many of the New schools established in Tehran in the 1890s.[64] Consciously modeled on Jean Jacques Rousseau's *Emile*, the book consists of short discussions for the ostensible purpose of educating the author's [fictitious] son—Ahmad. Using this method, Talebof presents a variety of topics, including history and sciences, as well as general information concerning European countries. Talebof ruminates at length concerning the reasons for Iran's backwardness vis-à-vis Europe, and proposes solutions to this problem.

Talebof begins his argument for the urgency of reform by pointing to the threat posed by European powers. He points out that in the past fifty years, Iran has lost much territory. Her independence, and indeed survival, therefore, depends on her ability to become competitive in the new international arena.[65] "Our era is the era of progress," declares Talebof. Iran must "pull the curtain of ignorance away" and adapt to the new era.[66] Even the legendary Iranian conquerors would not stand a chance against contemporary European powers, he writes, as strength

---

[63]Ibid, pp. 167, 35-37.
[64]Bakhash, *Iran*, pp. 346-47.
[65]'Abd al-Rahim Talebof, *Ketab-e Ahmad* 2 vols. (Tehran: Sazeman-e Ketabha-ye Jibi, 1346), vol. II, pp. 124-25.
[66]Ibid, vol. I, pp. 39, 74.

is not simply the result of the shah's capabilities. The secret of European strength is the rule of law.

Law is stressed as the necessary prerequisite for all progress. Indeed, the preamble to volume two of *Ketab-e Ahmad* declares that "wherever there is no law, there is no happiness and blessing."[67] Law engenders the benefits of "civilized" nations. Talebof wrote that "all those who love our nation know that if we had rule of law (*qanun*) we would be masters of knowledge, wealth, order and independence."[68]

Although throughout *Ketab-e Ahmad* Talebof uses the term "*qanun*" to designate law, his meaning includes government organization and regularization, and the establishment of uniform rights.[69] Constitutional law is also implied. This becomes clear in his discussion of the various types of government. According to Talebof, in an absolute monarchy no real law exists, since all power resides in the person of the king. This then necessarily results in oppression and injustice. A better system, he argues, is that of constitutional monarchy.[70]

Talebof's argument for the institution of constitutional law in Iran is premised on the distinction between temporal and spiritual realms. There are two types of law, he states, that which pertains to the soul, the *shari'a*, and that which pertains to the physical world, the qanun. Just as body and soul are unable to exist without each other, so too does Iran need both the religious and temporal legal systems.[71] This distinction attempts to further solidify the customary separation of legal realms into the religious (*shar'*) and governmental (*'urf*) law as practiced in Iran. Furthermore, it implicitly amounts to the effective reduction of the realm of law covered by the *shari'a*, and conversely, the expansion of the realm of authority accorded to *'urf* law. Talebof further legitimizes the expansion of the law overseen by the government— and thus the realm effected by the establishment of a constitution— by insisting that it would ultimately benefit religion as well as Iran. The purpose of a constitution, he assured the reader, is to ensure the maintenance of national honor, the empowerment of the *shari'a*, and the honor of the Qur'an. The establishment of a

---

67Ibid, vol. II, p. 89.
68Ibid, vol. II, p. 136.
69Ibid, vol. II, p. 99.
70Ibid, vol. II, pp. 127-28.
71Ibid, vol. II, pp. 125-27.

constitution in Iran will neither endanger the *shari'a*, nor will it constitute blind imitation of Europe.[72]

Talebof pinpointed education as a necessary prerequisite for legal reform. Only with the development of a literate citizenry, Talebof argues, will Iran be able to institute rule of law. Educational reform, therefore, is directly and causally related to the ability to establish constitutional government and to regularize the legal system. This argument had already been made by Mirza Yusef Khan Mostashar al-Dowleh and others in the 1870-90 period. What distinguishes Talebof's conception of the role of educational reform, however, was his much more sophisticated understanding of the role of a citizenry in the shaping of governmental systems. He believed that the political participation of an educated citizenry was the key to European progress, and the salvation of Iran. In *Ketab-e Ahmad* he wrote that in "civilized" nations where governments are based on the rule of law, education is compulsory for all since illiterate people are excluded from most of the privileges of civilization. Not only are illiterate children (both boys and girls) less desirable marriage partners, but they will not be able to join the military, independent associations, or Parliament.[73] Talebof thus goes much further than advocating general literacy. The type of education previously advocated for the better training and functioning of Iran's administrative and diplomatic elite was now deemed important to be spread amongst a much more socially and economically diverse population. Education emerges as a social and political panacea, and the fountainhead of strength. For example, in *Ketab-e Ahmad*, when Ahmad asks what the reason for the wealth and prosperity of European nations is, his father replies that universities are responsible for Europe's greatness. Through knowledge, Europe changed from being the wildest place on earth, to the most civilized.[74] Because European countries have more knowledge than anywhere else in the world, all other countries are subservient to them.[75] Talebof laments that "we do not have universities, we do not have schools.

[72]Ibid, vol. II, pp. 99-100.
[73]Ibid, vol. II, p. 92.
[74]Ibid, vol. II, pp. 122-23.
[75]Ibid, vol. II, pp. 103-4.

Except for books of fables, we do not have any books, any patrons, or educators. Because of all this, we do not have wealth."[76]

Talebof also stressed the importance of education as a means of acquiring commercial skills and of developing Iran's industrial capacity. He insists that "if we do not open schools and our children remain illiterate, if we do not establish commercial societies, our industries will not make progress. We will be dependent on foreign imports" and Iran will remain servile to the advanced nations of Europe.[77] A literate public could support effective government, uniform commercial laws, and security of personal property, which in turn would lead to capital investment.[78] Talebof insisted that the leaders of European nations, by way of newspapers, were able to encourage progress of industry and commerce and counter oppression.[79]

Talebof was very specific in terms of the type of education necessary to engender reform. He promoted "New," European-style education as the most effective means of developing a citizenry. The curriculum of the New schools as described in *Ketab-e Ahmad* included: Iranian history, religious principles and duties, introduction to geometry, arithmetic, geography, physics, chemistry, literature, German and English languages.[80] It is interesting to note the reasons given by Talebof for the importance of different subjects. Due to the advent of the train and the telegraph, Iran has been brought into close contact with European nations. European languages are thus necessary both for diplomatic and commercial purposes.[81] Sciences and mathematics provide skills necessary for industry and commerce. It is no coincidence that, given the close connection between the regularization of laws and development of industry and commerce on the one hand, and the belief in the need for "New" schools (or at least additional, "useful" subjects) on the other, that many large merchants supported the "New" schools and educational reform.[82]

---

[76]Ibid, vol. II, p. 136.
[77]Ibid, vol. II, pp. 98-99.
[78]Ibid, vol. II, p. 120.
[79]Ibid, vol. II, p. 92.
[80]Ibid, vol. II, p. 93.
[81]Ibid, vol. II, pp. 93-94.
[82]Iranian merchants living in Istanbul supported a Persian school there. The merchant community attempted to organize on their own, and established a Council of Merchants in 1883. This experiment, however, was short-lived.

The "New" school is favorably compared to the limited curriculum of the traditional *maktab*. According to Talebof, his son Ahmad learned more in four months at the New school than his older brother had after three years in a traditional school. Talebof also maintained that the methods used in the New schools were more effective in teaching children to read and write. Like Mirza Malkom Khan, Talebof pointed to the difficulty of the Arabic alphabet as a reason for the slow progress of Iranian students in general. Children in European countries learn their alphabet with games and can read and write even before they begin school. In contrast, because of the complexity of the Arabic alphabet and poor methods of instruction, Iranian children fail to learn the alphabet even after five years in school. Talebof lamented that "it is too bad that those with power (*bozorgan*) do not reform the errors of this important problem, which is the essence of the progress of the nation and the best guarantor of the range of influence of the religion of Islam."[83]

Indeed, Talebof asserts that the shah and government, as well as the ulama, have thus far failed to lead Iran in the direction of strength and progress. In contradistinction to many previous condemnations of political and social leadership, Talebof concludes from this that it is up to the individual citizens of Iran to take charge of promoting change. We expect the state to do everything, he laments, but the state is made up of individuals; we ourselves need to gather together the means for progress.[84] Talebof calls on the citizens of Iran to actively participate in Iran's rejuvenation. The individual emerges not only as the focus of reform efforts, but the agent of change as well. In fact, this promotion of the individual's responsibility firmly establishes a mutual, contractual relationship between the government, nation, and the individuals who

---

See Adamiyat and Nateq, *Afkar*, pp. 299-371; Shireen Mahdavi, *For God, Mammon, and Country: A Nineteenth-Century Persian Merchant, Haj Muhammad Hasan Amin al-Zarb* (Boulder, Westview Press, 1999), pp. 92-94; Adamiyat and Nateq *Afkar-e Ejtema'i va Siyasi va Eqtesadi*, pp. 299-371; and Janet Afary, *The Iranian Constitutional Revolution, 1906-1911: Grassroots Democracy, Social Democracy, and the Origins of Feminism* (New York: Columbia University Press, 1996), pp. 30-31.

[83]Talebof, *Ketab-e Ahmad*, vol. I, p. 22. In addition to Talebof, Mirza Malkom Khan, Mirza 'Ali Khan Amin al-Dowleh, Mirza Aqa Khan Kirmani and Mirza Fath 'Ali Akhundzadeh were all concerned with the issue of alphabet reform.

[84]Talebof, *Ketab-e Ahmad*, vol. II, pp. 121-22.

comprise it. This marks the beginning, albeit in nascent form, of state responsibility towards the individual as a primary objective of justice.[85]

The nation replaces the shah as the focus of loyalty and duty. The duty of everyone, Talebof asserts, is the welfare of the nation, and Iranians must be willing to sacrifice for the betterment of the nation. He hopes that the New, European-style schools will teach children their rights and responsibilities towards the nation, religion, society, and fellow citizens.[86]

Talebof's emphasis on the rights and duties of individuals toward the nation is also indicative of the general shift in reform initiative in the 1890s. In contrast to earlier reformers' espousal of the "doctor-patient" scenario of change, with the state assuming a top-down role, Talebof promotes a bottom-up approach. Iran's saviors will be its citizens, not necessarily its government leaders. The same holds true for Iran's relationship to Europe. Rather than expecting change from without, Iran should rely on its own resources. In direct contrast to Mirza Hosayn Khan and Mirza Malkom Khan's promotion of European sponsorship of Iranian reform measures, and of European capital investment for the development of Iranian infrastructure (particularly railroads), Talebof urges the development of indigenous capacities and self-reliance. He does not look to Great Britain to champion reform. Indeed, in *Ketab-e Ahmad*, one of the principal benefits arising from European-style education is believed to be the development of Iranian industry and commerce. Iran's ability to become self-sufficient and competitive with European powers is considered a primary foundation of national strength. As Talebof declares, the nationhood (*melliyat*) of each people depends on their independence.[87]

Talebof's outline of the "indigenous solution" involves more than Iranian self-sufficiency and motivation. He believed that Iranian cultural traditions must be safeguarded against foreign inroads. He is very sensitive to the problem of maintaining cultural integrity despite the importation of European institutions. He insists that modernization is distinct from and need not involve Westernization. It is imperative,

---

[85]Ibid, vol. II, p. 92.
[86]Ibid.
[87]Ibid, vol. II, p. 124.

Talebof asserts, to carefully and selectively adapt European social and political institutions to Iran's own needs.

Talebof proffers two arguments for the distinction between modernization and Westernization. First, he simply asserts that since the adoption of European technology, education and a constitution would lead to Iranian strength, self-reliance and ultimately defense, they must be adopted. Second, parallel to his distinction between temporal and spiritual spheres of legal authority, Talebof posits that there clearly is a difference in kind between material and spiritual culture.[88] Essentially, this reiterates Mirza Malkom Khan's argument for the universality (and therefore attainability) of progress. According to Talebof, any program of modernization must remain true to Iranian identity. As evidence for this assertion, Talebof points to educational reform programs in the Ottoman Empire. In *Ketab-e Ahmad*, he describes how the Ottoman Empire has established European-style schools.[89] Significantly, Talebof also cited the Japanese experience. The Japanese emperor opened several thousand schools and promulgated a European-style constitution. In this way, Japan made enormous progress and is no longer considered a backward country like Iran.[90] At the same time, however, Japan did not loose any of her indigenous culture. It is no accident that Japan emerged as a potential model of reform amongst proponents of the "indigenous solution"— replacing and in some sense supplanting the earlier prominance of Russia and the Ottoman Empire as models.

Cultural sensitivity is also evident in Talebof's discussion of the ulama, and in his treatment of the issue of *maktab* reform. *Ketab-e Ahmad* contains one of the only discussions in nineteenth-century reform literature of the failure of the religious establishment to implement educational reform. In the preface, Talebof praises the ulama for its past efforts and achievements in education, and for promoting knowledge and learning. However, he asserts that the traditional educational system is no longer fulfilling its function of producing individuals capable of meeting contemporary needs. Despite this fact, the ulama is taking no measures to incorporate new

---

[88]Feridun Adamiyat, *Andishehha-ye Talebof-e Tabrizi* (Saarbrücken: Nawid, 1363), p. 26.
[89]Talebof, *Ketab-e Ahmad*, vol. I, pp. 85-86.
[90]Ibid, vol. I, p. 61.

knowledge and subjects of study into the traditional system. Although Talebof fails to state his position explicitly, he implies that unless the traditional system is adapted to contemporary needs, it will be replaced by a new system with a more European-style curriculum and will become increasingly obsolete.

Talebof and Maragheh'i's articulation of an indigenous solution to Iran's backwardness was particularly significant as it constituted an important departure from much of the previous reform literature. In fact, their sensitivity to the real problems of modernization and its effects on Iran's cultural traditions, and their espousal of bottom-up mobilization and change had an enormous impact on the parameters of reform in Iran—politically, but more importantly, in terms of the social, cultural and intellectual challenges that this indigenous solution posed to traditional elites, justice, law, and the basis of knowledge.

Cultural Symbolism— Women

The European-style schools established by Iranian reformers in the 19th century (both secondary and subsequently primary) were intended exclusively for boys. Parents who wished their daughters to receive other than a traditional education either sent them to missionary schools, or hired private tutors. It was not until the constitutional period that educational activists attempted to open "New" schools for girls. Women's societies (*anjomans*), which emerged beginning in 1906 in Tabriz and the following year in Tehran, were pivotal in the promotion of women's education. However, the political turmoil of the revolutionary period effectively delayed school openings. Despite resolutions calling for women's education passed as early as 1907, it was not until 1910 that the first "New" school for women opened. The Constitutional Revolution of 1906-11 effectively marks the beginning of the rapid growth both of "New" schools for women, and of the debate concerning women's education in general.

"The Woman Question," as it was called, however, emerged in the course of the 19th century, in large part due to increased cultural and political interaction with Europe. Some of the educational activists and reform theorists of the 1860-1906 period discussed above advocated women's education. For example, Yahya Dowlatabadi mentions how he hoped to educate his daughter.[91] He also mentions, without elaborating on it, that the *Anjoman-e Ma'aref* began to discuss the importance of women's education in 1903.[92] Mirza Malkom Khan, like Talebof, included women in his call for universal education, although he did not specifically address the education of women as a separate issue. It was not until the turn of the century, with the establishment of revolutionary newspapers and journals, that women's education emerged as an important issue of reform.

There were two principal arguments for the necessity of education for women. The first based itself on the traditional role of women as wife and mother. An educated woman could fulfill these roles better than her uneducated counterpart, and thus contribute to both her family's and her country's advancement. The emphasis on women's roles as wife and mother as their primary contribution to the nation is in stark contrast to the role for men proffered by educational activists and theorists. In Talebof's *Ketab-e Ahmad*, for example, men are urged to become educated in order to actively participate in Iran's political life. Educational activist Yahya Dowlatabadi hoped that the New schools would create a new political leadership cadre.

The second argument perceived of women as a symbol of the nation. Educated women were a symbol of Iran's progress toward "civilization." The education of women, like rule of law and industrial development as conceived by many reform advocates, constituted a component of "progress" and a sign of modernization. It is not surprising that the intensely controversial book *Tahrir al-Mara'* (The Liberation of Women) by Egyptian Qasim Amin was translated into Persian almost as soon as it was published in 1899. In it, Amin argued that women, as embodiments of the nation, national honor, "progress," and "civilization," must be educated and (not incidentally), de-veiled.[93]

---

[91]Yahya Dowlatabadi, *Tarikh-e Mo'aser ya Hayat-e Yahya Dowlatabadi* 4 vols. (Tehran: Ferdowsi, 1362), vol. I, p. 353. Dowlatabadi's sister, Sadiqeh Dowlatabadi was a leading educational activist for women in the post-constitutional period.

[92]Ibid, p. 331. See also chapter VI, above.

[93]See Qasim Amin, *The Liberation of Women: a document in the history of Egyptian feminism* (trans) Samiha Sidhom Peterson (Cairo: American University of Cairo Press, 1992); and Afsaneh Najmabadi, "Crafting an Educated Housewife in Iran," in Lila Abu Lughod (ed) *Remaking Women: Feminism and*

Both these arguments are illustrated by one of the first public appeals for women's education. On December 30, 1906, the journal *Majles* published an appeal by a woman to Sayyid Mohammad Tabataba'i for women's education. In it, the writer asked the government to establish schools for girls, since women's lack of education was a primary cause for Iran's backwardness vis-à-vis Europe. The response to her request printed in *Majles* illustrates the limited view of the benefits of education for women. Women were not suited to politics and should not concern themselves with such matters. Education for women should therefore be limited to what they needed to prepare them for the "raising of children, home economics, preserving the [family] honor and other such sciences that deal with the issue of morality and means of livelihood of the family."[94]

Significantly, both proponents and opponents of women's education conceived of it in highly symbolic terms. For proponents, women's education was symbol of Iranian "progress" and "civilization;" opponents saw it as a symbol of lawlessness and the "Christianization" of Iran. Moreover, both symbols centered on the issue of morality. For proponents, women's education was a "veil of chastity" the acquisition of which served to internalize virtue and modesty in women.[95] Education, in this conception, emphasized the development of the individual person. Opponents countered that "new" education would result in women's licentiousness and immorality, as exemplified by the negative image of European women. For both sides, the issue of education for women became a central point of reference for the political and ideological divisions between proponents and opponents of modernization cum Westernization.[96]

Modernity in the Middle East (Princeton: Princeton University Press, 1998), pp. 91-125.

[94]*Majlis* vol. 6, 30 December 1906), p. 3, as quoted in Janet Afary, "The Debate on Women's Liberation in the Iranian Constitutional Revolution, 1906-1911," in *Expanding the Boundaries of Women's History: Essays on Women in the Third World,* (eds) Cheryl Johnson-Odim and Margaret Strobel (Bloomington: Indiana University Press, 1997). See also Afary, *Revolution,* pp. 10, 181, 207.

[95]See Afsaneh Najmabadi's discussion in "Veiled Discourse – Unveiled Bodies," *Feminist Studies,* vol. 19, no. 3 (Fall 1993), pp. 487-518.

[96]For the development of "The Woman Question" and it's symbolic centrality, see Mohammad Tavakoli-Targhi, "Women of the West Imagined: The *Farangi* Other and the Emergence of the Woman Question in Iran," in

Crisis and Tradition— The Intellectual Threat of Educational Reform

Throughout the nineteenth century, many reform arguments rested on the assertion that the world had entered a new era. Reform texts are replete with mention of the new era, *"asr-e jadid."* This notion began simply as an observation on the growing disparity between Middle Eastern weakness and the commercial, political, and military might of European nations, and thus as a call to action. Over time, the idea of a new era developed into the concrete notion that the world had experienced a break in time— a break between tradition and modernity, stagnation and "progress." Accordingly, skills, knowledge, statecraft and even political institutions were associated with either the traditional or the modern era. Reformers consciously distinguished between the two, and believed in the absolute necessity of bringing Iran into line with the exigencies of the modern age. Such views are apparent in the travel accounts of Mirza Saleh Shirazi and Mirza Mostafa Afshar written in the first decades of the century. The distinction in eras also intimated a parallel distinction in types of knowledge. Although Shirazi and Afshar did not go so far as to make this claim, it is increasingly evident in the reform texts written in the second half of the century. Mirza Malkom Khan, for example, based his argument for the adoption of European institutions and knowledge on this distinction. Talebof, too, argued for the separation of material and spiritual culture, as well as knowledge, and even legal spheres of authority in order to distinguish between modernization and Westernization, and to maintain the possibility of adaptation of foreign institutions to the Iranian context.

In practical terms, the distinction between types of knowledge surfaced with the teaching of European sciences and medicine at the *Dar al Fonun* beginning in the 1850s. European sciences were differentiated by new, European terminology, and their practitioners were accorded special intellectual and even social status. By the end of the century, with the establishment of the New schools and the increased visibility of the impact of modernization in the form of the spread of

(ed) Valentine M. Moghadam *Identity Politics and Women: Cultural Reassertions and Feminisms in International Perspective* (Boulder: Westview Press, 1994), pp. 98-120, and Mohammad Tavakoli-Targhi, "Imagining Western Women: Occidentalism and Euro-eroticism," *Radical America*, vol. 24, no. 3 (1993), pp. 73-87.

European-style education, tensions between the two bases of knowledge emerged into the open. As the ramifications of the split in types
of knowledge became more apparent, the split became bound to issues
of reform and opposition to Westernization. This was especially
apparent with regard to the intellectual threat that this distinction posed
to the religious establishment as the creator and purveyor of
knowledge.

From the outset of the introduction of European knowledge,
technology and expertise into Iran in the nineteenth century,
technology was perceived as lacking cultural content. This view
persisted throughout the century. Reformers insisted that the adoption
of European knowledge and technology would in no way threaten
existing traditional customs or institutions. Reformers also argued for a
distinction in types of knowledge in order to decontextualize European
institutions and rid them of cultural (and religious) content. It was
particularly important, in order to legitimize modernization, to maintain
the absence of a moral quality in European knowledge and institutions.
Indigenous values therefore could be grafted on to institutions of
European origin.

By the end of the century, new, European knowledge was
distinguished from traditional, Islamic knowledge both epistem-
ologically and metaphysically. New, scientific knowledge was
empirically based, and validated for its utilitarian applicability. Indeed,
the scientific revolution in Europe was identified as the "pursuit of
scientific knowledge as something validated in terms of its utilitarian
applicability rather than as knowledge for its own sake."[97] Scientific
knowledge moreover was secular knowledge, and therefore not
intuitive. The possibility always existed that it could be refuted,
challenged and made obsolete by new discoveries and/or research. It
was taught in new institutions (the *Dar al Fonun* and the New schools),
according to new methods, and by texts that were not sacred, or even
religiously based. Traditional, Islamic knowledge, on the other hand,
was based on an intuitive relationship to the Divine, and validated as
sacred, irrefutable, and immutable Truth. It was linked to a moral
system of religion, and the ulama played important roles as mediators in

---

[97]David Ralston, *Importing the European Army: The Introduction of European
Military Techniques and Institutions into the Extra-European World, 1600-1914*
(Chicago: University of Chicago Press, 1990), p. 11.

the understanding of sacred texts and ultimately as the guardians of Truth. The distinction between scientific and Islamic knowledge was further mirrored by the linguistic differentiation between *'ilm* and *ma'arefat*, with *ma'arefat* increasingly taking on the connotation of scientific, non-religious oriented knowledge.

The distinction between new and traditional knowledge, while aimed at making the introduction of the former less threatening, had quite the opposite effect. The European positivist and empirical approach in general threatened the all-encompassing ontological foundation of Islamic science. Indeed, in the context of the history of European science, it has been described as an "intellectual acid" which acted as a "disastrous disolvent of holistic concepts, traditional beliefs, and socially integrative certainties."[98] The fact that in Iran European knowledge was valued purely on utilitarian terms served to reinforce its identification as "useful" knowledge, in contradistinction therefore to Islamic knowledge which was increasingly relegated to the realm of "non-useful" knowledge. Reform texts calling for the marginalization of religious instruction and the establishment of a universal system of education with predominantly European curriculums (such as put forward by Mirza Malkom Khan and Abu Taleb Behbehani) illustrated this divergence. Even Talebof's "indigenous solution" and the New schools' synthesis of the European and traditional curriculums reinforced the distinction in types of knowledge, and stressed European sciences as "useful" and religious sciences as implicitly or explicitly "non-useful."

Islamic sciences, unlike European empirical and profoundly secularized sciences, had not undergone a process of separation from their religious, and therefore sacred and irrefutable, bases.[99] The challenges posed by the introduction of European sciences, therefore, threatened the religious basis of Islamic sciences. This is readily apparent in both the fields of medicine and astronomy. For instance, the issue of vaccination was intimately tied to the question of free will versus God's determinism. For this reason, many European attempts at vaccination were opposed. Similarly, European heliocentric astro-

---

[98]Fritz K. Ringer, *Max Weber's Methodology: The Unification of the Cultural and Social Sciences* (Cambridge: Harvard University Press, 1998), p. 22.

[99]Said Amir Arjomand, (ed) *The Political Dimensions of Religion* (Albany: SUNY Press, 1993), pp. 70-75.

nomical theory was initially denounced as inimical to the geocentric organization of the universe attested to in the Qur'an and prophetic traditions. It was devastating when these religious texts were found to no longer provide adequate and/or true explanations for physical phenomena.[100]

The distinctions between new and traditional, secular and religious knowledge, were echoed in the realm of law. Once reformers accepted the assumption that modernization consisted of more than the adoption-adaptation of European-style institutions, law, and education, modernization became firmly anchored to the process of secularization and rationalization of the judicial and educational systems (as well as the establishment of constitutional government).[101] Throughout the century, the process of reform and modernization was integrally connected to attempts at centralization and the expansion of monarchical authority. 'Abbas Mirza, Amir Kabir, Mirza Hosayn Khan, and Amin al-Dowleh all emphasized the importance of reducing the judicial prerogatives of the ulama in order for centralization to proceed. Reform texts also consistently emphasized the need to reduce the sphere of religious, shar', law and concomitantly, expand the sphere of customary, 'urf, law— in other words, to increase the government's judicial powers at the expense of those of the ulama. This plan was argued on the basis of the distinction between types of knowledge, the dawn of a new era, and basically the belief that the shari'a could not serve as a comprehensive basis for a modern constitutional state. Although reformers insisted that the shari'a would inspire constitutional law and that the principles underlying the two systems were inherently reconcilable, this debate called into question the very basis of religious law. Was, as Shaykh Fazlollah Allah Nuri would argue during the Constitutional Revolution, the very idea of manmade law (qanun) a direct challenge of the prophetic mission and an implicit denial of the sufficiency of God's provisions for mankind— as embodied in the

---

[100]Kamran Arjomand, "The Emergence of Scientific Modernity in Iran: Controversies Surrounding Astrology and Modern Astronomy in the Mid-Nineteenth Century," *Iranian Studies*, vol. 30, nos. 1-2 (Winter/Spring 1997), p. 20.

[101]For a refinement of the process of secularization and its relationship to modernization in a comparative perspective, see Nikki Keddie, "Secularism and the State: Towards Clarity and Global Comparison," *New Left Review*, vol. 226 (Nov/Dec. 1997), pp. 21-40.

shari'a?[102] The debate itself also challenged the dominance, both practical and theoretical, of the ulama (and specifically the jurists—*fuqaha*) in the judicial domain.

Most importantly, the very fact that reformers called for a reinterpretation of the underlying principles, or essence, of religious law as part of their attempt to reconcile it with European-style constitutional law, meant that the prerogative of *interpretation* of Islam and of religious texts was wrested from the sole preserve of religious scholars. The foundations, and even intent, of Islam thus were opened up to debate, discussion, and theoretically, criticism. This thus entailed the thorny issue of deciding who had the authority to reinterpret Islamic texts, and in arriving at a consensus concerning the essence of Islamic laws and traditions. Although in the pre-constitutional period advocates of this approach were not fully aware of the depth and breadth of conflict between the two legal traditions (Islamic and European), underlying tensions over delicate questions of political legitimacy and religious authority surfaced during the Constitutional Revolution and the related drafting of legislation.[103]

Questions concerning the role of Islam also emerged due to the tactical approach of some reformers towards Islam as an important basis of social cohesion, one that could and should be reinterpreted and reformulated to serve the interests of modernization.[104] As a result, the ulama's monopoly on the basis of knowledge, the interpretation texts, and the shaping of identity and values was severely undermined by the distinction between types of knowledge.

---

[102]This was nowhere more apparent than in the battles over the authority of Islam in the framing of the constitution. Polar positions on this issue are exemplified by Sayyed 'Abd al- Azim Imad al-Ulama Khalkhali's "A Treatise on the Meaning of Constitutional Government," on the one hand, and Shaykh Fazlollah Nuri's "The Book of Admonition to the Heedless and Guidance for the Ignorant," on the other. Both are translated and edited by Hamid Dabashi, "Two Clerical Tracts on Constitutionalism," in Said Amir Arjomand (ed) *Authority and Political Culture in Shi'ism* (Albany, 1988), pp. 334-70.

[103]Ibid.

[104]On the tactical use of Islam see especially Algar, *Mirza Malkum Khan*; and Nikki Keddie, *An Islamic Response to Imperialism* (Berkeley: University of California Press, 1983).

The Battle for Iran— The Threat of Educational Reform to the Elites

Despite the limited practical successes of the reform movement in Iran, the call for universal literacy, an educated citizenry, and their connection to constitutionalism, had enormous ramifications on the predominance, and even existence, of the social, cultural, and political elites. The theoretical basis of educational reform raised questions concerning the roles of the ulama, governmental elites, and even the legitimacy of the monarchy.

The emergence of nationalism and the importance of the individual added a new pillar to the traditional basis of justice and monarchical legitimacy. The nation, in conscious distinction with the monarch, became a new focus of citizens, and individuals', loyalty. The citizen's reciprocal contract with the government (as embodied ultimately in the monarch) meant that both parties enjoyed rights, as well as responsibilities. The government was charged with promoting progress. "Progress" remained loosely conceived of as constituting prosperity and strength. However, in the late nineteenth century, one of the aims of progress became the happiness of the individual.[105] As a result, the promotion of "progress" and "civilization" and the welfare of the individual emerged as a new pillar of justice, joining the ancient Persian "covenant of kingship." Naser al-Din Shah failed to satisfactorily uphold either of these two pillars of justice, and thereby lost both traditional and modern bases of legitimacy.[106] Mozaffar al-Din Shah also failed to uphold his end of the monarchical contract. His reign witnessed a growing willingness amongst reform-minded individuals to work outside of government channels for change, and for the first time, to begin advocating a change in the *type* of government itself.

The new basis of political legitimacy was accompanied by the emergence of new areas of public space and discourse. The founding of newspapers and journals provided new venues for political discussion and debate, as well as for the dissemination of information and

---

[105]See, for example Talebof's discussion of the individual in *Ketab-e Ahmad*, vol. II, p. 92.

[106]Abbas Amanat, *Pivot of the Universe: Nasir al-Din Shah Qajar and the Iranian Monarchy 1831-1896* (Berkeley: University of California Press, 1997), p. 442.

mobilization of support. The government maintained control of both the content and management of the newspapers published in the first three quarters of the nineteenth century, such as the *Ruznameh-ye Vaqaye'e Ettefaqiyyeh* and its successor, the *Ruznameh-ye Dowlat-e 'Aliyeh-ye Iran*. However, with the publication of journals and newspapers outside of Iran such as *Akhtar* (est. 1875 in Istanbul), *Sorayya* (est. 1899 in Cairo), and others, the government lost control of an important medium of political debate, and the influx of information to Iran. The publication of the newspaper *Qanun* by Mirza Malkom Khan in London from 1890 to 1896-97 marked a turning point as the journal openly advocated a change in type of government, and sought to mobilize widespread support amongst the ulama, the political elite, and other socioeconomic groups. Despite all attempts at preventing the dissemination of journals into Iran, neither Naser al-Din Shah nor Mozaffar al-Din Shah managed to regain control of the press. The establishment of secret societies in the last decades of the century marked an additional loss of control of the growing social and political discourse and activity on the part of the government.

Educational reform also created new, contested social, political and cultural spaces. The European-style schools (both the elite secondary schools and the more socially integrative New schools), directly challenged the existing social and political elites. Educational activists in the 1890s intended to generate a new cadre of political leaders in the New schools. The New schools were not simply utilitarian in purpose, but additionally sought to form the children according to new models of social and political behavior (in Persian: *adamsazi*).[107] According to Dowlatabadi, a major educational reformer, general primary education was a prerequisite for the development of a constitutional government, and for the formation of new leadership for Iran. The children educated in the New schools would, in his view, become the future leaders and proponents of the end of oppression. In fact, Dowlatabadi placed his hopes for what he termed "the salvation of Iran" on the results of the New schools.[108] Another central figure in the educational

---

[107]Dowlatabadi, *Hayat-e Yahya*, vol. I, p. 193.
[108]Ibid, vol. I, pp. 198, 338.

reform movement, Ehtesham al-Saltaneh, expressed similar hopes.[109] Talebof too, lauded the founders of the New schools as patriots, and emphasized the importance of a European-style curriculum in the training of citizens capable of effecting progress— commercially, socially and politically. It was no coincidence that Talebof's *Ketab-e Ahmad* served as a standard text in many of the New schools.

The New schools also threatened the cultural and social hegemony of the ulama. The texts used in the New schools differed enormously from that of the traditional schools. Many were written by educational activists, or translated from the Turkish (Ottoman) or European languages. As a result, the ulama were neither the creators, interpreters, or mediators of the new information, knowledge, or ideas expressed in these texts. The possession of new, scientific knowledge and the status and prestige associated with it also translated into a degree of cultural and moral authority in society, outside of the preserve of the ulama.[110] The New schools, as providers of primary education, contested the ulama's traditional role in forming, defining and transmitting morals and values. Apart from very basic religious instruction, the New schools imparted a radically different curriculum than the traditional primary schools. Together with the notion of citizen-formation, the New schools thus promoted the secularization of morality and responsibility.

The inclusion of subjects such as history (European, classical and Iranian), geography and Persian literature in the New schools (and the *Madraseh-ye 'Olum-e Siyasi*) was due to the reformers' changing conception of their own historical tradition, and its role in the regeneration of Iran, as well as of a consciousness of Iran's place in the international arena.[111] The emphasis on, and indeed reconstruction or creation of, Iran's pre-Islamic past served a dual function of extirpating the source of contemporary "backwardness" and establishing the cultural foundation of a modern Iran. As an attempt to identify an authentic

---

[109]Mirza Mahmud Khan Ehtesham al-Saltaneh, *Khaterat-e Ehtesham al-Saltaneh*, (ed) Sayyed Mohammad Mahdavi-Musavi (Tehran: Zavvar, 1366), p. 315.

[110]Adeeb Khalid, *The Politics of Muslim Cultural Reform: Jadidism in Central Asia* (Berkeley: University of California Press, 1998), p. 9.

[111]For an argument concerning the causal connection between Iran's loss of territory and the instruction of geography and history in Iran, see Kashani-Sabet, *Frontier Fictions*.

cultural identity that could serve as a model for the adaptation of modernization to the Iranian context, it in fact amounted to the *creation* of tradition.

Reformers gradually succeeded in usurping some of the ulama's social authority as well. The political elites and the ulama were criticized for failing to resolve Iran's backwardness, if not condemned for having caused it. This called into question their social authority. The very act of calling for reform and modernization was to some extent subversive of the status quo. However, throughout much of the century, the reformers were unable to refute claims that they advocated the Westernization of Iran. They never successfully distinguished between modernization and Westernization. A principal stumbling block thus became how to legitimize secularization, given the obvious resistance to this process, both ideologically and institutionally, on the part of the ulama. The lack of a clear distinction between Islamic and other, non-religious, bases of Iranian identity further complicated attempts at legitimation of modernization cum secularization.

Consciously or not, proponents of the "indigenous solution" partially resolved this dilemma, and in so doing made a convincing bid for social leadership. Their claim was put forward in several ways. First, their emphasis on the importance of adapting modernization to indigenous needs, paired with their overt call for national regeneration and defense against the ever present European threat, successfully silenced any attempt to dismiss or delegitimize them for being pro-European, or pro-Christian. This in turn, allowed them to present themselves as the guarantors of cultural integrity and the champions of the national interest— a claim that reformers up to this point had never successfully been able to substantiate due to their association with Westernization and Iran's loss of political and economic autonomy at the hands of European powers.

Advocates of the "indigenous solution" in a sense proposed (without fully realizing it) nationalism as a partial replacement, or substitute, for Islam as a pillar of identity— not to the extent of advocating irreligion, but to the degree that secularization of institutions would not be considered an attack on Iranian cultural traditions. In other words, the call for privatization of religion, or at least the elimination of the religious establishment in the legal, administrative and educational arenas, would thus allow for indigenous-based modernization. One strand of nationalism thus initially took on a pronounced anti-clerical (and sometimes even anti-Islamic) tenor.[112]

Second, the very fact that they debated on issues of knowledge, culture and education which were formerly the preserve of the religious establishment, constituted a bid for social leadership. Particularly alarming were reformer's reinterpretations of religious texts and traditions and their attempts to identify irrevocable principles of Islam which could then be reconciled to modernization and the importation of a constitution. Moreover, by proposing to synthesize tradition with modernization, Islam with constitutionalism, and religious instruction with sciences and foreign languages— by orienting Iranians' loyalty towards the nation not the monarch— by rebuking the religious establishment for having failed to lead the country in the direction of progress— and by publishing journals which sought to reach directly to the public, these theorists usurped the moral and cultural authority of the traditional elites and effectively ended their monopoly on the creation and interpretation of culture.

---

[112]Mirza Fath 'Ali Akhundzadeh exemplified the anti-Islamic strain of emerging Iranian nationalism.

CONCLUSION
CRISIS AND TRANSLATION

In the nineteenth century Iran began a process of reform and modernization. Modernization, as it entailed centralization and secularization, affected all spheres of government and society. New institutions were established, social and political elites challenged, and the basis of authority, legitimacy, and identity debated and fiercely contested. The introduction of elements of European education was conceived of from the outset of this process as a means of effecting change and modernization.

The historical context of nineteenth-century Iran gave shape to the parameters of the modernization process and associated discourse, which continued to characterize it throughout the century. The conjunction of increasing European international aggression (political, military, and commercial) with the reestablishment of central authority and control by the newly established Qajar dynasty served as the backdrop for the beginning of the modernization process. As a result, modernization in Iran, much like the process in neighboring states of Egypt and the Ottoman Empire, assumed several key characteristics: First, reform involved a process of state-sponsored centralization. It thus entailed the advancement of central government objectives at the expense of local, regional and informal political and social structures of authority. Due to the natural resistance of political and social elites to a reduction of prerogatives, reform (and thus centralization) in Iran necessitated strong monarchical commitment.

Second, the modernization of the military required an unprecedented degree of financial resources and central administrative control that further enhanced the drive for centralization.

Third, reform was defensive, initiated as a result of military defeats by Russian armies. The international environment of European imperialist expansion lent a strong element of urgency to the reform agenda. Reformers argued that, failing substantive restrengthening, Iran would be unable to resist foreign encroachment. This alarm contributed to the focus of reformers on convincing the monarch to undertake modernization.

Fourth, reform entailed the rationalization of administrative institutions in the form of accountability, formalization of offices, the establishment of governmental responsibility for the educational system and judicial systems and simply put, the end of irrational, informal, and arbitrary government. The centrality of educational and judicial reform to the success of the reform endeavor more generally also meant that the notion of the assumption of governmental authority, supervision and control over these institutions necessarily involved their secularization and regularization.

Fifth, modernization in Iran largely involved the importation of foreign (read European) political institutions and technology. This was partly due to the nature of defensive military reform and the adoption of military technology and training. It was also because European countries were demonstrably more powerful. Therefore, reform involved an attempt to identify and imitate the "secret of European strength."

The equation of the reform process— modernization as centralization, secularization, and administrative rationalization— with the adoption of European institutions and technology had an enormous impact on the articulation of the discourse surrounding modernization, and consequently on the ability to legitimize this process. The negative association of Europe with Christianity and imperialism meant that the model of change was itself questioned. Advocates were thrust into the awkward and essentially defensive position of trying to legitimize reform by distinguishing between modernization and Westernization. The modernization dilemma— namely the desire to adopt European material and technological (and eventually also institutional) advances without a concomitant absorption of cultural and intellectual tenets— dominated the discourse of modernization throughout the century. It led to the fixing of bipolar categories of modernization-Westernization versus traditional-indigenous. This explicitly privileged the indigenous and rejected the foreign institutions. The equation of Islam with Iranian cultural identity further legitimized opposition to reform. The problem of differentiating between modernization and Westernization became especially difficult later in the century when reformers began promoting the secularization of education, and, to some extent, of the judicial system as well. Modernization thus was particularly threatening to the ulama on a multitude of fronts.

The genesis of the modernization dilemma occurred in conjunction with the initiation of a defensive military reform (and centralization) program— the *Nezam-e Jadid*— by Crown Prince 'Abbas Mirza (d. 1833), and its continuance under his son and successor, Mohammad Shah (r. 1834-48). Although the *Nezam-e Jadid* reforms were predicated on the perception of Iranian military and technological "deficiency" vis-à-vis Europe, travel literature in this early period reveals that this "deficiency" was believed to be largely superficial in nature. It did not entail any sense of fundamental "backwardness" or social or cultural inferiority. No responsibility was attributed to Iranian political or social institutions for current military weakness. For this reason, it was believed that the adoption of elements of European technology and training would suffice to place Iran on the path towards "progress" and renewed strength. Proponents of reform were not aware of the cultural and historical contexts of European technology or educational systems. Devoid of context, advocates of limited reform believed that European education and technology could be easily transferred to Iran with no ensuing cultural cost. For example, Mirza Mostafa Afshar writing from Russia in 1829, argued that it would be "a simple matter" for Iran to establish European-style schools to train military and government elites. This decontextualization proved not to be so simple, however, even with regard to the *Nezam-e Jadid*.

The *Nezam-e Jadid* directly threatened a number of vested interests in the political status quo. It is clear that the principal opponents, both in the time of 'Abbas Mirza and Mohammad Shah, were local authorities (regional governors and princes), tribal leaders, and high ranking ulama whose prerogatives were threatened by centralization. While in no way seeking to minimize the very real antipathy on the basis of sartorial and other visible forms of Westernization associated with the military reforms, it is nevertheless the case that opposition was *articulated using the language of Islam— regardless of its basis*. Both 'Abbas Mirza and Mohammad Shah agreed with their opponents that Westernization as such was undesirable. Neither intended for the students dispatched to Europe to adopt European culture or social customs. To the contrary, 'Abbas Mirza expressly told the students to maintain traditional Iranian dress. Mohammad Shah warned students on their way to Europe to guard against a "loss of religion." 'Abbas Mirza and Mohammad Shah moreover tried to harness Islamic legitimization to their own cause, by portraying their reforms as having Islamic precedents and justification— whether by citing specific Qur'anic texts, or by pointing to the example of the Prophet Mohammad and his military victories. Mohammad Shah claimed that the European-style military uniforms

253

had both Islamic and non-Islamic precedents. The attempt to identify the intent of the Qur'an and Islamic tradition more generally as legitimizing reform (as modernization) was a tactic employed throughout the century by their like-minded successors. *Both* proponents and opponents of modernization vied to represent themselves as the guarantors of religious and cultural traditions and the defenders of Iranian honor and territory. This, too, remained a defining characteristic of the reform debate. Interestingly, the dispatch of students abroad to Europe was not the focus of opposition, as it neither threatened political prerogatives, nor were the students *perceived* to be carriers of European culture back to Iran.

Ambivalence by reformers concerning modernization and its connection to Westernization also continued, unresolved. This is aptly illustrated by the Iranian reaction to the establishment of missionary and foreign schools by European and Americans beginning in the mid 1830s and increasing dramatically in the last third of the century. Monarchical support and protection for such schools wavered, depending on the schools' association with foreign powers, and their political, commercial, and cultural objectives. European countries supported the schools diplomatically (and often financially), and interceded with the Iranian monarchs on their behalf. At the same time, the schools attempted to present themselves as having no ulterior objectives, although their directors and founders clearly understood their commercial, cultural and political ramifications. In fact, the missionary and foreign schools often described their mission as cultural and civilizing— although they never admitted as much to the Iranians themselves. Their attempts at dissimulation, however, were entirely unsuccessful and the Iranian government and local communities remained unconvinced by the missionaries' protestations of purely altruistic motives. Not surprisingly, therefore, monarchical support for these schools varied depending on royal diplomatic objectives. When the schools were identified with cultural inroads— proselytization and teaching of Muslims in particular— they were closed or their privileges reduced by royal decree. In order to maintain operation, schools primarily limited their activities to non-Muslim (Christian and Jewish) minorities, and exempted Muslims from religious instruction. Despite fierce resistance to these schools by Armenians and other Christian communities, Mohammad Shah, Naser al-Din Shah, and Mozaffar al-

Din Shah all extended official protection in order to further their own diplomatic agendas.

The *Dar al Fonun*, as the first state-sponsored European-style educational institution in Iran, served as a watershed in the history of educational reform. It embodied the modernization dilemma, and illustrated the difficulty in separating European sciences from their historical and cultural contexts. Its foundation in 1851 by Prime Minister Amir Kabir signified the gradual shift from a perception of technological "deficiency" to the beginnings of the perception of institutional "backwardness" vis-à-vis Europe. Amir Kabir realized that Iran needed not only new European technology, but also a general reform of the governmental apparatus. He also believed that the success of his political reform agenda depended on the creation of educated government cadres who would staff new administrative institutions and support continued reform. The establishment of the school thus illustrated the growing connection between educational reform and larger reform objectives.

The results of the *Dar al Fonun* both exceeded and fell short of expectations. On the one hand, the cultural, social and intellectual threats generated by the instruction of a European-style curriculum at the *Dar al Fonun* were largely unanticipated. Amir Kabir envisioned the establishment of the school as a necessary element in restoring effective government, military strength, and diplomatic self-sufficiency. He deliberately sought to limit further student dispatches abroad as he saw them as channels of European influence in Iran. Paradoxically, the *Dar al Fonun* became a conduit for European ideas into Iran. It emerged as the physical locus of proponents of modernization. Although Amir Kabir correctly perceived that students dispatched to Europe were in fact bearers of European culture and political ideas back to Iran, he failed to understand that educating students in a European-style institution and curriculum in Iran would have similar effects. Amir Kabir, like Mirza Mostafa Afshar some twenty years before, was unaware of the cultural context of European education.

Moreover, Amir Kabir dismissed Naser al-Din Shah's concerns that the *Dar al Fonun* would generate serious opposition from the ulama, insisting that they would be the first to send their sons to the new schools. To the contrary, had Amir Kabir lived long enough to witness the results of his labors, he would have certainly acknowledged that the threat posed by the *Dar al Fonun* to the religious establishment went far beyond anything engendered by other reforms thus far. The teaching of European sciences, particularly medicine and astronomy, directly challenged the ulama and the traditional doctors on a professional, intellectual and cultural basis.

At the same time, the *Dar al Fonun* failed to serve its intended role as an institutional foundation for substantive administrative reform. This was principally due to the fact that Naser al-Din Shah did not allow the school to develop its potential. The reform manifesto published in the *Ruznameh-ye Vaqaye'-e Ettefaqiyyeh* in 1860 indicated the many educational and institutional objectives which it was intended to bring about at that time. These included the establishment of a set curriculum, remedial courses to assist students with insufficient preparation, a guarantee of government employment for graduates, and the enrollment of students from a wider socioeconomic spectrum, as well as from other provinces in Iran. Most of these goals were not achieved. Instead, Naser al-Din Shah allowed the school to languish. Memoirs of students and others testify to the deterioration of the school throughout Naser al-Din Shah's long reign. Mirza Hosayn Khan unsuccessfully attempted to reform the school during his tenure as prime minister from 1871-73. He also established several additional schools to train government officials. Nonetheless, the Naser al-Din Shah period was notable for the absence of substantive educational reform measures. The *Dar al Fonun* remained institutionally isolated, with no supportive educational institutions. In addition, the relatively small number of graduates, in the absence of larger reform, meant that the *Dar al Fonun* never generated a new socioeconomic group that was invested in modernization. In the absence of much broader modernization, the effects of the *Dar al Fonun* were not surprisingly limited.

Naser al-Din Shah's failure to institute educational reform measures illustrates the twin problems of monarchical commitment and reform impetus that plagued the reform movement throughout the Qajar period. There were many obstacles to meaningful reform in nineteenth-century Iran.[1] First, Iran did not enjoy a strong centralized government. Tribes, which made up a substantial percentage of the population

---

[1]For a general discussion of obstacles to reform in Qajar Iran, see Nikki Keddie, *Qajar Iran and the Rise of Reza Shah, 1796-1925* (Costa Mesa: Mazda, 1999).

(roughly 50% at the outset of the nineteenth century and 25% by the end), were only marginally under central control.[2] Naser al-Din Shah, like his predecessors, depended on the tribes for military force throughout his reign and therefore could not afford to alienate them. Provincial governors (often royal princes) also enjoyed a great deal of autonomy, and the system for tax appraisal and collection was irregular and increasingly dysfunctional in the Qajar period. Concessions made to foreign governments, years of famine, and loans obtained from Great Britain and Russia also contributed to a worsening of Iran's financial health throughout the century. In addition, while Naser al-Din Shah did have telegraph lines at his disposal, neither the British nor the Russians, the most likely sources of capital, encouraged the development of a railroad network in Iran.[3] The Iranian government was therefore not in a position to enforce reform measures effectively.

Second, weakness of the central government was exacerbated by the large amount of autonomy enjoyed by regional powers, as well as by the religious establishment.[4] It was only in Naser al-Din Shah's reign (unlike that of Fath 'Ali and Mohammad Shah) that that provincial governors regularly submitted revenues to the central government in Tehran. The ulama capitalized on weak central authority during the decline of the Safavid state in the second half of the seventeenth century, and were never subject to government control under the Qajar dynasty to the extent that they had been in the Safavid period. Unlike their Sunni counterparts in the Ottoman Empire and Egypt, the Shi'ite ulama received funds directly from the population as payment for religious duties and as custodians of large endowments (*vaqf*). Most of them were therefore neither dependent on the government for employment nor for funding. The educational and judicial systems, as

---

[2]Charles Issawi, *The Economic History of Iran* (Chicago: University of Chicago Press, 1971), p. 20.

[3]It was not until the 1920s that the railroad was developed in Iran.

[4]This has been amply documented elsewhere. See for example Nikki Keddie, "The Roots of the Ulama's Power in Modern Iran," *Studia Islamica*, vol. 29 (1969), pp. 31-53. See also Said Amir Arjomand, *The Shadow of God and the Hidden Imam: Religion, Political Order, and Social Change in Shi'ite Iran From the Beginning to 1890* (Chicago: University of Chicago Press, 1984), and Hamid Algar, *Religion and State in Iran 1795-1906* (Berkeley: University of California Press, 1969). For a comparison between Iranian ulama and those Shi'ite scholars in Najaf and Karbala, see Meir Litvak, *Shi'i Scholars of Nineteenth-Century Iraq* (Cambridge: Cambridge University Press, 1998).

well as social services, were largely the prerogatives of the ulama. Furthermore, major centers of ulama power lay outside Iran. Moreover, the informal and diffuse nature of Shi'ite authority (despite the triumph of Usulism), meant that the religious establishment resisted domination and control— either from the state, or from within its own ranks.[5] These factors combined to enable Iranian ulama to resist government attempts to curtail their activities and power.

The Iranian ulama, as the staunchest opponents of new, European-style education, were in a position to hinder educational reform measures. As evidenced by the Tobacco Revolt of 1891-92, the ulama's ties to the community, and to the merchant classes in particular, enabled them to successfully present themselves as the representatives of the country, in opposition to the shah and the government.

Naser al-Din Shah, thus, more than his royal counterparts elsewhere in the Middle East, had to contend with very strong traditional sources of power and opposition that resisted cooption and/or control. Rulers in Egypt and the Ottoman Empire, on the other hand, had already largely succeeded in neutralizing or eliminating competing sources of power, and of forcing reform measures through by means of a strong central authority. For example, Mohammad 'Ali (r. 1805-49) succeeded in monopolizing military power, and in marginalizing the Egyptian ulama. The process of modernization commenced in the Ottoman Empire much earlier than Iran. By 1826 Mahmud II (r. 1808-39) had successfully abolished the semi-autonomous Janissary corps and had curtailed the independence of the religious establishment. Naser al-Din Shah did not enjoy the same latitude in instituting reform, and was therefore unable to effect a coordinated and sustained program of modernization— particularly in the realms of education and law that were controlled by the ulama.

Nevertheless, while these barriers to reform may well explain the *difficulty* of effecting substantive reform in Iran, they do not explain the lack of monarchical *commitment* to doing so. Certainly, centralization is in every ruler's interest. However, Naser al-Din Shah never displayed a firm and lasting commitment to reform and modernization. He repeatedly endorsed limited attempts at reform designed by prime

---

[5]Litvak, *Shi'i Scholars*, pp. 9-11; and Michael Fischer, *From Religious Dispute to Revolution* (Cambridge: Harvard University Press, 1980), pp. 136-37.

ministers and others, only to back away and abandon these reformers when the opposition became too strong. The explanation for this pattern lies largely in the particular nature of the modernization process in Iran, as well as in Iran's relationship with the European powers.

Naser al-Din Shah was convinced that Iran's territorial integrity depended on his ability to ensure a balance of power between Great Britain and Russia in Iran.[6] He therefore refined the policy developed by his predecessors of playing these two powers off against each other. At the same time, he believed that Russia posed the greater threat, and so consistently requested that Great Britain guarantee Iran's protection in the event of Russian invasion. Great Britain, while refusing to officially guarantee Iran's territorial integrity, in effect had promised to do so on a number of occasions.[7]

Another reason for the lack of monarchical commitment to reform in Iran was that opposition was skillfully articulated by the ulama in symbolic terms. Court adversaries of reform also employed the *language of Islam* to justify and strengthen their positions. Opponents (ulama and otherwise) presented themselves as protectors of Islam and of Iran" cultural traditions. The ulama's power meant that opposition to reform could be voiced effectively, and carried great weight. It was therefore difficult for reformers to legitimize reform while evading the accusation of selling out the country to foreigners. Reformers were in constant competition with those opposed to reform to present themselves as champions of the national interest. Naser al-Din Shah deliberately hesitated to support educational change in order to avoid alienating the ulama.

Finally, Naser al-Din Shah himself must bear much of the responsibility for failure to enact substantive reform. His treatment of the *Dar al Fonun* was indicative of his attitude towards reform in general. He viewed the *Dar al Fonun* with a mixture of approbation and alarm. On the one hand, Naser al-Din Shah was aware of Iran's

---

[6]This tactic appealed to others as effective, too. For example, a French minister in Tehran advised Naser al-Din shah to balance Great Britain and Russia against each other as the best means of guaranteeing her independence and territorial integrity. See Firuz Kazemzadeh, *Russia and Great Britain in Persia, 1864-1914* (New Haven: Yale University Press, 1968), p. 17.

[7]On Naser al-Din Shah's repeated requests to this effect, see Henry Creswicke Rawlinson, *England and Russia in the East* (London: John Murray, 1875), pp. 73, 99-100, 128.

political and military (and increasingly financial) weakness vis-à-vis Europe. He himself traveled to Europe on three separate occasions (1873, 1878, and 1889), and witnessed first-hand European advancements and strengths—many of which he appreciated. He was also sensitive regarding European opinion of Iran. He was eager to dispel European notions that Iran was "uncivilized and barbarian."[8] In his view, the *Dar al Fonun* served as a symbol of Iran's "progress."

At the same time, Naser al-Din Shah was concerned about the negative effects of European political ideas. This is evidenced by charges of "Republicanism" which were leveled against individuals suspected of harboring reformist designs. This is also clear from the limitations Naser al-Din Shah placed on the *Dar al Fonun*, and his abiding suspicions concerning the students' and teachers' political tendencies. Naser al-Din Shah took concrete measures to stem the flow of European political ideas into Iran. Three examples of this were his closure of the *Faranushkhaneh* in 1861, the ban on study abroad instituted in 1867, and his attempt to prevent the flow and dissemination of Persian journals into Iran such as *Akhtar* and *Qanun*. Educational reform in particular was viewed as undesirable by the shah due to the association of European-style education with foreign, particularly (revolutionary) French political ideas. Despite the urging of many reform-minded individuals and ministers that he spearhead educational reform, Naser al-Din Shah's reign is notable for the *absence* of concrete educational change.

It is also clear that the monarch himself had an intensely schizophrenic relationship to the system of government in Iran. Although as Amanat has pointed out, Naser al-Din Shah skillfully managed a precarious balancing act between multiple vested interests, powers and court factions, he in fact never fully managed to control the system itself. Despite a workable equilibrium, the Pivot of the Universe did not succeed in fully rising above the system, nor of holding firm the reigns of governance. Lacking the *willpower*, he also recognized that he lacked the requisite *ability* to institute major change. Nor did he always stand to benefit from reform in the short term. The shah himself was so enmeshed in the quagmire of factionalism and patronage systems, that any attempt at systemic rationalization endangered his own interests as

---

[8]Shaul Bakhash, *Iran: Monarchy, Bureaucracy and Reform under the Qajars 1858-1896* (London: Ithaca Press, 1978), p. 134.

well. For example, as pointed out by Matthee with regard to reform of the royal mint, the shah stood to gain from the traditional system in ways that *could not* and would not be the case under a new, rationalized system.[9] Naser al-Din Shah thus equated reform with a certain loss of benefits, if not control. Rationalization after all is clearly antithetical to arbitrary rule. In a typically candid assessment of the shah, Sir Henry Drummond Wolff, British Minister to Iran, wrote: "the shah fears the approach of civilization as being likely to curb his power and to check his autocratic and arbitrary tendencies."[10]

As a result of his paradoxical relationship to reform, Naser al-Din Shah failed to champion the efforts of his prime ministers, Amir Kabir, and later, Mirza Hosayn Khan Sepahsalar, despite his initial protestations of support and encouragement. Nor did he adequately endorse the private initiative of the Council of Merchants spearheaded by the wealthy and energetic Hajj Mohammad Hasan Amin al-Zarb in 1884-86.[11] Particularly after the opposition to Mirza Hosayn Khan's reform proposals and his ouster from the office of prime minister in 1873, Naser al-Din Shah's reign grew increasingly conservative and repressive. Reform-minded individuals concluded that monarchical commitment to reform would not be forthcoming. They therefore increasingly abandoned hopes of effecting change.

The death of Naser al-Din Shah in 1896 and the accession to the throne of Mozaffar al-Din Shah provided a major new impetus to the reform effort in Iran. The more relaxed political climate led reform-minded individuals to renew hopes of securing monarchical support for modernization. The easing up of political restrictions and censorship

---

[9]Rudi Matthee, "Changing the Mintmaster: The Introduction of Mechanized Minting in Qajar Iran," *Itinerario*, vol. 19, no. 3 (1995), pp. 109-127.

[10]Sir Henry Drummond Wolff in (eds) Kenneth Bourne and D. Cameron Watt, *British Documents on Foreign Affairs: Reports and Papers from the Foreign Office Confidential Print*, Part I, Series B, the Near and Middle East 1856-1914, Persia, Britain and Russia 1886-1907, volume 13, p. 25 as cited by Kashani-Sabet, *Frontier Fictions: Shaping the Iranian Nation, 1804-1946* (Princeton: Princeton University Press, 1999), p. 77.

[11]On the Council of Merchants, see Shireen Mahdavi, *For God, Mammon, and Country: A Nineteenth-Century Persian Merchant, Haj Muhammad Hasan Amin al-Zarb* (Boulder, Westview Press, 1999, pp. 92-94, and Feridun Adamiyat and Homa Nateq, *Afkar-e Ejtema'i va Siyasi va Eqtesadi dar Asar-e Montasher Nashodeh-ye Dowran-e Qajar* (Saarbrücken: Nawid, 1989), pp. 299-371. The Council of Merchants was formed in 1884 and dissolved less than two years later.

enabled educational reformers to achieve results on their own initiative. In fact, the Mozaffar al-Din Shah period is notable for the dual processes of politicization and popularization which led to the emergence of a full-fledged reform movement. Due in part to anxiety concerning the urgency of effecting reform, and in part to the growing disaffection with the arbitrary and autocratic nature of government, the numbers of proponents of reform increased. This was accompanied by a broadening of their socioeconomic background to include low-ranking and/or unorthodox ulama, merchants, and an expanding group of the literate pubic. For all of these reasons, the late 1890s witnessed a shift in the *initiative behind* the reform movement away from the highest levels of government and into the hands of private individuals (many of whom of course were in the government, but many others— like Dowlatabadi and Amin al-Zarb— were not). However, reform in the Mozaffar al-Din Shah period suffered from the same obstacles as it had under Naser al-Din Shah. Despite new and broader impetus, the reform movement was unable to plow through the monstrous barriers of systemic resistance and vested interests nor disengage from the infuriating quagmire of informal, non-rationalized government.

The history of the *Anjoman-e Ma'aref* aptly illustrates these developments. During its brief period of operation (1898-1903), the *Anjoman-e Ma'aref* succeeded in establishing and maintaining more than a dozen New schools in Tehran. Educational activists believed in the piecemeal, or "catalyst" approach to reform, whereby modernization in one area would spawn a similar process in others.[12] Education was viewed as an agent of change and modernization. Despite its educational achievements, however, the *anjoman* was unable to fulfill its founders' hopes of becoming a fountainhead of broader social and political reform. Gradually, the *anjoman* was coopted by the government, and subsumed by the Ministry of Science and Education. The failure of the *anjoman* to survive as an independent organization, however, was not surprising for a number of reasons. First, many of the members simultaneously held positions in the government. This resulted in an overlap of duties and responsibilities, and drew the government into the affairs of the *anjoman*. Second, in any event there were no clear distinctions between governmental and private spheres of authority. The shah enjoyed the prerogative, therefore, of determining

---

[12]I am borrowing this term from Bakhash, *Iran*.

and limiting the activities of the *anjoman*. Third, prominent members of the *anjoman* themselves continually looked to the government to play a leadership role in the reform movement. Despite their desire for the shah to lead the reform effort, monarchical commitment was not forthcoming. When Mozaffar al-Din Shah returned from a trip to Europe in 1902, all hopes for top-down government initiative were abandoned. Reformers correctly understood that in the absence of such commitment, substantive modernization and rationalization could not be achieved.

The New schools established by the *Anjoman-e Ma'aref*, its members, and others, increased the degree and nature of the threat to the existing educational system, and to the religious establishment which controlled it. The focus on primary education was a major challenge to the political status quo, as it was essentially a means of restructuring the political system. Primary education also represented a threat to the traditional educational system controlled by the religious establishment, both institutionally, and culturally. In contrast to the elite secondary schools such as the *Dar al Fonun* which were purely *supplementary* to the existing educational system, the New schools constituted a bid to *replace* the traditional system. Just as in Mirza Malkom Khan's educational blueprint outlined in his essay *Ketabcheh-ye Ghaybi*, the entire educational system would be dominated by a European-style curriculum. The new curriculum, by including Persian and Arabic language and basic religious principles along with sciences, foreign languages, geography, and mathematics, attempted to render the traditional system obsolete. Inevitably, traditional schools would serve only as specialized schools for the training of religious scholars. At the same time, the New schools challenged the ulama's cultural dominance, by ending their monopoly over primary education and the inculcation of attitudes and beliefs.

It is noteworthy that there is no discussion in reform literature of the issue of the reform of the *existing maktab-madraseh* system. Talebof and Maragheh'i both fault the ulama for the failure to incorporate European-style subjects into the new curriculum, but do not take the issue any further. Educational reformers believed that it was easier to establish new schools, than to reform existing ones. It would also have been virtually impossible to initiate widespread reform of traditional schools at that time, as there was no governing body or institution that could effect such changes. The Ministry of Sciences and Education did not enjoy authority over traditional schools, and thus was not in a position to dictate reforms. The relatively informal nature of the religious establishment mitigated against it undertaking reform of the traditional educational system, and conversely, for the government to coopt and control it. On the other hand, it also made it more difficult for the ulama to coordinate efforts aimed at preventing the spread of New schools.

Religion, Tradition and the Ulama

The role of the ulama in the process of modernization, and in the discourse surrounding it, is a complex one. Paradoxically, apart from their role in the Constitutional Revolution, investigations into the ulama's response to modernization have been largely neglected. Worse, the ulama has been depicted as backward, reactionary, and as resisting all attempts at modernization. The reasons for this overly simplistic account are not difficult to identify. Ideological predilections concerning the more recent Iranian Revolution of 1978-79 and the ensuing establishment of the Islamic Republic of Iran have clouded the historiography of the nineteenth century, and have resulted in the dehistoricization of the ulama's initial responses to modernization.

However, contemporary attitudes alone are not responsible for the totalization of the ulama reaction prior to the Constitutional Revolution. The relative scarcity of textual evidence of ulama response to modernization is also to blame. The dearth of texts should not be viewed as indicating a failure of the ulama to address questions of modernization (centralization, rationalization, and secularization) and to recognize the significance and import of reform. This position fails to take into account the context of reform literature. Until the late nineteenth century, reform texts were written largely by government officials and reform activists. Reform literature thus circulated primarily amongst government cadres, not the general public or scholarly circles. Even proponents of the "indigenous solution," and the growing number of journals, targeted the educated elite. Reformers dominated the new public and politicized space. By and large, the ulama refrained from participation in the growing public sphere of journals and reform literature that burgeoned in the late 1890s. This is not to say that there is no textual evidence of ulama attitudes towards modernization and reform. For example, members of the ulama sent *fatuas* and letters to the shahs protesting reforms undertaken by various prime ministers, including educational initiatives. However, in terms of scholarly debate, the ulama's audience remained *themselves*. For example, when directly confronted with the teaching of European sciences at the *Dar al Fonun* in the 1850s, members of the ulama wrote treatises debating the new scientific theories, and ultimately *succeeded* in reconciling them with their own religious doctrines by the end of the century.

In order to more accurately recomplicate and recontextualize the ulama response and reaction to modernization, one must distinguish not only between *types* of opposition, but amongst the ulama as a *group*. For a variety of historical, theological, and political reasons, the ulama can not be considered a monolithic group with a formal, centralized, and universally recognized leadership. As a result, it is misleading to talk of "*the* ulama response" since it was more a question of individuals, or small groups acting in concert. Furthermore, the ulama were divided amongst themselves in multiple ways— socially, economically, ideologically, and in degrees of scholarship. It must also be stressed that some of the most ardent reformers outside of government circles were members of the ulama. Many lower-ranking and heterodox members of the ulama were active in the educational reform movement (Dowlatabadi, Malek al-Motekallemin, Jamal al-Din Va'ez, Hadi Najmabadi, and Mirza Hasan Roshdiyyeh). And several high-ranking ulama were prominent leaders in the Constitutional Revolution.

Bases of ulama opposition to modernization can be divided into the following categories: material/technological innovation; centralization; secularization and administrative rationalization; cultural/intellectual conflict. There was little serious resistance to the adoption of technological advances, as long as they were not equated with cultural transgressions. For example, the ulama recognized the need to improve communications and transportation networks (telegraph and railroad) and for the government to operate more effectively in the international commercial and diplomatic arenas.[13] Famous instances of opposition, for example to Mirza Hosayn Khan's proposed railroad, were partly a

[13]Willem Floor, "The Ulama's Response to Modernization," unpublished paper, 1998.

result of deliberate misinformation (the rumor that the railway line would run through the middle of the *Shah 'Abd al-Azim* shrine), and partly due to ulama opposition to the prime minister's administrative reforms (centralization and rationalization), which was then *articulated* using Islamic symbols and arguments.

The religious establishment, along with local government officials and others with vested interests in the political status quo, was directly threatened by many of the centralizing and rationalizing reforms proposed by a series of prime ministers and other reformers. More important yet, the ulama enjoyed special prerogatives in both the judicial and educational systems. Both of these institutions were prime targets of secularization and rationalization throughout the century— which de facto meant a reduction of ulama control. Reformers certainly recognized that in identifying educational and judicial reforms as necessary prerequisites to substantive political and social change they were taking on the ulama's privileges and powers.

The ulama also opposed modernization when it infringed on religious and/or cultural mores, traditions and values. There is no question that educational reform in particular touched on the sensitive area of the instillation of belief systems and values. It was the combination of institutional and *ideological* threats posed by the introduction of European-style schools that made them so potent. For this reason, the *Dar al Fonun* never engendered the same degree or intensity of opposition as did the New schools, since it provided supplementary training for a small number of the elite. The primary European-style curriculum of the New schools was more radical and potentially destructive of both the traditional educational *institution* as well as of traditional values and *Weltanschauung* dominated by the ulama.

Despite these obvious threats, or rather because of them, members of the ulama reacted differently, particularly on the issue of educational reform. Much of the opposition was geared towards resisting the establishment of European-style schools, or at least attempting to limit their popularity and effects. In Tabriz, for example, religious authorities often supported the opposition of *tollab* to the establishment of the *Roshdiyyeh* and subsequently, the New schools. Individual action moreover, could and did have important results. The preacher Yazdi repeatedly instigated riots that destroyed some of the New schools. In 1903 several religious authorities in Najaf attempted to limit the impact of cultural "Europeanization" by issuing a *fatwa* forbidding Muslim attendance at schools which instructed foreign (European) languages. This had little effect, however, on student attendance at the schools.

Other ulama actions with regard to the New schools evidence a more complex and inherently ambivalent attitude towards educational reform. In 1903, several *mujtaheds* in Tabriz tried to make traditional religious instruction mandatory in all New schools, in an attempt to safeguard the inculcation of an Islamic-based value system in the New primary schools. Nonetheless, it was the very *synthesis* of traditional and European-style curriculums (at the primary level, but also as illustrated with the teaching of *fiqh* at the *Madraseh-ye 'Olum-e Siyasi*), that proved to be the most formidable threat to the traditional educational system.

The ulama were not alone in expressing cultural antipathy towards blatant Westernization. Secular reformers, too, concurred that there were drawbacks associated with modernization cum Westernization. Blind imitation of the West, and the cultural Europeanization of some individuals was deemed repugnant. For example, Majd al-Molk, in his essay *Resaleh-ye Majdiyeh*, while urging the government to undertake administrative reforms and greater rationalization, decried Iranian students who returned from abroad Europeanized yet still largely "useless" to the government.[14] E'tezad al-Saltaneh, while director of the *Dar al Fonun*, had one student physically punished for his insistance on speaking a pretentious admixture of French and Persian. Even Mirza Malkom Khan, who lived in Europe much of his adult life and was an avid "Westernizer," described many students abroad as wasting government funds and becoming sissified. Reform essays by Abu Taleb Behbehani, Talebof, and others made a point of recognizing the problems associated with modernization and the importation of European institutions— and not simply for tactical reasons.

Despite the growing depth and breadth of perceived "deficiency" throughout the century, there remained a consensus that this "deficiency" did not involve Iranian cultural traditions. Reformers do not display a sense of cultural inferiority vis-à-vis the West. Similarly, there was agreement across the spectrum of both reformers and their

---

[14]Mirza Mohammad Khan Majd al-Molk Sinaki, *Resaleh-ye Majdiyeh* (ed) Said Nafisi (Tehran: Chapkhaneh-ye Bank-e Melli-ye Iran, 1321).

opponents, that Iran needed to be strengthened to prevent foreign aggression. The debate concerned the remedy.

The crux of the discourse on modernization centered on the reformers' approach to tradition generally, and to the place of religion more specifically. Modernization entails the evaluation of traditions and their viability in a modern polity and society. Which traditions (whether in the form of institutions or attitudes) are essential, which modifiable/adaptable and which expendable? The answers to these thorny questions involves not simply the *identification* of tradition, but more subtly, the *creation* or invention of tradition, as the essential is combined with the adapted, the modified and the new. The important place reserved for the teaching of Iranian history, literature, and geography in the New schools, in the *Madraseh-ye 'Olum-e Siyasi* and in the educational blueprints of Malkom Khan and Behbehani testify that this process of creation and evaluation was underway.

Opponents of reforms were clear in their defense of Iran's cultural and religious traditions. Proponents of reforms, however, were less sure-footed— particularly on the slippery terrain of Islamic traditions and the role of the ulama. On this issue, the discourse of modernization remained a broad spectrum of responses. On one side of the spectrum stood those like Mirza Malkom Khan (and to a lesser extent al-Afghani) who proffered the idea of Islam as a *means* of social solidarity and political mobilization. Malkom Khan's insistence— echoed throughout the century in various permutations— that both Islamic and Western traditions could be stripped of incidental cultural (and in the case of Europe— religious) elements, meant that the two could be reconciled. European institutions thus could be modified, or adapted, to the Iranian context. Talebof's distinction between "material" and "spiritual" culture similarly allowed Western advances (technological and institutional) to be adapted into the Iranian context without endangering Iranian cultural traditions.

On the other hand, Talebof and other advocates of an "indigenous solution" (Maragheh'i and Behbehani) recognized the importance of modifying and adapting European institutions and insisted on Iran remaining the standard. Unlike Malkom Khan, they were more discriminating in their evaluation of tradition, and less willing to eliminate or radically reshape tradition to facilitate the importation of foreign institutions.

Somewhere towards the other end of the spectrum were those who believed that it was imperative to *adapt* any juridical reforms to the specifics of the *shari'a* law— with the *shari'a* remaining the standard. Others were less clear whether the importation of a European-style constitution and/or legal code need in fact be reconciled with the *shari'a*, or if a reconciliation only entailed a general accommodation with vaguely conceived notions of "the guiding principles of Islam." Those reformers, like Malkom Khan, Mirza Yusef Khan and others who called for a reinterpretation of Islamic texts and traditions and a throwing the debate out into the public arena were particularly threatening to the ulama's monopoly on the interpretation of sacred texts and traditions.

Reformers disrupted and challenged the ulama's social and cultural leadership, but did not succeed in dislodging their prominence at this time. Despite the successful articulation of social leadership inherent in the "indigenous solution," reformers recognized the ulama's role in the pre-constitutional period. In fact, many reformers reserved a special position for the ulama as translators and interpreters of tradition, and as mobilizers of popular opinion and political support. Talebof, in maintaining the importance of Iran's cultural and religious identity, left open the possibility of an important role for the ulama in the process of modernization. Behbehani was more straigtforward in reserving a key role for the ulama in the task of adapting a European-style constitution and educational system to fit Iran's needs. Despite the growth of nationalism and the emphasis on constructing identity on pre-Islamic pillars, and despite the limited secularization of morality and individual responsibility, Islam retained its potency— both as a basis of morality, and as a pillar of Iranian identity.

Clarity and Consensus

By the turn of the twentieth century, modernization in Iran had developed into an established movement, replete with a theoretical reform agenda. However, prior to the Constitutional Revolution of 1906-11, these goals remained highly abstract. While advocates of modernization called for the reinterpretation of Islamic texts and traditions, they failed to draw up specific plans to do so. Many of the most fundamental issues of modernization were unresolved, and, for reasons of political expediency, the reformers themselves maintained a deliberately vague reform platform. The general lack of clarity of reform goals was not entirely a matter of political tactics, however. Despite some agreement on the outlines of educational and other reform objectives, there remained no concrete consensus. The debate on modernization developed many shared elements and characteristics, but remained a broad spectrum of responses.

There were two reasons for the continued absence of both consensus and clarity in reform texts. First, the perpetual urgency of reform in the face of aggressive European powers created an environment where reformers' first priority remained the mobilization of support, and advocacy for reform. The splintering of the coalition of constitutionalists during the Constitutional Revolution (especially over the formulation of specific legislation), revealed many of the fundamental tensions and emerging fault lines in the process of modernization.

Second, the fact that modernization was associated with Westernization, or at the very least, with the importation and subsequent adaptation of foreign institutions and knowledge, made the task of legitimizing such reform more difficult. The key element in the legitimation of reform, and of educational reform in particular, remained the resolution of the modernization dilemma. Initially, reformers denied that there was any moral, religious or cultural component in modernization. This contention became difficult to maintain when modernization became connected to the introduction of political institutions and education into Iran, and the problems of contextuality and transferability became inescapable. This was particularly the case after the establishment of the *Dar al Fonun*, and more so even with the New schools in the late 1890s. The modernization dilemma and the cultural and religious concerns associated with it clouded the issues, and hindered the process of critical evaluation, understanding, and analysis that is a prerequisite in developing a workable solution and plan of action.

The Legacy of Nineteenth-Century Reform

The introduction of European-style education in Iran before 1906, despite many achievements, is also a history of failed initiatives, aborted reforms, and frustrated change. In absolute terms, both the numbers of European-style schools and the students they produced were too small to make much of an impact outside of reformist circles. They Iranian educational reform movement never, in the Qajar period, succeeded in producing a government corps or in establishing institutions which would spearhead political and social reform, and transform Iran into a "modern" nation. Indeed, the paucity of actual, substantive change in Iran during this period is most noticeable when compared with similar reform movements in the Ottoman Empire and Egypt. Failure to enact reform, in turn, meant that the political system in Iran continued to be dominated by factionalism and uncertainty. The shah at all times remained the ultimate arbiter. The obstacles to change were too great to be overcome by private initiative (e.g. the Council of Merchants), or even concerted attempts by private groups, such as the *Anjoman-e Maaref*. The shah himself was unable and unwilling to rise above the system itself. Without the shah's active and firm support for reform measures, however, they were bound to fail. Reformers correctly understood that, given the political environment, monarchical commitment was a necessary prerequisite for substantive reform.

It was not until the Pahlavi period that the barriers to reform were breached. Reza Shah forcefully eliminated competing centers of power, and effectively established a strong central government. This in turn enabled him to push forward, at times ruthlessly, his program of administrative rationalization and nation-state building. It was not until his reign, thus, that modern, European-style education was firmly established as the general, universal system of education in Iran. Reza Shah intensified the need for "new" European-style education by expanding and modernizing the bureaucracy, and satisfied this need by expanding and "Europeanizing" the educational system.

Both the achievements and the failures of educational reform in the pre-constitutional period provided an important background for later reform in two ways. First, the obstacles to reform, although not surmounted, were identified. The failures served as poignant lessons concerning necessary prerequisites and components of reform. In particular, it became clear that piecemeal educational reform could not serve as a means of social and political change in the absence of substantive political and administrative reform. Strong, centralized government was understood as the necessary first step in any reform program. Second, many of the educational goals and the schools established in the pre-constitutional period served as models in the constitutional and Pahlavi periods. For example, the emphasis on universal, compulsory, primary education continued. Although the Pahlavi period witnessed growing attention to secondary and higher education, the primary level was recognized as the essential building block of an educated, politicized citizenry.

More importantly even than its political consequences, educational reform in the pre-constitutional period has left an enduring intellectual and cultural legacy on subsequent Iranian history. The introduction of European-style education in Iran in the 1800-1906 period illustrates the historical experiences, cultural tenets and intellectual beliefs that shaped Iran's first response to the question of modernization. In particular, the conflict and competition among the creators of intellectual traditions and cultural identity that first emerged in this period became a dominant theme in subsequent Iranian history. It certainly shaped the emerging secular, socially engagé intelligentsia, as it did Iranian nationalism. The issue of the preservation of cultural integrity, although dormant in the early Pahlavi period, reemerged in the 1860s as central to the political and cultural discussions concerning identity, tradition and continued change. In many important ways, this first response continues to shape these paradigms to the present day.

BIBLIOGRAPHY

Abir, Muhammad. "Modernization, Reaction and Muhammad Ali's 'Empire'." *Middle Eastern Studies* vol. 13, no. 3 (1977), pp. 295-313.

'Abd al-Sabbar, Mohammad ibn. *Jame' al-Hekmatayn va Mojama' al-Tibbayn*. Tabriz, n.d. Paris: Bibliotèque Nationale de France. supplément persian.

Abdolhusayn, Nahid. *Zanan-e Iran dar Jonbesh-e Mashruteh*. Tabriz: Nashr-e Ahya, 1360.

Abdollahpur, Ahmad. *Vozara-ye Ma'aref-e Iran*. Tehran: Rudaki, 1369.

Abu-Ghazaleh, Adnan. *American Missions in Syria*. Brattleboro: Amana Books, 1990.

Abu-Lughod, Lila, (ed) *Remaking Women: Feminism and Modernity in the Middle East*. Princeton: Princeton University Press, 1998.

Adamiyat, Feridun. *Amir Kabir va Iran*. 2d ed. Tehran: Amir Kabir, 1955.

_____. *Andishehha-ye Talebof-e Tabrizi*. Saarbrücken: Nawid, 1363.

_____. *Andishehha-ye Mirza Aqa Khan Kermani*. Tehran: Amir Kabir, 1969.

_____. *Andisheh-ye Taraqqi va Hokumat-e Qanun-e 'Asr-e Sepahsalar*. Tehran: Kharazmi, 1351.

_____. *Andishehha-ye Mirza Fath 'Ali-ye Akhundzadeh*. Tehran, 1970.

_____. *Fekr-e Azadi va Moqademeh-ye Nahzat-e Mashrutiyat dar Iran*. Tehran, 1340.

Adamiyat, Feridun and Homa Nateq, (eds) *Afkar-e Ejtema'i va Siyasi va Eqtesadi dar Athar-e Montasher Nashodeh-ye Dowran-e Qajar*. Tehran: Aghah, 1977.

BIBLIOGRAPHY

Adib al-Molk. 'Abd al-'Ali Khan: *Safarnameh-ye Adib al-Molk beh Atabat.* Tehran: Golzari, 1985.

Afari, Janet. *The Iranian Constitutional Revolution, 1906-11: Grassroots Democracy, Social Democracy and the Origins of Feminism.* New York: Columbia University Press, 1996.

_____. "On the Origins of Feminism in Early 20th Century Iran." *Journal of Women's History* vol. 1, no. 2 (1990), pp. 65-87.

_____. "The Debate on Women's Liberation in the Iranian Constitutional Revolution, 1906-11." In *Expanding the Boundaries of Women's History: Essays on Women in the Third World,* (eds) Cheryl Johnson-Odim and Margaret Strobel, 101-21. Bloomington: Indiana University Press, 1997.

Afshar, Iraj. *Rejal-e 'Asr-e Mashrutiyat.* Tehran: Asatir, 1363.

_____. (ed) *Amir Kabir va Dar al Fonun: Majmu'eh-ye Ketabha-ye Iradshodeh dar Ketabkhaneh-ye Markazi va Markaz-e Asnad-e Daneshgah-e Tehran.*

_____. "Bahthi dar Asnad Marbut beh Farrokh Khan." *Yaghma* vol. 18, no. 11 (Bahman), pp. 583-91.

_____. "Talebov." *Yaghma* vol. 4, pp. 214-21.

Afshar, Mirza Mostafa. *Safarnameh-ye Khosrow Mirza beh Petersburg.* (ed) Mohammad Gulbun. Tehran: Ketabkhaneh-ye Mostowfi, 1349.

Al-Jabarti. *Napoleon in Egypt.* Princeton: Markus Wiener, 1995.

Alavi, Bozorg. *Geschichte und Entwicklung der modernen persischen Literatur.* Berlin: Akademie-Verlag, 1964.

Algar, Hamid. *Religion and State in Iran.* Berkeley: University of California Press, 1969.

_____. *Mirza Malkum Khan: A Study in the History of Iranian Modernism.* Berkeley: University of Califormia Press, 1973.

_____. "An Introduction to the History of Freemasonry in Iran." *Middle Eastern Studies* vol. 6, no.3 (1970), pp. 276-96.

BIBLIOGRAPHY

Amanat, Abbas. *Pivot of the Universe: Nasir al-Din Shah Qajar and the Iranian Monarchy, 1831-1896.* Berkeley: University of California Press, 1997.

_____. "Russian Intrusion into the Guarded Domains." *Journal of Asian and Oriental Studies* vol. 113, no. 3 (1993), pp. 39-56.

_____. "The Downfall of Mirza Taqi Khan Amir Kabir and the Problem of Ministerial Authority in Qajar Iran." *International Journal of Middle East Studies* vol. 23, no. 4 (1991), pp. 577-99.

Amin al-Dowleh, Farrokh Khan. *Majmu'eh-ye Asnad va Madarek-e Farrokh Khan Amin al-Dowleh.* 3 vols. (ed) K. Esfahanian and Q. Rowshani. Tehran, 1346-50.

Amin, Qasim. *The Liberation of Women: a document in the history of Egyptian feminism (Tahrir al-Mara')* (trans) Samiha Sidhom Peterson. Cairo: American University of Cairo Press, 1992.

Amin al-Dowleh, Mirza 'Ali Khan. *Khaterat-e Siyasi-ye Mirza 'Ali Khan Amin al-Dowleh.* (ed) Hafez Farmafarma'ian. Tehran: Persian Book Co., 1962.

Amini, Iradj, *Napoleon and Persia: Franco-Persian Relations under the First Empire.* (French original, 1995; English translation Mage, 1999).

Anonymous. *Shaykh va Shukh.* (ed) Ahmad Mojahed. Tehran: Entesharat-e Ruzaneh, 1373.

Anwar, A. "Anjoman-e Ma'aref," *Encyclopaedia Iranica* vol. 2, pp. 86-88.

Arasteh, Reza. *Education and Social Awakening in Iran.* 2d ed. Ithaca: Cornell University Press, 1969.

Arjomand, Kamran. "The Emergence of Scientific Modernity in Iran: Controversies Surrounding Astrology and Modern Astronomy in the Mid-Nineteenth Century," *Iranian Studies* vol. 30, nos. 1-2 (Winter/Spring 1997), pp. 5-24.

Arjomand, Said Amir. *The Shadow of God and the Hidden Imam: Religion, Political Order and Societal Change in Shi'ite Iran From the Beginning to 1890* Chicago: Chicago University Press, 1984.

_____.*The Turban For the Crown*. Oxford: Oxford University Press, 1988.

_____."The Ulama's Traditionalist Opposition to Parliamentarism, 1907-1909." *Middle Eastern Studies* vol. 17, no. 2 (1981), pp. 174-91.

_____. (ed) *The Political Dimensions of Religion*. Albany: SUNY Press, 1993.

Ashraf, Ahmad. "The Roots of Emerging Dual Class Structure in 19th Century Iran." *Iranian Studies* vol. 14, nos. 1-2 (1981), pp. 5-29.

Atai, Mohammad Farhad. "The Sending of Iranian Students to Europe, 1811-1906." Ph.D. dissertation, University of California, Berkelely, 1992.

Atkin, Muriel. *Russia and Iran, 1780-1828*. Minneapolis: University of Minnesota Press, 1980.

Avery, Peter. *Modern Iran*. London: E. Nenn, 1965.

_____. "Printing, the Press, and Literature in Modern Iran." *Cambridge History of Iran* vol. 7, pp. 815-69.

Avigdor, Levy. "Military Reform and the Problem of the Centralization in the Ottoman Empire in the 18th Century." *Middle Eastern Studies* vol. 18, no. 3 (1982), pp. 227-49.

Bakhash, Shaul. *Iran: Monarchy, Bureaucracy and Reform Under the Qajars, 1858-96*. (London: Ithaca Press, 1978).

_____. "The Evolution of Qajar Bureaucracy: 1779-1879." *Middle Eastern Studies* vol. 7, no. 1 (1971), pp. 139-68.

Bamdad, Badr al-Muluk. *From Darkness Into Light: Women's Emancipation in Iran*. Hicksville, NY: Exposition Press, 1977.

Bamdad, Mehdi. *Sharh-e Hal-e Rejal-e Iran dar Qarn-e 12-14 Hejri*. Tehran: Navar, 1347.

Balay, Christophe. *La genèse du roman persan moderne*. Tehran: Institut Francais de Recherche en Iran, 1998.

Banani, Amin. *The Modernization of Iran: 1921-1941.* Stanford: Stanford University Press, 1961.

Barzegar, Ali. "Mehdi Qoli Hedayat: A Conservative of the Late Qajar Era." *Iranian Studies* vol. 20, no. 1 (1987), pp. 55-76.

Bassett, James. *Persia: The Land of the Imams: a Narrative of Travel and Residence, 1871-1885.* London: Blackie & Sons, 1887.

Bayat, Mangol. *Iran's First Revolution: Shi'ism and the Constitutional Revolution of 1905-1909.* Oxford: Oxford University Press, 1991.

_____. "Mirza Aqa Khan Kermani: A 19th Century Persian Nationalist." *Middle Eastern Studies* vol. 10, no. 1 (1974).

_____. "Women and Revolution in Iran, 1905-1911." In *Women in the Muslim World*, (eds) Lois Beck and Nikki Keddie. Cambridge: Harvard University Press, 1978.

Behbehani, Aqa Ahmad ibn Mohammad 'Ali. *Mer'at al-Ahval-e Jahannameh.* Tehran: Amir Kabir, 1370/1991.

Berberian, Houri. "Armenian Participation in the Iranian Constitutional Revolution." Ph.D. dissertation, University of California, Los Angeles, 1997.

Bell, Daniel. "The Return of the Sacred? The Argument on the Future of Religion," *The Winding Passage: Essays and Sociological Journeys 1960-1980.* Cambridge: ABT Books, 1980, pp. 324-54.

Berkes, Niyazi. *The Development of Secularism in Turkey.* Montreal: McGill, 1964.

Bill, James Alban. *The Politics of Iran: Groups, Classes and Modernization.* Columbus, OH: Charles Merill Press, 1972.

Binder, Leonard. *Iran: Political Development in a Changing Society.* Berkeley: University of California Press, 1962.

Board of Foreign Missions of the Presbyterian Church in the USA. *A Century of Missionary Work in Iran, 1834-1934.* Beirut American Press, 1935.

Bonine, Michael and Nikki Keddie, (eds) *Continuity and Change in Modern Iran*. Albany: State University of New York Press, 1981.

Boré, Eugène. *Correspondance et mémoires d'un voyageur en Orient*. 2 vols. Paris: Olivier-Fulgenie, 1840.

Boroujerdi, Mehrzad. *Iranian Intellectuals and the West: The Tormented Triumph of Nativism*. Syracuse: Syracuse University Press, 1996.

Bosworth, Edmond and Carol Hilleband, (eds) *Qajar Iran: Political, Social and Cultural Change, 1800-1925*. Edinburgh: Edinburgh University Press, 1983.

Bourdieu, Pierre. "Cultural Reproduction and Social Reproduction." In *Knowledge, Education and Cultural Change*, (ed) Richard Brown, 71-112. London, 1973.

_____. "The Genesis of the Concepts of Habitus and Field." *Sociocriticism* vol. 2 (1985), pp. 11-24.

_____. "Systems of Education and Systems of Thought." *International Social Sciences Journal* vol. 19 (1967), pp. 338-58.

Bozorg Omid, 'Abd al-Hasan. *Az Mast keh bar Mast*. Tehran: Donya-ye Ketab, 1955.

Browne, Edward Granville. *Press and Poetry in Modern Persia*. Cambridge: Cambridge University Press, 1914.

_____. *A Year Amongst the Persians*. London: Adam & Charles Black, 1893.

_____. *Arabian Medicine*. Cambridge: Cambridge University Press, 1962.

_____. *A Literary History of Persia*. 2 vols. Cambridge: Cambridge University Press, 1951.

Bruézière, Maurice. *L'Alliance Française: Histoire d'une Institution*. Paris: Hachette, 1983.

Brydges, Sir Harford Jones. *An Account of the Transactions of His Majesty's Mission to the Court of Persia in the Years 1807-11*. London: 1834.

Bulliet, Richard W. *The Patricians of Nishapur*. Cambridge: Harvard University Press, 1972.

Burgess, Charles and Edward Burgess. *Letters From Persia Written by Charles and Edward Burgess, 1828-1855*. New York, 1942.

Butrus, Abu-Manneh. "The Sultan and the Bureaucracy: The Anti-Tanzimat Concepts of Grand Vizier Mahmud Nedim Pasha." *International Journal of Middle East Studies* vol. 22, no. 3 (1990), pp. 257-74.

Chambers, Richard. "The Ottoman Ulama and the Tanzimat." In *Scholars, Saints and Sufis: Muslim Religious Institutions in the Middle East Since 1500*, (ed) Nikki Keddie, 33-46. Berkeley: University of California Press, 1972.

_____."Notes on the Mekteb-i Osmani in Paris, 1857-1874." In *Beginnings of Modernization in the Middle East: the Nineteenth Century*, (eds) William Polk and Richard Chambers, 313-29. Chicago: Chicago University Press, 1968.

Chardin, Sir John. *Travels in Persia, 1643-1713*. London: 1927.

Chehabi, Houchang E. "Staging the Emperor's New Clothes: Dress Codes and Nation-Building under Reza Shah." *Iranian Studies* vol. 26, nos. 3-4, Summer/Fall 1993, pp. 209-33.

Chodzko, Aleksander Edmund Boreyko. *Théatre Persan: Choix de Téaziés*. Paris: Ernst Leroux, 1878.

Chouraqui, André. *L'Alliance Israélite Universelle et la Renaissance Juive Contemporaine 1860-1960*. Paris: Presses Universitaires de France, 1965.

Cole, Juan, R. I. "Iranian 'Orientalism' in Early 19th-Century India." *Critique* no. 8 (Spring 1996), pp. 41-60.

_____. "Marking Boundaries, Marking Time: The Iranian Past and the Construction of the Self by Qajar Thinkers." *Iranian Studies* vol. 29, nos. 1-2 (Winter/Spring 1996), pp. 35-56.

_____. "Invisible Occidentalism: Eighteenth-Century Indo-Persian

Constructions of the West," *Iranian Studies* vol. 25, nos. 3-4 (1992), pp. 316.

Confino, Albert. *L'action de l'Alliance Israélite Universelle en Perse.* Algiers, 1942.

Confino, Michael. "On Intellectuals and Intellectual Traditions in Eighteenth-and Nineteenth-Century Russia." *Daedalus* vol. 101, no. 2 (1972), pp. 117-49.

Creceliuis, Daniel. "Nonideological Responses of the Egyptian Ulama to Modernization." In *Scholars, Saints and Sufis: Muslim Religious Institutions 1500 to the Present*, (ed) Nikki Keddie, 167-210. Berkeley: University of California Press, 1972.

Curzon, George. *Persia and the Persian Question.* London: 1892.

Dabashi, Hamid. "Two Clerical Tracts on Constitutionalism." In *Authority and Political Culture in Shiism*, (ed) Said Amir Arjomand, 334-70. Albany: SUNY Press, 1988.

Davison, Roderic. *Reform in the Ottoman Empire, 1856-76.* Princeton: Princeton University Press, 1963.

_____."Westernized Education in Ottoman Turkey." *Middle Eastern Journal* vol. 15, no. 3 (Summer 1961), pp. 289-301.

_____."The Advent of the Principle of Representation in the Government of the Ottoman Empire." In *Beginnings of Modernization in the Middle East: The Nineteenth Century*, (eds) William Polk and Richard Chambers, 93-108. Chicago: University of Chicago Press, 1968.

_____. *Essays in Ottoman and Turkish History, 1774-1923: The Impact of the West.* Austin: University of Texas Press, 1990.

Delrish, Bashri. *Zan dar Dowreh-ye Qajar.* Tehran: Daftar-e Motale'at-e Dini-ye Honar, 1375.

Dodge, Bayard. *Muslim Education in Medieval Times.* Washington DC: Middle East Institute, 1962.

Dodwell, H. *The Founder of Modern Egypt: A Study of Muhammad Ali in Egypt*. Cambridge: Cambridge University Press, 1931.

_____."The Beginning of Modernization Among the Rectors of al-Azhar, 1798-1879."In *Beginnings of Modernization in the Middle East: The Nineteenth Century*, (eds) William Polk and Richard Chambers. Chicago: University of Chicago Press, 1968.

Donbali, 'Abd al-Razzaq. *Ma'athir al-Soltaniyyeh*. Translated by Sir Harford Jones Brydges as *Dynasty of the Kajars*. London, 1833.

Dowlatabadi, Yahya. *Tarikh-e Mo'aser ya Hayat-e Yahya Dowlatabadi*. 4 vols. Tehran: Ferdowsi, 1362.

Drouville, Colonel Gaspard. *Voyage en Perse pendant les anées 1812 et 1813*. 2 vols. Paris, 1828.

Dupré, Adrien. *Voyage in Perse fait dans les années 1807, 1808 et 1809 en traversant l'Anatolie et la Mesopotamie*. Paris, 1819.

Ebrahimnejad, Hormoz. " Introduction de la médicine européenne en Iran au XIXè siècle." *Sciences sociales et santé* vol. 16 (14 décembre 1998), pp. 69-96.

Ehtesham al-Saltaneh, Mirza Mahmud Khan. *Khaterat-e Ehtesham al-Saltaneh*. (ed) Sayyed Mohammad Mahdavi-Musavi. Tehran: Zavar, 1366.

Ekbal, Kamran. *Der Briefwechsel Abbas Mirzas*. Freiburg, 1977.

Ekhtiar, Maryam. "The Dar al-Fonun: Educational Reform and Cultural Development in Qajar Iran." Ph.D. dissertation, New York University, 1994.

_____. "An Encounter with the Russian Czar: The Image of Peter the Great in Early Qajar Historical Writings." *Iranian Studies* vol. 29, nos. 1-2 (Winter/Spring 1996), pp. 57-70.

Elgood, Cyril. *A Medical History of Persia and the Eastern Caliphate from the Earliest Times until the Year A.D. 1932*. Cambridge: Cambridge University Press, 1951.

_____. *Safavid Medical Practice*. London: Lazac & Co., 1970.

_____. *Medicine in Persia*. New York: Paul B. Hoeber, 1978.

Esdaile, Charles J. *The Wars of Napoleon*. New York: Longman, 1995.

E'temad al-Saltaneh, Mohammad Hasan Khan. *Chehel Sal-e Tarikh-e Iran dar Dowreh-ye Padeshahi-ye Naser al-Din Shah*. (ed) Iraj Afshar. Tehran, 1983.

_____. *Ruznameh-ye Khaterat-e E'temad al-Saltaneh*. (ed) Iraj Afshar. Tehran, 1345.

_____. *Al-Ma'athir va al-Athar*. Tehran: 1306.

Fahmy, Khaled. *All the Pasha's Men: Mehmed Ali, His Army and the Making of Modern Egypt*. Cambridge: Cambridge University Press, 1997.

Faksh, Mahmud. "The Consequences of the Introduction and Spread of Modern Education: Education and National Integration in Egypt." *Middle Eastern Studies* vol. 16, no. 2 (1980), pp. 42-56.

Farahani, Mirza Mohammad Hossein. *A Shi'ite Pilgrimage to Mecca 1885-1886*. (eds) Hafez Farmayan and Elton L. Daniel. Austin: University of Texas press, 1990.

Farmanfarma'ian, Hafez. "The Forces of Modernization in 19th Century Iran." In *Beginnings of Modernization in the Middle East: The Nineteenth Century*, (eds) William Polk and Richard Chambers, 115-51. Chicago: Chicago University Press, 1968.

Fasa'i, Hasan ibn Hasan. *Farsnameh-ye Naseri*. Translated by Herbert Busse as *History of Persian Under Qajar Rule*. (ed) Ehsan Yarshater. New York: Columbia University Press, 1972.

Feuvrier, Joannes. *Trois ans à la cour de Perse*. Paris: F. Juven, 1899.

Findley, Carter. *Ottoman Civil Officialdom*. Princeton: Princeton University Press, 1989.

Fischer, Michael. *Iran: From Religious Dispute to Revolution*. Cambridge: Harvard University Press, 1980.

Flandin, Eugène, and Paul Coste. *Voyage en Perse de M.M. Eugène Flandin et Paul Coste, 1840-1*. 2 vols. Paris, 1851.

Floor, Willem. "Chap." *Encydopaedia Iranica* vol. 6, pp. 760-4.

_____. "The Economic Role of the 'Ulama in Qajar Persia." unpublished article, 1998.

_____. "The First Printing Press in Iran." *Zeitschrift der Deutschen Morganländischen Gesellschaft* vol. 130 (1980), pp. 369-71.

Forughi, Muhammad 'Ali. "Farhang-e Now Cheguneh dar Iran Aghaz Shod." *Amuzesh va Parvaresh* vol. 25, nos. 8-9.

Fraser, David. *Persia and Turkey in Revolt*. London: William Blackwood, 1910.

Fraser, James Baillie. *Narrative of the Residence of the Persian Princes in London in 1835 and 1836 with an account of their journey from Persia and subsequent adventures*. 2nd ed. London: Richard Bentley, 1838.

_____. *Narrative of a Journey Into Khorasan in the years 1821 and 1822*. Oxford: 1984.

Frey, Frederick. *The Turkish Political Elite*. Cambridge: MIT Press, 1965.

Gardane, Alfred de. *Mission du General Gardane en Perse*. Paris, 1865.

_____. *Journale d'un voyage dans la Turquie d'Asie et la Perse*. Paris: 1809.

Garrusi, Amir Nezam. *Amir Nezan dar Sefarat-e Faranseh va Engolestan*. (ed) Ahmad Sahili Ansari. Tehran: Iqbal, n.d.

Gerth, H. H. and C. Wright Mills (eds) *From Max Weber: Essays in Sociology*. New York: Oxford University Press, 1958, 1970 printing.

Ghanoonparvar, Mohammad. *In a Persian Mirror: Images of the West and Westerners in Iranian Fiction*. Austin: University of Texas Press, 1993.

Ghani. "Tarikh-e Ruznamehnegari dar Iran." *Yadegar* vol. 1, no. 6 (Bahman 1323), pp. 6-17.

Gheissari, Ali. *Iranian Intellectuals in the 20th Century*. Austin: University of

Texas Press, 1998.

Ghougassian, Vazken. *The Emergence of the Armenian Diocese of New Julfa in the Seventeenth Century.* Atlanta, 1998.

Gibb, H.A.R. and Harold Bowen. *Islamic Society and the West: A Study of the Impact of Western Civilization on Moslem Culture in the Near East.* 2 vols. London: Oxford University Press, 1950.

Giddens, Anthony. *The Consequences of Modernity.* Stanford: Stanford University Press, 1990.

Gobineau, Joseph Arthur de. *Trois ans en Asie.* Paris: 1859.

_____.*Les religions et les philosophies dans l'Asia Centrale.* Paris: 1865.

Gocek, Fatma Muge. *East Encounters West: France and the Ottoman Empire in the \Eighteenth Century.* Oxford: Oxford University Press, 1987.

_____.*Rise of the Bourgeoisie, Demise of Empire: Ottoman Westernization and Social Change.* Oxford: Oxford University Press, 1996.

Gurney, John and Negin Nabavi. "Dar al-Fonun." *Encyclopedia Iranica* vol. 6, pp. 662-8.

Haag-Higuchi. "A Topos and Its Dissolution: Japan in Some 20th-Century Iranian Texts." *Iranian Studies* vol. 29, nos. 1-2 (Winter/Spring 1996), pp. 71-83.

Hadidi, Djavad. "French Schools in Persia." *Encyclopaedia Iranica* vol. 10, pp. 178-181.

Hairi, 'Abdul-Hadi. "The Legitimacy of Early Qajar Rule as Viewed by the Shii Religious Leaders." *Middle Eastern Studies* vol. 24, no. 3 (1988), pp. 271-87.

_____."Shaykh Fazlollah Nuri's Refutation of the Idea of Constitutionalism."*Middle Eastern Studies* vol. 13, no. 3 (1977), pp. 327-29.

Halpern, Manfred. *The Politics of Social Change in the Middle East and North Africa.* Princeton: Princeton University Press, 1963.

Hedayat, Mehdi Qoli Khan, Mokhbar al-Saltaneh. *Khaterat va Khaterat: Tusha'i as Shesh Padeshah va Gosha'i az Dowreh-ye Zendegi-ye Man.* Tehran, 1965-66.

Hedayat, Reza Qoli. *Rowzat al-Safa-ye Naseri.* Tehran, 1284.

Hekmat, Ali Reza. *Amuzesh va Parvaresh dar Iran-e Bastan.* Tehran: Mo'asseseh-ye Motele'at va Tahqiqat-e Ejtema'i, Daneshgah-e Tehran, 1972.

Heper, Metin. "Political Modernization as Reflected in Bureaucratic Change:The Turkish Bureaucracy and a 'Historical Bureaucratic Empire' Tradition. "*International Journal of Middle East Studies* vol. 7, no. 4 (1976), pp. 507-21.

Heyd, Uriel. "The Ottoman Ulema and Westernization in the Time of Selim III and Mahmud II." Scripta Hierosolymitana, Studies in Islamic History and Society. (ed) Uriel Heyd. Jerusalem: Magnes Press, Hebrew University, 1961.

Heyworth-Dunne, J. *An Introduction to the History of Education in Modern Egypt.* London, 1968.

Hillman, Michael. "The Modernist Trend in Persian Literature and Its Social Impact." *Iranian Studies* vol. 15, nos. 1-4 (1982), pp. 7-29.

Hourani, Albert. *Arabic Thought in the Liberal Age, 1798-1939.* London: Oxford University Press, 1962.

Ingram, Edward. *Britain's Persian Connection 1798-1828: Prelude to the Great Game in Asia.* Oxford: Clarendon Press, 1992.

Iqbal, Abbas. *Mirza Taqi Khan Amir Kabir.*Tehran, 1340.

_____."Tarikh-e Ruznamehnegari dar Iran." *Yadgar* vol. 1, no. 7 (1944-45), pp. 6-17.

_____. "Dastani az Moballeghayn-e Isavi dar Iran." *Yadegar* vol. 3, nos. 6-7 (1325), pp. 60-6.

Isfahani, Abu Taleb Khan. *The Travels of Abu Taleb Khan in Asia, Africa and Europe during the years 1799, 1800, 1801, 1802 and 1803.* 2 vols.

BIBLIOGRAPHY

Translated by Charles Stewart. London: Longman, 1810.

_____. *Masir-e Talebi fi Belad-e Afranji*. Calcutta, 1812.

Issawi, Charles. *The Economic History of Iran*. Chicago: University of Chicago Press, 1971.

Jahangir Mirza. *Tarikh-e Now*. (ed) A. Iqbal. Tehran, 1327.

Jaubert, Amedée. *Voyage en Arménie et en Perse fait dans les années 1805 et 1806*. Paris: 1821.

Jomard, E.F. "L'école égyptienne de Paris." *Nouveau Journal Asiatique* vol. 2, August 1828, pp. 96-116.

Kamshad, H. *Modern Persian Prose Literature*. Cambridge: Cambridge University Press, 1966.

Karabel, Jerome and A. H. Halsey, (eds) *Power and Ideology in Education*. New York: Oxford University Press, 1977.

Kashani-Sabet, Firoozeh. *Frontier Fictions: Shaping the Iranian Nation, 1804-1946*. Princeton: Princeton University Press, 1999.

Kasravi, Ahmad. *Tarikh-e Mashruteh-ye Iran*. Tehran: Amir Kabir, 1984.

Kazamias, Andreas M. *Education and the Quest for Modernity in Turkey*. Chicago:Chicago University Press, 1966.

Kazemzadeh, Firuz. *Russia and Britain in Persia, 1864-1914*. New Haven:Yale University Press, 1968.

Keddie, Nikki. *Qajar Iran and the Rise of Reza Khan, 1796-1925*. Costa Mesa: Mazda, 1999.

_____. "Iranian Politics 1900-1905: Background to Revolution." *Middle Eastern Studies* vol. 5, no. 1 (1969), pp. 3-31.

_____. "Secularism and the State: Towards Clarity and Global Comparison." *New Left Review* vol. 226 (Nov./Dec. 1997), pp. 21-40.

_____. "The Iranian Power Structure and Social Change 1800-1969: An Overview." *International Journal of Middle East Studies* vol. 2, no. 1 (1971), pp. 3-20.

_____.*Sayyid Jamal al-Din al-Afghani: A Political Biography*. Berkeley: University of California Press, 1972.

_____. *An Islamic Response to Imperialism*. Berkeley: University of California Press, 1983.

_____. "Religion and Irreligion in Early Iranian Nationalism." *Contemporary Studies in Society and History* vol. 4 (1962), pp. 265-95.

_____. *Religion and Rebellion in Iran: The Tobacco Protest of 1891-2*. London, 1966.

_____."Class Structure and Political Power in Iran Since 1796." *Iranian Studies* vol. 11 (1978), pp. 305-30.

_____. "Iranian Politics 1900-1905: Background to Revolution." *Middle Eastern Studies* (part 1) vol. 5, no. 1 (1969), pp. 3-31; (part 2) vol. 5, no. 2 (1969), pp. 151-67; (part 3) vol. 5, no.3 (1969), pp. 234-50.

_____. "The Roots of the Ulama's Power in Modern Iran." *Studia Islamica* vol. 29 (1969), pp. 31-53.

_____. "Religion, Society, and Revolution in Modern Iran." In *Continuity and Change in Modern Iran*, (eds) Michael Bonine and Nikki Keddie. Albany: SUNY Press, 1981.

Kedourie, Elie, and Sylvia Haim, (eds) *Towards a Modern Iran: Studies in Thought, Politics and Society*. London: Cass, 1980.

Khalid, Adeeb. *The Politics of Muslim Cultural Reform: Jadidism in Central Asia*. Berkeley: University of California Press, 1998.

Kia, Mehrdad. "Nationalism, Modernization and Islam in the Writings of Talibov-e Tabrizi." *Middle Eastern Studies* vol. 30, no. 2 (1994), pp. 201-23.

_____. "Constitutionalism, Economic Modernization and Islam in the Writings of Mirza Yusef Khan Mostashar al-Dowleh." *Middle Eastern Studies* vol. 30, no. 4 (1994), pp. 751-77.

Kirmani, Nazem al-Islam. *Tarikh-e Bidari-ye Iranian.* Tehran: Entesharat-e Amir Kabir, 1731.

Lachini, Abu al-Qasem. *Ahvalat va Dastkhatha-ye 'Abbas Mirza Na'yeb al-Saltaneh.* Tehran, 1326.

Lambton, Ann. "Secret Societies and the Persian Revlution of 1905-6." *St. Anthony's Papers* vol. 4 (1958).

_____. *Qajar Persia.* London: I.B. Taurus, 1987.

_____. "Some New Trends in Islamic Political Thought in Late 18th and Early 19th Century Persia." *Studia Islamica* vol. 39 (1977), pp. 95-128.

Laurie, Thomas. *Dr. Grant and the Mountain Nestorians.* Boston: Gould and Lincoln, 1853.

Lerner, Daniel. *The Passing of Traditional Society: Modernizing the Middle East.* Glenco, IL: The Free Press, 1958.

Levy, Habib, *Tarikh-e Jame'-e-ye Yahudiyan-e Iran* (Beverly Hills: Cultural Foundation of Habib Levy, 1997).

Lewis, Bernard. *The Emergence of Modern Turkey.* Oxford: Oxford University Press, 1961.

_____. *The Middle East and the West.* New York: Harper & Row, 1964.

_____. "The Impact of the French Revolution on Turkey." *Cahiers d'Histoire Mondiale* vol. 1 (July 1953), pp. 105-125.

Litvak, Meir. *Shi'i Scholars of Nineteenth-Century Iraq.* Cambridge: Cambridge University Press, 1998.

Lonca, Anouar. *Voyageurs et écrivins égyptiens en France au XIXe siècle.* Paris, 1970.

Lorentz, John. "Modernization and Political Change in Nineteenth Century Iran: The Role of Amir Kabir." Ph.D. dissertation, Princeton University, 1974.

Madani, Jalal al-Din. *Tarikh-e Tahvelat-e Siyasi va Ravabet-e Khareji-ye Iran: az Aghaz-e Qajariyeh ta Enqelab-e Mashrutiyat*. 2 vols. Tehran: Islami, 1990.

Mahbubi-Ardakani, Husayn. *Tarikh-e Mo'asesat-e Tamaddoni-ye Jadid dar Iran*. 3 vols. Tehran: Tehran University Press, 1975.

_____. "Dovvomin Karevan-e Ma'refat." *Yaghma* vol. 18, pp. 592-8.

_____. "Sevvomin Karevan-e Ma'refat." *Yaghma* vol. 19 (1345), pp. 516-19.

_____. "Karamuzan va Daneshjuyan-e Irani dar Rusiyeh dar Zaman-e Qajariyeh." *Rahnema-ye Ketab* vol. 6, no. 10 (1346), pp. 564-76.

_____. "Seyyed Mohammad Tabataba'i." *Rahnema-ye Ketab* vol. 21, nos. 1-2 (1357), pp. 25-36.

Mahdavi, Shireen. *For God, Mammon and Country: A Nineteenth-Century Persian Merchant, Haj Muhammad Hassan Amin al-Zarb*. Boulder: Westview Press, 1999.

_____. "Taj al-Saltaneh: An Emancipated Qajar Princess." *Middle Eastern Studies* vol. 23, no. 2 (1987), pp. 188-94.

_____. "Women and Ideas in the Qajar Period." *Asian and African Studies* vol. 19 (1985), pp. 187-97.

_____. "Social Mobility in Qajar Iran: Haj Muhammad Hassan Amin al-Zarb." *Middle Eastern Studies* vol. 26, no. 4 (1990), pp. 582-96.

Makdisi, George. "Muslim Institutions of Learning in 11th Century Baghdad." *British Society for Oriental and African Studies* vol. 24 (1961), pp. 1-56.

Malcolm. *History of Persia*. London: John Murray, 1815.

Malek Khan Sasani, Ahmad. *Siyasatgaran-e Dowreh-ye Qajar*. Tehran, 1960.

_____. *Yadbudha-ye Sefarat-e Istanbul*. Tehran: Entesharat-e Babak, n.d.

Malkom Khan, Mirza. *Majmu'eh-ye Athar*. (ed) Mohammad Mohit Tabataba'i. Tehran: Elmi, 1327.

_____. *Kulliyat-e Malkom Khan*. (ed) Hashem Rabi'zadeh. Tabriz, 1325.

_____. "Persian Civilization." *Contemporary Review* vol. 59 (1891), pp. 239-43.

Maraghe'i, Zayn al-'Abedin. *Siyahatnameh-ye Ibrahim Beg*. Tehran: Asfar, 1364.

Mardin, Serif. *The Genesis of Young Ottoman Thought: A Study in the Modernization of Turkish Political Ideas*. Princeton: Princeton University Press, 1962.

_____. "Super Westernization in Urban Life in the Ottoman Empire in the Last Quarter of the Nineteenth Century," in (eds) Pewter Benedict et al, *Turkey: Geographical and Social Perspectives*. Leiden: Brill, 1974, pp. 403-46.

Martin, Vanessa. "An Evaluation of Reform and Development of the State in the Early Qajar Period." *Die Welt des Islams* vol. 36, no. 1 (March 1996), pp. 1-24.

_____. "The Anti-Constitutionalist Arguments of Shaykh Fazlullah Nuri." *Middle Eastern Studies* vol. 22, no. 2 (1986), pp. 181-96.

Matthee, Rudi, "Firearms," *Encyclopaedia Iranica* vol. 9, pp. 623-24.

_____. "Changing the Mintmaster: The Introduction of Mechanized Minting in Qajar Iran," in *Itinerario* vol. 19, no. 2 (1995), pp. 109-27.

_____. "Between Aloofness and Fascination: Safavid Views of the West." *Iranian Studies* vol. 31, no, 2 (Spring 1998), pp. 219-46.

_____.Meftah al-Molk, Mirza Mahmud Khan. *Ramz-e Mahmudi.*

Menashri, David. *Education and the Making of Modern Iran.* Ithaca: Cornell University Press, 1992.

Meredith, Colin. "The Qajar Response to Russia's Military Challenge, 1804-28." Ph.D. dissertation, Princeton University, 1973.

Milani, Farzaneh. *Veils and Words: The Emerging Voices of Iranian Women Writers.* New York: Syracuse University Press, 1993.

Millward, William. "Traditional Values and Social Change in Iran." *Iranian Studies* vol. 4, no. 1 (1971), pp. 2-36.

Minovi, Mojtaba. *Tarikh va Farhang.* 3 vols. Tehran, 1973.

Minovi, Muhammad. "Avvalin Karevan-e Ma'refat." *Yaghma* vol. 4, pp. 181-5, 231-2, 274-8, 314-18.

Mitchell, Timothy. *Colonizing Egypt.* Cambridge: Cambridge University Press, 1988.

Molk-Ara, 'Abbas Mirza. *Sharh-e Hal-e 'Abbas Mirza Molk Ara.* (ed) 'Abd al-Husayn Nava'i. Tehran, 1325.

Mo'ayer al-Mamalek, Dust 'Ali Khan. *Rejal-e 'Asr-e Naseri.* Tehran: Nashr-e Tarikh-e Iran, 1361.

Mohit-Tabataba'i, Seyyed Mohammad. "Moshir al-Dowleh: Mard-e Siyasat." *Rahnema-ye Ketab* vol. 15, nos. 10-12.

_____. "Tarikhcheh-ye E'zam-e Mohsel beh Urupa." *Shafaq-e Sorkh* (July 6--Aug 29, 1933).

Mojtahedi, Mehdi. *Rejal-e Azarbayjan dar 'Asr-e Mashrutiyat.* Tehran, 1327.

Momtahen al-Dowleh, Mirza Mehdi Khan. *Khaterat-e Momtahen al-Dowleh.* Tehran: Amir Kabir, 1362.

Morier, James. *A Journey Through Persia, Armenia, and Asia Minor to Constantinople.* London, 1812.

_____. *A Second Journey Through Persia, Armenia, and Asia Minor to Constantinople, 1810-1816.* London, 1818.

Moshiri, 'Ali. "Avvalin Ruznameh-ye Irani," *Sokhan* vol. 14, no. 7 (1963-64), pp. 609-11.

_____."Avvalin Framasunha-ye Irani dar Avayel-e Nuzdahom." In *Histoire de la Franomasonnerie,* (trans) Ja'far Shahid. Tehran.

Moshir-Salimi, 'Ali Akbar. *Zanan-e Sokhanvar.* Tehran: Elmi, 1956.

Mostashar al-Dowleh. *Yaddashtha-ye Tarikhi-ye Mostashar al-Dowleh.* (ed) Iraj Afshar. Tehran: Ramin, 1361.

Mostashar al-Dowleh, Mirza Yusef Khan. *Yek Kalameh.* (ed) Sadeq Sajadi (Tehran: Nashr-e Tarikh-e Iran, 1364.

Mostawfi, Abdollah. *Sharh-e Zendegi-ye Man ya Tarikh-e Ejtemai va Edari-ye Dowreh-ye Qajariyeh.* 3 vols. Tehran, 1982-83.

Motia-Esfahani, Safreddin. "Sayyid Hasan Taqizadeh: The Emergence of Modern Iran." Ph.D. dissertation, University of Michigan, 1987.

Nafisi, Said. *Tarikh-e Ejtemai va Siyasi-ye Iran.* vol. 1. Tehran, 1335.

Najaf-Kuli Mirza. *Joural of residence in England and of a journey from and to Syria of their royal highnesses Reeza Koolee Meerza, Najaf Koolee Meerza, and Taymoor Meerza, of Persia, 1835, 1836.* 2 vols. (trans) Assad Y. Kayat. printed for private circulation, n.d..

Najmabadi, Afsaneh. "Veiled Discourse -- Unveiled Bodies." *Feminist Studies* vol. 19, no. 3 (Fall 1993), pp. 487-518.

_____. "Crafting an Educated Housewife in Iran," in Lila Abu Lughod, (ed) *Remaking Women: Feminism and Modernity in the Middle East.* Princeton: Princeton University Press, 1998, pp. 91-125.

Najmabadi, Mahmud. "Tebb-e Dar al Fonun va Kotub-e Darsi-ye An." In *Amir Kabir va Iran,* (ed) Iraj Afshar, 202-37.

Najmi, Nasir. *Iran dar Miyan-e Tufan: Sharh-e Zendegi-ye 'Abbas Mirza Na'yeb al-Saltaneh va Jangha-ye Iran va Rus.* Tehran: Qanun-e Mo'arraf, 1957.

Naraqi, Ehsan. *Enseignement et changements sociaux en Iran du VIIe au XXe siècle.* Éditions de la Maison des sciences de l'homme, Paris: 1992.

Naser al-Din Shah. *Ruznameh-ye Safar-e Farangestan.* Tehran, 1291.

_____. *Ruznameh-ye Safar-e Dovvom-e Farangestan.* Bombay, 1295.

_____. *Khaterat-e Naser al-Din Shah dar Safar-e Sevvom-e Farangestan.* (ed) I. Rezvani. Tehran, 1369.

Nashat, Guity, ed. *Women and Revolution in Iran.* Boulder: Westview Press, 1983.

_____."Women in Pre-Revolutionary Iran: A Historical Overview."In *Women and Revolution in Iran,* (ed) Guity Nashat, 5-35. Boulder: Westview Press, 1983.

_____.*The Origins of Modern Reform in Iran, 1870-80.* Urbana: University of Illinois Press, 1982.

Nateq, Homa. ed. *Qanun.* Tehran: Amir Kabir, 1976.

_____. "Negahi beh Barkhi Neveshteha va Mobarezat-e Zanan dar Dowran-e Mashrutiyat." *Ketab-e Jomeh* vol. 30 (1979), pp. 45-54.

_____. *Karnameh-ye Farhangi-ye Farangi dar Iran.* Tehran: Khavaran, 1375.

_____. *Iran dar Rahyabi-ye Farhangi.* Tehran: Khavaran, 1990.

_____. *"A Short History of the Alliance Francaise and Alliance Israélite in Iran."* In (ed) Homa Sarshar, *Yahudian-e Irani dar Tarikh-e Mo'aser.* Beverly Hills: Markaz-e Tarikh-e Shafahi-ye Yahudian-e Irani, 1997.

Nouraie, Fereshteh. "The Constitutional Ideas of a Shiite Mujtahed: Muhammad Husayn Na'ini." *Iranian Studies* vol. 8, no. 4 (1975), pp. 234-48.

Olivier, Georges. *L'Alliance Israélite Universelle, 1860-1960.* Paris: Librarie

Française, 1959.

Olivier, Guillaumme Antoine. *Voyage dans l'Empire Ottoman, l'Egypte et la Perse.* Paris, 1807.

Omid, Hosayn. *Tarikh-e Farhang-e Azarbayjan.* 2 vols. Tabriz: Farhang, 1332.

Ouseley, Sir Gore. *Biographical Notices of Persian Poets.* London: W.H. Allen, 1846.

_____. *Travels in Various Countries of the East; More Particilarly Persia.* London, 1819.

Pahlavan, Changiz. *Hoquq-e Asasi: Ya'in Adab-e Mashrutiyat-e Dowl.* 1368.

Paidar, Parvin. *Women and the Political Process in Twentieth-Century Iran.* Cambridge: Cambridge University Press, 1995.

Pakdaman, Homa and William Royce. "Abbas Mirza's Will." *Iranian Studies* vol. 6, nos. 2-3 (1973), pp. 136-52.

Perkins, Justin. *Historical Sketch of the Mission to the Nestorians.* Boston: American Board of Commissioners for Foreign Missions, 1866.

Perry, John R."Language Reform in Turkey and Iran." *International Journal of Middle East Studies* vol. 17, no. 3 (1985), pp. 295-311.

Petrov, G.M., Vladimir Minorsky, M.N. Pokrovskiy and V.O. Klucheskiy. "The Murder of Griboyedov." *Central Asian Review* vol. 7, no. 4 (1959), pp. 382-86.

Piemontese, Angelo M. "An Italian Source for the History of Qagar Persia: the Reports of General Enrico Andreini (1871-1886)." *East and West* vol. 19, no. 1 (1969), pp. 147-75.

Pirzadeh, Hajji Mohammad 'Ali. *Safamaneh-ye Hajji Mohammad 'Ali Pirzadeh.* 2 vol. (ed) Hafez Farmanfarma'iyan. Tehran, 1963.

Pistor-Hatam, Anja. *Iran und die Reformbewegung im Osmanischen Reich.* Berlin: Klausschwartz Verlag, 1992.

_____. "Progress and Civilization in Nineteenth-Century Japan: The Far Eastern State As a Model for Modernization." *Iranian Studies* vol. 29, nos. 1-2 (Winter/Spring 1996), pp. 111-26.

Polak, Jakob. *Persien: das Land und seine Bewohner.* Hildesheim, 1976.

_____.*Die Östereichischen Lehrer in Persien.* Wein: Hölder, 1876.

Polk, William and Richard Chambers, (eds) *Beginnings of Modernization in the Middle East: The Nineteenth Century.* Chicago: Chicago University Press, 1966.

Porter, Robert Ker. *Travels in Georgia, Persia, Armenia, Ancient Babylonia during the years 1817, 1818, 1819, and 1820.* London: 1821.

Qavami, Fakhri. *Kamameh-ye Zanan-e Mashur-e Iran.* Tehran: Entesharat-e Vezarat-e Amuzesh va Parvaresh, 1973.

Quchani, Muhammad Hasan Najafi. *Siyahat-e Sharq ya Zendeginameh-ye Aqa Najafi Quchani.* Tehran: Entesharat-e Amir Kabir

Raeff, Marc. *Origins of the Russian Intelligentsia: the Eighteenth-Century Nobility.* New York: Harcourt, Brace & Jovanovich 1966.

Ra'iss-Tousi, Reza. "The Persian Army 1880-1907." *Middle Eastern Studies* vol. 24, no. 2 (1988), pp. 206-29.

Ralston, David. *Importing the European Army: The Introduction of European Military Techniques and Institutions into the Extra-European World, 1600-1914.* Chicago: Chicago University Press, 1990.

Rawlinson, Henry Creswicke. *England and Russia in the East.* London: John Murray, 1875.

Razvani, Mohammad Isma'il. "Enqelab-e Fekri-ye Iran dar Dowran-e Fath 'Ali Shah." *Rahnema-ye Ketab* vol. 7, no. 1 (1343), pp. 3-18.

Reid, Donald. "Educational Career Choices of Egyptian Students, 1882-1922." *International Journal of Middle Eastern Studies* vol. 8, no. 3 (1977), pp. 349-78.

Reza'i, Shaykh Aniseh. "Madares-e Faransavi." *Ganjineh* vol. 2, nos. 3-4

(1371), pp. 95-109.

Richard, Yann. (ed) *Entre l'Iran et l'Occident: Adaptation et assimilation des idées et techniques occidentales en Iran*. Paris: Editions de la Maison des sciences de l'homme, 1989.

Richter, Julius. *A History of Protestant Missions in the Near East*. London : Fleming H. Revell Co., 1910.

Rieff, Philip, ed. *On Intellectuals: Theoretical Studies, Case Studies*. Garden City, NY: Doubleday & Co., 1969.

Ringer, Fritz. *Max Weber's Methodology: The Unification of the Cultural and Social Sciences*. Cambridge: Harvard University Press, 1997.

_____. *Education and Society in Modern Europe*. Bloomington: Indiana University Press, 1979.

_____. *Fields of Knowledge: French Academic Culture in Comparative Perspective, 1890-1920*. Cambridge: Cambridge University Press, 1992.

Ringer, Monica. "The Quest for the Secret of Strength in Iranian Nineteenth-Century Travel Literature: Rethinking Tradition in the Safarnameh." In (eds) Nikki Keddie and Rudi Matthee, *Iran and the Surrounding World Since 1500: Cultural Influences and Interactions* (forthcoming).

Riyadi, Muhammad Amin. "Do Nameh-ye Mohem-e Siyasi va Tarikhi az 'Abbas Mirza Na'yeb al-Saltaneh." *Yadegar* vol. 4 (1327), p. 20.

Rochechouart, C. J. *Souvenirs d'un Voyage in Perse en 1867*. Paris: Challemel Aine, 1867.

Roshdiyyeh, Fakhr al-Din. *Zendeginameh-ye Pir-e Ma'aref-e Roshdiyyeh: Bonyangozar-e Farhang-e Novvin-e Iran*. Tehran: Hirmand, 1370.

Roshdiyyeh, Shams al-Din. *Savanih-ye Omr*. Tehran: Nashr-e Tarikh-e Iran, 1362.

Rypka, Jan, et. al. *A History of Iranian Literature*. Dordrecht: Reidel, 1968.

Sadavandian, Mansureh Ettehadiyeh and Sirus, (eds) *Khaterat-e Taj al-Saltaneh*. Tehran: Nashr-e Tarikh-e Iran, 1982.

Sadiq, Issa. *Yadegar-e Omr*. Tehran: Maravi, 1974.

_____. *Tarikh-e Farhang-e Iran*. Tehran: Daneshgah-e Tehran, 1976.

Sadr, M. K. *Relations de l'Iran avec l'Europe*. (Paris, 1937).

Sadr-Hashimi, Muhammad. *Tarikh-e Jara'id-e Majalat-e Iran*. Tehran, 1948.

Safa'i, Ibrahim. *Rahbaran-e Mashruteh: Mushtamil bar 24 Biyugrafi va Sharh-e Jaleb va Shegeftehangiz-e Kuliyeh-ye Havad va Vaqaye'-e Nehzat-e Mashruteh-ye Iran*.

Sanasarian, Eliz, *The Women's Rights Movement in Iran: Mutiny, Appeasement, and Repression From 1900 to Khomeini*. New York: Praeger Publishers, 1982.

Sarabi, Hossein ibn 'Abd Allah. *Safamaneh-ye Farrokh Khan Amin al-Dowleh Makhzan al-Asfar, Makhzan al-Vaqaye'*. (ed) K. Esfahaniyan. Tehran, 1982.

Sarshar, Homa, (ed) *Yahudiyan-e Irani dar Tarikh-e Mo'aser*. Beverley Hills: Markaz-e Tarikh-e Shafahi-ye Yahudiyan-e Irani, 1997.

Sayyah, Hajj. *An Iranian in Nineteenth Century Europe: The Travel Diaries of Haj Sayyah 1859-1877*. Translated by Mehrbanoo Nasser Deyhim. Bethesda: Ibex, 1998.

Sepehr, 'Abd al-Hosayn Khan. *Merat al-Vaqaye'-e Mozafari va Yaddasht-ha-ye Malek al-Movarekhayn*. (ed) 'Abd al-Hosayn Nava'i, Tehran: Zarin, 1328.

Sercey, Conte Félix Eduard. *Une ambassade extraordinaire: La Perse en 1839-1840*. Paris: Artisan du livre, 1928.

Shafiei-Nasab, Djafar. *Les Mouvements Revolutionnaires et la Constitution de 1906 en Iran*. Berlin: Klaus Schwarz Verlag, 1991.

Shalaby, Ahmad. *History of Muslim Education*. Beirut: Dar al-Sashhaf, 1954.

Shaw, Sanford Jay. "Some Aspects of the Aims and Achievements of the Nineteenth-Century Ottoman Reformers." In *Beginnings of Modernization in the Middle East: The Nineteenth Century*, (eds) William Polk and Richard Chambers, 29-39. Chicago: Chicago University Press, 1968.

_____. *Between Old and New: The Ottoman Empire Under Sultan Selim III, 1789-1807*. Cambridge: Harvard University Press, 1971.

_____. "The Origins of Balkan Military Reform: the Nizam-i Jedid Army of Sultan Selim III." *Journal of Military History* vol. 37, no. 3 (1965), pp. 290-305.

Shayegan, Daryush. *Qu'est-ce qu'un révolution religieuse?* Paris: Les presses d'aujourd'hui, 1982.

Sheikh al-Islami, Pari. *Zanan-e Ruznamehnegar va Andishmand-e Iran*. Tehran: Mazgraphic, 1972.

Sheil, Lady Leonora Mary. *Glimpses of Life and Manners in Persia*. New York: Arno Press, 1973.

Shils, Edward. *The Intellectual Between Tradition and Modernity: The Indian Situation*. The Hague: Mouton & Co., 1961.

_____. *The Intellectuals and the Powers, and Other Essays*. Chicago: Chicago University Press, 1972.

_____. *Center and Periphery: Essays in Macrosociology*. Chicago: Chicago University Press, 1975.

_____. "The Intellectual in the Political Development of the New States." *World Politics* vol. 12 (April 1960), pp. 329-30.

Shirazi, 'Abd al-Hassan Khan. *A Persian at the Court of King George 1809-10: The Journal of Mirza Abdul Hassan Khan*. (trans and ed) Margaret Moris Cloake. London: Barrie & Jenkins, 1988.

Shirazi, Mirza Saleh. *Majmu-eh-ye Safamaneh-ye Mirza Saleh Shirazi*. Tehran: Nashr-e Tarikh-e Iran, 1985.

Sinaki, Mirza Mohammad Khan Majd al-Molk. *Resaleh-ye Majdiyeh*. (ed) Sa'id Nafisi. Tehran: Bank-e Melli-ye Iran, 1321.

Shustari, 'Abd al-Latif Jazayeri Musavi. *Tofaht al-Alam va Dhayl al-Tohfeh.* Tehran: Tahuri, 1363/1984. Bombay: 1263.

Siassi, Ali Akbar. *La Perse au Contact de L'Occident: étude historique et sociale.* Paris: Ernest Leroux, 1931.

Sivera, Alain. "The First Eyptian Student Mission to France Under Muhammad Ali." *Middle Eastern Studies* vol. 16, no. 2 (1980), pp. 1-23.

Slaby, Helmut. *Bindenschild und Sonnenlöwe: Die Geschichter der Österreichischen-Iranischen Beziehungen bis zur Gegenwart.* Graz, 1982.

Soroudi, Sorour. "Sur-e Esrafil, 1907-1908: Social and Political Ideology." *Middle Eastern Studies* vol. 24, no. 2 (1988), pp. 230-48.

Sparroy, Wilfred. *Persian Children of the Royal Family: The narrative of an English tutor at the court of H.I.H. Zillu's-Sultan.* London: John Lane, 1902.

Steppat, Fritz. "National Education Projects in Egypt Before the British Occupation." In *Beginnings of Modernization in the Middle East: The Nineteenth Century,* (eds) William Polk and Richard Chambers, 281-97. Chicago: University of Chicago Press, 1968.

Sykes, Sir Percy. *A History of Persia.* London, 1915.

_____. *Ten Thousand Miles in Persia, or eight years in Iran.* New York: Scribner, 1902.

Szyliowicz, Joseph. "Education and Political Development in Turkey, Egypt, and Iran." *Comparative Education Review* vol. 13 (1969), pp. 150-66.

_____. *Education and Modernization in the Middle East.* Ithaca: Cornell University Press, 1973.

Tabrizi, Mirza Reza Khan. *Sharh-e Hal-e Prins Arfa' Danesh.* (ed) Mohammad Javad Hushmand.

Taj al-Saltaneh. *Crowning Anguish: Memoirs of a Persian Princess From the Harem to Modernity.* (ed) Abbas Amanat. Washington, DC: Mage,

1993.

Talebof, 'Abd al-Rahim. *Ketab-e Ahmad*. Tehran: Sazeman-e Ketabha-ye Jibi, 1346.

Taqizadeh, Hasan. *Zaban va Farhang*. (ed) Iraj Afshar. Tehran: Sherekat-e Sahami-ye Afsat, 1973.

_____. Ma'ni va Din-e u beh Endemam-e Motun-e Arabi va Farsi Darbareh-ye Ma'ni va Manaviyat. Tehran: 1335.

Tarbiyat, Muhammad 'Ali. "Tarikh-e Matba'eh va Matbu'at-e Iran." *Ta'lim va Tarbiyat* vol. 4, pp. 658-71.

Tavakoli-Targhi, Mohammad. "Women of the West Imagined: The *Farangi* Other and the Emergence of the Woman Question in Iran." In *Identity Politics and Women: Cultural Reassertions and Feminisms in International Perspective*, (ed) Valentine Moghadam, 98-120. Boulder: Westview Press, 1994.

_____. "Imagining Western Women: Occidentalism and Euro-eroticism," in *Radical America* vol. 24, no. 3 (1993), pp. 73-87.

Tavernier, Jean-Baptiste. *The Six Voyages of Jean-Baptiste Tavernier*. London, 1878.

Tibawi, A. L. "Origin and Character of Al-Madrase" *Journal of the British Society of Oriental and African Studies* vol. 25 (1962), pp. 225-38.

Tritton, A. S. *Materials on Muslim Education in the Middle Ages*. London: Luzac & Co., 1957.

unknown. "Mirza Sayyed Ja'far Khan Moshir al-Dowleh." *Yadegar* vol. 2, no. 6.

Volodarsky, Mikhail. "Persia and the Great Powers, 1856-1869." *Middle Eastern Studies* vol. 19, no. 1 (1983), pp. 75-92.

Walcher, Heidi. "In the Shadow of the King: Politics and Society in Isfahan, 1874-1907." Ph.D. dissertation, Yale University, 2000.

Waldman, Marilyn. *Toward a Theory of Historical Narrative: A Case Study in Perso-Islamicate Historiography.* Columbus: Ohio State University Press, 1980.

Watson, Robert Grant. *A History of Persia from the Beginning of the Nineteenth Century to the Year 1858.* London, 1866.

Wilberforce, Reverend S., (ed) *Journals and Letters of the Reverend Henry Martyn.* London, 1821.

Wright, Denis. *The Persians Amongst the English.* London: IB Taurus, 1985.

_____. *The English Amongst the Persians.* London: Heinemann, 1977.

Yaghma'i, Habib. "Roshdiyyeh Pir-e Ma'aref." *Amuzesh va Parvaresh* vol. 14, p. 543.

Yagma'i, Iqbal. "Madraseh-ye Dar al Fonun." *Yagma* vol. 22 (1969-70); *Yagma* vol. 23 (1970-71).

_____. "Dastani az Moballeghayn-e 'Isavi dar Iran." *Yadegar* nos. 6-7, pp. 60-6.

Yasami, Rashid. "Talebov va Ketab-e Ahmad." *Iranshahr* vol. 2, pp. 283-97.

Yeganeh, Nahid. "Women's Organizations in Iran." In *In the Shadow of Islam: The Women's Movement in Iran,* 201-30. London: Zed Press, 1982.

Zarcone, Thierry and Fariba Zarinebaf-shahr, (eds) *Les Iraniens d'Istanbul.* Paris, 1993.

Zell al-Soltan, Mas'ud Mirza. *Safarnameh-ye Farangestan.* Tehran: Entesharat-e Asatir, 1368.

Ziai, Hossein, (ed) "19th Century Persian Medical Manuscripts: A Description." microfilms at the bio-medical library, University of California, Los Angeles.

Zirinsky, Michael. "Missionaries, Education, and Social Change in Iran, 1834-1941." Paper presented at the Middle East Studies Association conference, 1996.

INDEX